CRITICAL THINKING

AN ANNOTATED BIBLIOGRAPHY

by
Jeris F. Cassel
and
Robert J. Congleton

The Scarecrow Press, Inc.
Metuchen, N.J., & London
1993

British Library Cataloguing-in-Publication data available

Library of Congress Cataloging-in-Publication Data

Cassel, Jeris F. (Jeris Folk), 1952-
Critical thinking : an annotated bibliography / by Jeris F. Cassel and Robert J. Congleton.
p. cm.
Includes indexes.
ISBN 0-8108-2635-6 (acid-free paper)
1. Critical thinking--Bibliography. 2. Critical thinking in children--Bibliography. I. Congleton, Robert J. (Robert James), 1956- . II. Title.
Z5814.C88C37 1993
[B1590.3]
016.16--dc20 92-35306

Manufactured in the United States of America
Printed on acid-free paper

TABLE OF CONTENTS

ACKNOWLEDGEMENTS

The joy in working on a project of this magnitude is the contact with colleagues and friends who willingly provide their able assistance and expertise. We are most appreciative to the following colleagues and friends who reviewed and edited preliminary rough drafts of the chapters: Emily Fabiano, Reference Librarian/Education Specialist, Rutgers University; Mel Gelfand, Reference Librarian/Communications Bibliographer, Temple University; Lola Januskus, Social Science Bibliographer, Temple University; Elizabeth W. Kaschins, Senior Reference and Curriculum Librarian, Luther College; Virginia Nordstrom, Head Librarian of the Curriculum Resource Center, Bowling Green State University; Pamela Thaxter, Social Science Bibliographer, Temple University; Bob Warwick, Bibliographic Database Manager, Rutgers University Libraries; and Barbara Wright, Business Librarian, Temple University.

We extend our gratitude to the interlibrary loan and circulation personnel of the Rutgers University and Temple University Library Systems for handling our many requests graciously and fastidiously and to Drue Williamson, Rutgers University Libraries, for checking the accuracy of bibliographic citations. Special thanks goes to Rives Cassel for his helpful editorial comments and his love, patience, and support during this project.

INTRODUCTION

Upon sharing our research and work with others, the inevitable question that follows is "*What is critical thinking?*" This is the question that spurred us into approximately four years of research, reading, discussion, and attending critical thinking conferences. Beyond curiosity about the definition of critical thinking, we were also interested in how an individual becomes a critical thinker, whether critical thinking can be taught and learned in a classroom, the prerequisites for teaching or learning to be a critical thinker, and the most effective ways for teaching and learning critical thinking. We have found a diversity of answers to these questions.

In the last ten years, the term "critical thinking" has become prevalent in philosophy, education, and psychology to the extent that it is considered a buzzword. The concept itself is not new. It dates back to Socrates in ancient Greece and has been a goal of education reformers throughout history. Twentieth century efforts at integrating critical thinking into the forefront of education can be found in the writings of John Dewey, Edward Glaser's *Experiment in the Development of Critical Thinking* (1941), and Max Black's textbook *Critical Thinking* (1952). The current critical thinking movement can be traced back to 1962 with Robert Ennis's landmark article "A Concept of Critical Thinking" published in *Harvard Educational Review* 32, no. 1 (Winter 1962): 81-111. In that article, Ennis defined critical thinking as "the correct assessment of statements." This definition began the current dialogue among scholars and educators regarding the nature and teachability of critical thinking. While the dialogue reflects a lack of consensus regarding many aspects of critical thinking, proponents of critical thinking generally encourage exposure, recognition, and acceptance of multiple viewpoints by individuals and encourage providing opportunities for individuals to use critical thinking.

This annotated bibliography of 930 selected periodical articles, monographs, essays, conference papers, and chapters from anthologies provides an opportunity for individuals to explore critical thinking. It is intended for anyone interested in critical thinking and is geared especially to teachers, administrators, and researchers in elementary, secondary, and higher education. Theoretical and practical literature on or related to critical thinking from the fields of philosophy, psychology, and education is represented in this volume. Although we have surveyed the literature from the 1960s to the present, the bibliography covers selected representative literature from 1980 through 1991. During this period, critical thinking has become a well-supported goal of educational reform and research. The literature contained in this bibliography represents past and current trends in the concepts, research, and teaching of critical thinking.

Eight chapters, an author index, and a subject index make up this volume. The first chapter, "General," contains publications that cover numerous aspects of critical thinking and that were difficult to place judiciously in one of the topical chapters. It is within this chapter that literature on the history of critical thinking, the Critical Thinking Movement, and overviews of critical thinking literature are found. Chapter 2, "Definitions and Concepts," includes the wide range of views on critical thinking and reflects the dialogue among scholars on the idea of critical thinking and its relation to other types of thinking. Literature describing research projects related to critical thinking is in Chapter 3. Research areas covered include cognitive studies, experimental classroom projects and programs, investigations of the problem-solving strategies of experts versus novices, effective teaching techniques, and the transferability of critical thinking abilities. Sources in Chapter 4, "Theory," cover primarily the curriculum issues related to teaching critical thinking. Topics include whether critical thinking should be taught within current subject courses or as a separate course, how critical thinking should be integrated into the curriculum, what issues should be addressed when initiating a critical thinking program, the transferability of critical thinking, the role educators and education administrators play in integrating critical thinking into the curriculum, and other factors that should be considered before beginning to teach critical thinking in a classroom.

Movement toward the practical begins with Chapter 5, "Professional Development and Teacher Training," which includes a mix of theoretical and practical literature on how teachers, librarians, lawyers, and other professionals can become critical thinkers and employ critical thinking in their professions. The sources in this chapter cover descriptions and experiences with critical thinking programs and workshops, developed in-house by a school system or developed commercially. Literature on teacher training covers what reforms are needed and what reforms have been implemented in various college and university programs.

Chapter 6, "Testing and Evaluation," offers a guide to information on ways to evaluate or assess critical thinking proficiency, including analyses of commercial tests, research evaluating their effectiveness at measuring critical thinking, as well as in-house programs developed to assess the effectiveness of the direct teaching of critical thinking and of evaluative procedures developed by practitioners in the classroom.

Literature covering practical examples of teaching and fostering critical thinking in and outside of the classroom is included in Chapters 7 and 8 on instructional methods. The sources in these chapters cover descriptions of how the teaching of critical thinking has been or should be approached. Specific strategies, techniques, and in-house and commercial programs developed in particular schools or colleges and by experts are covered in this chapter. Frequently, the literature includes the theories and goals underlying methods or approaches, as well as comparative information on different programs or approaches, such as CoRT, Philosophy for Children, and Instrumental Enrichment. The focus in Chapter 7 is on literature that covers instructional techniques, strategies, methods, approaches, and programs that, for the most part, have broad applications. Chapter 8 covers the application of specific instructional methods and approaches to specific disciplines or curriculum units. The literature in Chapter 8 is categorized according to the broad areas of Reading and Writing, Library Instruction, Humanities, Social Sciences, and Science and Mathematics.

The Subject Index should be used to find entries for specific subject areas. By the same token, the Subject Index should be used for entries for specific instructional methods and approaches or specific instructional level referred to in the literature. Unless instructional levels were apparent in the literature, they were not included in the annotation and were indexed under general headings. The Author Index should be used to find the entry numbers for publications by a specific author. References to entries of publications within which authors are referred to are found in the Subject Index.

To help readers more readily follow the dialogue among scholars in the theoretical chapters, references to related articles are given. **Reply, Reply to,** or **See** precede these related references which are given with the author's name followed by the corresponding entry number in *Critical Thinking: An Annotated Bibliography* in curly brackets. **Reply** is followed by the author of the publication who responded to the specific entry publication. **Reply to** is followed by the author of the publication to which the entry is responding. **See** is followed by the author of related publications or the publications referred to in the specific entry publication.

We hope that learners and teachers of all instructional levels and disciplines will find this annotated bibliography of selected representative literature on various aspects of critical thinking valuable in forming their own community of inquiry.

1

GENERAL

001 Blair, J. Anthony, and Ralph H. Johnson. "The Current State of Informal Logic." *Informal Logic* 9, no. 2-3 (Spring-Fall 1987): 147-151. [17 Refs.]

The authors address the origins of the informal logic movement, expressing disappointment that some individuals sympathetic to the movement do not understand the distinction between the logic of argumentation and formal deductive logic. With some hesitation, Blair and Johnson provide a characterization of informal logic. They outline eight issues related to informal logic, including its relation to critical thinking, and the extent to which they have been and have not been addressed. In the discussion of these issues, the authors pose research tasks and opportunities.

002 Blair, J. Anthony, and Ralph H. Johnson, eds. *Informal Logic: The First International Symposium*. Inverness, CA: Edgepress, 1980. 172 pp.

This anthology of nine papers on informal logic is divided into five sections that cover historical development, fallacies, formalism, pedagogy, and the philosophical significance of informal logic. Eight of the papers were presented at the First International Symposium on Informal Logic (Ontario, 1978). The ninth paper, written for this book, is an essay on informal logic/critical thinking tests. The introduction identifies twelve characteristics of informal logic that distinguish it from formal logic and link it to the study of reasoning or critical thinking. A 151-item bibliography of journal articles, textbooks, monographs, reviews of textbooks and monographs on informal logic is provided at the end of the text.

003 Johnson, Ralph H., and J. Anthony Blair. "Informal Logic: The Past Five Years 1978-1983." *American Philosophical Quarterly* 22, no. 3 (July 1985): 181-196. [90 Refs.]

Johnson and Blair provide a general review of informal logic monographs, journal articles, and textbooks published between 1978 and 1983. They note that the significant increase in publications compared to 1970-1978 reflects the growth of the informal logic movement. The common feature of the literature is the attempt to rethink the nature of argument, focusing on arguments as they appear in everyday life and natural language. Johnson and Blair recommend that informal logic research begin addressing questions and theories discussed in related philosophical areas and integrate relevant research being done in fields such as rhetoric and cognitive psychology.

004 Johnson, Ralph H., and J. Anthony Blair. "The Recent Development of Informal Logic." *Informal Logic: The First International Symposium*, edited by J. Anthony Blair and Ralph H. Johnson, 3-28. Inverness, CA: Edgepress, 1980. [151 Refs.]

In this review of informal logic literature published between 1953 and 1978, the authors discuss the limited number of monographs on the subject, chart the relevant journal articles, note growth in journal literature after 1970, and review relevant textbooks. The authors contrast the textbooks published between 1953 and 1969 with those published after 1970. They found that the 1953-1969 texts emphasized a global approach and were organized into three parts: (1) language, (2) deduction, and (3) induction. The textbooks of post-1970 emphasize a critical thinking approach, focusing on practical skills for clear reasoning in everyday life. These post-1970 textbooks use realistic examples while the early texts used abstract ones. Johnson and Blair found little interplay between the approach in the textbooks and the theoretical work of the articles.

005 Kennedy, Mellen, Michelle B. Fisher, and Robert H. Ennis. "Critical Thinking: Literature Review and Needed Research." Chapter 1 in *Educational Values and Cognitive Instruction: Implications for Reform*, edited by Lorna Idol and Beau Fly Jones, 11-40. Hillsdale, NJ: Lawrence Erlbaum, 1991. [124 Refs.]

The authors discuss the history, definitions, and theories of the critical thinking movement, followed by an overview of the teaching and learning of critical thinking. This overview includes an examination of subject matter specificity, student characteristics, prior knowledge, transfer, teacher training, and the testing and evaluation of critical thinking. The authors summarize the research needs in each area.

006 McPeck, John E. *Critical Thinking and Education*. Oxford, UK: Martin Robertson, 1981. 170 pp. [77 Refs.]

McPeck defines critical thinking as the propensity and skill to use "reflective skepticism" when engaged in some specific activity. He believes that critical thinking is subject-specific and is not necessarily transferable between subject areas or activities. McPeck criticizes theories, teaching methods, and tests that depict critical thinking as general skills or logic rather than epistemology. The skills/logic concept is found in the writings of Robert Ennis, Edward D'Angelo, the Informal Logic Movement, in programs such as Edward de Bono's CoRT, and in critical thinking tests such as the Watson-Glaser Critical Thinking Appraisal and the Cornell Critical Thinking Tests. McPeck believes that critical thinking should be a goal of education and that the analysis of a subject's epistemology should be the core of teaching critical thinking. Other aspects of the subject should stem from this core. According to McPeck, the elementary school should concentrate on providing the prerequisites and background knowledge needed for critical thought and not on incorporating critical thinking into the curriculum. A 20-item bibliography of sources for further reading is provided.

007 McPeck, John E. *Teaching Critical Thinking: Dialogue and Dialectic*. New York, NY: Routledge, 1990. 135 pp. [45 Refs.]

In this collection of essays, McPeck criticizes standard conceptions of critical thinking and approaches to teaching critical thinking as a separate subject. He argues that the standard approaches to critical thinking by the informal logic movement do not sufficiently recognize the importance knowledge and information have for reasoning. Informal logic approaches reduce critical thinking to a set of logic skills which, once learned, are transferable across the disciplines. McPeck presents a Wittgensteinian conception of critical thinking as subject-specific or knowledge-dependent and non-transferable as an alternative to the standard view. The best avenue for teaching critical thinking is a general liberal arts curriculum, not a separate course. McPeck criticizes tests for critical thinking and suggests ways teachers may encourage the development of critical thinking in the classroom. Essays by Stephen Norris, Harvey Siegel, and Richard Paul criticizing McPeck's position are included, along with McPeck's responses to those essays.

008 Pauker, Robert A. *Teaching Thinking and Reasoning Skills: Problems and Solutions*. AASA Critical Issues Reports, no. 20. Arlington, VA: American Association of School Administrators, 1987. 80 pp.

Pauker provides brief analyses of the issues, history, leaders, and programs involved in the development of the movement to teach thinking or critical thinking. He covers such topics as the need to teach thinking and reasoning, the pioneers and practitioners of the movement, cognitive science research on critical thinking and creative thinking, how to choose the right thinking program, reports from several school districts that have initiated thinking skills instruction, and the assessment of thinking tests.

009 Paul, Richard W. "The Critical-Thinking Movement: A Historical Perspective." *National Forum: Phi Kappa Phi Journal* 65, no. 1 (Winter 1985): 2-3, 32.

Paul reflects on the growth of the Critical Thinking Movement and on education in the United States from the 17th century through the 1970s. He emphasizes the biased rote-learning, unquestioning atmosphere traditionally found in most schools and asserts that this atmosphere is changing as the Critical Thinking Movement gains in influence.

010 Sproule, J. Michael. "Ideology and Critical Thinking: The Historical Connection." *Journal of the American Forensic Association* 24, no. 1 (Summer 1987): 4-15. [46 Refs.]

Sproule traces the concept of critical thinking within a historical context from the late 1800s (with the revival and development of argumentation courses focusing on message analysis and construction or rationalistic and objectivistic approaches to argumentation theory) to the post-World War I era (with curricular focus on propaganda analysis or an ideological approach to argumentation in the 1920s and 1930s). The social solidarity movement of the 1940s caused a return to a rationalistic, nonideological approach to critical thinking in education. McCarthyism provided further impetus for this approach in the 1950s. Sproule observes ambiguity in the role of ideology in critical thinking today with instructional programs oriented toward objectivism, emphasizing generalized reasoning or thinking. With the increased interest in ideology among humanists and social scientists, Sproule predicts greater attention to ideological dimensions of reasoning-giving in the next decade.

011 Sternberg, Robert J. "Critical Thinking: Its Nature, Measurement, and Improvement." Chapter 3 in *Essays on the Intellect*, edited by Frances R. Link, 45-65. Alexandria, VA: Association for Supervision and Curriculum Development, 1985. [33 Refs.]

Sternberg defines critical thinking as comprising "the mental processes, strategies, and representations people use to solve problems, make decisions, and learn new concepts" (p. 46). He critically reviews several theories, tests, and instructional training programs found in the philosophical, psychological, and educational approaches to critical thinking.

2

DEFINITIONS AND CONCEPTS

012 Bailin, Sharon. "Belief, Doubt and Critical Thinking: Reconciling the Contraries." In *Philosophy of Education 1989: Proceedings of the Forty-Fifth Annual Meeting of the Philosophy of Education Society*, edited by Ralph Page, 315-319. Normal, IL: Philosophy of Education Society, 1990. [8 Refs.]

Reply to Garrison and Phelan {032}

Bailin argues that the poetic dialectic concept of critical thinking proposed by Garrison and Phelan entails a considerable misconstruing of contemporary theories of critical thinking. She believes the concept does not attempt to reconcile contradictions and seems to end inquiry rather than encourage it.

013 Bailin, Sharon. "Critical and Creative Thinking." *Informal Logic* 9, no. 1 (Winter 1987): 23-30. [12 Refs.]

Refuting the view that critical and creative thinking are distinct and separate, Bailin argues that they are complementary and connected in thinking well in any area. She believes that the separatist view is based on the traditional concept of ordinary thinking as analytic, convergent, and functioning within rigid frameworks while creative thinking demands imagination to transcend the frameworks. This view depicts subject disciplines as static bodies of knowledge containing facts to be memorized and recalled. Students are led to believe that knowledge is complete, definite, fixed, and centered in an authority, rather than open-ended and dynamic. Bailin advocates that teachers not only stress subject matter or disciplinary knowledge, but also principles and methods of inquiry and investigation.

014 Bailin, Sharon. "Putting Our Heads Together: Reason, Innovation and Critical Thinking." In *Philosophy of*

Education 1988: Proceedings of the Forty-Fourth Annual Meeting of the Philosophy of Education Society, edited by James M. Giarelli, 403-406. Normal, IL: Philosophy of Education Society, 1989. [3 Refs.]

Reply to Missimer {049}

Bailin argues that Missimer does not understand the Individual View of critical thinking nor does she recognize critical thinking as having multiple levels. Missimer's support of the Social View of critical thinking is untenable for it requires accepting several points she criticizes in the Individual View.

015 Baron, Jonathan. "Reflective Thinking as a Goal of Education." *Intelligence* 5, no. 4 (October-December 1981): 291-309. [42 Refs.]

Baron proposes a theory of reflective thinking and five phases of thinking modeled after Dewey's theory and phases. He explains and discusses the five phases (problem recognition, enumeration of possibilities, reasoning, revision, and evaluation) in the context of parameters that govern the operation of each phase. Baron suggests rules for setting these parameters for optimal behavior (or good thinking) and recommends them as the basis for teaching thinking.

016 Battersby, Mark E. "Critical Thinking as Applied Epistemology: Relocating Critical Thinking in the Philosophical Landscape." *Informal Logic* 11, no. 2 (Spring 1989): 91-100. [18 Refs.]

Critical thinking, or informal logic, has epistemological norms rather than rules of logic as its philosophical core. Battersby believes that a better term for informal logic would be "applied epistemology." To show the value that studying critical thinking has for epistemology, Battersby develops an analogy of ethics and epistemology that illustrates that the similarities between applied ethics and traditional ethical theory parallel the relationship of critical thinking and epistemology. He argues that applying epistemological understanding to practical problems should be the focus of a new epistemological field of Critical Thinking/Applied Epistemology. Battersby includes several epistemological difficulties and examples of applied epistemological solutions.

017 Beyer, Barry K. "Critical Thinking: What Is It?" *Social Education* 49, no. 4 (April 1985): 270-276. [33 Refs.]

Beyer believes critical thinking has been defined in terms that are either too vague, too broad, or that are confused with other kinds of thinking, such as inquiry, logical reasoning, decision making, or problem solving. He elaborates on the definition used by most critical thinking scholars--the "assessing of the authenticity, accuracy and/or worth of knowledge claims and arguments" (p. 271) and identifies ten most commonly used skills and two important dimensions of critical thinking (a frame of mind and specific mental operations). Beyer discusses historical descriptions of critical thinking, emphasizing analyses by social studies educators. He outlines a concept of individual critical thinking skills as consisting of a set of procedures, distinguishing criteria, and a set of rules that a teacher can use to teach a particular skill.

018 Blair, J. Anthony. "Recent Developments in Critical Thinking in Anglophone North America." *Thinking* 7, no. 2 (1987): 2-6. [33 Refs.]

Blair identifies four main perspectives of critical thinking: (1) the political, (2) the educational, (3) the ethical, and (4) the philosophical. He outlines the main characteristics, historical development, and concepts of each perspective.

019 Blair, J. Anthony, and Ralph H. Johnson. "Informal Logic: A Thematic Account." Chapter 5 in *Thinking, Reasoning, and Writing*, edited by Elaine P. Maimon, Barbara F. Nodine, and Finbarr W. O'Connor, 93-110. New York, NY: Longman, 1989. [71 Refs.]

Blair and Johnson delineate the concept of informal logic through a discussion of disagreements within the Informal Logic Movement regarding its nature, its historical development as a reaction to formal logic, its treatment in three current textbooks, and its relation to critical thinking. Blair and Johnson view informal logic as the study of nonformal methods and standards for analyzing, evaluating, and constructing arguments in natural language. Informal logic is a field of study, whereas critical thinking is a process which includes, but is not limited to, argument assessment. Informal logic makes important contributions to critical thinking, but the two are distinct.

020 DeNitto, John, and James Strickland. "Critical Thinking: A Skill for All Seasons." *College Student Journal* 21, no. 2 (Summer 1987): 201-204. [3 Refs.]

The authors discuss basic attitudes, skills, and strategies common to critical thinkers that should be nurtured in students before high school. They suggest using the Givens-Operations-Goals paradigm and the Scientific Method paradigm for learning to apply critical thinking strategies to a variety of problematic situations.

021 Ennis, Robert H. "A Conception of Critical Thinking--With Some Curriculum Suggestions." In *Conference 85 on Critical Thinking, Christopher Newport College*, edited by John Hoaglund, 13-40. Newport News, VA: Christopher Newport College Press, 1985. [11 Refs.]

Defining critical thinking as "reasonable reflective thinking that is focused on deciding what to believe or do" (p. 14), Ennis outlines thirteen dispositions and twelve abilities that make up this concept. He discusses four basic areas of critical thinking ability (clarity, basis, inference, and interaction), drawing upon his experience as a juror in a murder trial to exemplify how each of the basic areas are used in subjects not studied in school. He discusses the pros and cons of teaching critical thinking either within subject areas or as a separate course and the need to teach for transfer.

022 Ennis, Robert H. "A Logical Basis for Measuring Critical Thinking Skills." *Educational Leadership* 43, no. 2 (October 1985): 44-48. [8 Refs.]

Ennis defines critical thinking and relates it to higher order thinking skills and Bloom's taxonomy. He provides a comprehensive outline of dispositions and abilities important for curriculum decisions, teaching, and evaluation.

023 Ennis, Robert H. "Rational Thinking and Educational Practice." Chapter 7 in *Philosophy and Education: Eightieth Yearbook of the National Society for the Study of Education, Part I*, edited by Jonas F. Soltis, 143-183. Chicago, IL: National Society for the Study of Education, 1981. [15 Refs.]

This is a discussion of the proficiencies and tendencies which identify a rational thinker. Ennis uses five examples to illustrate how these skills are applicable in education as a guide for making judgments. In the discussion of the examples, Ennis focuses on the common fallacies of equivocation and impact equivocation. In the last half of the paper, he gives a more detailed presentation of the concept of rational thinking. In addition to proficiencies or skills, Ennis believes that a rational thinker must have tendencies or dispositions to use the skills with good judgment.

024 Ennis, Robert H. "The Rationality of Rationality: Why Think Critically?" In *Philosophy of Education 1989: Proceedings of the Forty-Fifth Annual Meeting of the Philosophy of Education Society*, edited by Ralph Page, 402-405. Normal, IL: Philosophy of Education Society, 1990. [3 Refs.]

Reply to Siegel {075}

Ennis argues that Siegel's assertion that rationality is self-justifying assumes that rationality consists of accepting the use of reasons for decision making. He poses two objections to Siegel's position: (1) not all reasons are good ones, for some could be irrational, and (2) Siegel's concept of good reason could be disputed. Ennis asserts that if Siegel had tried to justify critical thinking rather than general rationality, these objections would have been avoided. Ennis believes critical thinking is more deliberately discriminating than general rationality and has a practical justification that assumes making better decisions about practical real life situations is good. Using critical thinking would more likely lead to better decisions, but Siegel wants to resolve the justification problem in a theoretical rather than practical context.

025 Ennis, Robert H. "A Taxonomy of Critical Thinking Dispositions and Abilities." Chapter 1 in *Teaching Thinking Skills: Theory and Practice*, edited by Joan Boykoff Baron and Robert J. Sternberg, 9-26. New York, NY: W.H. Freeman, 1987. [18 Refs.]

Ennis defines critical thinking as "reasonable reflective thinking that is focused on deciding what to believe or do" (p. 10). He briefly compares critical thinking to Bloom's taxonomy and informal logic and discusses some of the advantages of critical thinking. Ennis identifies four basic areas of critical thinking abilities (clarity, basis, inference, and interaction) and describes selected skills under each. He outlines the role played by dispositions for critical thinking and provides a table listing the dispositions and abilities of critical thinking.

026 Facione, Peter A. "Toward a Theory of Critical Thinking." *Liberal Education* 70, no. 3 (Fall 1984): 253-261.

Facione focuses on the questions of how critical thinking can be theoretically and operationally defined, the applicability of critical thinking to various disciplines, and skills that should be taught for evaluating and constructing arguments. His intention is to suggest a direction for more systematic research on critical thinking. After outlining several flawed definitions, Facione defines critical thinking (1) theoretically as argument or a set of statements, one of which forms a conclusion implied or justified by the others and (2) operationally as "the development and evaluation of arguments" (p. 257). He identifies aspects of arguments that a critical thinker should be able to identify and defines a preliminary set of generic argument-building skills found in the methodologies of all disciplines.

027 Finocchiaro, Maurice A. "Critical Thinking and Thinking Critically: Response to Siegel." *Philosophy of the Social Sciences* 20, no. 4 (December 1990): 462-466. [3 Refs.]

Reply to Siegel {072}

See: Finocchiaro {028}

Siegel {341}

Finocchiaro asserts that the distinction Siegel makes between negative and neutral critical thinking is significant. However, the distinction does not address the criticisms Finocchiaro made of Siegel's equation of critical thinking, rationality, and reasoning. Finocchiaro concedes that Siegel's claims that (1) reasoning is a form of evaluation and (2) all thinking is reasoning may be true, but argues that Siegel has given no justification for either. Finocchiaro poses that all reasoning or all evaluative thinking is not critical thinking, but he believes it probable that all thinking that is reasoned, evaluative, and self-reflective is critical thinking.

028 Finocchiaro, Maurice A. "Siegel on Critical Thinking." *Philosophy of the Social Sciences* 19 (December 1989): 483-492. [27 Refs.]

Reply: Siegel {072}
See: Finocchiaro {027}
Siegel {341}

Finocchiaro addresses the arguments for equating critical thinking, reasoning, good reasoning, and rationality made by Harvey Siegel (*Educating Reason: Rationality, Critical Thinking, and Education* {341}). Finocchiaro identifies and analyzes two relatively explicit arguments for the equation: the conceptual and the critical. He argues that neither argument presents an actual reason that justifies equating the four concepts. Finocchiaro also examines several implicit arguments for Siegel's identification, but contends that none of them justify Siegel's position. He concludes that in spite of Siegel's efforts, the relationship of critical thinking, reasoning, and rationality remains problematic.

029 Freeman, James B. "The Human Image System and Thinking Critically in the Strong Sense." *Informal Logic* 11, no. 1 (Winter 1989): 19-40. [24 Refs.]

Freeman sketches the notion of critical thinking in the strong sense as conceived by Robert Ennis, Harvey Siegel, and Richard Paul. He focuses on Paul's description of strong sense critical thinkers as being able to transcend their world views, egocentricity, and sociocentricity. Egocentricity and sociocentricity are linked to one's image system which develops from experiences, social environment, and the need to make meaning of the world as a structured, organized, and consistent universe. Freeman considers some pedagogical implications for teaching critical thinking. He also discusses the nature of good reasons and how the relativism postulated by Hartry Field fails to provide an epistemological basis for good reasoning or critical thinking.

030 Gagné, Robert M. "Some Reflections on Thinking Skills." *Instructional Science* 17, no. 4 (1988): 387-390. [14 Refs.]

Gagné addresses the question of "Are there any thinking skills?" by outlining five points to consider for arriving at a reasonable answer: (1) a skill should have a concrete reference in human performance, (2) a skill should have a specific use, (3) problem solving requires flexibility of thought, (4) thinking involves idiosyncratic elements, and (5) thinking calls upon prior knowledge. Gagné views thinking as a process involving the flexible adoption and discarding of sets. He acknowledges thinking and skills, but questions the existence of thinking skills.

031 Gallo, Delores. "Empathy, Reason, and Imagination: The Impact of Their Relationship on Education." Chapter 18 in *Thinking: The Second International Conference*, edited by David N. Perkins, Jack Lochhead, and John C. Bishop, 305-322. Hillsdale, NJ: Lawrence Erlbaum, 1987. [9 Refs.]

Gallo challenges the philosophical and psychological tradition of distinguishing thought from feeling. She examines the theoretical and empirical relationship between reason and imagination. Gallo concludes that the distinction between critical and creative thinking is one of differing proportions and sequencing of convergent and divergent operations. This dual nature correlates with the cognitive and affective dimensions of empathy. Empathy provides engagement with a variety of culturally identified truths, beliefs, and procedures which enhances one's intellectual exposure to ideas, events, persons, and multiple perspectives. Empathic role playing facilitates the development of an individual's reason and imagination and should be a classroom strategy.

032 Garrison, James W., and Anne Phelan. "Toward a Feminist Poetic of Critical Thinking." In *Philosophy of Education 1989: Proceedings of the Forty-Fifth Annual Meeting of the Philosophy of Education Society*, edited by Ralph Page, 304-314. Normal, IL: Philosophy of Education Society, 1990. [13 Refs.]

Reply: Bailin {012}

New scholarship on ways of knowing has renewed interest in the role played by unreconciled paradoxes, contradictions, and contraries in rational thinking and can be used to overcome gender biases. The logic of paradoxical thinking is grounded in intersubjectivity, shared conversation and community, and in two modes of knowing (separate and connected). The paradox of critical thinking lies in the contrary but complementary relationship of doubting and believing. Separate knowers rely on argumentative reasoning and objective facts for doubting, characterized as traditionally masculine. Connected knowers build on subjective personal experience and empathy to see others in the other's terms, characterized as feminine and linked to believing. The dialectic of critical thinking should be poetic, directed toward disclosing meaning and enhancing understanding rather than determining truth. By recognizing the doubting and believing paradox a more gender sensitive concept of critical thinking can be constructed.

033 Glatthorn, Allan A., and Jonathan Baron. "The Good Thinker." Chapter 13 in *Developing Minds. Vol. 1: A Resource Book for Teaching Thinking*, rev. ed., edited by Arthur L. Costa, 63-67. Alexandria, VA: Association for Supervision and Curriculum Development, 1991. [4 Refs.]

Also printed in Costa {505}, pp. 49-53.

Glatthorn and Baron present a model of the good thinker based on a conception of critical thinking as a search for goals, possibilities, and evidence. They identify common types of thinking, contrast good thinking with poor thinking, and offer suggestions for fostering good critical thinking in the classroom.

034 Govier, Trudy. "Critical Thinking as Argument Analysis?" *Argumentation* 3, no. 2 (May 1989): 115-126. [22 Refs.]

The Informal Logic Movement and the Critical Thinking Movement have many close connections, but should not be construed as identical. Critical thinking should not be reductively defined as the analysis and criticism of argument. Critical thinking is interior, involving reasons, deliberation, judgment, hypothesizing, and is not necessarily expressed. Critical thinking entails intellectual evaluation, involving language, point of view, and selection of facts, in all forms of modern communication. Govier provides examples of critical analysis of non-argumentative aspects of discourse and discusses problems in applying critical thinking to different communications media such as speech, written discourse, and visual imagery. She believes that courses on informal logic could be enriched and enlivened by broadening their scope and including aspects of critical thinking beyond argument analysis.

035 Halstead, Robert. "Response to Stephen Norris." *Philosophy of Education 1983: Proceedings of the Thirty-Ninth Annual Meeting of the Philosophy of Education*

Society, edited by Robert E. Roemer, 191-195. Normal, IL: Philosophy of Education Society, 1984. [3 Refs.]

Reply: Norris {057}

Halstead argues that Norris successfully refutes Harvey Siegel's position that psychology is not relevant to epistemology. Siegel's position elevates knowledge claims to an ideal status where all relevant evidence has been validated. Halstead contends this is not the case in everyday life where prejudice, bias, and uncritical acceptance of authority exist. What is needed is improved critical thinking, beginning with self-criticism.

036 Hawes, Kenneth. "Understanding Critical Thinking." In *Varieties of Thinking: Essays from Harvard's Philosophy of Education Research Center*, edited by V. A. Howard, 47-61. New York, NY: Routledge, 1990. [9 Refs.]

Hawes explores the concept of critical thinking as "thinking which is characterized by some kind of reasoned or reasonable evaluation" (p.47). Evidence supporting this definition is found in the works of John Dewey, Richard Paul, John McPeck, and Robert Ennis who offer various meanings and descriptions of critical thinking. Hawes examines four aspects of critical thinking (purpose, method, result, and thing evaluated) in relation to their implications for education. He stresses the importance of developing a critical perspective and critical attitude in students.

037 Hostetler, Karl. "Community and Neutrality in Critical Thought: A Nonobjectivist View on the Conduct and Teaching of Critical Thinking." *Educational Theory* 41, no. 1 (Winter 1991): 1-12. [23 Refs.]

Hostetler argues for a nonobjectivist view of critical thinking. He pursues ethical and scientific inquiry to support and explain a nonobjectivist view. This view includes the Kantian notion of moral autonomy, that moral agents are autonomous beings who give themselves ethical standards rather than having them determined because they are accepted by other people; therefore, moral agents must be able to judge socially accepted norms critically. Hostetler believes that neutral standards are insufficient for pursuing a rational resolution of a dispute about ethical norms. He uses Thomas Kuhn's history and philosophy of science to further explicate the nonobjectivist view. Kuhn argues that there are shared norms across scientific communities which are necessary to prevent science from being merely arbitrary, but these norms will not resolve differences in interpretation of the values, aims, and purposes that should guide scientific efforts. It is through divergent views within a community that a resolution must be pursued. The implications for education for critical thinking are that (1) there must be a focus on a particular content and context rather than skills and (2) teaching should take the form of facilitation, coaching, and dialogue.

038 Kitchener, Karen Strohm. "Educational Goals and Reflective Thinking." *Educational Forum* 48, no. 1 (Fall 1983): 7-95. [47 Refs.]

Kitchener discusses the various concepts of reflective thinking, emphasizing John Dewey's role in the formulation of the initial concept of reflective thinking and its importance in education. She argues that critical thinking and reflective thinking are not synonymous. Critical thinking conceived as traditional logic or as a problem solving method involves the skills underlying reflective thinking, but leaves out the philosophical and theoretical assumptions upon which reflective thinking is based. Kitchener discusses the seven-stage reflective judgment model that she developed with Patricia King. The model implies that an individual must pass through seven stages of holding assumptions about reality and knowledge before their thinking becomes reflective. She identifies reflective judgment scores for sample high school juniors, college juniors, and doctoral level graduate students, identifying a discrepancy in educational goals and student ability to think reflectively. Kitchener offers three explanations for this discrepancy: (1) either reflective thinking is not being incorporated into classroom activity or is being taught poorly, (2) reflective thinking may be purely maturational, and (3) there is a sequentiality of dogmatism, skepticism, and rationality with appropriate educational experiences.

039 Langsdorf, Lenore. "Ethical and Logical Analysis as Human Sciences." *Human Studies* 11, no. 1 (January 1988): 43-63. [38 Refs.]

Langsdorf defines critical thinking as being "concerned with developing the ability to assess both explicit and implicit claims, so as to determine what I ought to do, or which claim I ought to accept, on the basis of good reasons for that decision..." (p. 45). As part of her definition, she distinguishes critical thinking from logic and argues that Husserlian phenomenology is a fruitful theoretical basis for critical thinking. Langsdorf discusses how the induction/deduction distinction and the fallacies must be grounded in the Husserlian lifeworld of egocentrism, linquistic imprecision, and contextual ambiguity before being retained in her concept of critical thinking. She criticizes philosophy and traditional logic for retreating away from the everyday world into scholarship intended only for fellow professionals. She then compares Richard Zaner's description of his activities as a critical ethicist with her concept of critical thinking. Langsdorf asserts that Zaner's activities should be described as critical thinking done from a phenomenological perspective.

040 Langsdorf, Lenore. "The Form of Television and the Possibility of Critical Thinking." Chapter 40 in *Argumentation: Analysis and Practice. Proceedings of the Conference on Argumentation 1986*, edited by Frans H. van Eemeren, Rob Grootendorst, J. Anthony Blair, and Charles A. Willard, 367-375. Dordrecht, The Netherlands: Foris Publications, 1987. [10 Refs.]

Langsdorf defends the distinction Richard Paul makes between "weak sense" and "strong sense" critical thinking. She realigns Paul's distinction with that between logic and critical thinking. Logic is the application of techniques to given premises, without attending to the context of either technique or premises. Logic results in "weak sense" critical thinking and is not linked to creative thinking. Critical thinking is concerned with the context of the techniques and the implicit premises supplied by the cultural and historical context in which the producers of the argument are situated. Paul places "strong sense" critical thinking in a context of imagined possible selves, multiple world views, and opposing arguments, where it is intrinsically creative thinking. Langsdorf also addresses the suppression of critical thinking by television that does not require the ego to transcend egocentricism through use of experience and imagination.

041 Lipman, Matthew. "Critical Thinking--What Can It Be?" *Educational Leadership* 16, no. 1 (September 1988): 38-43. [12 Refs.]

Lipman contends that current definitions of critical thinking stress outcomes, solutions, and decisions that are too narrow and vague. He argues that critical thinking is "skillful, responsible thinking that facilitates good judgment because it (1) relies upon criteria, (2) is self-correcting, and (3) is sensitive to context" (p. 39). He expands upon the meaning of these three characteristics and advocates cultivating all the cognitive skills necessary for mastering reading, writing, listening, speaking, and reasoning.

042 Marshall, Ernest. "Formalism, Fallacies, and the Teaching of Informal Logic." Chapter 42 in *Argumentation: Analysis and Practices. Proceedings of the Conference on Argumentation 1986*, edited by Frans H. van Eemeren, Rob Grootendorst, J. Anthony Blair, and Charles A. Willard, 386-393. Dordrecht, The Netherlands: Foris Publications, 1987. [4 Refs.]

Marshall argues that the critical thinking approach appears to rely, in crucial ways, on concepts or criteria of formal rather than informal logic. Critical thinking serves to determine the nature of an argument and what is not relevant to correctly evaluating the reasoning of an argument, but has difficulty in evaluating the actual reasoning without incorporating portions of formal logic. Informal fallacies seem to involve emotional or linguistic elements rather than logical errors per se. Both critical thinking and fallacies are important, but their importance does not make them independent of aspects of formal logic.

043 McPeck, John E. Chapters 1-4 in *Critical Thinking and Education*, 1-95. Oxford: Martin Robertson, 1981.

McPeck defines critical thinking as the propensity and skill to use "reflective skepticism" when engaged in some specific activity. He argues that critical thinking cannot be divorced from the skills that define an activity and is not necessarily transferable between subject areas or activities. He criticizes theories and teaching methods that define critical thinking as general skills or in terms of formal or informal logic rather than epistemology, focusing on the concepts of critical thinking found in the Informal Logic Movement and the writings of Robert Ennis and Edward D'Angelo.

044 McPeck, John E. "Critical Thinking and the 'Trivial Pursuit' Theory of Knowledge." *Teaching Philosophy* 8, no. 4 (October 1985): 295-307. [2 Refs.]

Also printed in McPeck {007}, pp.19-33.

McPeck criticizes the Informal Logic Movement, critical thinking literature, and critical thinking tests, such as the Watson-Glaser Critical Thinking Appraisal, for depicting critical thinking as content- and context-free. He argues that critical thinking is not a content-free general ability nor a set of specific skills, but consists of a knowledge component (knowledge-based skills whose applicability is limited to the kind of knowledge being called upon) and critical component (the ability to reflect upon, question, and suspend judgment or belief). The critical component is dependent on the knowledge component. McPeck believes that critical thinking ability varies with the amount of knowledge required by a problem. He asserts that only a broad liberal arts education can come close to supplying the breadth of cross-disciplinary understanding and knowledge needed for everyday problems or an informed critically thinking citizenry. McPeck believes that most critical thinking courses are unsatisfactory and that thinking skills are inherent in disciplines and should be taught as part of them. He offers general suggestions for teachers.

045 McPeck, John E. "Response to H. Siegel." In *Philosophy of Education 1985: Proceedings of the Forty-First Annual Meeting of the Philosophy of Education Society*, edited by David Nyberg, 73-77. Normal, IL: Philosophy of Education Society, 1986.

A version printed in McPeck {007}, pp. 86-101.
Reply to Siegel {071}

McPeck asserts (a) that Siegel's arguments do not show that the general activity of thinking is not connected to any object of thought and (b) that Siegel's examples of general reasoning describe specific skills rather than generalized ability. McPeck acknowledges value in learning logic, but believes Siegel overestimates the role of logic in critical thinking. Reason assessment is primarily an epistemic, not logical, matter to McPeck. Rationality is concerned with more than assessing reasons and, contrary to Siegel's position, is broader than critical thinking.

046 McPeck, John E. "Response to S. Norris." *Philosophy of Education 1985: Proceedings of the Forty-First Annual Meeting of the Philosophy of Education Society*, edited by David Nyberg, 89-96. Normal, IL: Philosophy of Education Society, 1986.

A version printed in McPeck {007}, pp. 86-101.
Reply to Norris, Stephen {056}

McPeck argues that Norris has confused causal questions (which are empirical) with questions of meaning (which are non-empirical) and by doing so, confuses scientific questions with philosophical ones. McPeck asserts that Norris's criticisms are based on a reductionist view of critical thinking as mental powers rising from certain mental structures and processes. To McPeck, reductionism addresses questions unrelated to a concept of critical thinking.

047 Meyers, Chet. "What Critical Thinking Means across the Disciplines." Chapter 1 in *Teaching Students to Think Critically: A Guide for Faculty in All Disciplines*, 1-10. San Francisco, CA: Jossey-Bass, 1986. [16 Refs.]

Meyers reviews and criticizes concepts that identify critical thinking with logic or general problem solving and that assume critical thinking to be skills separate from specific subjects. He sees critical thinking as the active consideration and analysis stemming from the underlying epistemology of a given discipline. Meyers supports his position by citing studies which show little transference of critical thinking skills from one discipline to another. He stresses the need for a motivational framework for analysis of materials in a discipline or a perspective that organizes and makes the discipline meaningful.

048 Missimer, Connie. "Perhaps by Skill Alone." *Informal Logic* 12, no. 3 (Fall 1990): 145-153. [19 Refs.]

Missimer questions the dominant view (the Character View) among critical thinking theorists that the critical thinker has certain character traits, dispositions, or virtues. She argues that its supporters do not agree on the attitudes, dispositions, or virtues that are necessary for critical thinking. The Character View excludes many thinkers, such as Newton and Marx, who display character traits at odds with those it advocates. In place of the Character View, Missimer proposes a "pure practiced-skill" conception of critical thinking in which critical thinking is acquired through practice and eventually becomes a habit. She discusses the historical evidence of this skill view, its advantage of theoretical simplicity, and its separation from ethical prescriptions entailed in the Character View.

049 Missimer, Connie. "Why Two Heads Are Better Than One: Philosophical and Pedagogical Implications of a Social View of Critical Thinking." In *Philosophy of Education 1988: Proceedings of the Forty-Fourth Annual Meeting of the Philosophy of Education Society*, edited by James M. Giarelli, 388-402. Normal, IL: Philosophy of Education Society, 1989. [11 Refs.]

Reply: Bailin {014}

Missimer distinguishes between the Individual View and Social View concepts of critical thinking. In the Individual View, critical thinking is the reasoned judgment of an individual, while in the Social View critical thinking is the reasoned judgment which considers other reasoned judgments or alternative views. Missimer criticizes the Individual View as being too dependent on logic or reasonableness (which assumes impartiality will produce correct judgments), for being divorced from content, for not considering the historical evolution of critical thinking important, and for impeding innovation. The Social View avoids the problems of the Individual View by stressing the importance of content and consideration of all views. Critical thinking is not subject-specific as John McPeck argues. Missimer asserts that McPeck confuses evidence (which is subject-specific) with theories (which are trans-disciplinary). Students should be taught information that forms part of the major theories of a subject, though not discouraging the exploration of minor theories.

050 Moros, Daniel A., Rosamond Rhodes, Bernard Baumrin, and James J. Strain. "Thinking Critically in Medicine and Its Ethics: Relating Applied Science and Applied Ethics." *Journal of Applied Philosophy* 4, no. 2 (1987): 229-243. [10 Refs.]

Two schemata outlining the elements in the evaluation of factual claims, judgments, and beliefs and the elements of moral reasoning in medical encounters form the framework for the discussion in this article. Each of the ten elements within each schema is specifically addressed and related to the technical or ethical aspects of medicine. The authors discuss the similarity between critical thinking in applied science and applied ethics, as well as between clinical science and the theoretical sciences.

051 Mucklow, Neale H. "A Case for Teaching Students to Think Critically in the Disciplines." In *Thinking about Thinking: Proceedings of the Thirty-First Annual Meeting of the South Atlantic Philosophy of Education Society*, edited by Samuel M. Craver, 39-48. Richmond, VA: South Atlantic Philosophy of Education Society, 1987. [5 Refs.]

Reply: Owen {298}

Mucklow argues that critical thinking is using methodological norms to evaluate the thinking, positions, and reasoning of another individual. Critical thinking is concerned with the logic and coherence of another's position, as well as the truth of that position. Methodological norms supply the critical thinker with guidelines and a perspective for understanding and criticism. These norms are grounded in particular disciplines and differ for each. Mucklow considers several objections to his position, focusing on the question of why the ontology of a discipline is related to what should be taught in that discipline.

052 Neimark, Edith D. "A Model of the Mature Thinker." *Thinking, Reasoning, and Writing*, edited by Elaine P. Maimon, Barbara F. Nodine, and Finbarr W. O'Connor, 47-68. New York, NY: Longman, 1989. [53 Refs.]

Neimark offers a model of the mature thinker. She identifies four necessary characteristics of thinking in the mature thinker: transformative, systematic, detached, and evaluative. These characteristics enable the mature thinker to deliberately transform key concepts, identify defining features, and evaluate the uniqueness or utility of the concepts. Neimark discusses implications for transforming students into mature thinkers and contrasts styles approaches with skills approaches.

053 Nickerson, Raymond S. *Reflections on Reasoning*. Hillsdale, NJ: Lawrence Erlbaum, 1986. 136 pp.

Nickerson discusses the nature of reason. He examines the relationship between reasoning and the concepts of language, logic, inventiveness/hypothesizing, knowledge, and truth in the second chapter. Nickerson contrasts reasoning and rationalizing, and identifies three categories of impediments to effective reasoning: natural limitations, knowledge impediments, and attitudinal impediments. In chapter three, Nickerson discusses the nature of beliefs. He outlines the distinction between belief and opinion, the basic properties of beliefs, how to decide what to believe, the consequences of false beliefs, and the need to appreciate opposing beliefs. Nickerson discusses the nature of assertions in chapter four. He identifies several types of assertions and describes methods for evaluating assertions. Nickerson deals with the nature of arguments in chapter five. He discusses the types of arguments, how to identify arguments, and how to evaluate them. In chapter six, Nickerson focuses on stratagems or approaches that are taken for the purpose of persuading or influencing someone to draw a desired conclusion or assertion. He identifies and discusses several common reasoning fallacies. In the concluding chapter of the text, Nickerson offers some rules or suggestions for reasoning.

054 Nolen, Donald M. "A Critical Theory of Critical Thinking." Chapter 38 in *Argumentation: Analysis and Practices. Proceedings of the Conference on Argumentation 1986*, edited by Frans H. van Eemeren, Rob Grootendorst, J. Anthony Blair, and Charles A. Willard, 349-357. Dordrecht, The Netherlands: Foris Publications, 1987. [11 Refs.]

Nolen attributes much of the confusion over the nature and justification of critical thinking to the relationships between technical, practical, and reflective thinking. He examines these three types of thinking, discussing the philosophical traditions from which they developed and the pedagogy of each type. Nolen outlines an alternative critical theory of critical thinking that emphasizes dialectical reasoning and methodology rather than the monological universalism of formal logic or the dialogical relativism of informal logic.

055 Norris, Stephen P. "The Choice of Standard Conditions in Defining Critical Thinking Competence." *Educational Theory* 35, no. 1 (Winter 1985): 97-107. [17 Refs.]

Norris outlines John McPeck's complaints about general critical thinking skills expressed in McPeck's book *Critical*

Thinking and Education {006}). Norris scrutinizes general logical competence as a possible general critical thinking skill, outlining Robert Ennis's account of it. He then discusses McPeck's criticisms of Ennis, detailing the epistemological and psychological assumptions in McPeck's position. Norris examines research evidence for each position and the problems and issues neither position resolves. He asserts that both concepts lack sufficient scientific evidence to justify their conclusions. Norris suggests that the notion of standard conditions used in the natural sciences may help in clarifying many of the problems found in definitions of human abilities. He believes all such definitions are interest-relative (dependent on the interests being served by the definition and knowledge of the underlying structures and processes of human reasoning). Further research on human reasoning is needed, but Norris believes it is unlikely that one definition of critical thinking ultimately will be accepted.

056 Norris, Stephen P. "Thinking about Critical Thinking: Philosophers Can't Go It Alone." In *Philosophy of Education 1985: Proceedings of the Forty-First Annual Meeting of the Philosophy of Education Society*, edited by David Nyberg, 79-87. Normal, IL: Philosophy of Education Society, 1986. [14 Refs.]

Reprinted in McPeck {007}, pp. 67-74, 127-128.
Reply: McPeck {046}

Three questions related to critical thinking are examined: (1) How should "critical thinking" be defined? (2) Is critical thinking ability generalizable across subject matter areas? (3) How ought the validity of critical thinking tests be determined? Criticizing the conceptual analysis method used by philosophers to define critical thinking, Norris proposes that the term be defined as mental powers rising from mental structures and processes. Since these structures are the result of being human, the same structures should be generalizable across subject areas.

057 Norris, Stephen P. "Trying Eyewitness Testimony, Validating Tests, and Teaching Critical Thinking." In *Philosophy of Education 1983: Proceedings of the Thirty-Ninth Annual Meeting of the Philosophy of Education Society*, edited by Robert E. Roemer, 179-189. Normal, IL: Philosophy of Education Society, 1984. [8 Refs.]

Norris disagrees with Harvey Siegel's argument that psychological information (i.e., effects of conflict of interest, excited emotional states, and leading questions) has no direct bearing on the assessment of authoritative-sounding statements. Norris argues that Siegel uses two different criteria of relevance--to be relevant psychological beliefs must justify a belief while epistemological information need only be supportive of that belief. Norris contends that both psychological and epistemological information need only be supportive of a belief to be relevant to the assessment of that belief. He presents a counterexample to Siegel's position based on Elizabeth Loftus's work on the influence of post-event experiences on remembering and interpreting remembrances. Norris claims that accepting Siegel's position would lead to the abandonment of sound practices of teaching and testing critical thinking.

058 Paul, Richard W. "Background Logic, Critical Thinking, and Irrational Language Games." *Informal Logic* 7, no. 1 (Winter 1985): 9-18. [1 Ref.]

Paul states that historically disciplines have emphasized one-dimensional, unquestioning procedures and abstract notation rather than self-critical, dialectical, cross-disciplinary intercourse. He asserts that most people reflect the background logic and language games implicit in their peer groups and society, presenting views that are irrational, confused, and biased. Paul believes that there are four dimensions of background logic and three language logic groups. From each language logic group emerges a different form of life, one being the reasoner or critical thinker. Only critical thinkers are capable of totalizing experiences rationally and understanding the influence of background logic on behavior and thought. They possess skills that are informal, dialectical, cross-disciplinary, rational, and self-critical.

059 Paul, Richard W. "Critical Thinking in the Strong Sense and the Role of Argumentation in Everyday Life." Chapter 35 in *Argumentation: Across the Lines of Discipline. Proceedings of the Conference on Argumentation 1986*, edited by Frans H. van Eemeren, Rob Grootendorst, J. Anthony Blair, and Charles A. Willard, 379-382. Dordrecht, The Netherlands: Foris Publications, 1987.

Paul distinguishes "weak sense" critical thinking from "strong sense" critical thinking. "Weak sense" critical thinking refers to extensive skills in constructing and analyzing arguments without applying those skills self-critically to beliefs, values and convictions. "Strong sense" critical thinking refers to the ability (a) to engage in self-reflexive Socratic questioning, (b) to reconstruct alien and opposing belief systems empathetically, and (c) to reason dialogically and dialectically. Paul asserts that there is a tacit infrastructure of logic underlying human behavior. Arguments justifying or defending behavior must be examined in relation to the background logic embedded in behavior. This examination can only be accomplished through overcoming egocentrism and sociocentrism through dialogical and dialectical reasoning.

060 Paul, Richard W. "Critical Thinking and the Critical Person." Chapter 22 in *Thinking: The Second International Conference*, edited by David N. Perkins, Jack Lochhead, and John C. Bishop, 373-403. Hillsdale, NJ: Lawrence Erlbaum, 1987. [24 Refs.]

Paul presents a concept of critical thinking and the critical person which links rationality, irrationality, education, socialization, and the critical society. He distinguishes philosophical approaches from the theoretical mode used by cognitive psychologists. Paul identifies two types of critical thinking: (1) weak critical thinking in which an individual thinks critically about only monological issues and does not critique personal bias or sociocentricism and (2) strong critical thinking in which an individual has developed self-criticism, an ability to construct strong opposing positions, and an ability to reason dialectically and multilogically. He describes alternative theories about strong sense critical thinking and the affective side of reason. Paul examines the sociocentrically critical person and the ideal critical society. He argues that critical habits of thought must be introduced into the classroom in order to overcome the egocentric and sociocentric curriculum presentation of world views. Paul critiques examples of such egocentrism and sociocentrism found in social studies and in a state department of education statewide testing program.

061 Perkins, David N. "Problem Theory." *Varieties of Thinking: Essays from Harvard's Philosophy of Education Research Center*, edited by V. A. Howard, 15-46. New York, NY: Routledge, 1990. [14 Refs.]

In examining the nature of problems, Perkins identifies features of formal problems and their role in defining the problematics of problems. He uses the features of formality, stability, transparency, simplicity, and deliberation to illustrate the problematic aspects of sports, games, and open-ended real problems such as writing an essay or running a business. Perkins also discusses the concept of challenge and examines six types, relating them to cognitive skills and specific problem domains. He outlines the benefits of formalizing and de-formalizing problems.

062 Peters, Roger. "Critical Thinking." Chapter 10 in *Practical Intelligence: Working Smarter in Business and Everyday Life*, 241-262. New York, NY: Harper & Row, 1987. [31 Refs.]

Peters summarizes his analysis of the critical thinking process into the mnemonic SOME LIP which symbolizes seven critical tasks: (1) considering Sources, (2) maintaining Open minds, (3) defining Meanings, (4) evaluating Evidence, (5) analyzing Logic, (6) examining Implications, and (7) unearthing Presumptions. He presents case studies of practical critical thinking by executives, lawyers, scientists, police officers, detectives, investigative reporters, and political columnists.

063 Price, Kingsley. "On Critical Thinking: Response to Professor McPeck." In *Thinking about Thinking: Proceedings of the Thirty-First Annual Meeting of the South Atlantic Philosophy of Education Society*, edited by Samuel M. Craver, 4-11. Richmond, VA: South Atlantic Philosophy of Education Society, 1987.

Price examines and criticizes several definitions of critical thinking. He defines critical thinking as "thinking about somebody's thinking in order to discover how one part should be connected with another in such a way as to make the whole of the objects revealed in awareness as good a whole as possible..." (p. 7). Price agrees with McPeck's position that critical thinking is subject-specific, but finds problems in the arguments McPeck uses to support that position. Price presents an alternative argument that avoids these problems. He views thinking as an ability humans have by nature. It cannot be taught in the sense of producing the ability, but by providing opportunities that encourage its use. He believes that students should be encouraged to think critically early in their formal education in subjects such as social studies and history.

064 Ranyard, Rob. "The Role of Rational Models in the Decision Process." Chapter 20 in *Lines of Thinking: Reflections on the Psychology of Thought. Vol. 1, Representation, Reasoning, Analogy, and Decision Making*, edited by K. J. Gilhooly, M. T. G. Keane, R. H. Logie, and G. Erdos, 289-298. New York, NY: John Wiley, 1990. [25 Refs.]

Ranyard identifies three concepts of rationality: (1) the super optimistic or olympian, which views human reasoning as almost infallible, (2) the pessimistic or primitive, which views human reasoning as seriously flawed and error-prone, and (3) the new optimist, which views human rationality more favorably than the pessimistic but less so than the super optimistic. He examines two rational models of choice for each concept, identifying the type of evaluation processes, judgment processes, and information integration supported by each concept.

065 Reeder, Harry P. "The Nature of Critical Thinking." *Informal Logic* 6 (July 1984): 18-22. [30 Refs.]

Reeder defines critical thinking as the "use of a combination of logical, rhetorical, and philosophical skills and attitudes which promotes the ability to discover intersubjectively what we should believe" (p. 18). He analyzes the elements of critical thinking in the context of rhetoric, logic, and philosophy. Comments by Richard Paul with responses from Reeder follow the article.

066 Sanders, James T. "Thinking without Reasoning, Reasoning without Virtue." In *Philosophy of Education 1988: Proceedings of the Forty-Fourth Annual Meeting of the Philosophy of Education Society*, edited by James M. Giarelli, 210-212. Normal, IL: Philosophy of Education Society, 1989. [2 Refs.]

Reply to Warren {079}

Warren is criticized for presenting rather than explaining his notion of thinking. Sanders argues that Warren's descriptions are often contradictory and unacceptable and that his concept presupposes a faculty psychology which has been wholly discredited.

067 Schrag, Francis. "Are There Levels of Thinking?" *Teachers College Record* 90, no. 4 (Summer 1989): 529-533. [3 Refs.]

Schrag explores the distinction between higher-order and lower-order thinking and concludes that efforts at distinguishing precise and operational levels of thinking have failed. The author cites ambiguities and inconsistencies of Lauren Resnick's characteristics of higher-order thinking and of the thinking behind Bloom's taxonomy of educational objectives in the cognitive domain. Shrag believes that the thinking required for tasks is not determined by the type of problem or task or by semantic or syntactical features of problems as suggested by Resnick and Bloom, respectively, but by the resources of the thinker.

068 Selman, Mark. "Another Way of Talking about Critical Thinking." In *Philosophy of Education 1987: Proceedings of the Forty-Third Annual Meeting of the Philosophy of Education Society*, edited by Barbara Arnstine and Donald Arnstine, 169-178. Normal, IL: Philosophy of Education Society, 1988. [8 Refs.]

Selman advocates reconceptualizing critical thinking in terms of established epistemological concepts such as understanding, judgment, and the evaluation of claims. He argues that current concepts of critical thinking, as delineated by Robert Ennis and Stephen Norris, have overemphasized the role of skills, abilities, and dispositions. Critical thinking should be taught as responsible decision making based on good reasoning, rather than as attacking and defending claims and actions.

069 Siegel, Harvey. "Educating Reason: Critical Thinking, Informal Logic, and the Philosophy of Education. Part One: A Critique of McPeck and a Sketch of an Alternative View." *American Philosophical Association Newsletter on Teaching Philosophy* (Spring-Summer 1985): 10-13. [9 Refs.]

Siegel identifies difficulties in John McPeck's position that critical thinking cannot be regarded as a generalized skill and should not be taught as a separate course. Siegel argues that McPeck (1) confuses thinking generally with specific acts of thinking, (2) presents a notion of critical thinking as "reflective skepticism" that is circular in its justification, (3) mistakenly asserts that informal logic is not relevant to critical thinking, neglecting the role informal logic plays in reason assessment, (4) does not undermine the practical necessity and utility of general critical thinking courses by distinguishing between logic and information, and (5) makes critical thinking a sub-species of rationality when it is a coextension of rationality. Siegel believes that McPeck raises important questions regarding the relation of critical thinking to informal logic even though his concept of critical thinking is flawed.

070 Siegel, Harvey. "Epistemology, Critical Thinking, and Critical Thinking Pedagogy." *Argumentation* 3, no. 2 (May 1989): 127-140. [9 Refs.]

Siegel believes a critical thinker bases beliefs and actions on reasons and a commitment to rationality. He argues that there is an epistemology underlying critical thinking that is fundamental to an adequate understanding of critical thinking. In this epistemology a belief in reasons and rational justification must be conceived as non-relativistic and independent of truth. Epistemology should be part of the critical thinking curriculum in order to examine the justification for thinking critically.

071 Siegel, Harvey. "McPeck, Informal Logic and the Nature of Critical Thinking." In *Philosophy of Education 1985: Proceedings of the Forty-First Annual Meeting of the Philosophy of Education Society*, edited by David Nyberg, 61-72. Normal, IL: Philosophy of Education Society, 1986. [14 Refs.]

Reprinted in McPeck {007}, pp. 75-85.

Although supporters of the Informal Logic Movement consider critical thinking as its central concern, Siegel believes they have not sufficiently explored the connection between critical thinking and logic or between critical thinking and education. He credits McPeck with raising questions about these two relationships and with attempting to clarify them. Yet, Siegel finds many difficulties in

McPeck's position: (1) he confuses thinking generally with specific acts of thinking, making thinking subject-specific, (2) his notion of reflective skepticism is opaque and defective, (3) he is ambivalent about the relevance of logic to critical thinking, (4) he overstates the need to know and understand the language of a discipline in order to do critical thinking in that discipline, and (5) his distinction between critical thinking and rationality is incompatible with his epistemological approach. Though McPeck has re-opened the examination of several important questions concerning critical thinking, Siegel asserts that McPeck's solutions to those questions are inadequate.

072 Siegel, Harvey. "Must Thinking Be Critical to Be Critical Thinking?: Reply to Finocchiaro." *Philosophy of the Social Sciences* 20, no. 4 (December 1990): 453-461. [3 Refs.]

Reply to Finocchiaro {028}
See: Finocchiaro {027}
Siegel {341}

Siegel criticizes Finocchiaro for failing to distinguish between negative and neutral critical thinking. Finocchiaro views critical thinking as negative evaluation whereas Siegel conceives critical thinking as unprejudged, neutrally reasoned evaluation. Siegel's concept equates critical thinking, rationality, and reasoning. Siegel presents four arguments defending his concept: (1) critical thinking, rationality, and reasoning involve reasons and the proper assessment of reasons, (2) competent reason assessment involves rationality, (3) the concept is consistent with use of "critical thinking" among critical thinking theorists, and (4) the concept makes the most sense if critical thinking is to be regarded as an educational ideal. Siegel also argues that the negative evaluation concept of critical thinking is part of the neutral evaluation concept.

073 Siegel, Harvey. "Psychology, Epistemology, and Critical Thinking." In *Philosophy of Education 1983: Proceedings of the Thirty-Ninth Annual Meeting of the Philosophy of Education Society*, edited by Robert E. Roemer, 197-200. Normal, IL: Philosophy of Education Society, 1984. [2 Refs.]

Reply to Norris {057}

Siegel states that Norris misinterpreted his position on beliefs. Siegel denies that a belief counts as evidence for a knowledge claim. He argues that Norris's counter-example of experiments by Elizabeth Loftus on the effect of post-event questioning on memory is not purely psychological. Loftus's causal law incorporates epistemological considerations and actually supports Siegel's position that psychological information does not contribute to the evaluation of knowledge claims. Principles of critical thinking incorporate epistemological components, not psychological information alone.

074 Siegel, Harvey. "Skills, Attitudes, and Education for Critical Thinking." Chapter 39 in *Argumentation: Analysis and Practices. Proceedings of the Conference on Argumentation 1986*, edited by Frans H. van Eemeren, Rob Grootendorst, J. Anthony Blair, and Charles A. Willard, 358-365. Dordrecht, The Netherlands: Foris Publications, 1987. [11 Refs.]

Siegel believes the defining characteristic of critical thinking is its focus on reasons and their power to justify or warrant beliefs, claims, and actions. In addition to cognitive skills, the critical attitude is an integral component of a conception of critical thinking. A critical thinker must have the disposition to engage in reason assessment and a willingness to conform judgment and action to principle. Siegel defines a critical thinker as one who is "appropriately moved by reasons."

075 Siegel, Harvey. "Why Be Rational? On Thinking Critically about Critical Thinking." In *Philosophy of Education 1989: Proceedings of the Forty-Fifth Annual Meeting of the Philosophy of Education Society*, edited by Ralph Page, 392-401. Normal, IL: Philosophy of Education Society, 1990. [4 Refs.]

Reply: Ennis {024}

Seigel considers two responses to the problem of justification for being rational: (1) the demand for a justification of rationality is bogus since such justification would be circular or question-begging and (2) the demand cannot be rationally answered. He rejects both positions, stating that rationality is self-justifying because serious inquiry, even by a skeptic, presupposes the justification of rationality. By justifying rationality, Siegel believes he provides an underlying rationale for fostering critical thinking.

076 Siegel, Marjorie, and Robert F. Carey. *Critical Thinking: A Semiotic Perspective*. Monographs on Teaching Critical Thinking, no. 1. Bloomington, IN: ERIC Clearinghouse on Reading and Communication Skills; Urbana, IL: National Council of Teachers of English, 1989. 55 pp. [49 Refs.]

The authors outline the basic skills definition of critical thinking proposed by Robert Ennis and summarize criticisms of this definition made by John McPeck and others. Siegel and Carey identify semiotic themes such as reflection, skepticism, and inquiry found in current definitions of critical thinking. They discuss the work of C.S. Pierce on semiotics and present a semiotic conception of critical thinking as a process of inquiry. Siegel and Carey stress the importance of providing a classroom environment that encourages discovery, risk taking, and reflective skepticism. They briefly describe a first grade classroom that exemplifies the semiotic perspective. The monograph includes an annotated bibliography on perspectives of critical thinking.

077 Smith, Frank. *To Think*. New York, NY: Teachers College Press, 1990. 181 pp. [231 Refs.]

Smith believes that most of the distinctions drawn between types of thinking are semantic rather than psychological. Remembering, understanding, and learning are terms that refer to different perspectives, points of view, or different subjects of thinking. Smith argues that critical thinking is not a generalizable skill or set of skills, for its application depends on the specific subject matter that is involved. Critical thinking requires experience, the ability to make judgments, and the disposition to know when to be critical. Smith believes that the teaching of thinking should focus on providing opportunities to think. Teachers should model thinking and provide a classroom environment that allows students to use their imagination to create alternative views and realities.

078 Wagner, Paul A. "Informing Critical Thinkers about Cognitive Science." In *Philosophy of Education 1987: Proceedings of the Forty-Third Annual Meeting of the*

Philosophy of Education Society, edited by Barbara Arnstine and Donald Arnstine, 179-183. Normal, IL: Philosophy of Education Society, 1988. [10 Refs.]

Reply to Selman {068}

Wagner asserts that Selman dislikes mixing philosophical epistemic justification with the tasks and processes of psychology. Wagner defends Robert Ennis against two of Selman's accusations: (1) ambiguous use of key terms and (2) the omission of explicit epistemological standards. Selman wants criteria for both the processes and the outcomes of critical thinking. Cognitive scientists, like Ennis, are concerned only with modeling the language of thought or the process of thinking. To Wagner, the inferential peculiarities unique to individual disciplines are nothing more than consequences of semantic nets and specific interests found in each discipline. Thinking is generalizable, but epistemic appraisal is not. Wagner asserts that both Selman and McPeck fail to recognize this distinction in their concepts of critical thinking.

079 Warren, Thomas H. "Critical Thinking beyond Reasoning: Restoring Virtue to Thought." *Philosophy of Education 1988: Proceedings of the Forty-Fourth Annual Meeting of the Philosophy of Education Society*, edited by James M. Giarelli, 200-209. Normal, IL: Philosophy of Education Society, 1989. [11 Refs.]

Reply: Sanders {066}

Warren views the pedagogical content of the critical thinking movement as focusing on reasoning rather than thinking. He equates reasoning with the skills of rationality, calculation, and measurement. He identifies thinking as reflection, wonderment, and a quest for meaning and self-fulfillment. Warren argues that thinking is always critical. He asserts that moral knowledge and behavior are exclusive properties of thinking, not reasoning. He suggests that the critical thinking movement may be a response to the growing technological superiority of other nations over the United States. While supporting the teaching of critical reasoning across the curriculum, he warns that critical reasoning alone is not sufficient to help America regain its economic leadership.

3

RESEARCH

080 Arlin, Patricia Kennedy. "Problem Finding and Young Adult Cognition." Chapter 2 in *Adult Cognitive Development: Methods and Models*, edited by Robert A. Mines and Karen S. Kitchener, 22-32. New York, NY: Praeger, 1986. [30 Refs.]

Arlin reviews three models she has used to describe the process of problem finding: (1) a cognitive processes model, (2) a cognitive development model, and (3) a cognitive science model. She discusses a unification of problem finding strategies and structures into a more comprehensive conception of adult cognition as a fifth stage or a stage of postformal thought beyond the Piagetian model. Arlin bases this fifth stage on L. Apostle's conception of postformal thought as representing both contractions and expansions of logical systems. Arlin also discusses her current research on the relationship between formal operations and the emergence of contractions and expansions of thought in a group of art and science students. The ongoing study indicates subtle new thought forms in young adulthood.

081 Bass, George M., Jr., and Harvey W. Perkins. "Teaching Critical Thinking Skills with CAI." *Electronic Learning* 4, no. 2 (October 1984): 32, 34, 96.

The authors investigated whether using computer-aided instruction (CAI) to teach critical thinking is more effective than using more conventional approaches. They designed an elective nine-week course to help seventh graders learn four critical thinking skills (verbal analogies, logical reasoning, inductive/ deductive reasoning, and word-problem analysis) through different instructional methods. Results of the study showed that the experimental group, students who received CAI, showed greater gains in verbal analogies skills and inductive/deductive reasoning skills, but did not show significantly greater gains in logical reasoning or word-problem skills than the control group who did not receive CAI.

082 Beatty, Michael J. "Increasing Students' Choice-Making Consistency: The Effect of Decision Rule-Use Training." *Communication Education* 37, no. 2 (April 1988): 95-105. [36 Refs.]

Beatty attributes the inability of college students to transfer the principles of problem solving and decision making to the lack of instruction in choice making or how to identify an alternative among possible solutions. A study of undergraduates given no instruction in decision rules revealed that one third of the subjects made inconsistent decisions ranging the three decision-rule options (maximum, maximax, maximin) as opposed to using one for all decisions. Beatty conducted a second study to investigate the factors leading to inconsistent decision-rule use. Results showed that (1) consistency in choice-making can be increased through decision making information presented in matrix form and in instruction in decision-rule theory and (2) the validity of decision-rule is dependent on an individual's perspective and philosophy underlying decision making. Beatty addresses the implications for the classroom and the need for further research using other variables.

083 Brabeck, Mary M. "Critical Thinking Skills and Reflective Judgment Development: Redefining the Aims of Higher Education." *Journal of Applied Developmental Psychology* 4, no. 1 (January-March 1983): 23-34. [31 Refs.]

Brabeck studied the relation between Kitchener and King's seven-stage reflective judgment model and the composite skills of critical thinking. A biographical Data Sheet, the Watson-Glaser Critical Thinking Appraisal Form A, and the Reflective Judgment Interview were administered to 119 female students from Catholic educational institutions (high schools, colleges, and graduate schools). Students were grouped according to educational level and high or low critical thinking scores. The groups were then compared on the basis of their Reflective Judgment Interview scores. The study showed that reflective judgment development is not contingent on critical thinking skills.

084 Braxton, John M., and Robert C. Nordvall. "Quality of Graduate Department Origin of Faculty and Its Relationship to Undergraduate Course Examination Questions." *Research in Higher Education* 28, no. 2 (1988): 145-159. [31 Refs.]

Braxton and Nordvall examined the relationship between graduate school training and the frequency at which faculty construct critical thinking questions for undergraduate course examinations. They found that (1) graduates from departments with faculty of higher scholarly quality more frequently use examination questions requiring both analysis and synthesis and (2) such questions are more frequent in courses in disciplines of lower paradigmatic development than those of higher paradigmatic development.

085 Bryden, David P. "What Do Law Students Learn? A Pilot Study." *Journal of Legal Education* 34, no. 3 (September 1984): 479-506. [14 Refs.]

Although law school professors aspire to teaching students how to think, Bryden believes they make little effort to determine their degree of success. Examination answers and class recitation are two major sources of evidence regarding teaching results, but are unreliable. Bryden proposes that functional analysis, the distinction between holding or dictum, and statutory construction are three aspects of thinking that can be tested and that can reveal information regarding teaching effectiveness. Bryden conducted a pilot project to examine the feasibility of testing these analytical skills. He constructed two examinations containing questions requiring these skills, which were administered to samples of third-year classes and first-year classes at three reputable law schools. The results confirmed that seniors are more adept at legal reasoning and more apt to notice potentially significant statutory phrases than novice law students, but indicated deficiencies in careful reading and in thoughtful reasoning. Bryden notes as problems the absence of a professional consensus on what skills to teach, how to teach such skills, and the failure to emphasize analytical skills on exams. He advocates pedagogical reform rather than curricular reform.

086 Burbules, Nicholas C., and Marcia C. Linn. "Response to Contradiction: Scientific Reasoning during Adolescence." *Journal of Educational Psychology* 80, no. 1 (March 1988): 67-75. [19 Refs.]

The authors analyzed the scientific reasoning of students in fifth, sixth, seventh, and eighth grades from ten schools to determine the influence of contradiction and awareness of variables on the restructuring of their scientific ideas. Their study focused on how students predicted displaced volume. After administration of the Predicting Displaced Volume pretest, 166 students were asked to predict how much water would be displaced by immersed objects and to test their predictions. A portion of the students were told the proper displacement rule. The findings from the study suggest that students learn principles more quickly when personally confronted with concrete contradictions counter to their expectations than by just being told a rule or principle. The study also showed that reasoning strategies for the task could be taught within twenty-minute interviews.

087 Byrne, Ruth M. J., and P. N. Johnson-Laird. "Models and Deductive Reasoning." Chapter 11 in *Lines of Thinking: Reflections on the Psychology of Thought. Vol. 1, Representation, Reasoning, Analogy and Decision Making*, edited by K. J. Gilhooly, M. T. G. Keane, R. H. Logie, and G. Erdos, 139-151. New York, NY: John Wiley, 1990. [26 Refs.]

Byrne and Johnson-Laird present their studies of three domains of deductive reasoning: (1) the construction of hypothetical scenarios, (2) two-dimensional spatial reasoning, and (3) reasoning based on multiple quantified premises. Experiments were designed to test three theories on the processes underlying deductive reasoning: (1) that the mind contains a set of formal rules of inference, (2) mental rules of inference have a specific content like those of an expert system, and (3) inference depends on a search for alternative semantic interpretations (models) of the premises. Experimental results suggest that the model-based theory gives the most plausible account of the process of inference.

088 Campbell, Christine M. "Guided Design: Critical Thinking and Proficiency in the University Foreign Language Classroom." In *Thinking across Cultures: The Third International Conference*, edited by Donald M. Topping, Doris C. Crowell, and Victor N. Kobayashi, 445-453. Hillsdale, NJ: Lawrence Erlbaum, 1989. [16 Refs.]

Campbell investigated the effect of Guided Design, a model and method for teaching cognitive abilities based on Bloom's taxonomy, on student foreign language proficiency in a third-semester college Spanish course. The results showed superior student language proficiency in writing in Spanish for students using Guided Design materials, but no significant difference in reading or evaluative capacity. Student attitudes toward instructors and the course favored use of Guided Design.

089 Cheng, Patricia W., Keith J. Holyoak, Richard E. Nisbett, and Lindsay M. Oliver. "Pragmatic Versus Syntactic Approaches to Training Deductive Reasoning." *Cognitive Psychology* 18, no. 3 (July 1986): 293-328. [37 Refs.]

In contrast to the two dominant views of how individuals reason (by syntactic, domain-independent rules of logic, and by domain-specific knowledge), the authors propose the individuals reason with pragmatic reasoning schemata. The authors conducted three experiments to investigate the influence of reasoning schemata on performance and the usefulness of various training procedures. Evidence from these investigations revealed that individuals typically reason using abstract knowledge structures organized pragmatically rather than syntactic rules of standard logic. Training in an entire course in standard logic or a brief training session in formal logic produced no substantial effects on individuals' ability to reason deductively. The authors contend that education in reasoning will more likely be effective in trying to refine pragmatically useful rules that individuals will have naturally induced from everyday experiences.

090 Chi, Michelene T. H., Miriam Bassok, Matthew W. Lewis, Peter Reimann, and Robert Glaser. "Self-Explanations: How Students Study and Use Examples in Learning to Solve Problems." *Cognitive Science* 13, no. 2 (April-June 1989): 145-182. [31 Refs.]

The authors studied the relation between the way individuals learn to solve problems and how students learn from or rely on examples. Student explanations for what they were learning were generated during talk-aloud protocols while studying examples and problems on Newton's Laws of Motion. College and university students were given declarative and qualitative questions and examples to compare their answers regarding critical facts, reasoning, and procedural skills. The authors found that students who have greater success at solving problems tend to study example exercises by refining and expanding the actions in the example, leading to the formulation of inferences for other problems. They seemed to understand the example and explain it to themselves. Students who had less success at problem solving tended to not explain the examples to themselves, nor connect the example with any understanding they might have of the principles and concepts in a textbook. Good students seemed able to monitor their comprehension failures and successes while studying examples. Poor students did little or no monitoring. The analysis concludes with a discussion of self-explanation and the adequacy of certain artificial intelligence models to account for this phenomenon.

091 Chipman, Susan F., Judith W. Segal, and Robert Glaser, eds. *Thinking and Learning Skills. Vol. 2: Research and Open Questions*. Hillsdale, NJ: Lawrence Erlbaum, 1985. 639 pp.

This is the second volume of a two-volume compilation of papers presented at a conference (sponsored by the National Institute of Education) on educational practices and scientific research on the cognitive abilities of students. The papers included in this volume deal with research on thinking and cognitive skills and are grouped into six topical areas: knowledge acquisition, problem solving, intelligence and reasoning, generality and specificity of cognitive skills, learning and development in the acquisition of cognitive skills, and approaches to the teaching of cognitive skills. The volume concludes with two chapters responding to the Conference on Thinking and Learning Skills as a whole.

092 Clinchy, Blythe. "On Critical Thinking & Connected Knowing." *Liberal Education* 75, no. 5 (November-December 1989): 14-19. [9 Refs.]

Clinchy believes that emphasizing critical thinking to the exclusion of other modes of thought is not effective for women students. She cites two studies to support her position: (1) a longitudinal study in which undergraduates were interviewed annually during their four years at college and (2) interviews with 135 women of different ages and social, educational, and ethnic backgrounds. Findings suggest that women have a proclivity towards connected knowing or attempting to understand an idea from the proponent's point of view by suspending disbelief, putting personal views aside, and seeing the logic in the idea. Unlike separate knowing (critical thinking) which is impersonal and detached, connected knowing involves both emotion and reason and an attempt to understand rather than evaluate. Teachers should help students develop an integrative approach to thinking--both detached and attached, critical and appreciative.

093 Colbert, Kent R. "The Effects of CEDA and NDT Debate Training on Critical Thinking Ability." *Journal of the American Forensic Association* 23, no. 4 (Spring 1987): 494-201. [33 Refs.]

Colbert conducted a study to determine (1) whether intercollegiate debating enhances the critical thinking ability of participants and (2) whether the CEDA (Cross Examination Debate Association) or the NDT (National Debate Tournament) style proved more effective for critical thinking. Experimental groups of debaters and control groups of nondebaters were drawn from undergraduate college students in eight institutions. The Watson-Glaser Critical Thinking Appraisal was given as a pretest and posttest. Results showed that the experimental groups had higher scores on the pretest, posttest, and on the differences between the pretest and posttest; that CEDA and NDT debate produce different effects in terms of critical thinking; and that both CEDA and NDT training are beneficial to critical thinking.

094 Crowell, Doris C., Karen Y. Aka, Karen Blake, Kanani Choy, and Gayle Mar-Chun. "Teaching Thinking Strategies: An Attempt to Promote Generalization." In *Thinking across Cultures: The Third International Conference*, edited by Donald M. Topping, Doris C. Crowell, and Victor N. Kobayashi, 409-416. Hillsdale, NJ: Lawrence Erlbaum, 1989. [12 Refs.]

Crowell presents a study on facilitating generalization and transfer of thinking strategies across content areas. The subjects were two groups of third grade children. The experimental group was taught thinking strategies through a variety of techniques from the Experience-Text-Relationship Method, Raphael's Question-Answer-Relationship Method, and CoRT. Opportunities for applying the reasoning strategies in other content areas were provided and the student efforts were observed. The results were mixed and inconclusive, but suggested ways to promote the generalization of thinking strategies that are taught directly. Generalization is achieved through sequences of lessons that provide opportunities for gradually practicing the strategies in contexts more and more dissimilar to the original instruction.

095 Daiute, Colette. "Play as Thought: Thinking Strategies of Young Writers." *Harvard Educational Review* 59, no. 1 (February 1989): 1-23. [41 Refs.]

In studying play of children in elementary classrooms over a three-month period, Diaute observed elements of critical thinking among fifteen pairs of third to fourth grade children involved in collaborative writing projects. Analyzing the children's tape-recorded composing sessions, Diaute discovered various types of play used in the writing process, including play with language, reality, composing, knowledge, imagery, and peers. The author provides excerpts of the sessions, followed by a discussion of the elements of analysis, synthesis, problem solving, self-monitoring, and evaluation evident in them. Diaute argues that play can be a catalyst to classroom learning and improved writing, providing illustrations of writing samples before and after collaboration. She suggests teaching approaches and strategies for encouraging playful thinking as a basis for more mature thinking.

096 Dreyfus, A., and E. Jungwirth. "A Comparison of the 'Prompting Effect' of Out-of-School with That of In-School Contexts on Certain Aspects of Critical Thinking." *European Journal of Science Education* 2, no. 3 (July-September 1980): 301-310. [16 Refs.]

The authors investigated the use of everyday contexts in promoting critical thinking abilities in secondary school students, especially in the less intellectually gifted students and in science education. Two multiple choice tests, each consisting of a Test A based on everyday content and a Test B based on biological content, were administered to two sample populations: ninth grade students in non-selective secondary schools and ninth grade students in highly selective secondary schools. Results indicated that presenting critical thinking problems in everyday contexts offered no advantage. The non-selective population did significantly worse in everyday contexts. Everyday context problems as prompts for recognizing logical fallacies in biological contexts were unsuccessful for both populations.

097 Dreyfus, A., and E. Jungwirth. "Students' Perception of the Logical Structure of Curricular as Compared with Everyday Contexts--Study of Critical Thinking Skills." *Science Education* 64, no. 3 (July 1980): 309-321. [37 Refs.]

Dreyfus and Jungwirth investigated the critical thinking ability of students confronting problems in science education and in real-life situations. They focused on whether there were commonalities between the two and if these commonalities could be used to promote transfer. After developing standards under which a study was to be conducted, Dreyfus and Jungwirth designed four multiple-choice tests based on eight logical fallacies which were administered to first term ninth grade students. From student responses, they identified five main categories of reasoning. The authors determined that students tend not to respond similarly when confronted with equivalent situations presented in different contexts. They concluded that with the existence of this tendency, transfer of critical thinking ability from one context to another is unlikely.

098 Edwards, John, and Richard B. Baldauf, Jr. "The Effects of the CoRT-1 Thinking Skills Program on Students." Chapter 26 in *Thinking: The Second International Conference*, edited by David N. Perkins, Jack Lochhead, and John C. Bishop, 453-473. Hillsdale: NJ: Lawrence Erlbaum, 1987. [26 Refs.]

The authors present a study of the effects CoRT materials had on seventh grade students and examine claims about the materials made by Edward de Bono. The study measured whether teacher and parental reinforcement had any affect on how well the students learned the material. Results of the study did not support several of de Bono's claims, in particular the claims that IQ should not increase and that reinforcement should improve CoRT results. While the study showed significant shifts in IQ, creativity, and self-concept as a learner, no measured effects on student performance from either parental or teacher reinforcement were demonstrated. All students showed improvement in thinking skills.

099 Edwards, John, and Richard B. Baldauf, Jr. "Teaching Thinking in Secondary Science." In *Thinking, the Expanding Frontier. Proceedings of the International, Interdisciplinary Conference on Thinking Held at the University of the South Pacific, January, 1982*, edited by William Maxwell, 129-137. Philadelphia, PA: Franklin Institute Press, 1983. [8 Refs.]

The authors report on a pilot study that investigated the effectiveness of the CoRT Thinking Skills Program in an Australian tenth grade secondary science program. Researchers used IQ scores, a pretest and posttest of two essays, homework, and results of end-of-year science examinations to evaluate the program. The results indicated improvement in thinking and a strong correlation between CoRT scores and end-of-year examination results, but found no correlation between IQ and improvement in thinking.

100 Farris, Pamela J., Rodney W. Kissinger, and Thomas Thompson. "An Analysis of Problem Solving in Elementary-Level Science Textbooks." *Capstone Journal of Education* 7, no. 4 (Summer 1987): 28-34. [13 Refs.]

The authors investigated the extent that responses to elementary level science textbook study questions require problem solving skills. A science educator and an elementary curriculum specialist examined fourth and sixth grade level textbooks from four series, each from a different publisher. They evaluated questions from two randomly selected chapters for evidence of the necessity for using problem skills. The evaluators classified the questions according to Bloom's hierarchical cognitive taxonomy of knowledge, comprehension, application, analysis, synthesis, and evaluation. They discovered that the majority of the questions required lower level thinking skills processes of knowledge and comprehension, not the higher level thinking processes of application, analysis, synthesis, and evaluation. The article includes tables showing the number and percentage of questions in each cognitive taxonomy level for each textbook. The authors conclude that teachers using the textbooks surveyed must incorporate higher level cognitive questions into their instruction to enhance the problem solving skills of their students.

101 Firestien, Roger L., and Richard J. McCowan. "Creative Problem Solving and Communication Behavior in Small Groups." *Creativity Research Journal* 1, no. 1 (December 1988): 106-114. [16 Refs.]

Firestien and McCowan explored the relationship between creative problem solving and interactive communication behavior within small problem solving groups. Subjects consisted of students from an introductory creative studies undergraduate course trained in creative problem solving and students from undergraduate courses in business, interdisciplinary sciences, and consumer studies and home economics who were not trained in creative problem solving. Subjects were randomly assigned into 40 groups of five members each with 22 trained groups and 18 untrained groups. The groups trained in creative problem solving exhibited greater participation, less verbal criticism of ideas, more verbal indications of idea support, more verbal indications of humor evidenced by laughter, more verbal indications of humor evidenced by smiles, and a higher quantity of ideas than untrained groups. These results indicate a synergistic relationship between creative problem solving and communication.

102 Fong, Geoffrey T., David H. Krantz, and Richard E. Nisbett. "The Effects of Statistical Training on Thinking about Everyday Problems." *Cognitive Psychology* 18, no. 3 (July 1986): 253-292. [22 Refs.]

The authors describe four experiments conducted to investigate the effects of statistical training on thinking about everyday problems. The results of the experiments showed that (1) statistical training increased the frequency of statistical reasoning in responses to posed problems, (2) statistical training increased the quality of statistical answers, (3) the frequency and quality of statistical responses varied with the degree of training, and (4) statistical training can enhance the use of statistical rules in reasoning about everyday life outside the context of training. The studies suggest that individuals use inferential rules in the form of statistical heuristics and support a formalist theory of reasoning--that people reason using abstract rules.

103 Freeman, Donald J. "State Guidelines Promoting Teaching for Understanding and Thinking in Elementary Schools: A 50-State Survey." *Educational Evaluation and Policy Analysis* 11, no. 4 (Winter 1989): 417-429. [33 Refs.]

Freeman explored state policies and practices designed to encourage elementary school teachers to teach for understanding and thinking in mathematics, sciences, social studies, literature, music, and art. He conducted telephone interviews with state department directors of elementary education in all fifty states and two or more curriculum specialists in seven states (California, Hawaii, Indiana, New York, North Carolina, Missouri, and Utah) considered active promoters of the teaching of higher order thinking in at least one subject area. Most of the efforts for encouraging the teaching of higher order thinking reported by forty-three states were expressed through primarily one or two policy initiatives, inservice, goals and objectives statements, and guidelines for local curriculum planners. Teaching higher order thinking was most strongly promoted in mathematics, followed by sciences, social studies, literature, and art/music. Most policies assumed the teaching of higher order thinking would occur within all academic subjects and that students must master basic skills before attempting higher order thinking.

104 Germann, Paul J. "Directed-Inquiry Approach to Learning Science Process Skills: Treatment Effects and Aptitude-Treatment Interactions." *Journal of Research in Science Teaching* 26, no. 3 (March 1989): 237-250. [22 Refs.]

Germann describes an investigation into the effectiveness of a directed-inquiry approach to learning science process skills and scientific problem solving. This directed-inquiry approach incorporated six teaching and learning methodologies determined effective by educational research, including the learning cycle (exploration, invention or concept introduction, and discovery or concept application), focusing, Gowin's Vee diagram, advance organizers, and concept maps. Four sections of ninth and tenth grade general biology classes were divided into two treatment and two control groups. Two measures of science process skills were administered as pretests and posttests. The treatment group exposed to the directed-inquiry approach had significantly lower mean scores on the pretests and posttests than the control group, indicating that the approach had no significant effect on learning science process skills or on cognitive development. An aptitude-treatment interaction analysis suggested that students with lower cognitive development would perform better with a directed-inquiry approach than students with higher cognitive development, who would perform better with traditional instructional approaches. Germann notes that this is consistent with Piagetian theory and implies that instruction should be matched to the learning abilities and skills of students.

105 Gibbs, Leonard E. "Teaching Critical Thinking at the University Level: A Review of Some Empirical Evidence." *Informal Logic* 7, no. 2-3 (Spring-Autumn 1985): 137-149. [27 Refs.]

In planning for a critical thinking program, a group from the University of Wisconsin--Eau Claire examined nine empirical studies which evaluated critical thinking and the effects of university programs for teaching critical thinking. The group reviewed the methodology, measures, and findings of each study. Since none of the studies used random assignment of experimental or control groups, Gibbs warns that inferences about the effects of university teaching on critical thinking should be made cautiously. He proposes more critical thinking research in the form of randomized studies which evaluate the different teaching approaches and the various aspects of classroom environment. Gibbs proposes that researchers get together to determine the major dimensions of critical thinking and standardized measures for these dimensions.

106 Gick, Mary L. "Transfer in Insight Problems: The Effects of Different Types of Similarity." Chapter 18 in *Lines of Thinking: Reflections on the Psychology of Thought. Vol. 1, Representation, Reasoning, Analogy and Decision Making*, edited by K. J. Gilhooly, M. T. G. Keane, R. H. Logie, and G. Erdos, 251-265. New York, NY: John Wiley, 1990. [27 Refs.]

Gick discusses recent research that focuses on the elements required for the transfer of insights gained from a source problem to a target problem. An experiment by Gick and Holyoak explored the effectiveness of using contrasting similarity to acquire a convergence schema using a combination of convergent and contrasting stories. The results indicated transfer did occur but showed no significant differences between the contrast and no contrast conditions. Two experiments conducted by Lockhart, Lamon, and Gick used similarity of conceptual operations to study transfer. The results indicated that transfer can occur if there is high similarity of information content or some similarity of conceptual operations.

107 Grant, Grace E. *Teaching Critical Thinking*. New York, NY: Praeger, 1988. 137 pp. [128 Refs.]

Grant uses her observations and interviews of four secondary classroom teachers as a basis for analyzing the knowledge base necessary for the teaching of critical thinking. Research results reveal two parts to this knowledge base: teacher knowledge and teacher actions. Teacher knowledge involves knowledge of pedagogy, subject matter, students, and self. Teacher actions involves instruction and strategies for classroom organization and management. Examples from the varying backgrounds and teaching methods and techniques of the teachers illustrate the interrelationship of teacher knowledge and teacher actions in the teaching of critical thinking. Grant briefly addresses the implications of research findings for the teaching of critical thinking and for teacher education.

108 Greeno, James G. "A Perspective on Thinking." *American Psychologist* 44, no. 2 (February 1989): 134-141. [43 Refs.]

Greeno finds that the research in the psychology of critical, productive, higher order, and creative thinking has lagged behind that in the psychology of thinking related to performance on specific tasks. He suggests that the relatively slow progress may be due to the theories and framing assumptions dominating scientific inquiry, namely that (1) the locus of thinking is in an individual's mind, (2) the processes of thinking and learning are uniform, and (3) thinking is an accumulation of knowledge and skills. Greeno proposes a different set of framing assumptions based on situation cognition, personal and social epistemologies, and conceptual competence. He supports these assumptions with research findings and discusses their relation to productive thinking, higher order thinking abilities, critical thinking, and creativity.

109 Guyton, Edith. "Critical Thinking and Political Participation: Development and Assessment of a Causal Model." *Theory and Research in Social Education* 16, no. 1 (Winter 1988): 23-49. [71 Refs.]

To examine the development and assessment of a conceptual model of the relationship between critical thinking and political participation, Guyton gathered data from 118 undergraduate and graduate students. The Watson-Glaser Critical Thinking Appraisal and measurements for personal control, political efficacy, self-esteem, democratic attitude, and political participation were administered to the students. Statistical assessment and path analysis of the data showed that critical thinking has a direct effect on self-esteem, personal control, and democratic attitude. Although a significant correlation between critical thinking and political participation was found, findings revealed no significant direct effect of critical thinking on political participation. Guyton determined that the variables of personal control, political efficacy, and democratic attitude were the most influential in the relationship between critical thinking and political participation.

110 Halpern, Diane F. "Analogies as a Critical Thinking Skill." Chapter 6 in *Applications of Cognitive Psychology: Problem Solving, Education, and Computing*, edited by Dale E. Berger, Kathy Pezdek, and William P. Banks, 75-86. Hillsdale, NJ: Lawrence Erlbaum, 1987. [24 Refs.]

Halpern reviews empirical studies of six approaches for assessing the effectiveness of critical thinking courses. She suggests that a better way of examining the effects of critical thinking instruction is to look at the components of a typical critical thinking course to ascertain whether they are effective aids to better comprehension and problem solving. Halpern presents one study focusing on the use of analogies in a college classroom. The experimental results indicated that analogies can be a useful tool in comprehending and recalling scientific information.

111 Hawkins, Jan. "The Interpretation of Logo in Practice." Chapter 1 in *Mirrors of Minds: Patterns of Experience in Educational Computing*, edited by Roy D. Pea and Karen Sheingold, 3-34. Norwood, NJ: Ablex, 1987.

See: Pea, Kurland, and Hawkins {154}

Hawkins details a study on the experiences and reflections of two teachers using Logo in their classrooms over a two year period. Data was gathered through interviews with the teachers throughout the two years and via journals the teachers kept during the first two months of the experiment. One teacher used Logo with a classroom of 25 third and fourth graders, the other in a classroom of 25 fifth and sixth graders. Both teachers found a lack of success in using Logo as an environment for discovery learning where students could freely explore with minimal guidance. They noted problems with individual differences in the student's commitment to working with Logo and became convinced that a more structured guidance of discovery by the teacher was needed. In the second year of the study, each teacher began to teach a structured sequence in which Logo concepts were presented and weekly lessons for the entire class were given. Both saw a conflict between a commitment to the importance of self-initiated, discovery-based learning and the need for a pedagogical structure for learning an abstract symbol system. Hawkins outlines the study results on the teachers' paradox, student differences in interest in Logo, students' varied difficulties in understanding the concepts and logic underlying Logo, and the problem of integrating Logo into ongoing classroom work.

112 Hudgins, Bryce B., and Sybil Edelman. "Children's Self-Directed Critical Thinking." *Journal of Educational Research* 81, no. 5 (May-June 1988): 262-273. [28 Refs.]

Hudgins and Edelman investigated the effects of training intermediate grade children in the use of self-directed critical thinking. Experimental and control groups of fourth and fifth graders were matched according to grade, gender, and scores on a critical thinking test. The experimental group received instruction in the four self-directed critical thinking roles: task definer, strategist, monitor, and challenger. Outcomes of the study confirmed the expectations that the experimental group would surpass the control group in (a) the application of thinking skills, (b) use of more available and relevant information, and (c) quality of response in solving problems.

113 Hughes, Thomas M., and Mary Costner. "Regression Analysis of Teacher Characteristics of Abstract Reasoning, Personality, Self, and Motivation." *Journal of Human Behavior and Learning* 6, no. 2 (1989): 67-71. [12 Refs.]

Hughes and Costner investigated whether there are significant predictive relationships between certain measures of personality and abstract/critical thinking. Their study of graduate students indicated a significant relation between motivation and critical thinking. Narcism drive levels (one's perceptions of personal well-being and accomplishment) are related to seeking higher levels of thought, as self-sentiment drives (drives toward self-awareness) are related to authenticating things such as problem solving and thinking about how things work.

114 Hultgren, Francine. "Using Interpretive-Critical Inquiry Perspective to Study Critical Thinking in Home Economics." *Journal of Vocational Home Economics Education* 7, no. 1 (Spring 1989): 10-35. [16 Refs.]

Hultgren presents a study of how critical thinking is experienced. The study was grounded in a phenomenological paradigm that views the experiencing of critical thinking as creating a transformation in the thinker's sense of self and world and uses a dialectic/dialogic process of inquiry. The bulk of the presentation consists of excerpts from conversations with students in a graduate course in home economics. The dialogues display the reflections, changes, and insights the students and Hultgren experienced as they engaged in critical thinking. The conversations cover several areas including the educational and social contraditions, transformation of self, and the use of selected models for teaching thinking.

115 Hutchinson, Richard T. "Teaching Problem Solving to Developmental Adults: A Pilot Project." Chapter 15 in *Thinking and Learning Skills. Vol 1: Relating Instruction to Research*, edited by Judith W. Segal, Susan F. Chipman, and Robert Glaser, 499-513. Hillsdale, NJ: Lawrence Erlbaum, 1985. [21 Refs.]

Hutchinson discusses the Cognitive Studies Project, a pilot project at Manhattan Community College designed to help academically underprepared adult students seeking higher education to become more effective thinkers and learners by teaching them to intervene in their own thinking and learning processes. The pilot program consisted of semester-long high school level courses in reading, mathematics, science, social science, and English, as well as a course in problem solving. Based on the paired problem solving approach developed by Whimbey and Lochhead, the trial problem solving course provided (1) students with instruction in problem solving skills believed to help them learn more effectively, (2) researchers with information about adult cognitive deficiencies, and (3) the opportunity to test instructional materials. The researchers found the Whimbey-Lochhead method not totally appropriate for the test groups due to its inclusion of many exercises requiring reading, verbal, and reasoning skills beyond the abilities of the test groups. Material from other sources, such as the Raven's Progressive Matrices, were incorporated to supplement the selected Whimbey-Lochhead exercises used in the project. Hutchinson includes general observations on the special needs of instructors dealing with developmental students and the changes that can occur in developmental students through participation in cognitive process instruction. He discusses the barriers to the introduction into higher education of the project's form of instruction.

116 Idol, Lorna. "A Critical Thinking Map to Improve Content Area Comprehension of Poor Readers." *Remedial and Special Education: RASE* 8, no. 4 (July-August 1987): 28-40. [29 Refs.]

Idol describes a study on a mapping strategy designed to teach critical thinking about expository texts to remedial and special education students. The mapping strategy requires the teacher to first model the use of the critical thinking map, lead each student through completion of the map, and have each student complete the map without assistance. Most participants demonstrated improvement in all areas covered by the study. Idol details each phase, includes the actual results and how the results were measured. She includes an outline for a ten-step procedure for using critical thinking maps.

117 Jaynes, Patsy A. "Using Thinking Skills in Modified ESL." *Thinking Skills Instruction: Concepts and Techniques*, edited by Marcia Heiman and Joshua Slomianko, 145-151. Building Students' Thinking Skills. Washington, DC: National Education Association, 1987.

The authors provide a description of an interdisciplinary critical thinking project developed to assist mainstreamed English as a Second Language (ESL) students and regular modified students in a senior high school. The teachers of these groups were assisted in developing common teaching techniques and in restructuring content material within the context of Bloom's taxonomy. Based on the data collected from several evaluation instruments, ESL students showed improvement in reading skills, course grades, total academic functioning, and English skills.

118 Kagan, Dona M. "The Social Implications of Higher Level Thinking Skills." *Research in Higher Education* 27, no. 2 (1987): 176-187. [55 Refs.]

Kagan explores theoretical and empirical research in support of her theory that skills in higher level thinking may enhance an individual's ability to communicate and interact with other individuals. She interrelates the fields of higher level thinking skills, social cognition, social competency, and communications. Kagan poses questions to which empirical answers would have practical implications for training professionals in these fields.

119 Keeley, Stuart M., M. Neil Browne, and Jeffrey S. Kreutzer. "A Comparison of Freshmen and Seniors on General and Specific Essay Tests of Critical Thinking." *Research in Higher Education* 17, no. 2 (1982): 139-154. [6 Refs.]

The authors posed a series of specific open-ended questions and a single broad essay question to college freshmen and seniors to determine the impact of college on critical thinking. Although findings indicated that seniors outperformed freshmen, the absolute differences were small. The authors contend that the insignificant difference reflects insufficient practice and reinforcement of the skills. An implication of the results is that there should be direct training in the development of critical thinking skills and clear feedback to students on their demonstration of specific skills.

120 Keeley, Stuart M., and M. Neil Browne. "How College Seniors Operationalize Critical Thinking Behavior." *College Student Journal* 20, no. 4 (Winter 1986): 389-395. [14 Refs.]

Keeley and Brown investigated how students operationalized "critically evaluate" at the end of four years of college. Thirty-seven (37) seniors were asked to critically evaluate a 550-word essay on why college attendance is a waste of time and money. Over half of the students failed to apply a questioning strategy that critically evaluated the author's reasoning and less than a quarter of the students identified a major value assumption. The students also failed to address important definitional issues and indicated limited awareness of assumptions other than those related to statistical arguments. The implications of this study include (1) the questionability of the assumption that students will internalize critical thinking skills through the experience of traditional curricula and (2) the necessity for stressing the skills of identifying assumptions and ambiguity in language. The authors advocate specific training in critical thinking skills via the application of skills to controversial issues.

121 King, Patricia M. "Formal Reasoning in Adults: A Review and Critique." Chapter 1 in *Adult Cognitive Development:*

Methods and Models, edited by Robert A. Mines and Karen S. Kitchener, 1-21. New York, NY: Praeger, 1986. [60 Refs.]

King describes the key features of Piaget's theory of formal operational thought (hypothetico-deductive reasoning, propositional thinking, and combinations) and the degree to which formal operational thinking is actually observed among adults. She reviews research on formal operational thought in adulthood and notes that the studies indicate that a sizable proportion of the normal adult population does not reason at formal levels. King discusses possible interpretations of these findings and the lack of standardized assessment procedures across the studies that hampers drawing generalized conclusions. She also discusses new theoretical developments that have grown out of attempts to understand and assess formal operations. A chart summarizing the incidence of formal operational thinking in adults indicated in the studies is included.

122 King, Patricia M., Philip K. Wood, and Robert A. Mines. "Critical Thinking among College and Graduate Students." *Review of Higher Education* 13, no. 2 (Winter 1990): 167-186. [48 Refs.]

The authors describe their investigation of differences by academic level, discipline, and gender in critical thinking between undergraduate and graduate students, using three critical thinking tests that reflect different degrees of problem structure. They obtained scores on the Watson-Glaser Critical Thinking Appraisal, the Cornell Critical Thinking Test, the Reflective Judgment Interview, and the ACT or SAT of forty college seniors and forty graduate students, representing social science and mathematical science majors. The researchers found significant effects for educational level and for gender on the three critical thinking tests and for discipline on the Reflective Judgment Interview. Graduate students scored higher than undergraduate students, graduate social science majors scored higher than other majors, and males scored higher than females.

123 Kitchener, Karen Strohm, and Patricia M. King. "Reflective Judgment: Concepts of Justification and Their

Relationship to Age and Education." *Journal of Applied Developmental Psychology* 2 (Summer 1981): 89-116. [55 Refs.]

The authors describe a seven-stage model of the development of reflective judgment and concepts of justification in post-adolescence. They identify the major assumptions about reality and knowledge and the forms of justification found in each stage. Following the discussion of the seven stages, the authors present a study on the correlation between higher reflective judgment levels and verbal fluency and socio-economic status. The study sample consisted of 20 high school juniors, 20 college juniors majoring in liberal arts, and 20 doctoral level graduate students in liberal arts disciplines and was evenly divided between male and female subjects. The reflective judgment levels of the sample were determined through the Reflective Judgment Interview. Verbal ability was determined by the Concept Master Test (CMT). Formal operational thinking was measured by the Combination of Colored and Colorless Chemical Bodies and the Oscillation of the Pendulum tasks. The socio-economic status of each subject was determined before the first session. Verbal fluency was measured by the number of words spoken during the Reflective Judgment Interview. Study results showed a consistent upward progression of reflective judgment scores from the high school students to the graduate students. This trend could not be statistically accounted for by verbal ability, formal operations, socio-economic status, or verbal fluency. Verbal ability was found to be closely related to the level of reflective judgment, but the differences in group scores could not be solely attributed to this factor. The authors hypothesize that differences in group scores may reflect differences in maturation, education, selection into higher educational programs, or a combination of these three factors.

124 Kitchener, Karen Strohm, Patricia M. King, Philip K. Wood, and Mark L. Davison. "Sequentiality and Consistency in the Development of Reflective Judgment: A Six-Year Longitudinal Study." *Journal of Applied Developmental Psychology* 10, no. 1 (January-March 1989): 73-95. [46 Refs.]

The authors present a study that evaluated the stage properties of the Reflective Judgment Interview scores. Subjects for the study were 57 individuals who had participated in two previous studies of the Reflective Judgment Model in 1977 and 1979. The subjects were grouped according to their age and educational level during the 1977 study. The participants were retested using the Reflective Judgment Interview to measure reflective judgment. The study results showed increased Reflective Judgment Interview scores by all participants. Davison's test of sequentiality was used to investigate the sequentiality of development indicated by Interview scores. The test supported the sequence outlined in the Reflective Judgment model. Stage skipping was observed in only 14% of the cases. Study results revealed a correlation between age and Interview scores. Results also indicated a cohort effect on epistemic cognition for same-aged subjects and greater growth in epistemic cognition for subjects who had attended college. An appendix listing the characteristic assumptions of Reflective Judgment model states is included.

125 Knight, Stephanie, Hersholt C. Waxman, and Yolanda N. Padron. "Investigating Hispanic Students' Cognitive Strategies in Social Studies." *Journal of Social Studies Research* 11, no. 2 (Fall 1987): 15-19. [17 Refs.]

The authors investigated the cognitive strategies used by Hispanic students in solving higher level thinking social studies problems and the existence of any correlation between cognitive strategies and gender, grade, or ability. One hundred and forty-one (141) third, fourth, and fifth grade English as a Second Language students from an urban elementary school in the Southwest were given the Social Studies Strategies Survey, containing a four-part critical thinking social studies task and questions regarding the use of twelve cognitive strategies. Data indicated that the cognitive strategies identified in the survey were not used extensively by the Hispanic students for solving critical thinking problems in social studies and that strategies reported differ according to gender and ability.

126 Kuhn, Deanna, Eric Amsel, and Michael O'Loughlin, with the assistance of Leona Schauble, Bonnie Leadbeater, and William Yotive. *The Development of Scientific Thinking*

Skills. New York, NY: Academic Press, 1988. 249 pp. [161 Refs.]

The authors present findings from six studies on the nature and development of some basic scientific thinking skills. The research points to three key abilities in coordinating theory and evidence: (1) to think about a theory and use it as a means of organizing and interpreting experience, (2) to encode and represent the evidence as distinct from any representation of the theory, and (3) to bracket or set aside acceptance or rejection of a theory in order to evaluate the evidence that is the only basis for making a judgment. The investigations identified several skills involved in interpreting evidence differentiated from theory: covariation, overcoming false inclusion, generating evidence for inclusion, prediction, mastering exclusion, interpreting mixed evidence, and overcoming false inclusion. The authors briefly outline implications for the teaching of thinking skills.

127 Kyllonen, Patrick C., and Raymond E. Christal. "Reasoning Ability is (Little More Than) Working-Memory Capacity?!" *Intelligence* 14, no. 4 (October-December 1990): 389-433. [53 Refs.]

Kyllonen and Christal present four investigations into the relationship between reasoning ability and working memory ability. In each study, a number of reasoning tests and working memory tests were given to large samples of Air Force recruits. The results showed a high correlation between reasoning ability and working memory ability. Working memory capacity seems responsible for differences in reasoning ability and may affect success across various component stages of reasoning tasks. The studies also revealed a differentiation between reasoning and working memory ability--reasoning correlated with general knowledge, while working memory capacity correlated with processing speed. The authors discuss the implications of the results for the nature of reasoning and of working memory.

128 Larkin, Jill H., and Ruth W. Chabay. "Research on Teaching Scientific Thinking: Implications for Computer-Based Instruction." Chapter 8 in *Toward the Thinking Curriculum: Current Cognitive Research*, edited by Lauren B. Resnick and Leopold E. Klopfer, 150-172.

1989 Yearbook of the Association for Supervision and Curriculum Development. [Alexandria, VA]: Association for Supervision and Curriculum Development, 1989. [21 Refs.]

This chapter is a summary of the research findings on learning and motivation as they relate to teaching science and for designing effective instructional activities. In research experiments on student learning, six common principles or features emerged: (1) develop a detailed description of the processes the student needs to acquire, (2) systematically address all knowledge included in the description of the process, (3) let most instruction occur through active work on tasks, (4) give feedback on specific tasks as soon as possible after an error is made, (5) let students encounter each knowledge unit several times, and (6) limit demands on student attention. Larkin and Chabay assert that these principles are ideal for computer-based instruction and may be used as guidelines for assessing and selecting effective software instructional programs designed to teach scientific thinking.

129 Lawrenz, Frances, and Robert E. Orton. "A Comparison of Critical Thinking Related Teaching Practices of Seventh and Eighth Grade Science and Mathematics Teachers." *School Science and Mathematics* 89, no. 5 (May-June 1989): 361-372. [19 Refs.]

The authors surveyed seventh and eighth grade mathematics and science teachers regarding their critical thinking teaching practices. They grouped responses into four general categories: (1) objectives and assessment techniques, (2) teaching preferences, (3) time spent on various activities, and (4) use of cooperative groups. Responses suggested that science teachers are more open to relevancy, diversity, and encouraging student thought, while mathematics teachers are more reflective on the nature of problem solving and the application of problem solving skills. Both science and mathematics teachers indicated enjoyment in teaching their disciplines, a positive belief in children's ability to learn the subject, and a desire to emphasize higher order thinking skills. Lawrenz and Orton advocate that science and mathematics teachers cooperate in integrating higher order thinking skills into their disciplines. They suggest some ways for collaboration and address potential problems.

130 Lehman, Darrin R. "The Effects of Graduate Training on Reasoning: Formal Discipline and Thinking about Everyday-Life Events." *American Psychologist* 43, no. 6 (June 1988): 431-442. [27 Refs.]

Late nineteenth and twentieth century psychologists, including William James, Thorndike, Piaget, and Wason, have believed that training in a formal discipline within which there is instruction in abstract rule systems has no effect on reasoning about everyday life events. Lehman discusses three studies in which this theory was tested. The effects of graduate education in psychology, medicine, law, and chemistry on statistical, methodological, conditional, and verbal reasoning were investigated at the University of Michigan through a cross-sectional and longitudinal study followed by a cross-sectional replication study at the University of California at Los Angeles. Significant effects on statistical and methodological reasoning in everyday life events were found to be a result of psychology and medical training, while significant effects on conditional reasoning were found to be a result of psychology, medical, and law education. Chemistry education had no effect on the four types of reasoning studied. These results show that formal discipline training can effect the reasoning ability of individuals on some types of problems. The article includes sample problems used in the studies and bar graphs representing calculated statistical results.

131 Light, Paul, and Martin Glachan. "Facilitation of Individual Problem Solving through Peer Interaction." *Educational Psychology* 5, no. 3-4 (1985): 217-225. [23 Refs.]

Light and Glachan conducted two sets of research studies to explore peer interaction as a facilitator of individual problem solving. The first set of studies involved seven- and eight-year-old children in a complex seriation task called the Tower of Hanoi. The second set of studies involved a group of seven- and eight-year-olds and a group of twelve- and thirteen-year-olds in a computerized version of Mastermind called Logic 5. Observations and videotapes were made of the children working individually and in pairs. Findings from the studies suggest that the experiences of working together in pairs can facilitate subsequent problem solving performance. The authors conclude that peer interaction is beneficial only when the task level is appropriate for the children and when steps are taken to alleviate possible dominance of interaction by one child.

132 Little, Joseph. "Student Responses to a Questionnaire about Their Philosophy Program." *Thinking* 3, no. 3-4 (1981): 47-49.

Little presents the quantified results of a survey given to children enrolled in Matthew Lipman's Philosophy for Children Program. He notes a marked increase in response sophistication as the students progress through the program's novels and includes select narrative responses.

133 Lohman, David F. "Predicting Mathemathanic Effects in the Teaching of Higher-Order Thinking Skills." *Educational Psychologist* 21, no. 3 (Summer 1986): 191-208. [66 Refs.]

Lohman provides a review of Aptitude X Treatment interaction research supporting the occurrence of negative effects from attempts to teach new ways of thinking, learning, problem solving, or studying via different instructional techniques to subjects of varied abilities. Based on the research studies, Lohman believes that direct instruction of cognitive skills or programs that attempt to teach new general problem solving (or thinking skills) in a content-reduced curriculum are more likely to produce negative effects in the performance of subjects already high in fluid ability (reasoning skill). Less direct instruction or programs that attempt to teach thinking skills within a specific domain are more likely to produce negative effects on the performance of subjects high in crystallized ability (achievement within that domain). Information on the fluid or crystallized abilities of subjects can be obtained through tests of those abilities. Lohman concludes that future research is needed to investigate the relationship between duration of instruction and the mathemathanic or negative effect.

134 Madland, Denise, and Marian A. Smith. "Computer-Assisted Instruction for Teaching Conceptual Library Skills to Remedial Students." *Research Strategies* 6, no. 2 (Spring 1988): 52-64. [8 Refs.]

Madland and Smith describe a study conducted to compare the effectiveness of a computer-assisted library instruction program with an oral class presentation. The program, based on a question analysis approach used in lecture/discussion library instruction sessions, was developed for undergraduate remedial English and study skills classes. Pretests and posttests were given to three classes, with one receiving the computer-assisted instruction program, a second receiving the class presentation by a librarian, and a third receiving no instruction. Students receiving the librarian's class instruction showed a greater increase in posttest mean scores than students receiving the computer-assisted instruction, but the difference was not statistically significant. The posttest mean score of the group who received no instruction decreased. The authors conclude that further work is needed on using computer-assisted instruction for teaching critical thinking or the conceptual approach to library instruction.

135 Matthews, Doris B. "The Effect of a Thinking-Skills Program on the Cognitive Abilities of Middle School Students." *Clearing House* 62, no. 5 (January 1989): 202-204. [18 Refs.]

Matthews investigated the effect of critical thinking skills instruction on student scores on the Cognitive Abilities Test. Sixty-seven (67) seventh and eight graders from a predominantly black laboratory school at a southern college participated in the study. Students were randomly assigned into two groups, one group taking the Cognitive Abilities Test, levels E through G, before critical thinking skills instruction and the other taking it after the instruction. Instruction in critical thinking skills took place in eighteen one-hour sessions over six weeks. Results showed that after instruction in critical thinking, students achieved higher scores on all subtests of the Cognitive Abilities Test, with significantly higher scores on three of the subtests that require abstract thinking--verbal analogies, number series, and figure analogies.

136 McCammon, Susan, Jeannie Golden, and Karl L. Wuensch. "Predicting Course Performance in Freshman and Sophomore Physics Courses: Women Are More Predictable Than Men." *Journal of Research in Science Teaching* 25, no. 6 (September 1988): 501-510. [21 Refs.]

Concerned with continual declining performance of students in introductory physics courses, physics and psychology faculty collaborated to determine the validity of thinking skills and mathematical competency as predictors of student performance in physics courses. The Watson-Glaser Critical Thinking Appraisal and the Primary Mental Abilities Test were used as measures for cognitive skills, while the Mathematics Anxiety Rating Scale and the Elementary Algebra Skills Test were used to measure mathematical competency. With students in freshman and sophomore level courses for physics majors and for non-physics science majors as subjects, the researchers discovered a positive correlation between cognitive skills and mathematical competence. Algebra and critical thinking measures were determined to be the best predictors of performance in introductory physics courses, but were determined to be successful only as predictors for women.

137 McGinley, William, and Robert J. Tierney. "Traversing the Topical Landscape." *Written Communication* 6, no. 3 (July 1989): 243-269. [66 Refs.]

McGinley and Tierney review theoretical and empirical research that supports their theory that learners who direct their own reading and writing activities in pursuit of other learning become familiar with the different perspectives and ways of thinking that will be useful in more elaborate combinations of these activities. The authors examine studies on reading, writing, and learning in literature, science, and social science and studies focusing on college student learning. They conclude that a diversity of reading and writing activities provides different ways of acquiring knowledge which enable learners to examine topics critically from multiple viewpoints. McGinley and Tierney believe that students' dynamic engagement in these activities characterize a critical examination of a topic. The authors stress the importance of exploring ways to help students direct their own reading and writing activities dynamically according to their particular needs.

138 McKnight, Curtis C. "Critical Evaluation of Quantitative Arguments." In *Assessing Higher Order Thinking in Mathematics*, edited by Gerald Kulm, 169-185. Washington, DC: American Association for the Advancement of Science, 1990. [27 Ref.]

McKnight contends that the ability to think critically through informative text with arguments containing quantitative or graphical data has become, and will continue to be, an essential skill. He describes a study on critical evaluation of graphical arguments. Seven adult subjects were given four graphical data examples typical of those found in popular media, texts, and monographs and were tested on the following taxonomy of information processing tasks: (1) observation of facts, (2) observation of relationships in the graphs as graphs, (3) interpretation of relationships in the graphs within the "real-world" context, (4) evaluation of the value of the graphical data as evidence for the truth of the related proposition, and (5) assessment of the basis on which each subject made his/her evaluation of the evidential value of the data. McKnight views these processing tasks as areas of potential research. Such research should be extended to other quantitative argument types and to a larger range of developmental levels.

139 McMillan, James H. "Enhancing College Students' Critical Thinking: A Review of Studies." *Research in Higher Education* 26, no. 1 (1987): 3-29. [59 Refs.]

McMillan reviews and analyzes 27 studies on the effect of instructional methods, courses, and programs on college students' critical thinking ability. He concludes that research needs a common definition of critical thinking, a demonstration of the conditions most enhancing for critical thinking, and good instrumentation for specific measurement of critical thinking. McMillan includes a table outlining the problem, design, subjects, instruments, and results of each study.

140 Meichenbaum, Donald. "Metacognitive Methods of Instruction: Current Status and Future Prospects." In *Facilitating Cognitive Development: International Perspectives, Programs, and Practices*, edited by Milton Schwebel and Charles A. Maher, 23-32. New York, NY: Haworth, 1986. [24 Refs.]

The author briefly examines the concept of metacognition as an individual's self-knowledge of their cognitions and their ability to control those cognitions. He reviews current research on metacognition and explores efforts at metacognitive instruction, focusing on strategy training for comprehension and self-control.

141 Mines, Robert A., Patricia M. King, Albert B. Hood, and Philip K. Wood. "Stages of Intellectual Development and Associated Critical Thinking Skills in College Students." *Journal of College Student Development* 31, no. 6 (November 1990): 538-547. [31 Refs.]

The authors investigated the relationship between reflective judgment and the skills constituting standardized critical thinking tests. Their research sample consisted of 100 students from freshmen, seniors, and graduate students representing a broad range of critical thinking skills and reflective judgment stages. The Watson-Glaser Critical Thinking Appraisal and the Cornell Critical Thinking Test were administered to the students as a group, while the Reflective Judgment Interview was administered individually. Each participant's scores from the American College Test, Scholastic Aptitude Test, or Graduate Record Examination were obtained as measures of academic aptitude. Results of the study indicated that the overall scores for each measure increased with educational level. Academic ability did not account for the educational level difference. A major finding of the study was that students who use the assumptions of the higher stages of reflective judgment to reason demonstrate better critical thinking skills than those using assumptions of the lower stages. Critical thinking skills distinguishing the reflective judgment stages were: (1) interpretation, weighing evidence, and identifying generalizations; (2) detecting fallaciously ambiguous arguments; (3) deduction; and (4) inference. This may indicate that these skills must be mastered for continual intellectual development through the reflective judgment stages.

142 Moshman, David, and Bridget A. Franks. "Intellectual Development: Formal Operations and Reflective Judgment." Chapter 1 in *Thinking, Reasoning, and Writing*, edited by Elaine P. Maimon, Barbara F. Nodine, and Finbarr W. O'Connor, 9-22. New York, NY: Longman, 1989. [13 Refs.]

The authors review Piaget's theory of intellectual development and formal operations and current research on the development of philosophical understanding, focusing on the reflective judgment research of Karen Kitchener and

Patricia King. The article includes a chart outlining the stages in the development of reflective judgment as determined by Kitchener and King.

143 Neumann, Yoram, and Edith Finaly. "The Problem-Solving Environment and Students' Problem-Solving Orientation." *Journal of Research and Development in Education* 22, no. 2 (Winter 1989): 22-29. [19 Refs.]

Neumann and Finaly explore three basic orientations to problem solving (rational, solution, and humanistic) and four profiles of problem environments based on degree of specificity and certainty components. They present a table of formal models showing the relationship between profiles of problem environment and problem solving orientation. They apply these models to the problem environments of university departments believed to influence students' orientation to problem solving. The authors use four academic areas (social work, political science, engineering, and physics) representing the four problem environment profiles to test the models of students' problem solving orientation. Three hundred and twenty (320) undergraduate students, representing the four disciplines, from five Israeli higher education institutions constituted the sample. Empirical tests supported sixteen of the researchers' eighteen hypotheses. Findings indicated a different pattern of problem solving orientations for each discipline.

144 Newell, George E. "Learning from Writing: Examining Our Assumptions." *English Quarterly* 19, no. 4 (Winter 1986): 291-302. [20 Refs.]

After reviewing research studies on writing and its relationship to learning, Newell presents a study of writing tasks and their connection to students' reasoning and comprehension skills. He investigated eight eleventh grade students' approaches to notetaking, study question exercises, and essay writing by having them think aloud while completing the tasks. The verbalizations of their thoughts were tape recorded, transcribed, and analyzed for writing and reasoning operations. Students were also tested for their understanding of specific concepts after the writing tasks. Newell found that notetaking and study question exercises promote routine learning by restricting students to factual information. Analytical essay writing provides opportunities for exploration and critical thinking of issues posed. Newell believes that writing must be seen as a learning tool in order for it to be valued as a higher order thinking task. He emphasizes the importance of assigning writing tasks that correspond with instructional goals.

145 Norris, Stephen P. "Research Needed on Critical Thinking." *Canadian Journal of Education* 13, no. 1 (Winter 1988): 125-137. [25 Refs.]

Norris asserts that research is still needed on topics in critical thinking mentioned by Robert Ennis in 1963. He focuses on two areas needing conceptual and empirical research: (a) the generalizability of critical thinking and (b) the evaluation of critical thinking ability. Norris presents specific questions related to general principles and strategies for making inductive inferences and the applicability of these general principles and strategies across the disciplines.

146 Norris, Stephen P. "Synthesis of Research on Critical Thinking." *Educational Leadership* 42, no. 8 (May 1985): 40-45. [36 Refs.]

Norris highlights critical thinking research related to definition, existence, instructional significance, instructional implications, and teaching effectiveness. Although Norris stresses the need for further research, he encourages teachers to teach critical thinking using available resources, but to think critically when selecting materials.

147 Nummedal, Susan G. "Developing Reasoning Skills in College Students." Chapter 7 in *Applications of Cognitive Psychology: Problem Solving, Education, and Computing*, edited By Dale E. Berger, Kathy Pezdek, and William P. Banks, 87-97. Hillsdale, NJ: Lawrence Erlbaum, 1987. [26 Refs.]

While the goal of improving students' reasoning is accepted by most educators, Nummedal finds disagreement about which reasoning skills should be taught and how they should be taught. She presents a study on correlational reasoning, one of the fundamental processes used in scientific and everyday reasoning. Results showed that students were unable to generate appropriate problem representation in cases containing the non-occurrence of a causal event that is usually unobservable in a natural environment. This difficulty did not necessarily prevent students from making correct covariational judgments. The author suggests that more simplistic judgment strategies utilizing only a portion of the relevant information are efficient and often lead to correct judgments.

148 Oakhill, Jane, Alan Garnham, and P. N. Johnson-Laird. "Belief Bias Effects in Syllogistic Reasoning." Chapter 10 in *Lines of Thinking: Reflections on the Psychology of Thought. Vol. 1, Representation, Reasoning, Analogy and Decision-Making*, edited by K. J. Gilhooly, M. T. G. Keane, R. H. Logie, and G. Erdos, 125-138. New York, NY: John Wiley, 1990. [23 Refs.]

The authors review studies showing the effects of belief bias on reasoning and outline conclusions that may be drawn from their results. They also detail two studies on whether beliefs affect performance, how beliefs affect premise models a person considers, and how such bias acts as a filter on conclusions. The studies indicate that prior belief has a significant influence on the deductive process.

149 Ormerod, T. C., K. I. Manktelow, A. P. Steward, and E. H. Robson. "The Effects of Content and Representation on the Transfer of PROLOG Reasoning Skills." Chapter 19 in *Lines of Thinking: Reflections on the Psychology of Thought. Vol. 1, Representation, Reasoning, Analogy and Decision Making*, edited by K. J. Gilhooly, M. T. G. Keane, R. H. Logie, and G. Erdos, 267-281. New York: John Wiley, 1990. [20 Refs.]

The authors examine how the manipulation of thematic content and representation can affect transfer in a PROLOG program comprehension task. They discuss the implications this research has for abstract reasoning skill training. The authors investigated the conditions under which performance with mismatched materials can be facilitated, particularly the issues of practice effects and transfer effects. Their experiment consisted of a pre-task in which participants received a task with either familiar-diagram, familiar-list, unfamiliar-diagram or unfamiliar-list materials, and a post-task in which the participants received a task with either familiar-list or unfamiliar-diagram materials. The pre-task and post-task were then compared. The results showed that the number of correct responses did not increase with practice, indicating that practice alone does not improve performance. The results also indicated that an unfamiliar-list pre-task produced positive transfer of performance. Since transfer occurred though no instruction was given, the results indicate that training in problems requiring procedural knowledge may not require or benefit from instruction. The authors conclude that procedural information coupled with practice, rather than instruction, seems more important for transfer to occur.

150 Owen, Elizabeth, and John Sweller. "Should Problem Solving Be Used as a Learning Device in Mathematics?" *Journal for Research in Mathematics Education* 20, no. 3 (May 1989): 322-328. [23 Refs.]

Reply: Lawson {903}

See: Sweller {177}

The authors examine the differences between experts and novices, focusing on the acquisition of mathematical problem solving schemas. Research indicates that experts possess domain specific schemas which can not be acquired by the means-ends searches or goal-oriented problem solving exercises used by most novices. Studies suggest that rule automation, as well as schema acquistion, is important to problem solving exercise and knowledge transfer. Research also indicates that expertise in problem solving is derived from domain specific skill rather than from superior heuristics. The authors conclude that solving many conventional goal-oriented problem exercises, as is currently done in mathematics classes, may not be the best way of acquiring expertise. They suggest that a better approach may be to have students solve goal-free problems or study problem solutions rather than solving the problem.

151 Paris, Scott G., and Peter Winograd. "How Metacognition Can Promote Academic Learning and Instruction." Chapter 1 in *Dimensions of Thinking and Cognitive Instruction*, edited by Beau Fly Jones and Lorna Idol, 15-51. Hillsdale, NJ: Lawrence Erlbaum, 1990. [120 Refs.]

Paris and Winograd review research on the importance of metacognition in cognitive development and academic learning.

152 Pascarella, Ernest T. "The Development of Critical Thinking: Does College Make a Difference?" *Journal of College Student Development* 30, no. 1 (January 1989): 19-26. [26 Refs.]

Pascarella discusses a longitudinal study of the changes in critical thinking in college and non-college students. The study matched a subsample group of college students and a subsample group of non-college students according to ethnicity, Watson-Glaser Critical Thinking Appraisal (Form A) scores, American College Testing Program composite scores, and family socioeconomic studies. One year later, the groups took the Watson-Glaser Critical Thinking Appraisal again and completed a questionnaire on specific experiences and activities of the previous year. The results showed that one year of college attendance produced a 17% improvement in critical thinking over no college attendance. Development in critical thinking was not influenced by any one specific experience in college, such as living on campus, hours spent studying, or extra-curricular activities, nor by the selectivity of the college, but did correlate positively with a composite measure of college activities.

153 Paul, Richard W. "Critical Thinking Research: A Response to Stephen Norris." *Educational Leadership* 42, no. 8 (May 1985): 46. [10 Refs.]

Reply to Norris {146}

Paul focuses on research areas which Norris failed to highlight: (1) the scope of the research, including that in sociology, anthropology, and psychology with potential contributions to critical thinking and (2) the importance of dialectical thinking. He offers considerations necessary for designing critical thinking instruction.

154 Pea, Roy D., D. Midian Kurland, and Jan Hawkins. "Logo and the Development of Thinking Skills." Chapter 9 in *Mirrors of Minds: Patterns of Experience in Educational Computing*, edited by Roy D. Pea and Karen Sheingold, 178-197. Norwood, NJ: Ablex, 1987.

Printed also in *Children and Microcomputers: Research on the Newest Medium*, edited by M. Chen and W. Paisley, Beverly Hills, CA: Sage, 1985. pp. 193-212.

See: Hawkins {111}

The authors explore whether learning to program affects the development of other cognitive skills. They discuss a series of studies conducted using the Logo symbol system for programming which focused on the effects of Logo learning on cognitive skills, particularly planning.

Over a two year period, the use of Logo in two elementary school classes, a fourth/fifth grade and a fifth/sixth grade, was studied. To assess planning skills during the first year of the study a classroom chore-scheduling task was assigned. Students were to devise a plan to accomplish six chores. The same task was given to a control group not involved in Logo training. Study results showed no significant influence of Logo training on planning. The authors did observe that the actual classroom practice with Logo programming seemed to be connected to the specific contexts in which they were learned and did not tend to transfer to other contexts. The authors devised a new version of the planning task that resembled programming in its deep structural features as well as on its surface. The new task was given to the experimental groups in the second year of the study. Results indicated that again no significant differences in planning could be ascertained between the control and experimental groups. The authors discuss several possible explanations, including a faulty design of the transfer tasks and the need for greater structure and teacher involvement in Logo programming activities.

155 Perkins, D. N. "Reasoning As It Is and Could Be: An Empirical Perspective." Chapter 14 in *Thinking across Cultures: The Third International Conference on Thinking*, edited by Donald M. Topping, Doris C. Crowell, and Victor N. Kobayashi, 175-194. Hillsdale, NJ: Lawrence Erlbaum, 1989. [32 Refs.]

Perkins reviews a program of six investigations conducted on informal reasoning through Project Zero (Harvard University Graduate School of Education). Unlike formal deductive reasoning that provides strict standards, informal reasoning involves the use of judgment calls. The studies indicate several factors about the situation modeling that occurs in informal reasoning: (1) informal argument is troubled more by problems of situation modeling than by either formal or informal fallacies, (2) people come to a reasoning task with certain skills and abilities which are reflected in the resulting situation models, and (3) conventional education only slightly improves informal reasoning, while instruction focusing on reasoning does increase reasoning skills. Perkins summarizes pertinent points about informal reasoning disclosed by the investigations and outlines three possible factors (disinterest, metacognitive shortfall, and confirmation bias) that inhibit the development of effective situation modeling.

156 Perkins, D. N., Richard Allen, and James Hafner. "Difficulties in Everyday Reasoning." In *Thinking, the Expanding Frontier. Proceedings of the International, Interdisciplinary Conference on Thinking Held at the University of the South Pacific, January 1982*, edited by William Maxwell, 177-189. Philadelphia, PA: Franklin Institute Press, 1983. [14 Refs.]

The authors discuss preliminary results of an ongoing study indicating that there are eight difficulties most common in everyday reasoning. These difficulties (contrary consequent, contrary antecedent, external factor, disconnection, scaler insufficiency, neglected critical distinction, counterexample, and alternative argument) reflect superficial models of situations rather than general logical lapses. Everyday reasoning seems often to imply a "make-sense" epistemology in which an intuitive feel that a proposition makes sense is used to judge the truth of a position. Skilled reasoning employs a large knowledge repertoire, efficient knowledge evocation, and a critical epistemology that incorporates justification skills, practical tactics, and skills for developing sound models of situations. The authors believe that critical epistemology should be teachable.

157 Pierce, Walter, Elmer Lemke, and Rolland Smith. "Critical Thinking and Moral Development in Secondary Students." *High School Journal* 71, no. 3 (February-March 1988): 120-126. [18 Refs.]

The authors describe a study of a secondary school curriculum model designed to foster critical thinking and moral development in secondary students. Students in control and treatment groups were given the Defining Issues Test and the Watson-Glaser Critical Thinking Appraisal. Students in the treatment group participated in the five-part program of discussion, debate, critical thinking exercises, value issues, and an independent learning project. Participating teachers were trained in Kohlbergian Theory, critical thinking skills, the independent study process, and other pertinent areas. At the end of the first project year, an analysis of pretest and posttest scores revealed a significant difference in the performance of the treatment group over that of the control group in the Defining Issues Test, but no significant differences were found in the Watson-Glaser Critical Thinking Appraisal. After the second project year, the treatment group performed significantly better on the critical thinking subtests of inference, deduction, and arguments than the control group. The results of the study suggests that curriculum changes can improve the scores of secondary school students on critical thinking and moral development measures. They also suggest that working in critical thinking and moral development simultaneously may have a mutual positive effect.

158 Pintrich, Paul R. "Student Learning and College Teaching." In *College Teaching and Learning: Preparing for New Commitments*, edited by Robert E. Young and Kenneth E. Eble. New Directions for Teaching and Learning, no. 33. San Francisco, CA: Jossey-Bass, 1988. [55 Refs.]

Pintrich reviews research on students' knowledge, learning strategies, and critical thinking and the implications for college teaching and learning. Research on students' knowledge describes how prior knowledge and experience affect how course content is learned, suggesting the importance of the instructor providing explicit discussion or direct instruction in his/her knowledge structure of the course material. Learning strategies research, focusing on cognitive processes used in learning, understanding, and remembering course material, suggests the instruction on appropriate learning strategies in all disciplines. Critical thinking research suggests that college courses must be designed and taught in a manner that fosters higher order thinking skills.

159 Ploger, Don. "Reasoning and the Structure of Knowledge in Biochemistry." *Instructional Science* 17, no. 1 (1988): 57-76. [11 Refs.]

Ploger investigated the relationship between reasoning strategy and the structure of knowledge in biochemistry. He examined the differences in the problem solving processes used by experts (biochemists) and novices (students) and in their explanations of the solutions. Two first-year medical students and two experts with Ph.D. degrees in a biological science were given a problem related to a metabolic disease to solve. The results of the study indicated that reasoning processes followed the organization of the knowledge of metabolism. Experts used both the known-pathology and normal function strategies, while novices used a variation of the normal function strategy only. Experts began with the known and progressed to the unknown in solving a problem, while novices moved from the unknown to the known. After arriving at the correct answer, the experts continued reasoning about the problem while novices terminated the process. Ploger believes this study has implications not only for the education of biochemists, but also for introducing biological science to laypersons.

160 Ploger, Don, and Richard Harvey. "Reasoning in Biochemistry: Problem-Solving in Metabolism." *Biochemical Education* 16, no. 2 (April 1988): 76-79. [8 Refs.]

In order to analyze the reasoning processes used by individuals to solve problems in biochemistry, Ploger and Harvey asked four expert biochemists and eight first-year medical students to think aloud about a specific problem involving metabolic diseases and explain their solutions. An analysis of the problem solving and explanation sessions revealed that the experts used more strategies for finding solutions and evaluated the solutions they found, whereas students stopped determining a solution. The authors see implications for more effective teaching strategies in biochemistry.

161 Plummer, Thomas G. "Cognitive Growth and Literary Analysis: A Dialectical Model for Teaching Literature." *Unterrichtspraxis* 21, no. 1 (Spring 1988): 68-80. [10 Refs.]

Plummer examines the responses of undergraduate and graduate students to an interview instrument designed to help determine (1) any relation between cognitive development level with attitudes toward literary analysis and (2) whether individuals at various cognitive levels shared patterns of response and ways of approaching and analyzing a specific text. Using Perry's model of cognitive development for college students and subjects' responses,

Plummer outlines three stages of development in students' acquisition of critical skills. He applies this model to the teaching of literary analysis to undergraduates, stressing that instructors must identify and address students' levels of critical development and teach methods of thinking about literature and weighing evidence. Instruction must focus on helping undergraduates develop from lower to higher levels of critical thinking (from noncritical, authority- or subject-oriented criticism to an understanding and acceptance of standards of judgment). Plummer suggests teaching critical analysis dialectically. He presents eight rules guiding the design of his courses in literary analysis.

162 Powers, Donald E., and Mary K. Enright. "Analytical Reasoning Skills in Graduate Study: Perceptions of Faculty in Six Fields." *Journal of Higher Education* 58, no. 6 (November-December 1987): 658-682. [34 Refs.]

Powers and Enright used a questionnaire to determine the reasoning or analytical abilities necessary for successful academic performance on the graduate level and the importance of these abilities among various academic disciplines. Two hundred and fifty-five (255) graduate faculty in six fields of study (chemistry, computer science, education, engineering, English, and psychology) responded to the questionnaire. Results showed significant differences among the six disciplines in the importance placed on the various skills and in the number of skills considered important in each field. The authors believe that these findings have implications for the development of general and subject-specific graduate admissions tests.

163 Prawat, Richard S., and Ariel L. H. Anderson. "Eight Teachers' Control Orientations and Their Students' Problem-Solving Ability." *Elementary School Journal* 89, no. 1 (September 1988): 99-112. [39 Refs.]

The authors investigated the relationship of autonomy granting by teachers with task demands and means-end problem solving ability by elementary school students. They assessed the means-end problem solving ability of 64 third and fourth grade students in meeting task and interpersonal demands. Results revealed that the students of less autonomy-granting teachers were better problem solvers. The authors acknowledge that their unexpected findings are consistent with research on parent socialization practices and on teaching from a social constructivist theoretical viewpoint. The article includes an appendix with sample problems from the problem solving ability measure.

164 Reusser, Kurt. "Problem Solving beyond the Logic of Things: Contextual Effects on Understanding and Solving Word Problems." *Instructional Science* 17, no. 4 (1988): 309-338. [41 Refs.]

Reusser presents findings from several experimental and thinking aloud studies. The findings demonstrate how the wording, content structure, and linguistic form of the text of a problem and the situational context within which the problem solving task takes place influence an individual's comprehension and solution to a problem.

165 Riding, R. J., and S. D. Powell. "The Effect on Reasoning, Reading and Number Performance of Computer-Presented Critical Thinking Activities in Five-Year-Old Children." *Educational Psychology* 7, no. 1 (1987): 55-65. [37 Refs.]

Riding and Powell studied the possibility of improving critical thinking in young children and the effect of improved thinking on reading and mathematics performance. Sixty-four (64) five-year-old children, divided into two treatment groups and two control groups, were given a reasoning test (Raven's Coloured Progressive Matrices), a reading-language scheme (Breakthrough to Literacy Reading Scheme), and a test of mathematics covering basic concepts of numbers, addition, and subtraction as pretests and posttests. For thirteen weeks, the treatment groups worked on computerized problem solving activities while the control groups worked on tasks related to the curriculum. Results showed a significant improvement on the reasoning test and reading language scheme by the treatment groups, but not on the mathematics test. The authors believe that the study suggests that thinking performance is generalizable to other activities, but that further study is needed to determine if it is generalizable to higher levels of basic subjects. An appendix provides a summary listing of critical thinking activities used on the computer.

166 Riding, R. J., and S. D. Powell. "The Improvement of Thinking Skills in Young Children Using Computer Activities: A Replication and Extension." *Educational Psychology* 6, no. 2 (1986): 179-183. [7 Refs.]

Riding and Powell replicated their 1985 study on the improvement of critical thinking skills in young children, using 60 rather than 36 four-year-old children and a female rather than male experimenter. They extended the study by setting a criterion of a minimum 70% accuracy for each activity performed. As in the previous study, children who participated in the critical thinking activities via computer improved their scores on the reasoning test (Raven's Coloured Progressive Matrices). It was also noted that the improvements in the pretest and posttest scores were greater which might be attributed to the minimum 70% accuracy criterion.

167 Riesenmy, Madonna R., Sybil Mitchell, Bryce B. Hudgins, and Debra Ebel. "Retention and Transfer of Children's Self-Directed Critical Thinking Skills." *Journal of Educational Research* 85, no. 1 (September-October 1991): 14-25. [38 Refs.]

The authors discuss the concept of critical thinking, its generalizability, the concept of self-directed critical thinking, and the retention and transfer of broad intellectual skills. They present their study of whether children trained in self-directed critical thinking retained and transferred their skills better than untrained children. A sample of 38 fourth and fifth grade students were divided into groups of four and trained in four thinking roles (task definer, strategist, monitor, and challenger) through twelve discussion sessions. Each student played a different role in each discussion. Discussion teachers participated in two inservice seminars given before the study to explain what their roles were to be. A pretest and posttest were given to the sample subjects and a control group of 28 fourth and fifth graders. In the posttest, the experimental group earned superior retention scores for self-directed critical thinking skills, amount of information used in solutions, and quality of answers than the control group. The experimental group also had higher scores on lateral and vertical transfer tasks. The authors conclude that the impact of the combined use of the thinking roles, small groups, special curriculum, and teaching was very strong. The two problems used for the pretest and posttest are included.

168 Ristow, Robert S. "The Teaching of Thinking Skills: Does It Improve Creativity?" *Gifted Child Today* 11, no. 2 (March-April 1988): 44-46. [14 Refs.]

Ristow conducted a study to determine whether direct teaching of thinking enhances creative thinking. The Torrance Test of Creative Thinking, Form A (1966) was verbally administered as a pretest and posttest to both a treatment group and a control group of third-grade children. The treatment group was exposed weekly to a 30-minute session of thinking activities, including brainstorming and SCAMPER techniques. Results showed that the direct teaching of thinking can significantly improve children's ability to create new ideas and to think in various ways.

169 Rogers, Theresa. "Exploring a Socio-Cognitive Perspective on the Interpretive Processes of Junior High School Students." *English Quarterly* 20, no. 3 (Fall 1987): 218-230. [19 Refs.]

Rogers conducted an exploratory study based on the socio-cognitive perspective which stresses the importance of the social context of classroom discourse in the development of critical and interpretive thought. Twenty-four (24) junior high school students divided into two groups (a response-centered group and a question-answer group), participated in discussion and essay writing assignments for the study. Discussions were taped, transcribed, and analyzed. Response patterns, sources used for responses, and interpretative processes were analyzed. Rogers found that the students in the question-answer group which used a teacher-centered approach were frequently not given time to develop a point and previously undeveloped topics re-emerged. The response-centered group which used a student-centered approach showed more qualitative change in their interpretations and their post-discussion theme essays were convergent and within a larger moral context. The author concludes with questions prompted by the study and proposes the hypothesis that dialectical discourse may be the preferred social context for higher level reading or thinking skills.

170 Ross, Gregory A., and George Semb. "Philosophy *Can* Teach Critical Thinking Skills." *Teaching Philosophy* 4, no. 2 (April 1981): 111-122. [13 Refs.]

Ross and Semb investigated whether philosophy can develop critical thinking skills. Two introductory philosophy course sections used George William's *Man Asks Why*, supplementary lectures, and quizzes. Other sections were taught conventionally. The critical thinking levels of all students were measured with the Watson-Glaser Critical Thinking Appraisal before and after the experiment. The results indicated a statistically significant increase in critical thinking abilities among the students in the two experimental sections. The authors conclude that philosophy can teach students to think critically.

171 Sadowski, Barbara R. "Critical Thinking and CAI." *Journal of Computers in Mathematics and Science Teaching* 4, no. 2 (Winter 1984-85): 12-13. [5 Refs.]

Sadowski summarizes three research studies on critical thinking and computer-assisted instruction. Two of the studies, conducted in 1984, involved seventh graders. One of these also included fifth and twelfth graders and was a replication of a 1980 study involving college students. Sadowski emphasizes the importance of educational researchers in mathematics and science clearly defining problem solving, critical thinking skills, and reasoning skills to alleviate the ambiguity and confusion in research on computer programming and problem solving.

172 Savell, Joel M., Paul T. Twohig, and Douglas L. Rachford. "Empirical Status of Feuerstein's 'Instrumental Enrichment' (FIE) Technique as a Method of Teaching Thinking Skills." *Review of Educational Research* 56, no. 4 (Winter 1986): 381-409. [80 Refs.]

The authors review the empirical research literature on Feuerstein's Instrumental Enrichment method for teaching thinking skills. The review includes studies conducted in Israel, Venezuela, Canada, and the United States. The authors list some of the generalizations and conclusions about the effects of the method, pose questions for future research, and make recommendations for improving such studies.

173 Simpkins, W. S. "The Way Examiners Assess Critical Thinking in Educational Administrative Theses." *Journal of Educational Administration* 25, no. 2 (Summer 1987): 248-268. [9 Refs.]

Simpkins analyzed fifty examiners' reports on theses in educational administration to determine whether they reflected a particular concept of critical thinking. The results revealed that the examiners subscribe to a common view of rational inquiry which includes the concepts of scientific method and critical thinking and to an idealized style of critical thinking which combines detached rationality with imaginative insight. A mixture of assumptions of the traditional and emergent research traditions is reflected in the application of the scientific method and critical thinking as assessment criteria for theses in educational administration.

174 Sinnott, Jan D., ed. *Everyday Problem Solving: Theory and Applications*. New York, NY: Praeger, 1989. 315 pp.

This anthology contains eighteen essays on key approaches used in studies on everyday problem solving. The essays are organized into three untitled sections dealing with (1) concepts, models and theories; (2) particular problems, issues and tests; and (3) memory and intervention. Issues covered include problem solving models, problem solving testing, consumer reasoning, intelligence and cognitive skills, and teaching/teacher preparation.

175 Sprafkin, Joyce, Kenneth D. Gadow, and Gail Kant. "Teaching Emotionally Disturbed Children to Discriminate Reality from Fantasy on Television." *Journal of Special Education* 21, no. 4 (Winter 1987-1988): 99-107. [25 Refs.]

Working under the assumption and hypothesis that critical viewing skills alleviate the negative impacts of television on children, the authors investigated the effectiveness of a critical viewing skills curriculum on the improvement of television-related perceptions and knowledge in emotionally disturbed children. They used the Stony Brook Videotest, a measure of children's perceptions of reality and fantasy of television content, as a pretest and posttest of two groups of emotionally disturbed children. The treatment group was exposed to a television viewing skills curriculum, consisting of 30-minute lessons on topics of television production, commercials, special effects, special effects for aggression, animation, and real and pretend. The critical viewing skills curriculum was effective in improving reality (fantasy discrimination and knowledge on special effects). It did not improve perceptions of commercials as persuasive messages which suggested to the authors that the curriculum should provide increased emphasis on advertising techniques. The results were consistent with research conducted with non-handicapped students. The authors advocate the incorporation of critical viewing skills in schools.

176 Statkiewicz, Walter R., and Robert D. Allen. "Practice Exercises to Develop Critical Thinking Skills." *Journal of College Science Teaching* 12, no. 4 (February 1983): 262-266. [13 Refs.]

Statkiewicz and Allen investigated the effectiveness of out-of-class exercises developed for a college biology course. Students were assigned ten to twelve out-of-class practice problems weekly, one was collected and graded. An examination was given every fourth week. The grades for the practice problems and examinations were correlated. The results indicated that students' analytical skills improve with practice and are transferable to new and unfamiliar problems. Statkiewicz and Allen concluded that out-of-class practice exercises are a productive component of learning activities. The authors include sample exercises and grading criteria.

177 Sweller, John. "On the Limited Evidence for the Effectiveness of Teaching General Problem-Solving Strategies." *Journal for Research in Mathematics Education* 21, no. 5 (November 1990): 411-415. [9 Refs.]

Reply to Lawson {903}

See: Owen and Sweller {150}

Sweller contends that research on artificial intelligence and expertise in physics and mathematics support the suggestion that domain-specific knowledge rather than general problem solving skills distinguishes novices from experts. He notes that there is little evidence (1) that experts have access to general problem solving strategies unavailable to novices and (2) of general problem solving strategies training being incorporated successfully into mathematics education. Sweller notes that the studies cited by Lawson as evidence for teaching general problem solving strategies to mathematics students are drawn primarily from research involving learning disabled or mentally retarded subjects and do not provide evidence for Lawson's position. Transfer is a complex process as Lawson indicates, but only theoretical analyses have been done on the topic. Sweller stresses the need for empirical evidence on the effectiveness and limits of the theory. He believes that any proposed reform of mathematics education should not take place until evidence and studies have been accumulated. He also believes that alternative techniques for improving problem solving performance that are supported by extensive data should be explored.

178 Thomas, Ruth G. "Alternative Research Paradigms: A Contrast Set." *Journal of Vocational Home Economics Education* 7, no. 2 (Spring 1989): 48-57. [9 Refs.]

See: Way {186}
Hultgren {114}

Thomas compares and contrasts the alternative critical thinking research paradigms presented in three articles in the preceding issue of the *Journal of Vocational Home Economics Education*. She identifies several questions she believed were unanswered in the articles.

179 Tierney, Robert J., Anna Soter, John F. O'Flahavan, and William McGinley. "The Effects of Reading and Writing upon Thinking Critically." *Reading Research Quarterly* 24, no. 2 (Spring 1989): 134-173. [43 Refs.]

The authors describe their extensive study on whether the combination of reading and writing prompts more critical thinking than each activity by itself or each activity in combination with questions or a knowledge activation activity. Each subject in the twelve treatment groups, formed from 137 undergraduate students, was randomly assigned one of two selected topics and one of twelve experimental conditions involving a combination of an introductory activity, a reading condition, and a question condition. Following the completion of the activities, all subjects wrote or revised an essay and answered debriefing questions. An analysis of the subjects' writing tasks, responses to questions, and debriefing comments showed that a combination of writing and reading activities produced more evaluative thinking and multiple perspectives than with either reading or writing activities alone or reading combined with a knowledge activation activity or questions.

180 Tweney, Ryan D., and Bonnie J. Walker. "Science Education and the Cognitive Psychology of Science." Chapter 9 in *Dimensions of Thinking and Cognitive Instruction*, edited by Beau Fly Jones and Lorna Idol, 291-310. Hillsdale, NJ: Lawrence Erlbaum, 1990. [77 Refs.]

While scientific thinking is generally regarded as a primary component in any attempt at integrating thinking skills instruction into school curriculum, Tweney and Walker assert that the nature of scientific thinking has been largely ignored or misrepresented by educators. In an attempt to rectify the misconceptions about science, the authors review relevant research in cognitive science, focusing on three areas of research: (1) the relation between the reasoning that occurs in science and the orthodox categories of formal reasoning that characterize early approaches to the philosophy of science, (2) the utilization of specialized expert knowledge in science, and (3) recent research on the problem solving process. They review studies on Karl Popper's theory of disconfirmed inference, the confirmation bias and heuristics, expert versus novice amount and organization of knowledge, and scientific problem solving contrasted with classroom conceptions of scientific thinking.

181 Udall, Anne J., and Mari Helen High. "What Are They Thinking When We're Teaching Critical Thinking?" *Gifted Child Quarterly* 33, no. 4 (Fall 1989): 156-160. [27 Refs.]

The authors investigated the effectiveness of teaching critical thinking in a middle school gifted program curriculum. They compared teacher intentions for student behaviors with student perceptions of teacher intentions. Two teachers from separate middle school programs in the same district were asked to design two 20 to 30 minute lessons, based on Taba strategies, to teach one of four critical thinking skills. Teachers and students participating in the lessons were interviewed after viewing videotapes of these lessons. Results indicated that students identified teacher intentions and articulated their use of the thought processes that teachers intended them to use.

182 Unks, Gerald. "Critical Thinking in the Social Studies Classroom. Do We Teach It?" *Social Education* 49, no. 3 (March 1985): 240, 244-246. [17 Refs.]

Unks conducted a study to measure the ability of social studies teachers in 75 high school systems throughout the United States to distinguish statements of fact from statements of opinion--a fundamental activity of critical thinking. The results indicated that almost half of the social studies teachers could not correctly make the distinction. Unks recommends future teachers be taught the basic operations of critical thinking and students having the most difficulty with critical thinking be identified and given special assistance.

183 Vandergrift, Kay E. "Critical Thinking Misfired: Implications of Student Responses to *The Shooting Gallery*." *School Library Media Quarterly* 15, no. 2 (Winter 1989): 86-91. [23 Refs.]

Vandergrift analyzes the assumptions and interpretations of *The Shooting Gallery* (a short film) given by junior high school students and graduate library school students which were unchallenged by teachers during class discussions. Vandergrift argues that educators must be willing to challenge student assumptions and explore the meaning making process students used to reach their conclusions. She believes that such an approach would help in developing higher order thinking skills.

184 Voss, James F. "On the Composition of Experts and Novices." Chapter 4 in *Thinking, Reasoning, and Writing*, edited by Elaine P. Maimon, Barbara F. Nodine, and Finbarr W. O'Connor, 69-84. White Plains, NY: Longman, 1989. [37 Refs.]

Voss reviews research on the solving of ill-structured problems by experts and novices. He explains that in well-structured problems, the givens, goals, and constraints are presented in the problem statement or easily derived from it; while in ill-structured problems, one or more of these components are missing. The author also reviews recent research on weak and strong problem solving methods and on informal reasoning. Voss draws two conclusions from the research review: (1) while weak problem solving methods and the strategies of informal reasoning are probably acquired by most people, the ability to use such strategies is greater when the individual has developed stronger intellectual ability or more formal education in subject matter content rather than a content-free reasoning course and (2) instruction in a particular context may be effective for learning to use that strategy in that particular content domain. Voss believes that there is no substitute for domain knowledge when performing a complex task in that domain.

185 Walvoord, Barbara E., Lucille Parkinson McCarthy, Virginia Johnson Anderson, John R. Breihan, Susan Miller Robison, and A. Kimbrough Sherman. *Thinking and Writing in College: A Naturalistic Study of Students in Four Disciplines*. Urbana, IL: National Council of Teachers of English, 1990. 269 pp. [154 Refs.]

The authors present a one semester study on thinking and writing in four college classes in different subject areas: biology, psychology, history and business. The research team focused on four areas: (1) teachers' expectations for good writing, thinking and learning, (2) what difficulties arose as the students attempted to meet the teacher's expectations, (3) how teachers' methods and students' strategies affected those difficulties, and (4) the differences and similarities among the four classes in the focus areas. The researchers tracked students in the history and business classes across the entire semester and gathered data on all writing assignments in those classes. Data gathered consisted of student's pre-draft writing, drafts and teachers' comments, student logs, think aloud recordings, peer interviews, peer responses to drafts, teacher logs, and classroom observations. Each course is examined individually in separate chapters. The researchers identify similarities and differences in the four focus areas and relate nine guiding principles for reshaping teaching in response to what the study revealed about student writing and thinking.

186 Way, Wendy L. "Examining Critical Thinking in Home Economics Education: An Empirical/Analytical Perspective." *Journal of Vocational Home Economics Education* 7, no. 1 (Spring 1989): 1-9. [30 Refs.]

Way examines the characteristics, potential contributions and limitations of the Empirical/Analytical or Positive methodological paradigm for knowledge production. She identifies three general goals for critical thinking research in home economics education that are consistent with the paradigm.

187 Woods, Donald R. "Novice vs. Expert Research Suggests Ideas for Implementation." *Journal of College Science Teaching* 18, no. 2 (September 1988): 77-79, 66-67.

See: Woods {188} and {189}

In this first of a series of three articles dealing with research on the "novice" versus "expert" problem solver, Woods presents a compilation of the approaches and attitudes characterizing the "novice" or unsuccessful problem solver and the "expert" or successful problem solver. The characteristics of each group are presented in comparative lists dealing with different aspects of problem solving: the overall problem solving process, the overall approach taken, attitudes, and reasoning skills.

188 Woods, Donald R. "Novice Versus Expert Research Suggests Ideas for Implementation." *Journal of College Science Teaching* 18, no. 2 (November 1988): 138-141.

See: Woods {187} and {189}

This second of three articles on novice versus expert research in the sciences and its implications for college science teachers examines the differences between successful and unsuccessful problem solvers in exploring a problem, translating the information into different forms, devising a problem solving plan, executing the plan, and reviewing their work.

189 Woods, Donald R. "Novice Versus Expert Research." *Journal of College Science Teaching* 18, no. 3 (December 1988-January 1989): 193-195. [26 Refs.]

See: Woods {187} and {188}

In this third of three articles comparing novice and expert problem solving, Woods focuses on research comparing the discipline specific, knowledge-use characteristics of unsuccessful and successful problem solvers, and the implications of this research for teaching. He lists characteristics of unsuccessful and successful problem solvers and outlines general procedures for helping students reflect on the integrated structure of knowledge and the process of problem solving.

190 Worsham, Antoinette W., and Gilbert R. Austin. "Effects of Teaching Thinking Skills on SAT Scores." *Educational Leadership* 41, no. 3 (November 1983): 50-51. [3 Refs.]

Worsham and Austin give the results of an experiment in a public school system in which a group of seniors participated in a program using *Think* language arts material. This group significantly increased their SAT verbal scores in comparison to the scores of a control group taken from the same school system. The authors conclude that additional research is needed to study the correlation of aptitude and achievement with teaching thinking skills.

191 Yeazell, Mary I. "A Report on the First Year of the Upshur County, West Virginia, Philosophy for Children Project." *Thinking* 3, no. 1 (1983): 12-14. [3 Refs.]

Yeazell presents the results of a one year experimental use of the Institute for the Advancement of Philosophy for Children (IAPC) materials, specifically *Harry Stottlemeier's Discovery*. The results indicate a significant increase in reading comprehension for those students using the IAPC materials compared to regular classes using a county school system's in-house reading program. Yeazell argues that the data shows the usefulness of incorporating logical and critical thinking into the elementary school curriculum.

4

THEORY

192 Adler, Jonathan E. "On Resistance to Critical Thinking." Chapter 15 in *Thinking: The Second International Conference*, edited by David N. Perkins, Jack Lochhead, and John C. Bishop, 247-260. Hillsdale, NJ: Lawrence Erlbaum, 1987. [30 Refs.]

Critical thinking has traditionally been taught as an activity of logic, but Adler asserts that teaching it as an epistemological enterprise would be more appropriate. He elaborates on cognitive, motivational, personal, and methodological obstacles to critical thinking and argues that attitudes such as dogmatism, bias, and engagement are both resistant to and required for critical thinking. The resistant attitudes are in tension with those accepted as virtues of critical thinking, such as openness to opposing viewpoints, impartiality, and detachment. The tension between these attitudes gives rise to conflicting judgments and exceptions to accepted logical principles of critical thinking. Adler presents several examples to illustrate this position. The teaching of critical thinking as an epistemological enterprise would incorporate the tensions of attitudes and teach the student to know when to think critically. He believes ultimate resolutions of conflicts should not be expected, but should lead to further inquiry and continued self-examination.

193 Adler, Mortimer J. "Why 'Critical Thinking' Programs Won't Work." *Education Week* (September 17, 1986): 28.

Reprinted in *Education Digest* 52, no. 7 (March 1987): 9-11.

Adler argues that current critical thinking programs are oversimplified versions of ineffective logic courses that rely on texts with stated laws and rules of thinking processes. He asserts that thinking cannot be taught in isolation.

Adler believes students should be coached in thinking in every course, preferably by teachers who know how to think.

194 Arons, Arnold B. "'Critical Thinking' and the Baccalaureate Curriculum." *Liberal Education* 71, no. 2 (Summer 1985): 141-157. [13 Refs.]

Reply: Garver {234}
See: Arons {195}

Adler believes that the term "critical thinking" must be unpacked in order to identify underlying processes of abstract logical reasoning common to many disciplines and capable of being cultivated in students. He examines ten thinking and reasoning processes: (1) asking what and how we know; (2) being aware of gaps in available information; (3) discriminating between observation and inference; (4) recognizing words as signs for ideas, not ideas themselves; (5) probing for assumptions; (6) drawing inferences; (7) performing hypothetico-deductive reasoning; (8) discriminating between inductive and deductive reasoning; (9) testing one's own line of reasoning and conclusions for internal consistency; and (10) developing self-consciousness concerning one's own thinking and reasoning processes. Arons believes that the cultivation of these processes would aid in the education of an enlightened democratic citizenry. Since research studies indicate that little transfer occurs from reasoning experience acquired from only one discipline, Arons asserts that instruction in abstract reasoning should be done in each course. Arons focuses on science curricula and suggests that the capacity for abstract logical reasoning can be enhanced by giving students hands-on experience and time to explore, test, theorize and inquire. He offers several explanations for why abstract reasoning is not taught, and outlines a faculty workshop where individuals from the various disciplines could meet and present their analyses of topics. He includes an example of one assignment.

195 Arons, Arnold B. "Critical Thinking as a Self-Conscious Activity." *Liberal Education* 72, no. 3 (Fall 1986): 251-252.

Reply to Garver {234}
See: Arons {194}

Arons clarifies several of his views that were criticized by Garver. Arons denies that he is a Piagetian and that self-conscious use of reasoning processes inevitably lead to "right answers" in all situations, though they are a necessary condition for the intellectual development desired. Educators should become sensitized to the opportunities for making necessary insights and awareness explicit for students. Arons proposes a faculty workshop with such sensitization as its goal.

196 Aucoin, Linda, and Jo Ann Cangemi. "Improving the Curriculum: Teach Critical Thinking Skills." *Louisiana Social Studies Journal* 13, no. 1 (Fall 1986): 18-21. [5 Refs.]

The authors argue in support of *A Nation at Risk*, the National Commission on Education's 1983 report recommending increased emphasis on teaching critical thinking skills. They outline a definition of thinking, list Robert Ennis's compilation of critical thinking skills, and summarize Barry Beyer's five-step outline of teaching critical thinking skills as a way of implementing the Commission's recommendations.

197 Baer, John. "Let's Not Handicap Able Thinkers." *Educational Leadership* 45, no. 7 (April 1988): 66-72. [27 Refs.]

Reply: Perkins {313}

While supporting the teaching of thinking, Baer cautions that programs to teach thinking have been developed even though the nature of thought and reasoning are not fully understood. He believes the approaches used in the programs may hinder students' thinking skills, especially those students who are already able thinkers, by inhibiting ways of thinking that differ from the procedures taught in the program. Baer argues that many teaching programs assume a relation between thinking and consciousness which has not been demonstrated or fully accepted by cognitive science researchers. He suggests that student teaching be assessed before planning for instruction in thinking is begun. Such planning should allow for alternative thinking styles and emphasize the product not the process. Two sidebar discussions of unconscious thinking and thinking as embedded in brain structure are included.

198 Baron, Joan Boykoff, and Robert J. Sternberg, eds. *Teaching Thinking Skills: Theory and Practice*. New York, NY: W. H. Freeman, 1987. 275 pp.

This collection of twelve essays provides an overview of the major modern viewpoints concerning the theory and practice of teaching thinking skills. The anthology contains five parts: Part 1, Foundation of Thinking Skills and Their Instruction; Part 2, General Approaches to the Teaching of Thinking Skills; Part 3, Programmic Approaches to the Teaching of Thinking; Part 4, Evaluating Thinking Skills; and Part 5, Integration.

199 Baron, Jonathan. "What Kinds of Intelligence Components are Fundamental?" Chapter 16 in *Thinking and Learning Skills. Vol. 2: Research and Open Questions*, edited by Susan F. Chipman, Judith W. Segal, and Robert Glaser, 365-390. Hillsdale, NJ: Lawrence Erlbaum, 1985. [60 Refs.]

Baron identifies three components of intelligence: processing components of skills, strategies, and styles. Of these three components, Baron argues that only styles (general behavioral dispositions that characterize performance in mental tasks) are teachable and transferable. Baron offers a framework for studying styles that analyzes dimensions or functions of style such as (1) a search for possibilities, (2) a search for evidence, (3) use of evidence, and (4) a search for goals. Teaching good thinking can be viewed as the changing of styles toward the optimum range on each style dimension. It involves the attempt to change personality and habits and motives in thinking situations, whereas teaching strategies usually entails having a student be able to use a desired strategy. Styles may account for transfer effects in studies of strategies. Baron offers suggestions for further research.

200 Barrow, Robin. "Skill Talk." *Journal of Philosophy of Education* 21, no. 2 (Winter 1987): 187-195. [8 Refs.]

Barrow asserts that teacher evaluation exams and research on teaching have emphasized generic teaching skills over mastery of subject matter. He argues for a distinction between "skill" and "ability." Skill is a subclass of ability and should refer to notions of physicality, training, and practice rather than understanding. Intellectual abilities such as critical thinking entail an understanding of particular domains or contexts and should not be considered a set of skills. Similarly, teaching is linked to understanding specific subjects and should not be thought of as a set of generic teaching skills.

201 Beck, Isabel L. "Improving Practice through Understanding Reading." Chapter 3 in *Toward the Thinking Curriculum: Current Cognitive Research*, edited by Lauren B. Resnick and Leopold E. Klopfer, 40-58. 1989 Yearbook of the Association for Supervision and Curriculum Development [Alexandria, VA]: Association for Supervision and Curriculum Development, 1989. [35 Refs.]

Beck notes that reading is a complex skill in which multiple mental operations must take place concurrently. Since the ability for humans to pay active attention to multiple processes at once, a number of processes must be developed to be carried out efficiently or automatically. She also notes that the current view of reading as an interactive process emphasizes comprehension as constructive. Word recognition must be developed so that it is carried out efficiently in the reading process allowing greater mental processing capacity for higher level processes of comprehension (e.g., constructing meaningful phrases and sentences). Beck contends that understanding (1) the importance and effects of word recognition efficiency, (2) how the construction of a text influences comprehension, and (3) how background knowledge that the reader has on the topic of a text has implications for classroom instruction. She emphasizes the importance of teachers understanding the reading process and having knowledge of individual students.

202 Bereiter, Carl. "How to Keep Thinking Skills from Going the Way of All Frills." *Educational Leadership* 42, no. 1 (September 1984): 75-77. [4 Refs.]

Bereiter asserts that successful teaching of thinking skills requires the integration of thinking skills activities into instructional objectives (contingency strategy) and throughout an instructional program (permeation strategy).

203 Beyer, Barry K. "Common Sense about Teaching Thinking Skills." *Educational Leadership* 41, no. 3 (November 1983): 44-49. [12 Refs.]

Beyer discusses three essential components for effective instruction in critical thinking: (1) a supportive learning environment in which information processing, rather than information receiving, is the major activity; (2) effective skill teaching strategies that are systematic, direct, integrated, and developmental; and (3) curriculum guidelines for the coordination and structure of effective thinking skills for kindergarten through twelfth grade and beyond. Beyer believes that thinking skills should be taught across the curriculum.

204 Beyer, Barry K. "Developing a Scope and Sequence for Thinking Skills Instruction." *Educational Leadership* 45, no. 7 (April 1988): 26-30. [5 Refs.]

Beyer suggests a framework for teaching thinking skills in kindergarten through twelfth grade. He outlines the scope and sequence for introducing specific thinking skills at each grade level and provides charts to illustrate the division of thinking operations and their appropriate introduction into the curriculum.

205 Beyer, Barry K. "Improving Thinking Skills--Defining the Problem." *Phi Delta Kappan* 65, no. 7 (March 1984): 486-490. [25 Refs.]

See: Beyer {206}

To improve the teaching and learning of thinking in schools, Beyer believes that the major obstacles to effective teaching of thinking skills must be confronted. He discusses five of the more significant obstacles: (1) lack of consensus on what thinking means and the thinking skills that should be taught, (2) lack of knowledge regarding the essential components of the thinking skills educators have chosen to teach, (3) inappropriate instruction on how to perform a given skill, (4) attempting to teach too many skills in too little time, and (5) inappropriate testing for thinking proficiency.

206 Beyer, Barry K. "Improving Thinking Skills--Practical Approaches." *Phi Delta Kappan* 65, no. 8 (April 1984): 556-560. [36 Refs.]

See: Beyer {205}

Beyer discusses five steps that educators can take to improve the teaching of thinking skills: (1) identify and define a core of thinking skills that should be taught, (2) identify components of each of the thinking skills, (3) provide direct instruction in how to use these thinking skills in all content areas and grade levels, (4) create and implement sequential, developmental curricula integrating the teaching of selected thinking skills within and across courses and grade levels, and (5) devise measures of thinking skills competency that are valid, reliable, and congruent with the skills taught.

207 Beyer, Barry K. "What Philosophy Offers to the Teaching of Thinking." *Educational Leadership* 47, no. 5 (February 1990): 55-60. [16 Refs.]

Reprinted in Costa {506}

Concerned that insights from philosophy are often excluded from the teaching of thinking, Beyer stresses the importance of including both psychological and philosophical perspectives in teaching thinking. Noting that philosophy is thinking, the author highlights and analyzes six concepts of philosophy (reasoning, critical judgment, criteria, point of view, dialogue, and dispositions) that are central to critical thinking and that should be incorporated into the kindergarten through twelfth grade curriculum.

208 Beyth-Marom, Ruth, Ruth Novik, and Michele Sloan. "Enhancing Children's Thinking Skills: An Instructional Model for Decision-Making under Certainty." *Instructional Science* 16, no. 3 (1987): 215-231. [35 Refs.]

Stressing the importance of thinking skills training in modern society, the authors establish a casc for a curriculum which promotes thinking skills. Emphasis is on decision making skills, specifically decision making under certainty. They present a decision making instructional model, developed as a curriculum project for ensuring the technological and scientific literacy of clementary and junior high students, as a framework for developing a curriculum intended to promote thinking skills. This model outlines five decision making steps, the cognitive abilities required for each step, and the educational objectives necessary for developing a curriculum for promoting the cognitive abilities. The authors advocate teaching decision making within a content area.

209 Binker, A. J. A., and Marla Charbonneau. "Piagetian Insights and Critical Thinking." *Informal Logic* 5 (June 1983): 10-15. [5 Refs.]

Binker and Charbonneau demonstrate ways in which Richard Paul's theory of critical thinking can be combined with Piaget's analysis of egocentric thought in children to help adults recognize their egocentric and sociocentric tendencies. They review Paul's theory, discussing the dangers involved with teaching critical thinking and how such dangers are addressed by Paul. Binker and Charbonneau draw parallels between Paul's theory and Piaget's descriptions of childish thought patterns and adult fallacious thinking. They identify aspects of egocentric thought and suggest ways students may learn to become more aware of their own egocentrism by exploring the egocentricity and sociocentricity of opposing views.

210 Binkley, Robert W. "Can the Ability to Reason Well Be Taught?" In *Informal Logic: The First International Symposium*, edited by J. Anthony Blair and Ralph H. Johnson, 79-92. Inverness, CA: Edgepress, 1980.

Binkley asserts that critical reasoning courses designed to improve reasoning abilities have been resisted by educators due to their perceived tedium and boring nature and the question of whether such a course can actually improve reasoning. He argues that the ability to reason well can be taught and, using the Platonic dialogue between Meno and Socrates concerning virtue as a springboard, outlines the foundations of a critical reasoning course. Such a course should teach not only a grasp of logical theory but also an intuitive logical sense, knowledge, and right opinion. It should foster a love of reasoning so that students will not only learn to reason well but want to do so. To achieve this goal, a critical reasoning course should include three aspects: (1) training of logical intuition by drilling, (2) pursuit of theoretical logical insight by some feasible substitute for Socratic dialect, and (3) an approach that will be conducive to the acquiring of a love of reason. Binkley offers several suggestions for course content: the deductive/inductive distinction, the concept of argument, propositional logic, and opportunities for the student to use their reasoning skills on important and interesting subject matters.

211 Blair, J. Anthony. "Some Challenges for Critical Thinking." In *Conference 85 on Critical Thinking, Christopher Newport College*, edited by John Hoaglund, 69-82. Newport News, VA: Christopher Newport College Press, 1985. [8 Refs.]

Blair identifies two challenges for the critical thinking movement: (1) formulating a clear conception of what constitutes critical thinking and (2) determining how critical thinking should be taught. Blair recommends that a practical and conceptually useful definition be accepted. He suggests that many of the premises raised by McPeck concerning the subject-specific nature of critical thinking are correct, but believes that there are aspects of critical thinking that are cross disciplinary and could be taught as a separate course. Blair asserts that the critical thinking movement needs to support the teaching of argumentation in a self-critical, open-minded way that focuses on argument as inquiry rather than advocacy or total criticism and has as its goal enlightenment rather than victory.

212 Blatz, Charles V. "Contextualism and Critical Thinking: Programmatic Investigations." *Educational Theory* 39, No. 2 (Spring 1989): 107-119. [21 Refs.]

Blatz asserts that critical thinking is applied reasoning and that the contexts of critical thinking exists within "communities of discussion" (p. 108). The individuals within this community are linked by common basic assumptions and procedures which provide guidelines for reasoning and for which individuals are held accountable. Blatz explores levels of generality of critical thinking principles and procedures based on contextual specificity. He argues that critical thinking should be incorporated into subject matter courses and that students should be initiated into the reasoning of the various communities within which they may participate throughout their lives. Separate courses of critical thinking should not be taught except to the more advanced thinkers who will be more ready to operationally transfer what is logically useful. Blatz discusses what aspects of critical thinking are logically and operationally transferable and provides suggestions for appropriately assessing critical thinking in terms of the "communities of discussion."

213 Block, Richard A. "Education and Thinking Skills Reconsidered." *American Psychologist* 40, no. 5 (May 1985): 574-575. [8 Refs.]

Reply to Glaser {241}

See: Sternberg {345}

Glaser {240}

Block argues that teaching thinking skills in domain-specific courses is problematic in regard to the transfer of these skills to other areas. He discusses the use of a special general thinking skills course that includes features that may be essential to transfer and adopts some of the more important characteristics of domain-specific training.

214 Brandon, E. P. "Deductive Reasoning Ability, Error, and Education." Chapter 17 in *Argumentation: Perspectives and Approaches. Proceedings of the Conference on Argumentation 1986*, edited by Frans H. van Eemeren, Rob Grootendorst, J. Anthony Blair, and Charles A. Willard, 155-161. Dordrecht, The Netherlands: Foris Publications, 1987. [21 Refs.]

Brandon examines the existence of deductive reasoning ability and the educational consequences of its possible existence. He believes a theory of deductive reasoning ability depends on what is the best explanatory theory of human behavior. Such a theory, as Stephen Norris and John McPeck point out, may or may not use a system of classical first order logic to explain how people think. Brandon argues that the neglect of non-standard rule systems by researchers skews the analysis and interpretation of cognitive research results in education. He shows the effects of this neglect by looking at what counts as an adequate grasp of a concept or rule and how assumptions about a rule influence evaluation of that rule's use. Educationally, Brandon believes that it is good to teach logic even if people do not actually think like that.

215 Brell, Carl D., Jr. "Critical Thinking as Transfer: The Reconstructive Integration of Otherwise Discrete Interpretations of Experience." *Educational Theory* 40, no. 1 (Winter 1990): 53-68. [20 Refs.]

Brell analyzes viewpoints on whether critical thinking should be taught as a set of general, transferable skills or as subject-specific sets of skills. Focusing on the positions of John McPeck, Robert Ennis and Richard Paul, he presents the positions in a dialogic fashion, outlining each viewpoint, and presenting criticisms and responses to the criticisms. Through this method, Brell identifies and clarifies several of the key interactions between the two sides. He finds McPeck's critique of the general skills approach reveals the important point that thinking can not occur or be taught independently of the epistemological norms of some frame of reference or knowledge domain, although there are general concepts and procedures that are teachable and useful for knowledge transfer. Brell concludes that while both approaches are useful, neither adequately addresses the problem of getting students to transfer their knowledge and skills. Drawing from the writings of Paul, Brell proposes a concept of critical thinking as transfer entailing "the ongoing construction, reconstruction, and integration of a person's world view and ways of knowing" (p. 67). Critical thinking instruction should be viewed as the fostering of rational inquiry habits leading to the disposition to strive for intellectual, emotional, and behavior integrity or the "critical spirit." He outlines some educational guidelines for fostering critical thinking and suggests that John Dewey's *How We Think* (Boston, MA: Heath, 1933) be studied.

216 Brod, Harry. "Philosophy Teaching as Intellectual Affirmative Action." *Teaching Philosophy* 9, no. 1 (March 1986): 5-13. [13 Refs.]

Attempts to maintain teacher neutrality when presenting material perpetuates the bias and prejudices already believed by students. Brod asserts that the neutrality position has as its hidden agenda the support of the societal status quo which neglects opposing views. He argues that the neutrality position is detrimental to the development of critical thinking and should be replaced by a pedagogy of advocacy. Brod distinguishes two types of advocacy: (1) liberal, or holding that minority views are in danger of being neglected by society, and (2) radical, or holding that society's intrinsic structure prevents consideration of minority views. Only the ideas of the political left truly oppose the status quo, and should be taught as serious, viable alternatives to the established society. Brod contends that critical thinking and self consciousness would be raised through the use of advocacy pedagogy.

217 Brown, Rexford. "Who is Accountable for Thoughtfulness?" *Phi Delta Kappan* 69, no. 1 (September 1987): 49-52. [16 Refs.]

Brown contends that thoughtfulness is not promoted in the schools and that there is too much reliance on textbooks, teacher domination, discrete pieces of knowledge, and factual tests. He attributes this to the existence of many incentives for minimum competence and performance (such as state and local use of tests to determine policy decisions or to insure that minimum standards are met) and too few incentives for thoughtfulness. Brown fears that instruction and curriculum become directed towards these tests. He calls for the development of a different kind of accountability system, one that values inquiry and thoughtfulness.

218 Campbell, Dennis E., and Carl L. Davis. *Improving Learning by Combining Critical Thinking Skills with Psychological Type*. Wright-Patterson Air Force Base, OH: School of Systems and Logistics, Air Force Institute of Technology, 1988. 22 pp. ED 306 250. [23 Refs.]

Campbell and Davis argue that student critical thinking skills can be improved by identifying the psychological type of the student and assigning tasks to strengthen the less preferred or inferior cognitive learning function. They examine the Myers-Briggs Type Indicator (MBTI) diagnostic assessment indicator and discuss its categories of cognitive functions. The authors relate the MBTI to critical thinking and suggest teaching strategies to develop the less preferred or inferior cognitive function. Campbell and Davis outline the implications these strategies have for learners, teachers, and learning systems.

219 Carbone, Peter F., Jr. "Thinking about Thinking: What Are We to Think?" In *Philosophy of Education 1990: Proceedings of the Forty-Sixth Annual Meeting of the Philosophy of Education Society*, edited by David P. Ericson, 410-414. Normal, IL: Philosophy of Education Society, 1991. [9 Refs.]

Reply to Sanders and McPeck {332}

Carbone contends that Sanders and McPeck tend to blur appropriate distinctions between thinking capacities, psychological processes, and cognitive performances, though Sanders and McPeck's skepticism about their teachability may be justified. Carbone raises several questions regarding thinking about thinking, the applicability of certain thinking skills within specific families of disciplines, and the need of developing a skeptical disposition in students.

220 Chambers, John H. "Teaching Thinking throughout the Curriculum--Where Else?" *Educational Leadership* 45, no. 7 (April 1988): 4-6. [6 Refs.]

Chambers argues that thinking and learning to think occur in contexts and that it is a philosophical mistake to believe that thinking can be taught as a formal course of general skills of thinking. He emphasizes the importance of knowing when to use ways of thinking in specific academic subjects. Children learn to think as they encounter problems and the structures and patterns of understanding those problems within a discipline. The author recommends good teachers who make learning interesting and who make children think within their specific discipline.

221 Collins, Cathy, and John N. Mangieri, eds. *Teaching Thinking: An Agenda for the Twenty-First Century*. Hillsdale, NJ: Lawrence Erlbaum, 1992. 362 pp.

The seventeen chapters of this anthology focus on issues concerning the teaching of thinking in elementary schools, middle schools, high schools and adult learning classrooms. Other subjects covered include literacy, achievement testing, and the teaching of thinking in children, adolescents, and adults.

222 Costa, Arthur L. "The Principal's Role in Enhancing Thinking Skills." Chapter 8 in *Developing Minds. Vol. 1: A Resource Book for Teaching Thinking*, rev. ed., edited by Arthur L. Costa, 35-38. Alexandria, VA: Association for Supervision and Curriculum Development, 1991. [11 Refs.]

Revision of Costa {505}, pp. 29-32.

Costa clarifies the principal's role in infusing thinking skills into the curriculum. He suggests ways principals can exert influence in enhancing students' development of thinking skills: (1) create intellectual stimulating school conditions for students and staff, (2) use available resources to support the teaching and development of thinking; and (3) model rational thinking.

223 de Bono, Edward. "Critical Thinking Is Not Enough." *Educational Leadership* 42, no. 1 (September 1984): 16-17.

De Bono asserts that critical thinking, emphasized in society and education, is reactive and lacks the creative, constructive, and design elements necessary for future living or social progress offered by lateral thinking. Critical thinking should not be taught at the exclusion of lateral thinking. Perception must be taught before logic. Once a thinker's perceptions have been changed and broadened and he/she uses lateral thinking to solve problems, the critical or evaluative aspect of thinking is needed. The CoRT (Cognitive Research Trust) thinking skills program teaches the lateral skills of breadth and change, two aspects of perception and of critical thinking.

224 Deever, Bryan. "Critical Pedagogy: The Concretization of Possibility." *Contemporary Education* 61, no. 2 (Winter 1990): 71-76. [9 Refs.]

Deever explains that the goal of critical pedagogy is helping students to think for themselves and to understand the social and moral implications of their beliefs and choices. He describes the basic principles and assumptions inherent in the traditional, interpretative, and critical discourses of schooling. Critical discourse is distinctive in its focus on emancipatory educational concepts, in developing students' critical awareness around specific social realities and the need for transformation from existing social inequality and injustice. Critical educators must be aware of these competing discourses, develop fluency in multiple discourses, engage in critical awareness on the multiplicity of interpretations and choices in the world and on the role of an educator, and understand and use various teaching techniques appropriate to advancing an agenda of personal growth and human justice.

225 Deshmukh, M. N. "Teaching the Unteachable: Some Pedagogical Considerations of Creativity." *Psycho-lingua* 15, no. 1 (1985): 33-40. [35 Refs.]

Deshmukh finds that research on the brain, creativity, learning, intelligence, and teaching approaches suggests that creative thinking can be developed through certain teaching techniques and programs, such as brainstorming, Synectics, Inquiry Training Technique, psychodrama, and the Productive Thinking Programme. To facilitate creative thinking, Deshmukh believes that blocks (e.g., fear of failure and risk, stereotype thinking, teaching for testing, and hostility toward divergent thinking) must be removed and conducive classroom conditions (e.g., psychological safety; freedom of expression, thinking, and action; and less authoritarian teachers) must be established.

226 Ennis, Robert H. "Critical Thinking and Subject Specificity: Clarification and Needed Research." *Educational Researcher* 18, no. 3 (April 1989): 4-10. [42 Refs.]

Reply: McPeck {283}
See: Ennis {228}

Ennis briefly identifies three general approaches to teaching critical thinking: (1) general, in which critical thinking is taught separately, (2) infusion, in which critical thinking is infused in instruction in existing subjects, and (3) immersion, in which students are immersed into the subject matter with no explicit teaching of critical thinking. Ennis focuses on the question of the subject specificity of critical thinking, examining three principle versions of subject-specificity (domain, epistemological, and conceptual). He finds that each version suffers from excessive vagueness in key concepts (domain, field and subject), though the domain and epistemological versions contain valuable insights concerning the importance of background knowledge, interfield differences on good reasons, and teaching for transfer. Ennis criticizes conceptual subject specificity as having no basis and for being too vague. In the course of the paper, he outlines areas needing both practical and theoretical research.

227 Ennis, Robert H. "Critical Thinking and the Curriculum." *National Forum* 65 (Winter 1985): 28-31. [12 Refs.]

Ennis examines the transferability of critical thinking and argues that a subject-specific view of critical thinking is incomplete. General principles such as conflict of interest, the strawman fallacy, and the ability of a hypothesis to explain the facts, are applicable to many subjects. He includes several examples that illustrate the application of these principles in situations where specific subject knowledge is not known. While these examples indicate transferability, Ennis acknowledges that firm evidence about transferability is difficult to obtain. He believes that critical thinking is best taught as a separate subject, though its integration into primary and secondary schools may best be handled by teaching it within existing subjects.

228 Ennis, Robert H. "The Extent to Which Critical Thinking Is Subject-Specific: Further Clarification." *Educational Researcher* 19, no. 4 (May 1990): 13-16.

Reply to McPeck {282}

See: Ennis {226}

Ennis summarizes his earlier article and addresses four points in McPeck's criticisms: (1) the vagueness of the concepts, 'domain', 'field', and 'subject', is a problem when referring to a basis for prediction; (2) the distinction between school-subject knowledge and everyday life is valid, even though there is some overlap; (3) the distinction between topic and subject made was designed to address the inference that all thinking is about some school subject rather than some topic; (4) relatively narrow general thinking abilities can be applied over a broad range. Ennis accuses McPeck of misrepresenting the position of the earlier paper and of creating a straw person to criticize.

229 Ennis, Robert H. "Logic and Critical Thinking." *Philosophy of Education 1981: Proceedings of the Thirty-Seventh Annual Meeting of the Philosophy of Education Society*, edited by Daniel R. DeNicola, 228-232. Normal, IL: Philosophy of Education Society, 1982. [10 Refs.]

Reply to McPeck {283}

Ennis repudiates McPeck's rejection of critical thinking and logic courses. While acknowledging the over-emphasis of deductive logic in thinking and logic courses, Ennis argues that knowing a field of study, understanding what constitutes a good reason in that field, and having a grasp of the field's semantic concepts do not sufficiently produce critical thinking. McPeck presents no empirical evidence against studies that indicate the helpfulness of a logic course in developing critical thinking, nor does he offer evidence in support of his assertions concerning the conceptual/ empirical distinction and the existence of different logics. With only limited empirical studies having been done on all aspects of thinking, Ennis contends that more research be performed, rather than simply debating the topic.

230 Erdman, Jean. "Reflecting on Teaching and Adult Education." *Lifelong Learning: An Omnibus of Practice and Research* 10, no. 8 (June 1987): 18-21, 27. [34 Refs.]

Erdman examines the value of reflection in the context of an adult education program. Reflection enables teachers to think critically about teaching strategies, improving teaching to facilitate learning, institutional and individual biases, and the relationship among social, cultural, and pedagogical practices. Such reflection leads to greater awareness of choices in teaching, renewal of energy, and teacher empowerment to improve programs.

231 Fischer, Kurt W., and Michael Jeffrey Farrar. "Generalizations about Generalization: How a Theory of Skill Development Explains Both Generality and Specificity." *International Journal of Psychology* 22, no. 5-6 (1987): 643-677. [69 Refs.]

Fischer and Farrar propose a skill theory framework for understanding generalization and specificity. The skill theory acknowledges that both organism and environment are inseparable in cognitive development and that a skill is characteristic of a person-in-a-context (a change in task produces a change in skill). Although research shows that an individual functions at different skill levels for different tasks and contexts, the authors believe that there is an order in the different skill levels and that the sequence of development with a specific context can be predicted. Generalization is maximized when (1) tasks are of similar complexity and content, (2) tasks are familiar, (3) individuals are given opportunities to practice tasks, (4) individuals are provided with high environmental support, (5) individuals have a long period of time at a particular optimal level (6) individuals have a high degree of intelligence, and (7) individuals have an emotional state that facilitates the skill. To characterize the range of generalization that varies with individuals and situations, research is needed to distinguish true generalization and apparent generalization (optimal-level co-occurrence) in which new capacities across domains emerge.

232 Fisher, Alec. "Philosophy and Transferable Thinking Skills." *Cogito* 4, no. 2 (1990): 123-128. [11 Refs.]

Fisher examines the claim that philosophy teaches transferable thinking skills. He outlines the general conceptions of thinking found in supporters and critics of the claim and examines the claim's evidential requirements. Fisher examines three attempts at teaching transferable thinking/reasoning skills (informal logic, the Philosophy for Children program, and Richard Paul's Critical Thinking Handbooks) and finds all but the Philosophy for Children program lack research supporting their effectiveness at teaching transferable thinking skills.

233 Furedy, Christine, and John J. Furedy. "Critical Thinking: Toward Research and Dialogue." In *Using Research to Improve Teaching*, edited by Janet G. Donald and Arthur M. Sullivan, 51-69. New Directions for Teaching and Learning, no. 23. San Francisco, CA: Jossey-Bass, 1985. [42 Refs.]

Acknowledging the prevailing lack of understanding surrounding critical thinking, the authors advocate (1) meaningful and relevant research on critical thinking in higher education that emphasizes clarifying the values, attributes, and attitudes essential to critical thinking and (2) discussion and reflection among colleagues regarding a concept of critical thinking in their disciplinary fields. The authors do not believe critical thinking is nonexistent or deteriorating in higher education, but believe that a stronger commitment to it is important. They examine the countervailing forces to critical thinking in higher education and encourage use of assignments and course structures known to facilitate critical thinking. The authors also urge the consideration of ways of incorporating the development of critical thinking beyond assignments.

234 Garver, Eugene. "Critical Thinking, Them, and Us: A Response to Arnold B. Aron's 'Critical Thinking and the Baccalaureate Curriculum'." *Liberal Education* 72, no. 3 (Fall 1986): 245-249. [8 Refs.]

Reply to Arons {194}
See: Arons {195}

Garver criticizes Arons's claim that life consists of a two-act play in which abstract, formal reasoning processes mark the ascent from more concrete means of working. While the detached formality of Arons's approach is desirable in the natural sciences, Garver argues that it becomes problematic in the humanities and social sciences where different cultural values and alternative positions of equal standing play important roles. In these disciplines, solutions are not based on performing operations correctly as in the natural sciences, making Arons's proposed two-part hierarchy inadequate. The ten critical thinking abilities outlined by Arons should be considered permanently challenging intellectual problems. To Garver, faculty development should concentrate on how to make critical thinking and abstract reasoning explicit in what is taught and should address analogous continuous problems in faculty scholarship.

235 Giddings, Louise R. "Beyond E. D. Hirsch and Cultural Literacy: Thinking Skills for Cultural Awareness." *Community Review* 8, no. 2 (Spring 1988): 5-13. [16 Refs.]

Giddings cites E.D. Hirsch's view of cultural literacy as narrow, traditional, and lacking cultural diversity. Concerned over the prevalence of this perspective in educational materials and mass media, Giddings calls for a broader, more diverse, and less traditional perspective, emphasizing the importance of cultural awareness--"the ability to respond at the more critical levels to the ideas, information and myths of cultural heritage" (p. 11). She suggests Benjamin Bloom's *Taxonomy of Educational Objectives, Handbook I Cognitive Domain* (New York, NY: David McKay,1956) as an aid to developing an educational environment to foster higher levels of intellectual activity or develop critical thinking skills that can be applied to all concepts of cultural knowledge or cultural literacy.

236 Giroux, Henry A. "Critical Literacy and Student Experience: Donald Graves's Approach to Literacy." *Language Arts* 64, no. 2 (February 1987): 175-181.

This article is based on a presentation made by Giroux at Miami University (Oxford, OH) regarding Donald Graves's work. Giroux believes Graves's approach to critical literacy links learning with the experiences, backgrounds, languages, and dreams of students. Graves stresses the importance of teachers acknowledging these elements as a confirmation of students' own sense of worthiness and their participation in their own learning. Giroux contrasts Graves' approach with that of the mainstream curriculum. Giroux advocates viewing schools as the cultural sites that they are, redefining curriculum as "a configuration of knowledge, social relations, and values" rather than as "a warehouse of knowledge" (p. 176), and developing a critical pedagogy. Teachers must critically examine cultural backgrounds, social formations, the construction of school knowledge, and themselves for inherent interests that may enable or disable student learning. Giroux suggests that the elements of a critical pedagogy include teachers (1) developing conditions in the classroom that allow and confirm diversity in students and that foster appreciation for differences as a basis for democratic tolerance, of critical dialogue, and for commitment to improving the quality of human life; (2) providing opportunities for interrogation and critical analysis; (3) introducing morality in relation to public life, community life, and individual and social commitment; and (4) providing opportunities for decision making and critical thinking which directly relate to community and global issues. According to Giroux, such an approach empowers students and teachers.

237 Giroux, Henry A. *Teachers as Intellectuals: Toward a Critical Pedagogy of Learning*. Grumby, MA: Bergin & Garvey, 1988. [273 Refs.]

This is a collection of previously published Giroux essays on critical pedagogy, many of which were revised for this anthology. The essays are organized into four units on different aspects of Giroux's theory of critical pedagogy: language, writing, teaching, and critiquing. The common thesis of each essay is Giroux's attempts at illuminating the specific conditions in which educators operate. He believes that schools should be used as democratic public spheres which prepare students for participation in the greater society. Schools must be constructed around forms of critical inquiry where students learn the discourse of social responsibility, and the language of freedom. The interrelationship of theory, fact, and knowledge, as well as argumentation and critical thinking should be a part of the curriculum.

238 Giroux, Henry A. *Theory & Resistance in Education: A Pedagogy for the Opposition*. Critical Perspectives in Social Theory. South Hadley, MA: Bergin & Gravey, 1983. 280 pp. [402 Refs.]

Giroux argues that a foundation for education can be found in the critical theory of the Frankfurt School, in the literature of the hidden curriculum, and in the theoretical work on the structural and interactional analysis of the process of schooling. He discusses the implications of a critical pedagogy on education and on the public sphere.

239 Glaser, Edward. "Critical Thinking: Educating for Responsible Citizenship in a Democracy." *National Forum: Phi Kappa Phi Journal* 65, no. 1 (Winter 1985): 24-27. [9 Refs.]

Glaser stresses the importance in developing critical thinking as an educational objective for helping individuals deal more effectively with problems encountered in their lives and to form more intelligent judgments on public issues. He identifies three principal elements of critical thinking: (1) an attitude of willingness and openness to consider problems thoughtfully and perceptively, (2) knowledge of the methods of logical inquiry and reasoning, and (3) skill in applying these methods. Through the results of controlled experiments, Glaser determined that these three elements could be substantially improved through certain types of instruction and guidance. He lists six factors which affect the efficacy of training and cites a number of texts and national tests on critical thinking.

240 Glaser, Robert. "All's Well That Begins and Ends with Both Knowledge and Process: A Reply to Sternberg." *American Psychologist* 40, no. 5 (May 1985): 573-574. [3 Refs.]

Reply to Sternberg {345}
See: Block {213}
Glaser {241}

Glaser identifies points in his original paper that he claims Sternberg overlooked in his reply. He also addresses Sternberg's criticisms of his overemphasis on domain-specific knowledge. Glaser agrees with Sternberg that both domain-specific and domain-general knowledge have significance, but asserts that domain-specific processes have been neglected in current instructional attempts.

241 Glaser, Robert. "Education and Thinking: The Role of Knowledge." *American Psychologist* 39, no. 2 (February 1984): 93-104. [58 Refs.]

Reply: Sternberg {345}
See: Glaser {240}
Block {213}

Glaser believes that the understanding of the nature of human thinking, reasoning, and problem solving gained through psychological research has implications for instructional practices designed to foster these higher order thinking abilities. He investigates these implications by discussing the implications of past theories on teaching thinking and several current programs designed to encourage thinking and problem solving. Most of these programs emphasize the teaching of general processes and use abstract tasks, puzzle-like problems, or informal life situations as their content and avoid subject matter information. Current research in cognitive science and developmental psychology indicate that domain-specific knowledge is important for the development of problem solving and reasoning skills. Glaser suggests that ways for developing thinking abilities in the context of knowledge and skill acquisition be examined and integrated into the classroom.

242 Goldman, Louis. "Intended Consequences: Louis Goldman's Reply." *Educational Leadership* 42, no. 1 (September 1984): 64-65.

Reply to Paul {309}
See: Goldman {243}

Goldman justifies his views on the dangers of teaching the Socratic method to children, answering Paul's criticism.

243 Goldman, Louis. "Warning: The Socratic Method Can Be Dangerous." *Educational Leadership* 42, no. 1 (September 1984): 57-62. [9 Refs.]

Reply: Paul {309}
See: Goldman {242}

Goldman explores the dangers of teaching the Socratic method to children before they: (1) have accumulated experience, (2) are capable of thinking analytically, and (3) have a grounding in the nature and values of their culture. Goldman suggests that it be taught in an idea-centered rather than a skill-centered curriculum, advocating the traditional liberal arts curriculum and faculty of diverse ideas, values, and teaching styles as the means most likely to develop critical thinking. Through continual discussion created by such diversity, the faculty will demonstrate to students the importance of critical thinking to successful living.

244 Grice, George L., and M. Anway Jones. "Teaching Thinking Skills: State Mandates and the K-12 Curriculum." *Clearing House* 62, no. 8 (April 1989): 337-341. [34 Refs.]

Stressing the importance of instruction in thinking skills, Grice and Jones review issues related to the implementation of thinking skills programs in public school curricula. They discuss various classifications of thinking skills evident in the literature and identify overlaps in the classifications. These overlaps suggest agreement on what should be taught. Grice and Anway examine three instructional frameworks for teaching thinking skills (the subject-matter-free course approach, the integrated approach, and the separate and integrated approach) in terms of advantages and disadvantages. They stress the importance of teacher training in and institutional commitment to a thinking skills curricula, providing an overview of suggested guidelines for teacher training found in the literature. From a survey they conducted of the fifty states, they found only ten of the forty-three states which responded reported a state mandate for teaching thinking skills, while one had a proposal under consideration, and only six require teacher training in thinking skills.

245 Gutteridge, Moira. "First Sit Down and Play the Piano Beautifully...: Reading Carefully for Critical Thinking." *Informal Logic* 4, no. 2-3 (Spring-Fall 1987): 81-91. [11 Refs.]

Gutteridge asserts that textbook writers and instructors of critical thinking tend to assume students to have an ability to read critically before learning critical thinking. Careful reading is supposed to entail that obvious implications and inferences of a passage are understood. Often, readers do not see these implications due to avoidable errors in reading. Instructors and textbooks assume the reader to be at fault. Gutteridge argues that the problem is not the student but the attitudes and presumptions that instructors and textbooks have regarding the "correct" interpretation of a passage and the level of critical thinking students have when entering a critical thinking class. Analyzing passages from several critical thinking textbooks, Gutteridge shows how interpretations differing from those presumed "correct" in the textbook could be drawn from those passages. The texts take any conclusions differing from the "correct" one to be correctable through careful reading, but treat instruction in careful reading by listing misinterpretations to avoid or as something to be taught in a remedial course. The texts assume background knowledge beyond a "minimum knowledge of the world" to be unnecessary for proper interpretation. Faulty interpretations comes from faulty reading techniques rather than gaps in background knowledge. Gutteridge asserts that this assumption stems from the presumption by instructors and textbooks that careful reading is both a prerequisite for and an end product of critical thinking.

246 Hall, Ann Hays. "Critical Readers: An Endangered Species?" *Georgia Journal of Reading* 13, no. 2 (Spring-Summer 1988): 10-16. [42 Refs.]

Hall argues that the goal of American education to enable students to become independent critical readers is being hindered by (1) the lack of instruction in higher level comprehensive skills; (2) textbooks and teacher guides which emphasize lower level skills; and (3) the school environment which focuses on test scores and avoids controversy by avoiding open discussion or exploration of ideas that might conflict with students' religious or cultural training. She notes that available studies and informed opinion on critical reading suggest that (1) the role of the teacher is crucial, (2) critical reading skills should be taught directly, (3) teachers should be aware of the effect of questions on thinking, (4) critical reading should be taught in all disciplines, and (5) integrating instruction in speaking, listening, writing, and reading facilitates critical thinking.

247 Hiland, Leah F. "Information and Thinking Skills and Processes to Prepare Young Adults for the Information Age." *Library Trends* 37, no. 1 (Summer 1988): 56-62. [19 Refs.]

Hiland finds numerous reports on educational reform emphasize the importance of information, but do not address the acquisition of the information skills and related thinking skills underlying information. Hiland stresses the importance of librarians preparing young adults in the broader scope of information, information skills, and information processes. She emphasizes the need for a change to an information process and skills curriculum by proposing three areas of activities that address the need. Hiland concludes by calling upon researchers to investigate the information behavior of young adults and librarians to take the initiative in developing their role in the improvement of education.

248 Hudgins, Bryce B., Madonna Riesenmy, Debra Ebel, and Sybil Edelman. "Children's Critical Thinking: A Model for Its Analysis and Two Examples." *Journal of Educational Research* 82, no. 6 (July-August 1989): 327-338. [19 Refs.]

The authors propose a prescriptive model of self-directed critical thinking for children. The model consists of a cognitive component of three intellectual skills (task definition, strategy formulation, and monitoring) and an interrelated motivational component of spontaneity and independence. The authors believe that children who are exposed to the model will be better able to engage in critical thinking than those who are not. They show the application of this model to two realistic problems, with the responses and desired or ideal protocols from fourth and fifth graders. The authors consider prior knowledge and the ability to recognize an appropriate application of that knowledge to a task important to the critical thinking process.

249 Hyland, J. T. "Instruction, Rationality and Learning to be Moral." *Journal of Moral Education* 15, no. 2 (May 1986): 127-138. [37 Refs.]

Hyland opposes moral education programs that focus on teaching critical thinking skills and rationality exclusively. Such programs concentrate on the formal methodological aspects of moral thinking rather than on the content of morality and overlook the two elements of rationality: (1) conformity to standards and (2) criticism of those standards' effectiveness and validity. Hyland discusses rationality's connection to morality and identifies two levels of moral thinking: the intuitive and the critical. It is the intuitive that forms the foundation of both moral principles and the context for criticism of those principles. Critical thinking emphasizes the critical level and ignores the intuitive. Hyland argues that teachers should include elements of moral instruction and moral content when teaching morality.

250 Johnson, David W., and Roger T. Johnson. "Collaboration and Cognition." Chapter 52 in *Developing Minds. Vol. 1: A Resource Book for Teaching Thinking*, edited by Arthur L. Costa, 298-301. Alexandria, VA: Association for Supervision and Curriculum Development, 1991. [14 Refs.]

The authors contend that the interpersonal exchange within cooperative learning groups promotes critical thinking, higher level reasoning, and metacognitive thought. They outline reasons why cooperative learning affects cognition and metacognition.

251 Johnson, Kenneth G. "Critical Thinking for Survival in the 21st Century." *Etc.* 43, no. 4 (Winter 1986): 358-362. [1 Ref.]

Johnson stresses the importance of understanding the nature of language and its embedded assumptions when performing critical thinking. General semantics promotes an awareness of the varying levels of abstraction in language and encourages more scientific and analytical thinking. Johnson provides a twelve-item bibliography on semantics.

252 Joyce, Bruce. "Models for Teaching Thinking." *Educational Leadership* 42, no. 8 (May 1985): 4-7. [19 Refs.]

Joyce emphasizes the pervasive approach as the best alternative for teaching thinking. This approach, favored over teaching thinking as subject matter or as enrichment, combines the teaching of intellectual process and content and makes the teaching of thinking an important component of every school activity. The teaching of thinking requires a commitment to using models appropriately and persistently in the classroom. A substantial number of effective, research-supported models for teaching thinking, subject matter, and academic skills are available. Staff development programs which provide sufficient time, opportunities, and training for teachers to master these teaching models must be supported by districts.

253 Kahane, Howard. "The Proper Subject Matter for Critical Thinking Courses." *Argumentation* 3, no. 2 (May 1989): 141-147. [3 Refs.]

Kahane discusses the nature of critical reasoning courses and the issues surrounding these courses. He argues that the purpose of these courses, which should emphasize the practical rather than the theoretical, is to help students improve their reasoning about everyday life problems. Intelligent reasoners in everyday life must have general kinds of background knowledge, including facts about important sources of information such as mass media and textbooks, the ability and inclination of human beings to reason well, and insight into the use of language to confuse and deceive. Kahane also addresses the fears of instructors in teaching critical reasoning or critical thinking courses.

254 Kaplan, Laura Duhan. "Teaching Intellectual Autonomy: The Failure of the Critical Thinking Movement." *Educational Theory* 41, no. 4 (Fall 1991): 361-370. [18 Refs.]

Kaplan finds that the typical critical thinking course in college takes the form of informal logic courses which do not live up to their potential to prepare students for the intellectual autonomy required in a democratic society. She believes that, according to criteria used in the critical pedagogy movement, informal logic courses tend to teach political conformity rather than political autonomy. Supporters of the critical pedagogy movement advocate a critique of lived social and political realities with the aim of changing those realities to allow greater freedom and action, whereas critical thinking/informal logic courses teach argument criticism. Kaplan identifies three ways educators often fall into teaching conformity: (1) substituting radical slogans for conservative ones, (2) interpreting the student's social reality for them, and (3) providing the students with a menu of possible political actions from which they are to chose. She looks at three widely used college-level critical thinking texts and shows how each falls into one of the conformity traps. Kaplan also argues that using logical analysis as a model of college-level reading may inhibit students from asking certain types of politically significant questions concerning a text that may reveal some of the forces that have shaped the author's or reader's reasoning.

255 King, Jonathan B. "The Three Faces of Thinking." *Journal of Higher Education* 57, no. 1 (January-February 1986): 78-92. [21 Refs.]

King justifies the inclusion of the humanities in higher education curriculum by exploring their contribution to the thinking process. He describes three dimensions or "faces" of thinking: empirical, interpretative, and evaluative. Although there is an understanding of the empirical, the same understanding does not exist for the evaluative and the interpretive. It is to these two "faces" of thinking that the humanities make a difference by contributing contexts and contents, such as analogies, metaphors, ideologies, stories, and myths. Thus, humanities are the means for practicing interpretive thinking. King explores the concepts of context, content, and the humanistic perspective which is equated with moral knowledge. He believes that humanities can lead to thinking about thinking.

256 King, Jonathan B., and David Bella. "Taking Context Seriously." *Liberal Education* 73, no. 3 (May-June 1987): 7-13. [33 Refs.]

King and Bella address the need for education and society to move away from the acontextual conceptions or foundationalist view of knowledge in which students are taught responsibility for their assigned tasks without thought of the larger contexts. They suggest how contextual thinking can be incorporated into the classroom by having students view problems from multiple perspectives and by using metaphors and the advantages in doing so. Contextual thinking allows students to comprehend interrelationships of concepts, knowledge, methods, behavior, and time.

257 Kinney, James J. "Why Bother? The Importance of Critical Thinking." In *Fostering Critical Thinking*, edited by Robert E. Young, 1-9. New Directions for Teaching and Learning, no. 3. San Francisco, CA: Jossey-Bass, 1980. [20 Refs.]

In addressing the importance of critical thinking, Kinney points out some of the barriers to teaching critical thinking in college, such as course materials and assignments that avoid critical issues or encourage analysis in a narrow context and a marketplace that demands narrowly defined, technical analytical skills. He stresses the conflict between how critical thinking is taught in higher education institutions and its application to other contexts. Kinney suggests a pedagogical and a structural approach to encourage the transfer of critical thinking skills.

258 Kitchener, Karen Strohm. "Cognition, Metacognition, and Epistemic Cognition: A Three-Level Model of Cognitive Processing." *Human Development* 26 (1983): 222-232. [37 Refs.]

Kitchener proposes a three-level model of cognitive processing to explain the ability of individuals to monitor their own problem solving when engaged in ill-structured problems. The three levels are: (1) cognition, (2) metacognition, and (3) epistemic cognition. Metacognition leads individuals to use different cognitive strategies and redefine a specific cognitive task, while epistemic cognition leads an individual to interpret the nature of a problem and to define the limits of any strategy to solve it. Kitchener illustrates the interrelationship of the three levels in considering an ill-structured problem by presenting the related issues of inflation and unemployment. She addresses research related to epistemic cognition and adult development, noting that investigators recognize developmental shifts in epistemic assumptions and the relationship between epistemic assumptions and problem solving in adolescents and adults.

259 Kitchener, Karen Strohm. "The Reflective Judgment Model: Characteristics, Evidence, and Measurement." Chapter 5 in *Adult Cognitive Development: Methods and Models*, edited by Robert A. Mines and Karen S. Kitchener, 76-91. New York, NY: Praeger, 1986. [37 Refs.]

Kitchener describes the characteristics of the Reflective Judgment Model and its relation to epistemic cognition. She relates the seven developmental stages of epistemic cognition described in the model and notes the relation different epistemic assumptions have to different solutions to puzzles and problems. Kitchener discusses assessing the model's stages by the Reflective Judgment Interview and reviews research supporting the Reflective Judgment Model and Reflective Judgment Interview. She distinguishes reflective judgment from other aspects of intellectual development such as Piaget's formal operations and critical thinking which emphasize deductive and inductive logical skills rather than epistemic cognition.

260 Kitchener, Karen Strohm, and Kurt W. Fischer. "A Skill Approach to the Development of Reflective Thinking." In *Developmental Perspectives on Teaching and Learning Thinking Skills*, edited by Deanna Kuhn, 48-62. Contributions to Human Development, vol. 21. Basel, Switzerland: Karger, 1990. [33 Refs.]

The authors argue that logic can not sufficiently characterize higher order reasoning or critical thinking in all areas of problem solving. Assumptions about knowledge play a crucial role in many solutions, particularly for ill-structured problems. Kitchener and Fisher discuss a skill model of the seven developmental stages of reflective judgment that address the collaboration between the developing person and the environment in which a behavior occurs. The model relates the nature of knowledge and justification to the type of behavior and skill level demonstrated at each stage. The authors discuss functional and optimal levels of reflective judgment and two ways it can be measured, the Reflective Judgment Interview (RJI) and the Prototypic Reflective Judgment Interview (PRJ). They summarize a study of the PRJ that indicates an age-related ceiling and development spurt exists for reflective judgment development. The authors suggest that educational systems should shift from emphasizing well-structured problems to ill-structured ones in order to give students the opportunity to work out new higher level coordinations through attempting to solve the contradictions in such problems.

261 Kuhn, Deanna, ed. *Developmental Perspectives on Teaching and Learning Thinking Skills*. Contributions to Human Development, 21. New York, NY: Karger, 1990. 134 pp.

This is an anthology of eight papers designed to illustrate the benefit cognitive and developmental psychological research has for educators interested in developing student thinking skills. Written by leading research psychologists, the papers address topics such as scientific thinking in children and adults, heuristics harmful to the improvement of thinking, approaches to teaching thinking skills, and the influences social relations, communities of learning, and context have on the development of thinking skills.

262 Kurfiss, Joanne Gainen. *Critical Thinking: Theory, Research, Practice, and Possibilities*. ASHE-ERIC Higher Education Report No. 2. Washington, DC: Association for the Study of Higher Education, 1988. 148 pp. [301 Refs.]

After defining critical thinking as "an investigation whose purpose is to explore a situation, phenomenon, question, or problem to arrive at a hypothesis or conclusion about it that integrates all available information and that can therefore be convincingly justified" (p. 4), Kurfiss explores three perspectives on critical thinking: informal logic, cognitive processes, and intellectual development. She examines critical thinking programs and specific disciplinary courses for fostering critical thinking in colleges and universities. Kurfiss addresses the issues of institutional support, faculty support, and student and faculty readiness for various critical thinking approaches in the college and university classroom. The work concludes with an emphasis on research needed on teaching critical thinking and related areas.

263 Kurfiss, Joanne Gainen. "Helping Faculty Foster Students' Critical Thinking in the Disciplines." In *The Department Chairperson's Role in Enhancing College Teaching*, edited by Ann F. Lucas, 41-50. New Directions for Teaching and Learning, no. 37. San Francisco, CA: Jossey-Bass, 1989. [16 Refs.]

Written for college department chairs, this essay provides basic information on critical thinking abilities and intellectual development levels as background for encouraging them to develop interest in and support faculty in teaching critical thinking. Kurfiss provides examples of how critical thinking has been incorporated into numerous disciplines by various teaching methods and assignments designed to strengthen students' knowledge base, to develop procedural knowledge, and to modify students' beliefs about knowledge. She offers suggestions for supporting and developing interest in the teaching of critical thinking within a department.

264 Langsdorf, Lenore. "Is Critical Thinking a Technique, Or a Means of Enlightenment?" *Informal Logic* 8, no. 1 (Winter 1986): 1-17. [14 Refs.]

Langsdorf proposes a foundation for practicing and teaching critical thinking conceived as both a technique and a "means for enlightenment." She links Ian Angus's concepts of instrumental reason and judgment with Richard Paul's "weak" and "strong" notions of critical thinking. Instrumental reason and weak sense critical thinking are concerned with the development of formal techniques for achieving defined ends by using already given means. Judgment and strong sense critical thinking are concerned with reasoning that examines those means and ends involving the integration of self, process, object, and reflection. Langsdorf suggests that Paul's proposal for teaching critical thinking would be strengthened by adding two aspects of Angus's notion of judgment: (1) a phenomenological analysis of the logical elements implicit in our reasoning and (2) the constitution of self and world as a particularization of constituting judgments. Langsdorf links imagination with critical thinking and the ability to move beyond ego to self and explores the functioning of imagination in the context of Paul Ricoeur's conception of ego, self, and text. Langsdorf believes that the teaching of literature, writing, and critical thinking should integrate philosophy, literature, and composition within the context of the students' lives rather than as abstract techniques. She also examines the way in which the form of television suppresses the development of imagination and critical thinking by impeding our capacity to go beyond egocentricity.

265 Larkin, Jill H., Joan I. Heller, and James G. Greeno. "Instructional Implications of Research on Problem Solving." In *Learning, Cognition, and College Teaching*, edited by Wilbert J. McKeachie, 51-65. New Directions for Teaching and Learning, no. 2. San Francisco, CA: Jossey-Bass, 1980. [33 Refs.]

Larkin, Heller, and Greeno review research related to the current cognitive theory of problem solving. They discuss knowledge of content and knowledge of procedures in relation to problem solving. The authors provide three kinds of examples of practical instruction in problem solving (direct teaching of procedural knowledge, development of qualitative representations, and the teaching of general strategies) which offer suggestions for instruction.

266 Lee, Okhee, and Andrew C. Porter. "Bounded Rationality in Classroom Teaching." *Educational Psychologist* 25, no. 2 (Spring 1990): 159-171. [30 Refs.]

Lee and Porter discuss H.A. Simon's concept of human rationality as bounded or limited by certain intrinsic characteristics of human perception and cognition, such as incomplete information regarding alternatives, risk or uncertainty about the consequences of alternatives, and complexities in the environment beyond the information processing capacities of humans as decision makers. Bounded rationality requires the individual to construct simplified mental models of real situations in order to deal with them. The authors examine bounded rationality as a concept for understanding the reasoning, problem solving, decision making, and behavior of teachers in dealing with complexities of the classroom. They use a study of the phenomenon of teacher expectations and differential treatment of students to demonstrate how bounded rationality can be used.

267 Levine, Daniel U., and Eric J. Cooper. "The Change Process and Its Implications in Teaching Thinking." Chapter 13 in *Educational Values and Cognitive Instruction: Implications for Reform*, edited by Lorna Idol and Beau Fly Jones, 387-410. Hillsdale, NJ: Lawrence Erlbaum, 1991. [53 Refs.]

In this discussion on successful implementation of innovation in educational institutions, Levine and Cooper outline some findings and considerations important for initiating projects to improve higher order thinking skills and other higher order mental processes. The discussion revolves around four fundamental issues: (1) adaptation versus fidelity, (2) top-down versus bottom-up mandates, (3) packaged versus locally developed materials and procedures, and (4) scope and planning. The authors present six conclusions regarding the implementation of higher order skills projects.

268 Lind-Brenkman, Jean. "Seeing Beyond the Interests of Industry: Teaching Critical Thinking." *Journal of Education* 165, no. 3 (Summer 1983): 283-294. [21 Refs.]

Lind-Brenkman argues that all knowledge is socially constructed and value-ladened. Research models of knowledge are produced out of ideological interests that emerge from socio-historical circumstances. Instructional materials produced by industry for distribution and use in school curriculum contain a hidden curriculum ideology supportive of industry. Lind-Brenkman discusses the knowledge content of the industry-created educational materials and argues that critical thinking must be taught in order to enable citizens to unveil the concealed interests in instructional materials. Education would then become a liberating and empowering activity aimed toward transformative social action. Lind-Brenkman discusses a procedure for teaching critical analysis of educational content and provides an appendix of critical questions to be used for detailed analysis.

269 Lipman, Matthew. "The Cultivation of Reasoning through Philosophy." *Educational Leadership* 42, no. 1 (September 1984): 51-56.

Lipman advocates a series of sequential philosophy courses throughout the kindergarten through twelfth grade curriculum for developing primary and higher order thinking skills in students and helping students to learn to think within the disciplines. Philosophy is the only discipline which provides the principles of logic and is experienced in teaching the role of reasoning in reflection and discourse. To cultivate reasoning and teach students the primary and higher order thinking skills needed for thinking in the disciplines, philosophy must become a central part of the elementary school curriculum.

270 Lipman, Matthew. "Philosophy for Children and Critical Thinking." *National Forum* 65 (Winter 1985): 18-23.

Lipman focuses upon the importance of reasoning skills for children and adults. He supports teaching these skills throughout the elementary and secondary curriculum within the context of a humanities discipline. Lipman advocates incorporating philosophy courses into all levels of education, beginning with elementary schools. He suggests using novels containing models of student thinking about problems, such as those in the Philosophy for Children series, instead of formal philosophy textbooks. Children should be encouraged to read and select problems found in the novels for classroom discussion. Lipman includes examples of reasoning skills for the elementary school level.

271 Lipman, Matthew. *Philosophy Goes to School.* Philadelphia, PA: Temple University Press, 1988. 228 pp. [93 Refs.]

Lipman discusses the educational significance of grade school philosophy and argues for its inclusion as the core subject in elementary and secondary school curricula. Philosophy should be viewed as the subject where students are taught to think logically, coherently, and productively in a community of inquiry. Students learn to think and reflect about the thinking in the disciplines and to think self-correctively about their own thinking. Lipman discusses the educational contributions of ethics and aesthetics and the impact and relevancy philosophy can have to learning subject areas such as language arts, science and social studies. He outlines strategies for constructing a curriculum to improve thinking and understanding through philosophical inquiry, and describes a teacher education program for training grade-school philosophy teachers. Selections from a Philosophy for Children program teacher's classroom log are included as examples of how philosophy can be taught to grade school students. Lipman also addresses the relationship between philosophical inquiry and creativity. An appendix containing examples of how a curriculum for values education would attempt to develop specific reasoning skills is included.

272 Lipman, Matthew. "The Role of Philosophy in Education for Thinking." In *Conference 85 on Critical Thinking, Christopher Newport College*, edited by John Hoaglund, 41-51. Newport News, VA: Christopher Newport College Press, 1985. [1 Ref.]

Lipman discusses the need for a discipline that improves the study of all disciplines and generates thinking by strengthening thinking skills. He argues that philosophy, rather than cognitive science is this discipline. Cognitive science studies thinking in other disciplines but does not generate thinking in them. Philosophy not only studies thinking, but generates thinking by pursuing the problematic and the controversial. The skills needed to think in other disciplines need to be learned before the discipline's subject matter. Lipman identifies two obstacles to improving thinking skills: the claim by testing services that reasoning cannot be taught, and the belief that thinking skills are domain-specific rather than general. He contends that there are generic thinking skills applicable in every discipline. These general skills are influenced by the specific rules and language of each discipline.

273 Lipman, Matthew. *Thinking in Education*. New York: Cambridge University Press, 1991. 280 pp. [200 Refs.]

In this four-part monograph, Lipman examines issues related to the development of a thinking-oriented educational process that integrates philosophy into the curriculum. In part one, he outlines a reflective or inquiry model of educational practice having the teaching of excellent or higher order thinking as its goal. Lipman discusses the general characteristics of higher order thinking, describing it as a fusion of critical and creative thinking. In part two, he discusses the origins of the critical thinking movement, offers a functional definition of critical thinking, examines the influences of criteria on critical thinking, and discusses obstacles to the teaching of thinking. In Part Three, Lipman examines the concept of creative thinking, and the use of narrative and schematically organized texts and the use of instructional manuals. In part four, he discusses the nature and uses of a community of inquiry and its political implications.

274 Maher, Frances A. "Toward a Richer Theory of Feminist Pedagogy: a Comparison of 'Liberation' and 'Gender' Models for Teaching and Learning." *Journal of Education* 169, no. 3 (Fall 1987): 91-100. [31 Refs.]

Maher asserts that feminist pedagogy emerged as a response to the traditional content and theory of knowledge dominant in the college classroom in which the experience, viewpoint, and goals of white, Western, elite males represent all human experience and the kind of thinking and problem solving found in generalized abstract reasoning, critical thinking, and the scientific method. Maher examines the theories of critical or liberation pedagogy and feminist theories of women's development as models for feminist pedagogy. She finds that the liberation pedagogy model emphasizes the analysis of power and relates different forms of oppression, focusing primarily on the public spheres of work and politics. It ignores the private sphere and women as oppressed in a particular way. Gender models of pedagogy emphasize the subjective roots of thinking processes and the relation of personal experiences, emotions, and values to knowledge, placing critical thinking and rational problem solving in a framework specific to the individual. Gender models ignore differences among women. Through a discussion of the contributions and limitations of liberation and gender models, Maher demonstrates the importance of synthesizing the models for developing an adequate theory of feminist pedagogy.

275 Maimon, Elaine P., Barbara F. Nodine, and Finbarr W. O'Connor, eds. *Thinking, Reasoning, and Writing*. New York, NY: Longman, 1989. 266 pp. [335 Refs.]

In this collection of essays, thinking is explored through the disciplines of cognitive psychology, informal logic, and composition. The essays are sorted into three units featuring each discipline: Thinking as approached by psychologists, Reasoning as approached by philosophers, and Writing as approached by teachers of composition. The editors attempt to show agreement and conflict between the disciplines, as well as actual and potential interdisciplinary collaboration by including introductory commentary to each unit that proposes ways each discipline would respond to the topic of that unit. Discipline specificity, kinds of knowledge, and the social/individual degrees of knowledge and learning are some of the issues covered.

276 Martinelli, Kenneth J. "Thinking Straight about Thinking." *School Administrator* 44, no. 1 (January 1987): 21-23. [13 Refs.]

Martinelli offers a conceptual framework of thinking skills intended to help educators make informed and effective program decisions. He presents thinking skills as a hierarchy with the general category of thinking and reasoning at the bottom, critical and creative thinking on the next level, and problem solving at the top. Enveloping the hierarchy or process is metacognition. Martinelli provides a sequence chart of thinking skills for kindergarten through twelfth grade as an example of a possible program.

277 Marzano, Robert J. "Creating an Educational Paradigm Centered on Learning through Teacher-Directed, Naturalistic Inquiry." In *Educational Values and Cognitive Instruction: Implications for Reform*, edited by Lorna Idol and Beau Fly Jones, 411-441. Hillsdale, NJ: Lawrence Erlbaum, 1991. [126 Refs.]

Marzano contends that the beliefs underlying the emphasis on the direct teaching of thinking must become part of the culture of education in order to effect a significant change. He discusses shifting to a new paradigm centered on learning that is organized around five types of thinking characteristic of an effective learning experience: (1) thinking that establishes and maintains the context for learning, (2) thinking that gives rise to the structuring of content, (3) thinking that generates the representation of content in long-term-memory, (4) thinking that changes existing knowledge structures, and (5) dispositional thought. Marzano believes that teacher-directed naturalistic inquiry about the learning process will lead to the development of this new paradigm.

278 Marzano, Robert J., Ronald S. Brandt, Carolyn Sue Hughes, Beau Fly Jones, Barbara Z. Presseisen, Stuart C. Rankin, and Charles Suhor. *Dimensions of Thinking: A Framework for Curriculum and Instruction*. Alexandria, VA: Association for Supervision and Curriculum Development, 1988. 166 pp. [291 Refs.]

The seven authors of this work provide a framework to be used for staff development programs and curriculum development planning for integrating thinking into the curriculum. This framework consists of five dimensions, incorporating the array of theories, definitions, and research on thinking found in philosophy and psychology. The authors discuss different aspects of the framework in seven chapters: (1) Thinking as the Foundation of Schooling, (2) Metacognition, (3) Critical and Creative Thinking, (4) Thinking Processes, (5) Core Thinking Skills, (6) The Relationship of Content-Area Knowledge to Thinking, and (7) Use of the Framework. The chapters include diagrams, charts, and other illustrative matter.

279 Marzano, Robert, and Daisy E. Arredondo. "Restructuring Schools through the Teaching of Thinking Skills." *Educational Leadership* 43, no. 8 (May 1986): 20-26. [50 Refs.]

Marzano and Arredondo call for the restructuring of education to meet the needs of a changing society by teaching students skills essential to accessing, organizing, and using information. They describe a thinking skills model which categorizes thinking skills as: (1) learning-to-learn skills, (2) content thinking skills, and (3) basic reasoning skills and which affects curriculum, instruction, testing, and student learning. The authors discuss the three categories and how each might be incorporated into a curriculum. If incorporated into a curriculum, they believe that such a thinking skills model provides an opportunity for all students to develop the skills necessary for success in an information age.

280 McCaulley, Mary H. "The Myers-Briggs Type Indicator: A Jungian Model for Problem Solving." In *Developing Critical Thinking and Problem-Solving Activities*, edited by James E. Stice, 37-53. New Directions for Teaching and Learning, no. 30. San Francisco, CA: Jossey-Bass, 1987. [20 Refs.]

McCaulley reviews the Jungian model and theory of psychological types, used as the basis for the Myers-Briggs Type Indicator's sixteen types. She includes a chart of the sixteen types and their theoretical characteristics as problem solvers, based on the priorities placed on four basic mental processes (sensing, intuition, thinking, feeling) and the attitudes (extraversion, introversion, judgment, perception) typically used with each process. McCaulley suggests strategies for using the Myers-Briggs Type Indicator model for problem solving and for teaching problem solving. The article includes information on correlations between types of college students and chosen fields of study.

281 McMurtry, John. "The History of Inquiry and Social Reproduction: Educating for Critical Thought." *Interchange* 19, no. 1 (Spring 1988): 31-45. [13 Refs.]

McMurtry illustrates how human societies have traditionally persecuted or tabooed the questioning of established structures by exploring the outcomes of such questioning found in the execution of Socrates; the absence of social criticism in the works of thinkers such as Augustine, Aquinas, Scotus, and Ockham; the repression of works that include such criticism; and afflictions placed upon writers of these works. He argues that though Rousseau, Marx, and Mill opened the way to critical thinking about social structures, human self-knowledge, and the educated person, the repression of critical thinking and inquiry toward social structures still exists in schools today despite the purported educational goals of developing independent, critical, and creative thinking. Fear of controversy, lack of academic freedom, and submission to external policies and conventional beliefs prevent critical inquiry and debate in schools. McMurtry purports that schools need to clarify what education is and is not, and recognize that an educational system is governed by disciplines of research and expression, rather than by special interests and political pressures.

282 McPeck, John. "Critical Thinking and Subject Specificity: A Reply to Ennis." *Educational Researcher* 19, no. 4 (May 1990): 10-12. [10 Refs.]

Reply to Ennis {226}
Reply: Ennis {228}

McPeck criticizes the position expounded by Ennis on the ambiguity of key concepts in subject-specific positions on critical thinking and transfer, the dichotomy between school-subject knowledge and everyday life, and McPeck's rejection of significant general critical thinking skills.

283 McPeck, John. "Critical Thinking without Logic: Restoring Dignity to Information." *Philosophy of Education 1981: Proceedings of the Thirty-Seventh Annual Meeting of the Philosophy of Education Society*, edited by Daniel R. DeNicola, 219-227. Normal, IL: Philosophy of Education Society, 1982. [5 Refs.]

Reply: Ennis {229}

Logic courses do not develop critical thinkers because logic can not deal with the different kinds of information used in arguments. The analysis of good reasons varies with different fields of study and is epistemological rather than logical in character. Logic is concerned with syntactical relations of propositions, epistemology is concerned with the semantic or meaning of statements. Practical reasoning on public issues depends more on determining the truth of premises rather than the argument's logical validity. Logic courses mask the complexity of empirical information by their emphasis on the conceptual/empirical distinction of propositions. The existence of diverse logics with different notions of validity undermines the universal application of logic across different areas of enquiry. McPeck stresses that though he is claiming only semantic and epistemic differences they still raise serious doubts about the relevance of training in logic for critical thinking.

284 McPeck, John. "Paul's Critique of Critical Thinking and Education." *Informal Logic* 7, no. 1 (Winter 1985): 45-54. [2 Refs.]

Reprinted in McPeck {7}, pp. 112-123, 131.

Reply to Paul {308}

McPeck addresses Paul's criticisms of his book, *Critical Thinking and Education* {6}. McPeck distinguishes between his own view which stresses the semantic and pragmatic features of logic and the Informal Logic Movement's emphasis on the formal, syntactical features of logic and reasoning. He clarifies his position, correcting what he interprets as Paul's misreadings about the broad domains of human understanding and the different kinds of reasoning particular to each domain. McPeck asserts that Paul fails to distinguish schooling from education. He argues that understanding the different contexts and perspectives available when approaching a problem requires a broad liberal arts education and knowledge base, not a specific course on critical thinking. McPeck also defends his critique of opposing views of critical thinking against Paul's criticisms.

285 McPeck, John E. "Picture Puzzles, Red Herrings, and Geometry." In *Philosophy of Education 1987: Proceedings of the Forty-Third Annual Meeting of the*

Philosophy of Education Society, edited by Barbara Arnstine and Donald Arnstine, 303-307. Normal, IL: Philosophy of Education Society, 1988. [2 Refs.]

Reply to Orton {297}

McPeck argues that Orton's discussion of the psychological theories of Piaget and of Pierre and Dina van Heile does not address Orton's stated theme, the transferability of critical thinking skills.

286 McPeck, John E. "Stalking Beasts, but Swatting Flies: The Teaching of Critical Thinking." *Canadian Journal of Education* 9, no. 1 (Winter 1984): 28-44. [7 Refs.]

McPeck criticizes the standard approach to teaching critical thinking for equating "reasoning ability" with "argument analysis," "everyday problems" with "everyday argument" and viewing critical thinking as general skills. He contends that supporters of the standard approach tend to view the information involved in everyday problems as common knowledge when it is often complex and specialized knowledge. Rather than teaching critical thinking as general skills transferable to all problems, McPeck proposes combining the teaching of a discipline's subject matter and philosophy to form the foundation for teaching critical thinking.

287 McPeck, John, Jack Martin, James Sanders, and Alan Slemon. "Aerobics for the Mind." *Interchange* 20, no. 3 (Fall 1989): 35-38. [5 Refs.]

Replies: Winne {368}
McPeck {288}

The authors note a historical shift in the conception of intelligence from an ability representing a potential for learning to a skill that can be improved or changed. The shift is reflected in the number of thinking skills programs which equate intellectual competence or cognitive skill with intelligence test performance rather than performance in subject domains. The authors argue that this shift may lead to teaching to the test, and teaching thinking skills without regard to subject context. They assert that thinking skills must be taught within the context of a subject domain in order to improve student performance.

288 McPeck, John, Jack Martin, and James Sanders. "More Aerobics for the Mind? A Reply to Winne." *Interchange* 20, no. 3 (Fall 1989): 53-57. [6 Refs.]

Reply to Winne {368}

See: McPeck, Martin, Sanders, Slemon {287}

The authors assert that Winne misinterpreted their position. They reaffirm their views on the teaching of intelligence, the stability of intelligence, teaching to the test, and the generalizability of thinking skills in correcting Winne's misinterpretations of them.

289 McTighe, Jay, and Rochelle Clemson. "Making Connections: Toward a Unifying Instructional Framework." Chapter 54 in *Developing Minds. Vol. 1: A Resource Book for Teaching Thinking*, rev. ed., edited by Arthur L. Costa, 304-311. Alexandria, VA: Association for Supervision and Curriculum Development, 1991. [28 Refs.]

McTighe and Clemson describe the differences in teaching for thinking, by thinking, and about thinking. They discuss cooperative learning, direct instruction of thinking skills, invitational education, metacognition, classroom climate, learning styles, instructional framework, and staff development.

290 Metzger, Devon J. "Coming to Terms with Citizenship Education." *Louisiana Social Studies Journal* 13, no. 1 (Fall 1986): 11-14. [1 Ref.]

Metzger accuses the education system of the United States of promoting anti-democratic attitudes, or indifference to democracy through its dictatorial approach to education. He argues that citizenship education should not be simply a memorization of various facts, but should develop critical thinking skills and prepare students to participate in a democracy.

291 Miles, Curtis. "Making Choices: It Ought to Be Carefully Taught." Chapter 14 in *Thinking and Learning Skills. Vol. 1: Relating Instruction to Research*, edited by Judith W. Segal, Susan F. Chipman, and Robert Glaser, 473-497. Hillsdale, NJ: Lawrence Erlbaum, 1985. [40 Refs.]

Miles argues that colleges would better prepare its students for post-graduate life if choice-making skills were fostered in the college curriculum. He identifies the types of students who would benefit from special instruction in choice-making and the dimensions of choice-making in academia and personal/social life that are difficult for many students. Miles discusses four categories of skills that should be incorporated into the curriculum: (1) basic reasoning tools, (2) choice-making techniques, (3) choice-making heuristics, and (4) choice-making attitudes. He outlines impediments to the implementation of choice making programs identified by researchers and lists questions requiring further research.

292 Newell, William H., and Allen J. Davis. "Education for Citizenship: The Role of Progressive Education and Interdisciplinary Studies." *Innovative Higher Education* 13, no. 1 (Fall-Winter 1988): 27-37. [8 Refs.]

Newell and Davis identify civic literacy, critical thinking, social conscience, toleration and respect for diversity, global citizenship, and political action as the anticipated requirements for world citizenship in the twenty-first century. They use the six requirements as the basis for arguing that a combination of progressive education and interdisciplinary studies is the best means for educating future citizens. Both forms stress the interrelatedness of knowledge, link learning inside and outside the classroom, deal with questions of value, and involve students in problem solving and independent inquiry. The authors conclude that the challenge facing higher education is to create an environment where critical thinking, values, and action can be fused and where students can experience participation and empowerment.

293 Newman, Fred M. "Higher Order Thinking in the High School Curriculum." *NASSP Bulletin* 72, no. 508 (May 1988): 58-64.

Newman address three questions: (1) What is higher order thinking? (2) Why is higher order thinking so hard to promote in secondary schools? and (3) What can principals do to help? Newman contends that higher order thinking is relative to an individual's prior knowledge and mental state. The effectiveness of teaching techniques depends on the kinds of students and nature of the challenges presented. Teacher-centered pedagogy, expansive coverage of subject matter, organizational structure, and cultural orientation are factors contributing to the lack of promotion of higher order thinking in secondary schools. Newman asserts that principals can promote higher order thinking in secondary schools by modifying these factors appropriately and by promoting a culture of thoughtfulness throughout all facets of the school.

294 Nickerson, Raymond S. "Kinds of Thinking Taught in Current Programs." *Educational Leadership* 42, no. 1 (September 1984): 26-36. [36 Refs.]

Nickerson summarizes five categories of programs designed to teach thinking: (1) cognitive-process, (2) heuristics-oriented or problem solving, (3) approaches focusing on the development of Piagetian formal thinking, (4) programs emphasizing language and symbol manipulations, and (5) thinking as subject matter. He identifies the main features and programs found in each category. Nickerson discusses learning strategies and the relation between thinking skills and knowledge. He concludes that more data is needed before the effectiveness of each program or approach can be evaluated.

295 Nickerson, Raymond S. "On Improving Thinking through Instruction." *Review of Research in Education* 15 (1988-1989): 3-57. [263 Refs.]

Nickerson reviews and discusses research on and approaches to the teaching of thinking. Areas discussed include basic thinking operations or processes, domain-specific knowledge, normative principles of reasoning, metacognitive knowledge, values, dispositions and beliefs, stand-alone versus integrated instructional approaches, thinking environments, and evaluations of approaches to the teaching of thinking.

296 Norris, Stephen P., and Linda M. Phillips. "Explanations of Reading Comprehension: Schema Theory and Critical Thinking Theory." *Teachers College Record* 89, no. 2 (Winter 1987): 281-306. [26 Refs.]

Printed as "Reading Well Is Thinking Well" in *Philosophy of Education 1986* (Normal, IL: Philosophy of Education, 1987), p. 187-197.

Norris and Phillips explore the theories of schema and critical thinking in the context of reading comprehension through the presentation of a thinking aloud process of two sixth-grade children reading a passage. The schema theory is product-oriented; comprehension occurs by matching elements in a schemata with pieces of information from the text read. The critical thinking theory is process-oriented by which it is iterative, interactive, creative and imaginative with background knowledge in relation to new information. In offering critical thinking theory as an alternative explanation to good reading, the authors point out the incompleteness of it since unresolved issues continue to exist. Norris and Phillips suggest that combining the theories offers a better understanding of reading. If it is correct that schemata are needed for comprehension, then perhaps the critical thinking theory could determine the selection and construction of appropriate schemata.

297 Orton, Robert E. "Geometry and the Generality of Critical Thinking Skills." In *Philosophy of Education 1987: Proceedings of the Forty-Third Annual Meeting of the Philosophy of Education Society*, edited by Barbara Arnstine and Donald Arnstine, 293-302. Normal, IL: Philosophy of Education Society, 1988. [17 Refs.]

Reply: McPeck {285}

Orton addresses the transfer of critical thinking skills through a discussion of the nature of deduction in high school geometry found in the psychological theories of Pierre and Dina van Heile, and Piaget. The van Heile theory hypothesizes that deduction arises from a need to organize a system of subject specific knowledge of geometric figures and properties. Piaget focuses on the logical operations underlying intellectual competence in general rather than any particular subject matter. Orton asserts that epistemologically there is no conflict between the two theories, but their implications for pedagogy are significant different. The van Hiele theory entails students learning specific geometric figures and properties before they are able to perceive the need for deduction. The Piaget theory might lead to the development of materials to teach general critical thinking skills. Research on both theories is inconclusive, but Orton believes the van Hiele theory to be more promising.

298 Owen, Roderic L. "What Does 'Teaching Students to Think Critically' Actually Mean?" *Proceedings of the Thirty-First Annual Meeting of the South Atlantic Philosophy of Education Society*, edited by Samuel M. Craver, 49-52.

Richmond, VA: South Atlantic Philosophy of Education Society, 1987. [6 Refs.]

Reply to Mucklow {51}

Owen enumerates responses and explanations regarding the increased emphasis on infusing critical thinking in undergraduate education and lists skills usually associated with critical thinking. He discusses questions raised directly and indirectly by Mucklow's paper on the meaning of critical thinking as an educational goal and the best means of teaching it in an undergraduate curriculum. Owen affirms that critical thinking should be taught, but does not think it is the highest achievable educational goal. He argues that the most successful approach to critical thinking instruction is effective teaching rather than whether it is integrated into disciplinary courses or taught as a separate course.

299 Passmore, John. "Teaching to Be Critical." Chapter 9 in *The Philosophy of Teaching*, 166-182. Cambridge, MA: Harvard University Press, 1980. [20 Refs.]

Passmore argues that critical thinking should not be viewed as a subject or skill to be taught, but as more akin to a character trait that can be fostered through the encouraging of the critical spirit and creating an enthusiasm for critical discussion. Passmore reviews three difficulties that inhibit the encouragement of critical discussion: (1) a teacher who is not prepared to submit to criticism their beliefs and rules, (2) social pressure against examining certain beliefs and practices, and (3) a teacher who lacks training in encouraging critical discussion. He believes critical thinking cannot be developed without the development of a body of knowledge in the great traditions. This information should be imparted in an atmosphere that encourages questioning the reliability and justification of information and that encourages the use of critical thinking at an early stage in schooling.

300 Pastin, Mark. "The Author Responds: Pastin to Willard." *Social Epistemology* 2, no. 2 (1988): 171-174. [1 Ref.]

Charles Willard's review of Pastin's book *The Hard Problems of Management: Gaining the Ethics Edge* is addressed. Pastin distinguishes between the typical philosophical emphasis on "bold ethical theories" that Willard supports, and his own position that ethics should be approached as a form of critical thinking concerned with the subject matter and subject of ethics. A discussion of stakeholder utilitarianism is used to illustrate Pastin's approach.

301 Paul, Richard. "An Agenda Item for the Informal Logic/Critical Thinking Movement." *Informal Logic* 5 (June 1983): 23-24.

Paul warns of danger in the efforts of the critical thinking movement to clarify and develop the role of critical thinking in education and everyday life. He sees the public schools using simplistic solutions for training teachers to teach critical thinking rather than educating them on the concept.

302 Paul, Richard W. "Bloom's Taxonomy and Critical Thinking Instruction." *Educational Leadership* 42, no. 8 (May 1985): 36-39. [4 Refs.]

Acknowledging the usefulness and influence of Benjamin Bloom's *Taxonomy of Educational Objectives: Affective and Cognitive Domains* (New York, NY: David McKay, 1974) in education, Paul focuses on its fallacies in relation to the critical thinking movement and its limitations in the construction of a critical thinking curriculum. He asserts that the work's neutrality to knowledge, cognition, and education and its one-way hierarchy of cognitive processes (in which knowledge is a product that presupposes comprehension) inhibit the fostering of critical thinking. To Paul, successful critical thinking instruction requires that (1) teachers possess insight into cognitive processes and their interrelationships, (2) Bloom's hierarchy becomes two-sided, and (3) teachers view rational learning as a process. A brief reply from Benjamin Bloom follows the article.

303 Paul, Richard W. "Critical and Reflective Thinking: A Philosophical Perspective." Chapter 14 in *Dimensions of Thinking and Cognitive Instruction*, edited by Beau Fly Jones and Lorna Idol, 445-494. Hillsdale, NJ: Lawrence Erlbaum, 1990. [13 Refs.]

Paul contrasts a philosophy-based approach to teaching critical thinking with a psychology-based approach. He asserts that the philosophy-based approach emphasizes a person-centered approach to thinking in which the individual begins to rationally analyze, assess and control their own thinking, and accurately understand and assess the thinking of others. Psychology-based approaches emphasize technical competence, empirical research, and expertise. Paul calls for greater cooperation and communication between proponents of both approaches. He discusses the need to have philosophically oriented teachers for critical thinking instruction and outlines a philosophy-based classroom approach for directly infusing philosophical thinking across the curriculum. The paper includes a chart outlining the criticisms of the didactic theory of knowledge and learning made by representatives of both the philosophy-based and psychology-based approaches.

304 Paul, Richard W. "Critical Thinking: Fundamental to Education for a Free Society." *Educational Leadership* 42, no. 1 (September 1984): 4-14. [13 Refs.]

An excerpt from this paper can be found in Costa {505}, pp. 152-160.

Paul discusses strategies and goals that would enable school systems and teachers to meet education mandates for teaching critical thinking. He asserts that developing a short term and a long term strategy for teaching critical thinking requires an analysis of (1) the current critical thinking skills of teachers and students, (2) the development of cognitive and affective processes, (3) the conditions and obstacles affecting this development, and (4) the difference between critical thinking skills extrinsic to individual character (critical thinking in a weak sense) and those intrinsic to individual character (critical thinking in a strong sense). Paul stresses the importance of the development of higher order thinking skills, specifically dialectical thinking skills for individual intellectual, emotional, and moral autonomy.

305 Paul, Richard W. "Critical Thinking in North America: A New Theory of Knowledge, Learning, and Literacy." *Argumentation* 3, no. 2 (May 1989): 197-242. [38 Refs.]

Paul compares the traditional didactic, monological theory of knowledge, learning and literacy to the multilogical, dialectical theory supported by the critical thinking movement. He examines several proposed definitions of critical thinking, identifying their strengths and weaknesses. Paul argues for retaining a number of definitions in order to maintain insights into the various dimensions of critical thinking highlighted in different definitions and to overcome the limitations of any one. Paul focuses on the definition of critical thinking as "disciplined, self-directed thinking which exemplifies the perfections of thinking appropriate to a particular mode or domain of thinking" (p. 214) and distinguishes two types of critical thinking: weak sense (or sophistic critical thinking) and strong sense (or fair-minded critical thinking). Paul believes that present day schooling impedes the development of autonomous thinkers by emphasizing uncritical lower order thinking rather than higher order thinking. He identifies seven interdependent traits of mind that should be cultivated in order to develop critical thinkers: (1) intellectual humility, (2) intellectual courage, (3) intellectual empathy, (4) intellectual good faith, (5) intellectual perseverance, (6) faith in reason, and (7) intellectual sense of justice. The article includes a bibliography of works reflecting North American perspectives on teaching critical thinking.

306 Paul, Richard W. *Critical Thinking: What Every Person Needs to Survive in a Rapidly Changing World*, edited by A. J. A. Binker. Rohnert Park, CA: Center for Critical Thinking and Moral Critique, Sonoma State University, 1990. 575 pp.

This collection of 39 theoretical and practical papers is divided into three sections: I: What is Critical Thinking?, II: How to Teach for It, and III: Grasping Connections --Seeing Contrasts. In Part I, Paul provides an overview and history of critical thinking and explores his concept of strong sense critical thinking as fundamental to a democratic society. In the papers of Part II, he examines assumptions about instruction, knowledge, and learning; explores dialogical and dialectical thinking; provides practical examples, model lessons, and strategies for incorporating critical thinking into elementary social studies, language arts, and science; and suggests guidelines, strategies, models, and approaches for developing staff development programs and learning centers. Part III includes theoretical papers covering the application of critical thinking across disciplines, the contributions and assumptions of philosophy and cognitive psychology to critical thinking, and the relation between Bloom's taxonomy and critical thinking instruction. The book includes a glossary of critical thinking terms and concepts and a list of 74 recommended readings on critical thinking.

307 Paul, Richard W. "Dialogical Thinking: Critical Thought Essential to the Acquisition of Rational Knowledge and Passions." Chapter 7 in *Teaching Thinking Skills: Theory and Practice*, edited by Joan Boykoff Baron and Robert J. Sternberg, 127-148. New York, NY: W. H. Freeman, 1987. [10 Refs.]

Paul compares a psychologist's and a philosopher's approach to teaching critical thinking. To Paul, cognitive psychologists tend to emphasize problems that are monological or settled within one frame of reference while philosophers tend to choose multilogical problems that use more than one frame of reference and set each frame dialectically against each other to determine their comparable logical strength. Paul argues that individuals approach issues of everyday life with an egocentric, monological frame of reference even though most of these issues are multilogical in nature. He accuses current schooling of encouraging authoritative, monological answers rather than giving students experience with dialogical reasoning. Paul urges schools to teach strong sense critical thinking and encourage students to examine their biases and egocentric views by allowing them to choose, organize, and shape their own ideas and living beliefs by means of critical principles. Critical and creative thinking must be seen as essential to each other rather than distinct abilities.

308 Paul, Richard W. "McPeck's Mistakes." *Informal Logic* 7, no. 1 (Winter 1985): 35-43. [2 Refs.]

Reprinted in McPeck {7}, pp. 102-111, 130.

Paul identifies the flaws he sees in John McPeck's *Critical Thinking and Education* {6}. McPeck conceives of critical thinking as subject specific and as teachable only within the context of a subject or discipline. Paul asserts that world problems and life experiences can not be categorized into distinct subjects or disciplines. He argues that individuals must learn to think critically about their total experience in relation to specific dimensions of their lives. Paul believes that the question to focus on is whether or not content restricts thinking within a category rather than free thinking between and among categories, not whether content is necessary to thought.

309 Paul, Richard W. "The Socratic Spirit: An Answer to Louis Goldman." *Educational Leadership* 42, no. 1 (September 1984): 63-64. [1 Ref.]

Reply to Goldman {243}

Paul refutes Goldman's view on the negative effects of teaching thinking to children. He cites the Philosophy for Children program as a way in which the Socratic method has been incorporated into teaching strategies that encourage and nurture children's thoughts and questions.

310 Pea, Roy D., and D. Midian Kurland. "On the Cognitive Effects of Learning Computer Programming." Chapter 8 in *Mirrors of Minds: Patterns of Experience in Educational Computing*, edited by Roy D. Pea and Karen Sheingold, 147-177. Norwood, NJ: Ablex, 1987. [80 Refs.]

Printed also in *New Ideas in Psychology* 2, no. 2 (1984): 137-168.

Pea and Kurland examine two beliefs about the mental activities engaged when programming a computer and the expected cognitive and educational benefits of this engagement. The first belief perceives learning to program to be the learning of the command vocabulary and the syntactic rules for constructing arrangements of commands. This belief views learning as an accumulation of facts. The second belief perceives learning to program leading to the acquisition of higher cognitive skills such as planning abilities and problem solving heuristics. The authors review the relevant cognitive science and developmental psychology research on the cognitive outcomes of learning to program and discuss the major issues confronting such research. They examine claims made about the effects of learning to program upon thinking, the developmental role of contexts in learning to program, and the cognitive restraints on such learning. Pea and Kurland identify several levels of programming skill development and argue that spontaneous transfer of higher cognitive skills does not develop from learning to program.

311 Pecorino, Philip A. "Critical Thinking and Philosophy." *Informal Logic* 9, no. 2-3 (Spring-Fall 1987): 143-145.

Pecorino argues against colleges and universities counting critical thinking or informal logic courses as philosophy courses that satisfy degree requirements in the liberal arts.

312 Perkins, D. N. "General Cognitive Skills: Why Not?" Chapter 15 in *Thinking and Learning Skills. Vol. 2: Research and Open Questions*, edited by Susan F. Chipman, Judith W. Segal, and Robert Glaser, 339-363. Hillsdale, NJ: Lawrence Erlbaum, 1985. [85 Refs.]

Perkins criticizes the notion that intellectual competence consists of a few cognitive-control strategies that can be taught. He discusses four hypotheses derived from this notion: (1) the strategies hypothesis that holds that having certain cognitive-control strategies is one way one can have general cognitive skills, (2) the comprehensiveness hypothesis that holds that cognitive-control strategies in combination with specific knowledge account for intellectual competence, (3) The economy hypothesis that holds that a few cognitive-control strategies account for most or all intellectual competence, and (4) the teachability hypothesis that assumes being able to assimilate cognitive-control strategies is accomplished through informing people about such strategies and allowing these strategies to be practiced. While these hypotheses are inadequate, Perkins asserts that general cognitive-strategies such as asking "Why not?" do exist. However, he believes such strategies provide only limited power for complex intellectual tasks and are hampered by the problem of context boundedness. Perkins suggests that identifying the general types of tasks having fundamental similarities that permit the use of common strategies, is a way to resolve many of the difficulties found in the four hypotheses.

313 Perkins, D. N. "Teaching Thinking Needn't Put Able Thinkers at Risk: A Response to John Baer." *Educational Leadership* 45, no. 7 (April 1988): 76-77. [6 Refs.]

Reply to Baer {197}

Perkins presents counter-arguments to Baer's positions on the effects a rigid program for teaching thinking can have on students who are already able thinkers, and the consciousness/unconsciousness controversy.

314 Perkins, D. N. "Thinking Frames." *Educational Leadership* 43, no. 8 (May 1986): 4-10. [42 Refs.]

Perkins examines three key questions regarding the teaching of thinking: (1) What are the components of thinking that cam be improved by education? (2) What sort of learning process teaches people to think better? and (3) How can we tell whether a particular approach to teaching thinking may be effective? Perkins characterizes intelligence as a compound of power, tactics, and content. He argues that thinking can be improved by improving students' tactics or thinking frames. Perkins defines thinking frames as "representations intended to guide the process of thought by organizing, supporting and catalyzing our course of thought" (p.7). Learning thinking frames requires attention to the acquisition, internalization, and transfer of frames, all of which have pitfalls that may impede effective learning. To judge whether a particular approach to teaching thinking is effective, Perkins advises an educator to consider its content of instruction: the frame content and range, and whether the frames are relevant and effective. An educator should also examine how the method of instruction teaches frame acquisition, internalization, and transfer.

315 Perkins, D. N. "Thinking Frames: An Integrative Perspective on Teaching Cognitive Skills." Chapter 3 in *Teaching Thinking Skills: Theory and Practice*, edited by Joan Boykoff Baron and Robert J. Sternberg, 41-59. New York, NY: W. H. Freeman, 1987. [58 Refs.]

Perkins addresses three questions: (1) what constitutes better thinking; (2) by what process can people learn to think better; (3) how can one tell whether a particular approach to teaching thinking is effective. Perkins reviews three concepts of intelligence which define intelligence as power, tactics, or content. He argues that the best opportunity for long-term intellectual competence is to improve a student's tactical intelligence or thinking frames. Perkins defines a thinking frame as "a guide to organizing and supporting thought processes" (p.47). He examines three broad aspects of learning and the bottlenecks they may create in building a larger repertoire of thinking frames: (1) initial acquisition of the thinking frame; (2) making a thinking frame automatic; (3) transferring the thinking frame across a wide range of contexts. Perkins suggests ways to evaluate the effectiveness of a particular teaching approach or program for teaching thinking frames and lists general concerns to be used in evaluating a particular frame.

316 Perkins, D. N., and Gavriel Salomon. "Are Cognitive Skills Context-Bound?" *Educational Researcher* 18, no. 1 (January-February 1989): 16-25. [73 Refs.]

Perkins and Salomon explore the contextual/generalizable nature of cognitive skills through a review of research and arguments. They note that these studies and arguments present cognitive skills as either exclusively general or contextual. The authors argue that there are general cognitive skills that function within a context and serve as general tools for retrieving, wielding, and adjusting domain-specific knowledge. Perkins and Salomon believe this concept of cognitive skills requires the integration of context-specificity and general cognitive skills in classroom instruction.

317 Perkins, D. N., and Gavriel Salomon. "Teaching for Transfer." *Educational Leadership* 46, no. 1 (September 1988): 22-32. [41 Refs.]

An adapted version appears in Costs {506}, pp. 215-223.

Perkins and Salomon present a model for transfer that distinguishes between two different mechanisms of transfer: "low road" transfer, or the automatic triggering of routines in circumstances similar to the original learning context, and "high road" transfer, or the deliberate mindful abstraction of skill or knowledge from one context to another. Perkins and Salomon discuss the conditions for successful low or high road transfer and possible reasons for transfer failure. They describe two techniques for promoting transfer: "hugging" or teaching to better meet the resemblance conditions for low road transfer, and "bridging" or teaching to meet better the conditions for higher road transfer. The authors argue that despite the problem of "local knowledge," opportunities for transfer do exist. They attribute this to (1) the fuzziness of boundaries between disciplines, (2) the existence of important crosscutting thinking strategies, and (3) numerous patterns of thinking of intermediate generality that cut across certain domains.

318 Perkins, D. N., and Gavriel Salomon. "Transfer and Teaching Thinking." Chapter 17 in *Thinking: The Second International Conference*, edited by David N. Perkins, Jack Lochhead, and John C. Bishop, 285-303. Hillsdale, NJ: Lawrence Erlbaum, 1987. [93 Refs.]

The authors present a perspective on transfer that addresses conflicting research findings and suggest tactics for promoting transfer when teaching thinking skills or other knowledge. They identify several types of transfer: (1) positive transfer or when transfer occurs, (2) negative transfer or when learning A impedes performance on B, (3) horizontal transfer where A and B are somewhat different tasks, and (4) vertical transfer where A is a part of B. Perkins and Salomon discuss two ways that transfer occurs: low road transfer where transfer occurs as the automatic consequence of varied practice, and high road transfer where transfer results from the mindful abstraction and application of principles. The authors examine the limits to and different opportunities for transfer entailed by four theories of intelligence: (1) power; (2) expertise; (3) tactics; and (4) cognitive style. They suggest that teachers do everything they can to promote both low road and high road transfer by incorporating all four theories into their approach so that no opportunity for transfer is omitted. The authors include a list of pitfalls and tactics for designing instruction for transfer.

319 Piro, Joseph M., and John E. Iorio. "Rationale and Responsibilities in the Teaching of Critical Thinking to American Schoolchildren." *Journal of Instructional Psychology* 17, no. 1 (March 1990): 3-10. [21 Refs.]

The authors review historical and contemporary views on the teaching of critical thinking and discuss the educational usefulness of critical thinking. They examine the expanded role of teachers in implementing the teaching of reasoning and outline guidelines for successful critical thinking programs.

320 Powell, Stuart. "Improving Critical Thinking: A Review." *Educational Psychology* 7, no. 3 (1987): 169-185. [86 Refs.]

Through a review of the relevant literature, Powell examines the meaning of critical thinking, its teachability as a problem solving skill, and its generalizability. He analyzes how children use thinking skills for problem solving, and discusses factors that should be considered by teachers when creating problem solving activities. He includes an outline of areas needing further research.

321 Prawat, Richard S. "Why Embed Thinking Skills Instruction in Subject Matter Instruction?" Chapter 35 in *Developing Minds. Vol. 1: A Resource Book for Teaching Thinking*, rev. ed., edited by Arthur L. Costa, 185-187. Alexandria, VA: Association for Supervision and Curriculum Development, 1991. [5 Refs.]

Prawat notes that there are three categories of thinking involved in embedding thinking skills instruction in subject matter instruction: executive control skills, learning skills, and critical thinking skills. Prawat discusses the role each plays in the processing of information.

322 Presseisen, Barbara Z., ed. *At-Risk Students and Thinking: Perspectives from Research*. Washington, DC: National Education Association; Philadelphia, PA: Research for Better Schools, 1988. 160 pp.

This collection of essays focuses on at-risk students, their learning difficulties, and the educational reforms needed in American schools to prepare them for living in a democratic society. The essays emphasize the effective integration of higher order cognitive skills instruction throughout the public school grade curriculum; effective pedagogical practices; the understanding, support, and collaboration of local, district, and state administrators and teachers on the issues related to at-risk students; and helping at-risk students become independent learners and critical thinkers. Topics covered include: curriculum models, thinking programs, intellectual assessment, and teaching strategies appropriate for at-risk students.

323 Presseisen, Barbara Z. "Avoiding Battle at Curriculum Gulch: Teaching Thinking and Context." *Educational Leadership* 45, no. 7 (April 1988): 7-8. [14 Refs.]

Emphasizing the importance of relating content and process for meaningful learning, Presseisen advocates curricula which integrate the teaching of thinking and content.

324 Presseisen, Barbara Z., Robert J. Sternberg, Kurt W. Fischer, Catharine C. Knight, and Reuven Feuerstein. *Learning and Thinking Styles: Classroom Interaction*. NEA Schooling Restructuring Series. Washington, DC: National Education Association, 1990. [152 Refs.]

This is an anthology on the attempt to restructure schooling using basic theories about how children think and learn. The first essay outlines questions that need to be answered in any educational paradigm shift: the purpose of schooling, the nature of intelligence, how students become competent thinkers, and the role of teachers and educators in an effective school. The next three essays discuss three theories of human learning and intelligence: (1) Sternberg's theory of intellectual styles and their implications for the classroom, (2) Fischer's and Knight's research on cognitive development levels in children and the different developmental pathways each child takes while acquiring skills, and (3) Feuerstein's theory of structural cognitive modifiability. The final essay attempts to supply answers to questions posed in the first essay by analyzing each theorist's position and its relation to current attempts to move schooling away from content coverage and knowledge accumulation to complex forms of thinking and meaning.

325 Proefriedt, William A. "Teaching Philosophy and Teaching Philosophically." *Clearing House* 58, no. 7 (March 1985): 294-297. [2 Refs.]

The Philosophy for Children Program developed by Matthew Lipman has successfully introduced philosophy into public schools, but should be viewed as only one way to introduce philosophical inquiry into the classroom. Proefriedt reviews the Philosophy of Children Program, focusing on the program's novel *Lisa* to exemplify the program's approach. He finds the program worthwhile, but advocates considering other approaches. Proefriedt offers an alternative model based on a teacher having a spirit of inquiry and developing a philosophical approach to teaching that sees philosophy as a self-empower activity. Students are encouraged to question and analyze arguments, inferences, concepts and other philosophical topics found in curriculum materials.

326 Quellmalz, Edys S. "Developing Reasoning Skills." Chapter 5 in *Teaching Thinking Skills: Theory and Practice*, edited by Joan Boykoff Baron and Robert J. Sternberg, 86-105. New York, NY: W.H. Freeman, 1987. [15 Refs.]

Quellmalz discusses philosophical and psychological models of fundamental higher order thinking skills. While philosophers have focused on the features and quality of the products of critical thinking, psychologists have focused on components of the process. Quellmalz compares the reasoning skills proposed in psychology and philosophy and identifies a core of thinking and reasoning skills and underlying operations that can be used as a framework for teaching reasoning skills across academic and practical areas. The framework serves as a basis for analyzing how skills and problem types are represented in the curriculum and the classroom. A Higher Order Thinking Skills (HOTS) project using writing to promote skill development exemplifies the framework approach. Quellmalz suggests designing tasks that allow multiple interpretations, require explanations of reasoning strategies, and develop transfer of learning. Such tasks should be assigned on a regular basis. The chapter includes charts listing skills and textbook material classifications.

327 Resnick, Lauren B., and Leopold E. Klopfer, eds. *Toward the Thinking Curriculum: Current Cognitive Research*. 1989 Yearbook of the Association for Supervision and Curriculum Development. [Alexandria, VA]: Association for Supervision and Curriculum Development, 1989. 221 pp.

The authors in this work advocate incorporating thinking into the traditional subject matter of elementary and secondary schools rather than teaching thinking as a separate part of the curriculum. Common themes running throughout the chapters include: learning is constructive, thinking skills and content should be taught by using concepts generatively, social communities have a role in teaching thinking, teaching thinking requires a real task and practice in context, and learning requires knowledge. Each chapter provides examples of how thinking skills and content can be incorporated into various subjects.

328 Richards, Thomas J. "Attitudes to Reasoning." *Informal Logic Newsletter* 3 (March 1981): 2-7. [2 Refs.]

Richards views the teaching of practical reasoning to be the most important activity in a curriculum. He believes that the primary way reasoning is currently taught is according to the "Received Theory of Reasoning," which limits reasoning to facts and does not deal with the rational evaluation of opinions. Richard argues that the "Received Theory" reflects general societal attitudes toward reasoning and contains three tenets (the Principle of Bastardized Liberalism, the Genetic Fallacy, and the Empathetic Theory of Evidence) that stifle practical reasoning.

329 Rogers, Peter. "'Discovery', Learning, Critical Thinking, and the Nature of Knowledge." *British Journal of Educational Studies* 38, no. 1 (February 1990): 3-14. [4 Refs.]

Rogers argues that viewing inquiry skills as general and easily acquired ignores the complexity of knowledge and variation in the nature of inquiry within subject disciplines. To show the relation of inquiry to subject-specific criteria, Rogers examines the critical thinking aspect of inquiry, focusing on Robert Ennis's identification of three interrelated analytical dimensions of critical thinking: the logical, the criterial, and the pragmatic. Ennis's approach emphasizes logical rather than epistemological criteria and implies that basic terms and statements can be understood apart from the field of study. Rogers argues that the approach is inadequate. He reiterates the necessity of subject matter knowledge and procedural skills for critical thinking and outlines a pedagogical model that recognizes the importance of studying the forms of knowledge, not just its logical structure.

330 Romanish, Bruce. "The American School and Prospects for Critical Thinking." *Journal of Educational Thought* 23, no. 1 (April 1989): 52-60. [31 Refs.]

Romanish asserts that the primary focus of critical thinking proponents has been on defining the term and describing the methods and strategies for teaching it. He believes this focus ignores the nature and influence that oppressive school experiences have on the development of critical thinking--the questioning and examining of one's social surroundings and institutions. Romanish examines the settings and effects of the school experience on student critical thinking and discusses the impeding influences the hierarchical, authoritarian nature of the school system has on the teaching of critical thinking. He concludes that the prospects for a critically empowered next generation are not good.

331 Sabini, John, and Maury Silver. "Critical Thinking and Obedience to Authority." *National Forum: Phi Kappa Phi Journal* 65, no. 1 (Winter 1985): 13-17.

Using the findings from experiments on destructive obedience reported in Stanley Milgram's *Obedience to Authority* (New York, NY: Harper & Row, 1974), Sabini and Silver suggest reasons why thinking and moral decision-making fail in situations where participants are to administer gradual painful bodily punishment to another person. The authors suggest that this failure or destructive obedience might be avoided by teaching individuals how to confront authority and by eliminating illusions about human nature (e.g., that only evil people do evil things).

332 Sanders, James, and John McPeck. "Teaching Johnny to Think." In *Philosophy of Education 1990: Proceedings of the Forty-Sixth Annual Meeting of the Philosophy of Education Society*, edited by David P. Ericson, 403-409. Normal, IL: Philosophy of Education Society, 1991. [14 Refs.]

Reply: Carbone {219}

Sanders and McPeck assert that cognitive research on thinking has tended to relate the descriptive complexity of the thinking process to difficulties in human cognitive performance. This perception has been interpreted as evidence for the possibility of teaching thinking directly. The authors argue that cognitive processes are more akin to common capacities than improvable skills and find no direct link between cognitive research and the possibility of teaching thinking. When thinking is construed as a skill, as in research on expert versus novice cognitive performance, it is the difference in knowledge, not common processes, that distinguishes performance. To Sanders and McPeck, the relevance of cognitive research to education remains problematic.

333 Schuler, Adrian L., and Linda Perez. "The Role of Social Interaction in the Development of Thinking Skills." *Focus on Exceptional Children* 19, no. 7 (March 1987): 1-11. [60 Refs.]

Schuler and Perez explore the role of language and social interaction in learning and cognitive development in relation to the development of self-regulatory and metacognitive skills in special education students. Increasingly, these students are viewed as deficient in metacognition and in effective use of problem solving strategies, rather than in attention, perception, and memory, as previously thought. Traditional treatments (medication, stimulus reduction, and behavior modification) are being seen as reinforcers of the basis of the problem of passivity. To counter this, such instructional methods as cognitive behavior modification, cognitive strategies, and instrumental enrichment for teaching self-regulatory skills and problem solving skills have arisen. The authors examine these methods in terms of effectiveness, student involvement, and mediating social interaction. They hypothesize that social cognitive skills and effective communication skills may be more critical to effective teaching, especially of special education students, than previously assumed.

334 Scriven, Michael. "Critical for Survival." *National Forum: Phi Kappa Phi Journal* 65, no. 1 (Winter 1985): 9-12.

Scriven argues that training in critical thinking should be the primary task of education. He offers three essential conditions for implementing a critical thinking program: (a) teacher supervision of the activity at all times, (b) a focus on the provision and improvement of coping strategies and not just "experiencing," and (c) a degree of realism. Scriven criticizes schools for not allowing free discussion of opposing viewpoints of controversial issues, especially by supporters of alternative or unpopular viewpoints. He believes critical thinking can not be taught unless such discussion and free inquiry take place.

335 Scriven, Michael. "Critical Thinking and the Concept of Literacy." *Informal Logic* 9, no. 2-3 (Spring-Fall 1987): 93-110. [4 Refs.]

Scriven asserts that the ability to think critically depends on the ability to understand and comprehend the meaning of paragraphs. He attributes literacy problems among students to poor teaching and indifferent attitudes about literacy. Educators erroneously emphasize high verbal fluency over the grammar, punctuation, spelling, and logic skills which the real world associates with literacy. Tests for literacy reflect the same error by their widespread use of composition exercises in which students are able to avoid words they cannot spell or use properly. Scriven advocates the use of proof-reading tests for grammar, punctuation, and spelling in addition to the composition tests. He argues that literacy in English should be a minimum requirement for passing any subject. He discusses ways a standard of literacy can be developed and outlines a "full treatment" program. The paper includes a literacy test for teacher trainees developed by Scriven.

336 Selman, Mark. "Ideology and What? A Response to Harvey Siegel." *Educational Theory* 38, no. 2 (Spring 1988): 261-265. [11 Refs.]

See: Siegel {342}

Selman criticizes Siegel's arguments for a rational justification of critical thinking as an educational ideal that transcends any ideology as vague and ambiguous. Selman asserts that Siegel's position reinforces the view that philosophers are interested only in the abstract and are remote from the real world. To Selman, thinking needs little justification to be an educational ideal. He supports a concept of rationality that encompasses the transcendental nature of reason as well as its immanent link to social and historical developments.

337 Sholseth, Richard D., and Diane Y. Watanabe. "How Do You Choose a Thinking Skills Program That Is Right for You?" Chapter 29 in *Developing Minds. Vol. 2: Programs for Teaching Thinking*, rev. ed., edited by Arthur L. Costa, 114-120. Alexandria, VA: Association for Supervision and Curriculum Development, 1991. [24 Refs.]

Sholseth and Watanabe recommend that a needs assessment be performed before a published thinking skills program is selected. They outline twelve ways programs differ and describe several programs that are typically included in long range plans in districts or schools.

338 Siegel, Harvey. "Critical Thinking as an Educational Ideal." *Educational Forum* 45, no. 1 (November 1980): 7-23. [23 Refs.]

Siegel discusses the nature of critical thinking and attempts to justify it as an educational ideal. He describes critical thinking as judging in an unarbitrary, impartial objective manner based on appropriate and properly assessed reasons. A critical thinker is one who recognizes the importance of reasons and has the disposition or critical attitude to be rational. Siegel presents three arguments to justify critical thinking as an educational ideal: (1) teaching should be done in accordance with the critical manner because it would be immoral to do otherwise, (2) education has the responsibility of preparing students to be self-sufficient, and empowered adults, and (3) education should initiate students into central human traditions such as science, literature and history. Siegel argues that critical thinking is not political. Its task is to liberate not indoctrinate. Siegel outlines several ramifications of accepting critical thinking as an educational ideal.

339 Siegel, Harvey. "Critical Thinking As An Intellectual Right." In *Children's Intellectual Rights*, edited by David Moshman, 39-49. New Directions for Child Development, no. 33. San Francisco, CA: Jossey-Bass, 1986. [9 Refs.]

Siegel elaborates upon four reasons supporting his claim that critical thinking is an intellectual right: (1) teachers have a moral obligation to treat students with respect which includes honoring students' right to question, challenge, and demand reasons and justifications for what is being taught, (2) education has the responsibility to prepare students for adulthood by fostering self-sufficiency and the ability to control competently their own lives, (3) education is an initiation into the rational traditions which help students understand the role and criteria of evaluation of reasons, and (4) students have the right to participate fully in a society committed to democratic living which requires the skills, attitudes, abilities, and traits of a critical thinker. Siegel addresses the issue of indoctrination, emphasizing that encouraging the development of critical thinking (inculcating beliefs without reasons while encouraging the development of rationality and an evidential style of belief) is not indoctrination.

340 Siegel, Harvey. "Educating Reason: Critical Thinking, Informal Logic, and the Philosophy of Education. Part Two: Philosophical Questions Underlying Education for Critical Thinking." *Informal Logic* 7, no. 2-3 (Spring-Fall 1985): 69-81. [37 Refs.]

See: Siegel {069}

Siegel uses three components of education to justify the consideration of critical thinking/informal logic as an educational ideal: (1) educators are morally obligated to treat students with respect and allow them to question, challenge and demand justifications for what is being taught; (2) education has the task of preparing students to manage their adult lives, and (3) education teaches students to appreciate the standards of rationality. Siegel argues that critical thinking promotes all three educational aspects by developing students' understanding about the role and criteria of the evaluation of reasons, leading to self-sufficiency and autonomy. He believes the focus of study should be how critical thinking manifests itself, rather then exploring a generalized skill of critical thinking. Siegel conceives critical thinking to be primarily a process of epistemology encompassing all criteria of reason assessment, subject-specific as well as general. He asserts that the dispute between John McPeck and Robert Ennis concerning the subject specific nature of critical thinking collapses once it is realized that they are concerned with different criteria for the assessment of reasons, not different concepts of critical thinking.

341 Siegel, Harvey. *Educating Reason: Rationality, Critical Thinking, and Education*. New York, NY: Routledge, 1988. 191 pp. [180 Refs.]

Siegel provides a philosophical inquiry into critical thinking as an aim of education. He reviews several conceptions of critical thinking, including those of Robert Ennis, Richard Paul, and John McPeck, and attempts to justify his own conception of critical thinking as an educational ideal and goal. After addressing objections of ideology and indoctrination, he discusses the relevance of critical thinking to curricular and educational policies and practices. Siegel criticizes Thomas Kuhn's anti-critical conception of science and science education, contrasting it with a critical thinking approach to science education.

Siegel illustrates the relevance of critical thinking to educational policy and practice through a discussion of minimum competency testing which he argues is incompatible with any educational aim. In the final chapter, he discusses the connection of critical thinking to rationality.

342 Siegel, Harvey. "Rationality and Ideology." *Educational Theory* 37, no. 2 (Spring 1987): 153-167. [28 Refs.]

Reply: Selman {336}

The central question addressed in this article is whether critical thinking can be rationally justified as an educational ideal without regard to a prior commitment to any ideology. Siegel approaches the question by exploring the nature of ideology and whether rational justification independent of ideology exists. He discusses whether education is fundamentally political in nature and whether ideology shapes consciousness in ways relevant for rational justification. Siegel argues that ideological determinism is question begging and in need of good reasons for its own position. Siegel concludes that rationality, not ideology, is fundamental. Critical thinking relies on rational justification, not ideological determination.

343 Simon, Roger I., and Don Dippo. "What Schools Can Do: Designing Programs for Work Education that Challenges the Wisdom of Experience." *Journal of Education* 169, no. 3 (1987): 101-116.

The authors argue that schools are sites of cultural politics where a sense of identity, place, worth, and value is formed and meanings organized. They believe cooperative education programs present the opportunity for combining work experience with a pedagogy designed to critique that experience. The authors outline several ways experience is understood and relate them to cooperative education programs. They explore the pedagogical implications of such understanding, using student interpretations of their work experience. The authors suggest ways school curricula can address the need for students to question and develop alternative interpretations of their work experiences.

344 Smith, Mike U., ed. *Toward a Unified Theory of Problem Solving: Views from the Content Domains*. Hillsdale, NJ: Lawrence Erlbaum, 1991. 164 pp.

This anthology consists of position papers on attempts at working towards a unified theory of problem solving by identifying commonalities in problem solving approaches within biology, chemistry, medicine, programming, mathematics, physics, and troubleshooting. Researchers and educators from each field discuss the nature of a problem, aspects of problem solving performance that are similar in other domains, and the transferability of problem solving skills.

345 Sternberg, Robert J. "All's Well That Ends Well, But It's a Sad Tale That Begins at the End: A Reply to Glaser." *American Psychologist* 40, no. 5 (May 1985): 571-572. [9 Refs.]

Reply to Glaser {241}
Reply: Glaser {240}
See: Block {213}

Sternberg expresses concern about Glaser's over-emphasis of domain-specific knowledge. He identifies and discusses psychological issues that seem to merit a domain-general approach to learning rather than a domain-specific one, problem finding and cognitive monitoring. Sternberg advocates the consideration of ways in which knowledge and process interact.

346 Sternberg, Robert J. "Teaching Critical Thinking: Eight Easy Ways to Fail Before You Begin." *Phi Delta Kappan* 68, no. 6 (February 1987): 456-459.

The author identifies eight fallacious assumptions regarding teaching and learning that are detrimental to critical thinking programs. Chief among these assumptions are that teachers are the teachers and students are the learners, it is the correct answer that is important, and the principles of mastery learning are applicable to critical thinking. Sternberg counters these assumptions by outlining teacher attitudes more appropriate for promoting critical thinking: teachers must view themselves as facilitators and learners, view their students as teachers and learners, think of critical thinking as having a limitless depth of achievement, and believe that what is important is the thinking process that underlies an answer.

347 Stice, James E. "Learning How to Think: Being Earnest Is Important, But It's Not Enough." In *Developing Critical Thinking and Problem-Solving Abilities*, edited by James E. Stice, 93-99. New Directions for Teaching and Learning, no. 30. San Francisco, CA: Jossey-Bass, 1987. [13 Refs.]

Stice testifies from personal experience as a college student and college teacher that too much time is spent teaching subject content and comprehension rather than problem solving or teaching students how to use what they know.

348 Swartz, Alma M. "Critical Thinking Attitudes and the Transfer Question." In *Thinking Skills Instruction: Concepts and Techniques*, edited by Marcia Heiman and Joshua Slomianko, 58-68. Washington, DC: National Education Association, 1987. [7 Refs.]

Swartz believes that the tendency toward critically thinking is innate. Educators should view critical thinking as something to be facilitated through the development of good attitudes or dispositions, rather than something to be taught. In order to integrate thinking skills into the curriculum, teachers need to understand and know critical thinking attitudes and dispositions and how to encourage their development and transfer to other subjects and to everyday life. Swartz emphasizes the need to evaluate the presence of these attitudes and dispositions in students. She recommends using the interview method and an inventory of critical and creative thinking dispositions and suggests ways they may be employed.

349 Swartz, Robert J. "Critical Thinking, the Curriculum, and the Problem of Transfer." Chapter 16 in *Thinking: The Second International Conference*, edited by David N. Perkins, Jack Lochhead, and John C. Bishop, 261-284. Hillsdale, NJ: Erlbaum, 1987. [19 Refs.]

Swartz examines two basic approaches for incorporating critical thinking into classroom teaching: the subject-specific skills approach and the general skills approach. Swartz argues that both approaches can be enhanced by explicitly teaching for transfer. He discusses the approach used by the Amherst Project of the 1970s to integrate critical thinking into traditional subjects and suggests ways the approach may be broadened to include teaching for transfer. Swartz suggests that teachers use techniques that motivate the understanding and use of critical thinking skills by students. He argues that John McPeck's advocacy of teaching critical thinking based on the epistemology of the separate fields of study makes sense educationally, though he believes McPeck's position that critical thinking skills are not transferable is too extreme. Swartz examines the California-based Project Impact program as an approach for teaching general critical thinking skills and discusses ways for broadening the program's lessons to encourage a critical attitude and transfer. He suggests that an integration of the fragmentary subject-by-subject approach and the unifying conceptual framework of a general program such as Project Impact would be the most effective approach for bringing critical thinking into the classroom.

350 Tanner, Laurel N. "The Path Not Taken: Dewey's Model of Inquiry." *Curriculum Inquiry* 18, no. 4 (1988): 471-479. [30 Refs.]

Tanner asserts that the teaching of critical thinking has "gone the canned and packaged way" (p. 471) using pre-determined, abstract problems that do not enhance student skills in handling real-life problems. She advocates a return to John Dewey's theory of teaching reflective thinking dealing with real problems (teaching children to inquire about the world) and arrive at useful solutions. Pre-packaged dialectical exercises are not substitutes for the discoveries of actual inquiry.

351 Tchudi, Stephen. "Invisible Thinking and the Hypertext." *English Journal* 77, no. 1 (January 1988): 22-30. [12 Refs.]

Tchudi examines critical thinking in the context of holistic learning and teaching, "invisible thinking," and hypertext. He views "invisible thinking" as "integrated, imaginative, spontaneous, responsive critical analysis that is inseparable from its content and thus does not call attention to itself" (p.25). Tchudi presents a scenario of a future with computer technology and electronic hypertext, where teachers are guides to exploring and evaluating the diversity of computer-based resources. Tchudi believes hypertext of the present exists in the form of currently available interdisciplinary resources, including print, nonprint, media resources, people, and institutions. He proposes an interdisciplinary curriculum which incorporates a joy of learning, traditional knowledge and information, and which encourages systematic disciplined inquiry.

352 Tennyson, Robert D., and Mariana Rasch. "Linking Cognitive Learning Theory to Instructional Prescriptions." *Instructional Science* 17 (1988): 369-385. [38 Refs.]

Tennyson and Rasch present an instructional design model that focuses on a learning environment in which students acquire knowledge and improve their cognitive abilities to employ and extend their knowledge. The model links the knowledge type to be acquired or employed, specific learning objectives, corresponding instructional strategies, and learning time allocation. In the model, the authors allocate 70% of instructional time to the acquisition of contextual knowledge and the development and improvement of thinking processes. The remaining time is devoted to the acquisition of content knowledge.

353 Trotter, Gwendolyn. "I Thought What?" *Clearing House* 60, no. 2 (October 1986): 76-78. [1 Ref.]

Trotter encourages administrators, teachers, and parents to link thinking with the intellectual, moral, and emotional well-being of learners. She believes helping learners view thinking in the context of their own beliefs, feelings, and ways of thinking will guide them toward realizing the importance of assuming responsibility for their own thinking. Trotter outlines the responsibilities of administrators, teachers, parents, and the learners themselves in helping learners become thinkers who act responsibly.

354 Van Eemeren, F. H., and Rob Grootendorst. "Teaching Argumentation Analysis and Critical Thinking in the Netherlands." *Informal Logic* 9, no. 2-3 (Spring-Fall 1987): 57-69. [3 Refs.]

After reviewing research in argumentation theory, Van Eemeren and Grootendorst relate argumentation theory to pragmatics, dialectus, and didactus. Advocating a dialectical approach over a rhetorical approach to argumentation analysis, the authors believe such an approach includes a critical rationalist attitude which has implications for instruction. Students should be viewed as already having certain skills and knowledge and as being active discussants who reflect on information and respond critically. Instruction should correspond with existing knowledge and precipitate further reflection and insight. Such instruction involves familiarizing students with the basics of dialectical analysis of argumentation through a systematic explanation of the major characteristics of verbal communication, interaction, argument, and discussion. The authors provide in-depth discussion and illustrations of the following three components of argumentation analysis: (1) the analysis of argumentative discourse, (2) identification of fallacies, and (3) the evaluation of argumentation. Believing that argumentation analysis should be incorporated into school curricula, the authors offer a sample analysis assignment and suggest instructional modes.

355 Vann, Allan S. "Let's Give Values Clarification Another Chance." *Principal* 68, no. 2 (November 1988): 15-18. [6 Refs.]

Vann calls for a re-examination of the 1960's values clarification approach to the teaching of basic values. He recalls that the pioneers of the values clarification movement called for the fostering of critical thinking in values education. He advocates the incorporation of values clarification into the elementary school curriculum to provide a systematic process by which children can discuss values-related issues openly. Vann stresses the importance of presenting various viewpoints and of helping students logically analyze decisions made throughout history.

356 Vold, Edwina Battle. "Critical Thinking: Strategy for Diversity." Chapter 11 in *Education & the American Dream: Conservatives, Liberals & Radicals Debate the Future of Education*, edited by Harvey Holtz, Irwin Marcus, Jim Dougherty, Judy Michaels, and Rick Peduzzi, 124-133. Critical Studies in Education Series. Granby, MA: Bergin & Garvey, 1989. [15 Refs.]

Vold emphasizes the need for a systematic and persistent instructional plan that encourages elementary and secondary school students to confront issues such as racism, ethnocentrism, and sexism in a critical manner, using analytical and evaluative processes. Voss believes this instructional plan must emphasize content, perceptual responses to society and environment, action processes, and informal logic or critical thinking processes.

357 Voss, James F., David N. Perkins, and Judith W. Segal, eds. *Informal Reasoning and Education*. Hillsdale, NJ: Lawrence Erlbaum, 1991. 498 pp.

This book is an anthology of papers on informal reasoning collected to provide a firmer knowledge base for instruction. The papers are organized into three parts: (1) Contexts for Informal Reasoning, (2) Modes and Models of Informal Reasoning, and (3) Informal Reasoning and Instruction. Each part concludes with a commentary on the respective papers.

358 Walsh, Debbie, and Richard W. Paul. *The Goal of Critical Thinking: From Educational Ideal to Educational Reality*. Washington, DC: American Federation of Teachers, Educational Issues Department, [1989]. 60 pp. [89 Refs.]

Walsh and Paul outline the issues related to developing critical thinking initiatives and transforming critical thinking from an educational ideal to an educational reality. They discuss the background and definitions of critical thinking, general research on critical thinking, and approaches to teaching and evaluating critical thinking. The authors recommend policy and practice for preservice and inservice teacher programs and for effective integration of critical thinking into the K-12 curriculum. In the appendix, Walsh and Paul provide sample subject-specific questions that can be formulated at various grade levels for fostering critical thinking.

359 Walters, Joseph M., and Howard Gardner. "The Development and Education of Intelligences." Chapter 1 in *Essays on the Intellect*, edited by Frances R. Link, 1-21. Alexandria, VA: Association for Supervision and Curriculum Development, 1985. [10 Refs.]

Walters and Gardner sketch the characteristics and criteria of intelligence. They argue that cognitive competence is better described as multiple intelligences consisting of a set or sets of problem solving abilities, talents, or mental skills rather than the traditional view which defines intelligence as logical or logical-linguistic capabilities. The authors believe each problem solving skill has a biological origin that is coupled with the cultural nurturing of that origin. They identify seven intelligences: musical, bodily-kinesthetic, logical-mathematical, linguistic, spatial, interpersonal, and intrapersonal. Walters and

Gardner characterize the intelligences as independent (a person may be strong in one area of problem solving or intelligence while weak in all others) and discuss the theory's educational implications.

360 Walters, Kerry S. "Critical Thinking and the Danger of Intellectual Conformity." *Innovative Higher Education* 11, no. 2 (Spring-Summer 1987): 94-102. [3 Refs.]

Walters argues that higher education overemphasizes critical thinking strategies as reductionistic analysis. Walters warns this overemphasis may result in methodological, psychological, and practical conformity to the reductionist approach. Such a development may foster an intolerance of alternative methods and conceptual models, which is the reverse of the goals of critical thinking. Walters calls for a more balanced curriculum in which students are exposed to non-reductionistic and open-ended strategies and that methodologies should be created.

361 Walters, Kerry S. "Critical Thinking in Liberal Education: A Case of Overkill?" *Liberal Education* 72, no. 3 (Fall 1986): 233-244. [15 Refs.]

Although an advocate for critical thinking in liberal arts curricula, Walters warns of overemphasizing a systematic program of critical thinking focusing on reductionist analysis as the best method for solving problems. Walters worries that an over-emphasis of critical thinking encourages students to (1) assume that it is the only approach to understanding claims about reality and expressions that do not conform to the method do not warrant serious consideration, (2) make unwarranted assumptions about reality and knowledge, and (3) become passive in thinking and intolerant toward other alternative models. Walters proposes balancing the curriculum with strategies that employ creative thinking and alternative approaches such as free-writing or journal writing, elective hands-on art classes, alternative methodologies to understanding reality, and stronger emphasis by instructors on the limitations of critical thinking techniques.

362 Wasserman, Selma. "Teaching for Thinking: Louis E. Raths Revisited." *Phi Delta Kappan* 68, no. 6 (Fall 1987): 460-466. [21 Refs.]

Wasserman reviews Louis Raths' theory of thinking as a basis for teaching thinking. Raths' theory associates certain behaviors with deficient thinking, stemming from inadequate opportunities to develop higher order mental functions. He theorized that such behaviors would diminish with extensive practice in thinking. Wasserman outlines the eight behavior patterns and the fourteen thinking operations identified by Raths and offers suggestions for assessing student behavior, teaching activities, and interactions that promote thinking.

363 Watkins, Peter. "Forecasting the Technological Future: Directions for Education." *Unicorn* 12, no. 2 (May 1986): 81-86. [25 Refs.]

Watkins argues that it is wrong to assume recent, rapid technological developments necessitate greater need for mathematical, scientific, and technical skills. He cites studies in Australia and the United States that show that the majority of high school and college graduates will work in low technology jobs that do not require high technical skills. Watkins urges educators to focus on teaching critical thinking skills that will enable students to examine and deal with the practices and repercussions of technology implementation.

364 Weddle, Perry. "Fact from Opinion." *Informal Logic* 7, no. 1 (Winter 1985): 19-26. [2 Refs.]

Weddle discusses ways "fact" has been distinguished from "opinion". He asserts that several distinctions break down under analysis. The failure of the distinctions presents problems for education programs having the separating of fact from opinion as one of the goals of critical thinking. Weddle proposes that the goal of distinguishing fact from opinion be shifted to evidence quality or assessing and producing support for contentions.

365 Weinstein, Mark. "Towards a Research Agenda for Informal Logic and Critical Thinking." *Informal Logic* 12, no. 3 (Fall, 1990): 121-143. [64 Refs.]

Weinstein recommends that concern with informal logic and critical thinking be redirected from a general philosophical focus towards an emphasis on the epistemologies, approaches to argumentation, and activities of other disciplines. He presents a concept of critical thinking and informal logic that incorporates this redirection. Weinstein sketches the circumstances in which critical thinking and informal logic developed and outlines critical thinking's relation to a discipline's language of inquiry and argument. He asserts that the educational framework for critical thinking and informal logic should entail that informal logicians and critical thinkers: (1) be proponents of educational reform in undergraduate education and (2) develop collaborative approaches involving all academic disciplines in an ongoing dialogue in which all are equally valued contributors. Weinstein proposes several questions derived from this concept of critical thinking and redirection of concern as a research agenda for the future.

366 Williams, Joseph M. "Afterword: Two Ways of Thinking about Growth. The Problem of Finding the Right Metaphor." *Thinking, Reasoning, and Writing*, edited by Elaine P. Maimon, Barbara F. Nodine, and Finbarr W. O'Connor, 245-255. New York, NY: Longman, 1989.

Williams discusses alternative approaches to diagnosing a person's cognitive ability and teaching cognitive skills by sketching two metaphorical models of cognitive growth: a holistic developmental model and a social model. The first metaphor characterizes cognitive development as a graph, a progression from uncritical/lower order thinking to critical/higher order thinking. In this metaphor, intellectual growth seems inevitable and normal. The second metaphor characterizes cognitive growth as an outsider interacting with an interpretive community. The interaction of outsider (or novice) thinking and insider (or expert) thinking opens both the individual and community to different perspectives and inquiry into their own views. Socialization of the outsider comes from thoughtful deliberation between the individual and the community. Williams believes the social metaphor encourages thinking and finds its conception of educational progress or cognitive development to be more engaging and more productive than the graph-like growth in the holistic model.

367 Wilson, Marilyn. "Critical Thinking: Repackaging or Revolution?" *Language Arts* 65, no. 6 (October 1988): 543-551. [6 Refs.]

Wilson expresses skepticism about whether many teachers claiming or attempting to teach critical thinking skills have considered the numerous issues inherent in selecting materials and methods for developing critical thinking in students. These issues concern the definition, teachability, and transferability of critical thinking skills, the social and political implications of students groomed as critical thinkers, and the implications for assessment of achievement or competency. Wilson asserts that teaching critical thinking demands a reorientation by teachers toward students, subjects, their roles, the nature of learning, and the purpose and methods of assessment of student achievement. She contends that collaborative learning best reflects the concepts in critical literacy and that standardized measures for student achievement and teacher accountability contradict such concepts.

368 Winne, Philip H. "Intelligence and Thinking Skills." *Interchange* 20, no. 3 (Fall 1989): 39-52. [27 Refs.]

Reply to McPeck, Martin, Sanders, Slemon {287}

Reply: McPeck, Martin, Sanders, Slemon {288}

Winne reviews the work of Herrnstein and colleagues and responds to the empirical and conceptual issues related to intelligence and thinking skills raised by McPeck, Martin, Sanders, and Slemon.

369 Wolman, Rebekah. "Technology and the Basic Skills Crisis." *Information Center* 6, no. 1 (January 1990): 16-24.

Wolman argues that computer technology has not only eliminated the need for previously required human skills, it has increased the demand for higher order thinking at all employee levels. Wolman reports that research indicates that only 16% of the work force currently possess the degree of literacy that will be required by 59% of the work force in the year 2000. Positions previously requiring low skill levels and in which thinking was discouraged, now require reading, thinking, problem solving, teamwork, judgment, self-regulation, and initiation. Literacy programs, including instruction in problem solving, decision making, and computer skills, are evolving in the workplace, while others are being formed through state and federal government initiatives.

370 Worsham, Toni. "From Cultural Literacy to Cultural Thoughtfulness." *Educational Leadership* 46, no. 1 (September 1988): 20-21. [6 Refs.]

This paper consists of responses to recommendations on cultural literacy related to the issues of content and process instruction, teacher education, and student assessment made by Ravitch, Finn, Hirsch, and Cheney. While the recommendations focus on factual knowledge for achieving cultural literacy, the respondents believe that both knowledge and processes such as decision making and problem solving should be incorporated into teaching.

371 Yinger, Robert J. "Can We Really Teach Them to Think?" In *Fostering Critical Thinking*, edited by Robert E. Young, 11-31. New Directions for Teaching and Learning, no. 3. San Francisco, CA: Jossey-Bass, 1980. [66 Refs.]

Yinger explores the concept of critical thinking by looking at various definitions of it and at aspects of thought. He believes that it is an essential component of everyday thought and deliberation. Yinger discusses four major factors affecting critical thinking: (1) knowledge and experience, (2) relevant intellectual skills and strategies, (3) appropriate attitudinal dispositions, and (4) the thinking environment. To foster critical thinking in students, teachers must: (1) be aware of how knowledge and skills develop, (2) acknowledge the nature of the problems that students will most frequently encounter, (3) integrate procedural techniques with knowledge, skills, and attitudes needed to solve uncertain practical problems, and (4) integrate efforts to improve critical and evaluative aspects of thought with those for improving productive and creative aspects.

372 Yocum, Michael J. "Planning for Critical Teaching." *Michigan Social Studies Journal* 2, no. 1 (Fall 1987): 19-22. [7 Refs.]

Yocum examines reasons for the failure of many teachers to adequately teach critical thinking. He argues that teachers should become aware of the social, moral, and political context of their curriculum, and recognize the influence of their own conceptions of knowledge on their construction of classroom curriculum.

373 Young, Robert E. "Moral Development, Ego Autonomy, and Questions of Practicality in the Critical Theory of Schooling." *Educational Theory* 38, no. 4 (Fall 1988): 391-404. [32 Refs.]

Young reviews child/adult communication, open discourse, and cases regarding distorted communication with an emphasis on institutionally bound distortion. He examines views of Habermas, Miller, Dewey, and others regarding the capacity for children to participate in moral argumentation, the development of this capacity and recent behavioral research on teaching and learning styles, and how these views and empirical research relate to teaching and to critical development in children.

5

PROFESSIONAL DEVELOPMENT AND TEACHER TRAINING

374 Andrews, Sharon Vincz. "A Student's Insights: Window on the Reflective Classroom." *Contemporary Education* 61, no. 2 (Winter 1990): 58-64. [17 Refs.]

Andrews believes that the core of teacher education methods courses should be formed of active and reflective strategies for teaching and learning in the college classroom--strategies that require active participation, promote dialogue, reflection, inquiry, and critical thinking. She stresses the effectiveness of strategies such as journal writing, interviews, classroom dialogue, and reflective writing assignments in helping students uncover assumptions and fears about teaching and learning, as well as in providing feedback for the assessment of and the planning of teacher education methods courses. Andrews analyzes one education student's reflections revealed in journals and interviews, summarizing the instructional themes that emerge from such reflections.

375 Arnstine, Barbara. "Rational and Caring Teachers: How Dispositional Aims Shape Teacher Preparation." *Philosophy of Education 1990: Proceedings of the Forty-Sixth Annual Meeting of the Philosophy of Education Society*, edited by David P. Ericson, 2-21. Normal, IL: Philosophy of Education Society, 1991. [15 Refs.]

Arnstine examines the type of teacher education program needed to achieve the dispositional educational aims of rationality and caring. She discusses the nature and role played by dispositional aims and the implications that casting educational aims in dispositional language has on the means to achieve or cultivate them. While current teacher training programs advocate rationality and caring, the curriculum inhibits their development. These inhibitions are carried over into the new teacher's classroom. Prospective teachers should be encouraged to form cooperative communities of teachers for rational inquiry into teaching purposes and the obstacles to and means for achieving those purposes. These activities would then more likely be carried over into teachers' classrooms.

376 Baldwin, Dorothy. "The Thinking Strand in Social Studies." *Educational Leadership* 42, no. 1 (September 1984): 79-80.

Baldwin describes a model inservice program for training kindergarten through twelfth grade teachers to become guides or resources in teaching, not mere providers of information. The program involves helping teachers to analyze, design, and evaluate a learning experience while practicing their ability to think logically, critically, and imaginatively. Baldwin describes and illustrates the incorporation of the Thinking Strand, a thinking skills program, into a ninth grade social studies class.

377 Bellanca, James A. "A Call for Staff Development." Chapter 5 in *Developing Minds. Vol. 1: A Resource Book for Teaching Thinking*, rev. ed., edited by Arthur L. Costa, 20-26. Alexandria, VA: Association for Supervision and Curriculum Development, 1991. [1 Ref.]

A revision of Costa {505}, pp. 13-19.

Bellanca presents a dialogue on designing a thinking skills program based on systematic staff development.

378 Beyer, Landon E. "Critical Theory and the Art of Teaching." *Journal of Curriculum and Supervision* 1, no. 3 (Spring 1986): 221-232. [24 Refs.]

Beyer describes the tensions between implementing a teacher preparation program based on critical reflection and the current practices in schools. He briefly describes a preparation program which exemplifies the problems between classroom theory and the realities of curriculum, teaching, and professional ethos of schools that a teacher experiences in the workplace. Administrative and technically oriented repetitive tasks dominate schools. Teacher creativity tends to be sacrificed for more standardized, deskilled curricula. Beyer identifies seven paradoxes embedded in teacher preparation programs and schools. He contends that teaching needs to be recognized as an artistic, political, and human act in order to transform the social and political realities of schools.

379 Beyer, Landon E. "Field Experience, Ideology, and the Development of Critical Reflectivity." *Journal of Teacher Education* 35, no. 3 (May-June 1984): 36-41. [39 Refs.]

Beyer sees a paradox being created within teacher education programs by the increasing emphasis on field work and the growing commitment to provide prospective teachers with more than vocational training by encouraging them to critically examine educational issues, ideas, and practices. He outlines the Knox College Teacher Preparation Program which incorporates a historical and social perspective of education, critical analysis of experiences of classroom phenomena, and the development of alternative principles and practices.

380 Biermann, Melanie J., Susan L. Mintz, and Laura L. McCullough. "*Cogito, Ergo Sum*: Reflection in the University of Virginia's Five-Year Teacher Education Program." Florida Conference on Reflective Inquiry: Contexts and Assessments, Orlando, FL, October 20-22, 1988. ED 307 264. [9 Refs.]

The authors describe a teacher education program model which emphasizes independent decision making and critical reflection. Classroom scenarios demonstrate three levels of teaching: technical competence, instructional decision making, and critical reflection. These three levels are developed in the program which focuses on the image of a teacher as a decision-maker.

381 Blachowicz, Camille L. Z. "Showing Teachers How to Develop Students' Predictive Reading." *Reading Teacher* 36, no. 7 (March 1983): 680-684. [11 Refs.]

Blachowicz describes a teacher training workshop on using the Directed Reading Thinking Activity (DRTA) to model a technique for developing student predictive strategies.

382 Bland, Carol, and Irene Koppel. "Writing as a Thinking Tool." *Educational Leadership* 45, no. 7 (April 1988): 58-60. [5 Refs.]

Bland and Koppel describe a staff development program initiated by the Bernards High School (Bernardsville, NJ) faculty to help junior and senior high school teachers in all subject areas develop students' critical and creative thinking through writing. The program involved a manual and a series of eight training sessions during which faculty were trained in (a) strategies for improving thinking through writing, (b) implementing and refining the strategies through peer coaching and inservice workshops, and (c) conducting evaluation activities for determining the effectiveness of the strategies on improving student thinking.

383 Bretz, Mary Lee, and Margaret Persin. "The Application of Critical Theory to Literature at the Introductory Level: A Working Model for Teacher Preparation." *Modern Language Journal* 71, no. 2 (Summer 1987): 165-170. [42 Refs.]

To alleviate students' deficiencies in comprehending and analyzing literary texts, Bretz and Persin contend that high school and college teachers need to instruct students in the various approaches to deciphering a text. They believe that teachers must be trained in the diverse critical approaches to literature and in the methodology for incorporating those approaches into introductory level curricula in high school and college. The authors propose a model for teacher preparation based on a course they developed, "Approaches to Hispanic Literature," in which theories are studied, applied to texts, and used in teaching exercises. They discuss the resources and techniques used in the course.

384 Christensen, Patricia S. "The Nature of Feedback Student Teachers Receive in Post-Observation Conference with the University Supervisor: A Comparison with O'Neal's Study of Cooperating Teacher Feedback." *Teaching & Teacher Education* 4, no. 3 (Summer 1988): 275-286. [3 Refs.]

In this 1985 study of the nature of the feedback received by University of Maryland student teachers from their university supervisors, Christensen found that the major evaluative feedback provided by supervisors involved helping student teachers to think critically about their interactions with students and to develop a way of thinking about teaching as a problem solving process. This differs from the findings of a similar study by O'Neal in 1983 of feedback from cooperating teachers to student teachers which emphasized the technical approach rather than the decision making approach to teaching.

385 Collison, Judith. "A Program for Teacher Education in Reasoning Skills." Chapter 44 in *Argumentation: Analysis and Practices. Proceedings of the Conference on Argumentation 1986,* edited by Frans H. van Eemeren, Rob Grootendorst, J. Anthony Blair, and Charles A. Willard, 404-409. Dordrecht, The Netherlands: Foris Publications, 1987. [4 Refs]

Even though most educators and administrators endorse the teaching of critical thinking, Collison contends that few programs in reasoning skills have been developed for teacher education. The typical form of teacher education programs has been after-school workshops provided by school systems. The emphasis and content of the programs range from formal logic, informal logic, and problem solving to developing a critical attitude. Collison discusses criticisms and successes of each approach. She identifies three goals of a teacher education program: (1) fostering clarity, insight and independence of thought; (2) encouraging the application of critical thinking skills; and (3) creating a model for teaching and learning critical thinking skills. Collison describes a high school teacher workshop program she conducted which included (a) an overview of cognitive theories and their educational implications, (b) a study of reasoning methods and analysis, (c) an examination of disciplines in relation to different reasoning methods, and (d) suggestions for reorganizing course materials to incorporate the teaching of reasoning skills.

386 Daniel, James O. "The Knowledge Base for Library Automation Personnel." *International Library Review* 21, no. 1 (January 1989): 73-82. [15 Refs.]

Asserting that the socioeconomic level of a nation is related to its capacity to mobilize and utilize information, Daniel discusses what is needed for library automation education in relation to the needs of Nigeria and other third world countries. Emphasis is on enhancing librarians' skills in critical judgment, decision making (especially under uncertainties), and human relations while imparting knowledge about technology and terminology.

387 Downs, Judy R. "What Critical Thinking Can Do for You as a Counselor." *TACD Journal* 16, no. 1 (Spring 1988): 41-48. [10 Refs.]

Downs discusses ways that critical thinking can be used in counseling. She compares the methodologies of critical thinking and counseling and suggests ways counselors can develop and use their thinking and problem solving skills with clients. Downs identifies possible consequences of employing critical thinking in counseling. She provides questions counselors can use when evaluating counseling programs that have implemented the use of critical thinking skills and includes a number of figures and charts for evaluating a counselor's personal philosophy of counseling and incorporating critical thinking into a counseling program.

388 Ford, Nigel. "Intellectual Development and the Organization of Knowledge." *Journal of Education for Librarianship* 24, no. 3 (Winter 1984): 157-173. [18 Refs.]

Ford argues that the study of the organization of knowledge within the context of specific subject knowledge taught in library and information science education contributes to the development of intellectual skills. Critical thinking should be explicitly emphasized given the increased need for generalizable problem solving and critical thinking skills for employment and the rapidity with which specific knowledge becomes outdated.

389 Goodman, Jesse. "The Political Tactics and Teaching Strategies of Reflective, Active Preservice Teachers." *Elementary School Journal* 89, no. 1 (September 1988): 23-41. [37 Refs.]

Goodman discusses the findings of a case study on the professional socialization of ten reflective, active elementary preservice teachers during student teaching. The findings showed student teachers believed that teachers (a) should be active decision makers, (b) wanted to promote self-discipline among children, (c) believed knowledge to be open to questioning, (9) that subjects should be integrated, and (10) that learning activities should promote critical thinking, creativity, and a desire to learn.

Interviews and observations were used to determine how student teachers interpreted the social world of their schools and classrooms and how these interpretations were used as the basis for their actions. Interviews were also conducted with the cooperating teachers, principals, and appropriate university personnel. Results indicated that the student teachers employed five political tactics (overt compliance, critical compliance, accommodative resistance, resistant alteration, and transformative action) in reconciling their beliefs with school systems' expectations and developed and implemented instructional strategies related to these tactics. The author addresses issues and implications for teacher training education related to reflective, active teaching.

390 Goodman, Jesse. "Teaching Preservice Teachers a Critical Approach to Curriculum Design: A Descriptive Approach." *Curriculum Inquiry* 16, no. 2 (Summer 1986): 179-201. [86 Refs.]

Goodman describes a critical approach to curriculum design taught to preservice elementary/middle school teachers. The author also describes a social studies curriculum methods course in which the approach is taught. The approach and course promote three goals: (1) empowering future teachers as creators of curriculum; (2) strengthening the link between progressive, critical viewpoints of education and curriculum practice; and (3) encouraging reflective analysis as an integral aspect of teaching and learning. Theory and practice are interrelated as preservice teachers are exposed to critical viewpoints on numerous educational topics (e.g., definition of knowledge, type of content studied, quality of learning experiences, nature of instruction, criteria for evaluation, and the role of the teacher) while learning to develop and implement a unit of study.

391 Huston, Mary M., and Willie Parson. "A Model of Librarianship for Combining Learning and Teaching." *Research Strategies* 3, no. 2 (Spring 1985): 75-80. [10 Refs.]

Huston and Parson contend that librarians must take part in intellectual inquiry and debate among a community of scholars in order to guide others effectively in question formulation, resources selection, and information evaluation. The authors discuss how their participation in such a community helped them better understand the inquiry process, the nature of disciplinary work, and the structure of disciplines. Huston and Parson re-evaluated librarianship and incorporated investigative problem solving, team teaching, faculty-student seminars, and small group work into a bibliographic instruction course emphasizing the development of students' ability to conduct independent research and problem solving skills.

392 King, Lean, and Rita King. "Tactics for Thinking in Action." *Educational Leadership* 45, no. 7 (April 1988): 42-44. [6 Refs.]

The authors describe the successful implementation of the Tactics for Thinking staff development program. The program focuses on integrating thinking into content areas, developing reasoning skills, and developing learning-to-learn skills.

393 Laff, Ned Scott, Howard K. Schein, and Deborah R. Allen. "Teaching, Advising, and Student Development: Finding the Common Ground." *NACADA Journal* 7, no. 1 (Spring 1987): 9-15. [5 Refs.]

The authors propose using developmental advising, which incorporates student development concerns and academic advising, as a means of helping students integrate their college experiences and teaching them to become self-directed learners. To alleviate the inadequacies in expertise felt by student affairs professionals and faculty academic advisers in the other's areas of expertise, the authors suggest using root concepts and critical thinking as frameworks for developmental advising. By employing the root concepts of relation, order, and structure, advisers help students see the interrelation of parts, to consider future possibilities, and gain insight into processes and outcomes. The authors believe critical thinking skills can be integrated into advising by consciously raising questions with students to help them clarify gaps in information, probe assumptions, draw inferences, and test conclusions.

394 Lambert, Linda. "Staff Development Redesigned." *Phi Delta Kappan* 69, no. 9 (May 1988): 665-668. [12 Refs.]

In order for the instructional ideas and innovations such as cooperative learning, critical thinking, mathematical problem solving, and global education to effectively occur in schools and in the minds and actions of students, Lambert argues that they must be incorporated first into the minds and actions of teachers. Staff development programs such as fieldwork, coaching, and formal programs organized outside of the school are ineffective because they overlook the value of teacher inquiry and expertise. Lambert advocates redesigning staff development into professional development where teachers develop not only as individuals, but also as professionals. She suggests ways to redefine teachers' roles and establish a professional culture offering a system of inquiry, multiple learning opportunities, and shared authority and decision making.

395 Lipman, Matthew. "Preparing Teachers to Teach for Thinking." *Philosophy Today* 31, no. 1 (Spring 1987): 90-96.

Lipman argues that the traditional approach to teacher education does not properly balance instructional methodology and knowledge of the discipline being taught. He notes that these deficiencies have been addressed in a program designed to train teachers to teach grade school philosophy. The program consists of seminars and workshops designed to teach teachers philosophy issues related to the curriculum, gain experience in the curriculum as students, model the curriculum in settings before other trainees, and participate in teacher evaluations.

396 MacDonald, Stephen C. "Critical Thinking 'Grokking the Fullness'." *College Teaching* 36, no. 3 (Summer 1988): 91-93. [2 Refs.]

In giving workshops on teaching critical thinking across the curriculum, MacDonald and his workshop co-director found college faculty unreceptive to presentations of William Perry's scheme of student intellectual and moral development until they tried a critical thinking approach. Faculty groups were asked to make inferences from samples of student papers about student attitudes toward learning and the nature of knowledge. Without having been exposed to Perry's scheme, the faculty groups developed schemes similar to Perry's. When they were then presented with Perry's scheme, the faculty acknowledged the framework for intellectual development of students and began confronting the phenomenon of human intellectual development within the context of a liberal arts education.

397 Mahler, Sophia, and Dan E. Benor. "Short and Long Term Effects of a Teacher-Training Workshop in Medical School." *Higher Education* 13, no. 3 (June 1984): 265-273. [17 Refs.]

The authors studied the effects of a four-day teacher training workshop designed to improve instructional behavior of medical school faculty by focusing on student-oriented instruction. Each of the 60 participants, representing clinical, basic, and behavioral sciences, was assigned to one of eight multidisciplinary groups. Each participant gave three fifteen-minute micro-presentations which were followed by group discussions. Participants could view videotapes of their presentations and discuss them on a one-to-one basis with a tutor. After the workshop, the researchers observed 161 lessons of each teacher over 500 days. Results indicated that (a) the workshop participants tended to stimulate and encourage higher cognitive levels of student verbal activities more after the training and (b) the training effect was sustained over a long period of time, suggesting that a new instructional pattern had been established.

398 Martin, David S. "Preparing Teachers to Teach Thinking." Chapter 9 in *Developing Minds. Vol. 1: A Resource Book for Teaching Thinking*, rev. ed., edited by Arthur L. Costa, 39-42. Alexandria, VA: Association for Supervision and Curriculum Development, 1991. [13 Refs.]

Originally published as "Preparing Thinking Teachers," *Teaching Thinking and Problem Solving Newsletter* 11, no. 3 (May-June 1989).

Martin stresses the importance of preparing teachers not only to teach for thinking, but also to teach thinking as an overt part of the curriculum and to teach students to focus on their own mental processes. The teaching of thinking and teaching about thinking should be a part of the teacher education curriculum, infused into both the course work and the practicum. Martin provides descriptions of models of such teacher education programs. He also gives a brief history of the actions of the Association Collaborative for Teaching Thinking (ACTT) and the National Council on the Accreditation of Teacher Education (NCATE) regarding teacher education standards. Martin offers six techniques that teacher education faculty might incorporate within their courses to foster the teaching of thinking and concludes with ten research questions about the relationship between teacher education and thinking skills that need to be investigated.

399 Michalak, Stanley J., Jr. "Enhancing Critical-Thinking Skills in Traditional Liberal Arts Courses: Report on a Faculty Workshop." *Liberal Education* 72, no. 3 (Fall 1986): 253-262. [4 Refs.]

To encourage "thinking across the curriculum" by helping college faculty integrate critical thinking within their disciplinary courses, Michalak conducted an extended workshop with faculty members from the Central Pennsylvania Consortium Colleges which he describes in this article. After discussing and reading on issues related to college teaching and critical thinking, participants analyzed and revised selected courses. The participants discussed the revisions and implemented them in the next academic year. At the end of the year, the participants discussed their experiences with the revised courses. The workshop resulted in more interactive teaching styles, greater explicitness in thinking about course goals and teaching techniques, and greater collegiality among faculty in various disciplines. Michalak offers suggestions to others at liberal arts colleges who wish to move into the practice of teaching thinking skills effectively.

400 Negin, Gary A. *A Primer in Inferential Reasoning for Teachers*. Dubuque, IA: Kendall/Hall, 1987. 110 pp.

Written to familiarize teachers with the characteristics of inferences, Negin describes the main features of generalizing, hypothesizing, and evaluating. In each of the three chapters, he focuses on one of the characteristics and posits suggestions on how to teach the characteristic. Each chapter concludes with exercises designed to improve the reader's use of inference by practicing the three characteristics.

401 Niles, Nancy, and Trudi E. Jacobson. "'Teaching Critical Thinking in Libraries': A Continuing Education Course." *Research Strategies* 9, no. 4 (Fall 1991): 198-201.

Niles and Jacobson describe a two-day course they developed for librarians on critical thinking, covering its theoretical background and application in libraries. They provide a course outline in an appendix to the article.

402 O'Hanlon, Nancyanne. "Library Skills, Critical Thinking, and the Teacher-Training Curriculum." *College & Research Libraries* 48, no. 1 (January 1987): 17-26. [4 Refs.]

O'Hanlon conducted a study of faculty in elementary education teacher training programs in Ohio to determine their views on library instruction. Results of the study showed that teacher education faculty support the teaching of the library research process in the education curriculum and believe that it would enhance the ability of future teachers to foster the development of research skills in their elementary school students. The results suggested that faculty did not view the development of library research skills as necessarily related to the development of critical thinking skills.

403 O'Hanlon, Nancyanne. "The Role of Library Research Instruction in Developing Teachers' Problem Solving Skills." *Journal of Teacher Education* 39, no. 6 (November-December 1988): 44-49. [34 Refs.]

O'Hanlon argues that library research skills instruction aids in developing critical thinking and problem solving skills. She reviews current methods for teaching thinking skills and asserts that those methods are not being included in curricula for training teachers. Thus, teachers often lack good research and critical thinking skills which impedes the development of such skills in students. She discusses the guided design model for incorporating reasoning and problem solving into the curriculum and reviews the benefits of including library research skills instruction into the training of teachers.

404 Olson, Julie, and Marsha Besch. "Teachers Teaching Teachers: An Inservice Model for Staff Development and School Improvement." *Journal of Staff Development* 4, no. 1 (May 1983): 101-108.

The authors relate the readiness, implementation, and internalization stages of a year-long staff development program on developing critical thinking skills. The program, based on teachers teaching peers, used inservice sessions to raise teachers' awareness of Bloom's six levels of thinking skills and to enable them to apply those skills in their classrooms. After attending the workshops, reinforcement of the concepts learned and continued encouragement to apply them was attempted through newsletters, memos, and teacher-development projects. Several questionnaires were distributed to participants throughout the initial year of the program in order to access the program's effectiveness. Responses to the program were generally positive.

405 Onosko, Joseph, and Robert B. Stevenson. "Effective Staff Development Practices for Higher-Order Thinking." Chapter 6 in *Developing Minds. Vol. 1: A Resource Book for Teaching Thinking*, rev. ed., edited by Arthur L. Costa, 27-30. Alexandria, VA: Association for Supervision and Curriculum Development, 1991. [6 Refs.]

Onosko and Stevenson outline five strategies determined as effective ways for helping secondary school teachers promote higher order thinking. These were gathered from written questionnaires and telephone interviews given to staff development personnel with extensive experience in the area. The authors provide descriptions of two exemplary staff development programs.

406 Parson, Willie L. "User Perspective on a New Paradigm for Librarianship." *College & Research Libraries* 45, no. 5 (September 1984): 370-373. [4 Refs.]

Parson advocates a paradigm for librarianship that includes proactive programs and an emphasis on critical thinking in bibliographic instruction programs. This paradigm requires a change from the identification of the library as an agency or institution to an identification with library users and their needs.

407 Paul, Richard W. "Staff Development for Critical Thinking: Lesson Plan Remodelling as the Strategy." Chapter 23 in *Developing Minds. Vol. 1: A Resource Book for Teaching Thinking*, rev. ed., edited by Arthur L. Costa, 124-130. Alexandria, VA: Association for Supervision and Curriculum Development, 1991. [7 Refs.]

Adapted from "Staff Development for Critical Thinking: Lesson Plan Remodelling as the Strategy," *Journal of Staff Development* 8, no. 3 (Fall 1987): 40-46.

Paul proposes lesson plan remodeling as a strategy for staff development in critical thinking. Through critiquing lesson plans using certain strategies and principles and formulating a new lesson plan, teachers will progressively develop their own critical thinking skills, reshape the curriculum, and develop their teaching skills. Paul suggests one approach to lesson plan remodeling and five basic goals for incorporating critical thinking into inservice design. He also provides examples of remodeling lesson plans and a taxonomy of critical thinking strategies.

408 Peterson, Donovan, Jeffrey Kromrey, Jean Borg, and Arthur Lewis. "Defining and Establishing Relationships Between Essential and Higher Order Teaching Skills." *Journal of Educational Research* 84, no. 1 (September-October 1990): 5-12. [43 Refs.]

The authors present the results and analysis of an exploratory investigation of a correlation (1) between essential and higher order thinking teacher performance and (2) between training in the teaching of higher order thinking skills and increased classroom performance in teaching higher order thinking. The Florida Performance Measurement System (FPMS) was used to measure teacher performance related to achievement and conduct (essential teaching skills) and a Teaching for Higher Order Thinking (THOT) instrument was used to measure teacher performance related to student acquisition of reasoning, problem solving, and critical thinking skills. A THOT training program was developed and administered to four teachers in eleven sessions over a twelve week period. Results indicated that (1) training for teaching higher order thinking improves higher order teaching performance, (2) scores on the essential teaching skills remained fairly stable between pretraining and posttraining, and (3) training in higher order thinking increased teacher performance, but did not affect essential teaching skills performance, suggesting that the teacher performances are independent of each other. The authors suggest implications for teacher training and teacher evaluation. They also emphasize the need for further study.

409 Smyth, John. "A 'Critical' Perspective for Clinical Supervision." *Journal of Curriculum and Supervision* 3, no. 2 (Winter 1988): 136-156. [50 Refs.]

Smyth contends that present day uses of clinical supervision impede teacher development and teaching reform by focusing on the evaluation and fine-tuning of teaching techniques rather than results. He advocates a reconstruing of clinical supervision, emphasizing the ends or effects of teaching, and having the supervision subjected to critical evaluation. Teachers would be encouraged to form collegial alliances to collaborate or discuss concerns about the historical and social contexts of teaching and how teaching has been shaped and constrained by these contexts. Teaching contexts would be critically evaluated, enabling teachers to observe where reforms in the structure of education and curriculum are needed. Smyth outlines stages in which teachers regain control over their professional lives under the recommended reconceptualizing of clinical supervision. He cites several theorists of clinical supervision recommending the conception of clinical supervision outlined by Goldhammer.

410 Stewart, William J. *How to Teach Decision-Making Skills to Elementary and Secondary Students*. Springfield, IL: Charles C. Thomas, 1988. 149 pp. [38 Refs.]

Considered suitable as a text for undergraduate and graduate education courses and as a reference source for inservice professionals, this work focuses on the importance of active student involvement in the classroom and of teachers in curriculum development. Half of the work focuses on specific aspects of the student-teacher decision making concept, including purposes, principles, design, and procedures. The other half addresses microcomputer applications to the decision making process, the individuality of students, curriculum decision making, and the development of teacher education preservice and inservice programs which focus on the decision making process. Each chapter is followed by references. A list of selected readings appears at the end of the work.

411 Stout, Candace Jesse. "Teachers' Views of the Emphasis on Reflective Teaching Skills During Their Student Teaching." *Elementary School Journal* 89, no. 4 (March 1989): 511-527. [45 Refs.]

Stout describes her study of the extent to which reflective teaching behaviors were taught and promoted by the college faculty and cooperating teachers during the student teaching experience of 98 elementary school practicing teachers. The subjects responded to a questionnaire composed of four clusters of questions which focused on the concepts of retrospective and predictive thought, critical inquiry, problem solving skills, and acceptance and use of feedback. Results indicated that as student teachers, the respondents were: (1) generally encouraged to reflect on their teaching practices and their effects on students; (2) moderately encouraged in areas such as (a) inquiry into curriculum, methods, and values, (b) generation of ideas, and (c) strategies for problem solving; and (3) only slightly encouraged in inquiry into ethical and political principles, application of research, and solicitation of student feedback. Tables with the results of the statistical analysis of the responses to the questionnaire and a copy of the questionnaire are provided.

412 Tabor, Marilyn. "Better Student Thinking through Changing Teacher Behaviors." *Educational Leadership* 45, no. 7 (April 1988): 49. [4 Refs.]

Tabor describes the implementation of and results of the Irvine (CA) Thinking Project. This project focused upon professional development in and application of questioning and responding strategies effective in promoting critical and creative thinking in the classrooms.

413 Wilcox, Ray T. "Teaching Thinking While Exploring Educational Controversies." *Clearing House* 62, no. 4 (December 1988): 161-164. [11 Refs.]

Drawing upon the literature of critical thinking, Wilcox designed a teacher education program course focusing on educational controversies. From this experience, he offers seven recommendations to other educators interested in incorporating critical thinking in their courses. Recommendations include making minimal use of the lecture method of teaching, incorporating thinking skills in the teaching of subjects, requiring interaction in the classroom, modifying traditional grading practice, sharing ideas and opinions, and allowing time for interactive methods.

414 Williams, Marion. "A Developmental View of Classroom Observations." *ELT Journal* 43, no. 2 (April 1989): 85-91.

Believing that teacher training classroom observations are usually one-sided evaluations containing little input from the trainee, Williams presents an approach in which the development of trainees' own critical judgments about their teaching methods is emphasized. The approach uses a series of self-evaluation forms to be responded to by the trainee and then discussed with the observer. The forms require the trainee to analyze teaching strategies, the meaningfulness of classroom assignments, classroom discussions, and the trainees' questioning and response techniques.

415 Yeazell, Mary I. "What Happens to Teachers Who Teach Philosophy to Children?" *Thinking* 2, no. 3-4 (1981): 86-88. [6 Refs.]

The author examines the teacher training program of Matthew Lipman's Philosophy for Children program. She focuses on a study designed to measure the effect the program has on teachers' critical thinking skills and self-actualization. The results indicated no significant difference in critical thinking skills, but a significant increase in self-actualizing values. Yeazell speculates that participants in the program would have a positive effect on the self-confidence and self-actualization of students.

6

TESTING AND EVALUATION

416 Anderson, Robert L. "California: The State of Assessment." Chapter 55 in *Developing Minds. Vol. 1: A Resource Book for Teaching Thinking*, rev. ed., edited by Arthur L.Costa, 314-325. Alexandria, VA Association for Supervision and Curriculum, 1991. [16 Refs.]

Anderson describes movements towards the improvement of assessments by the California State Department of Education through the California Assessment Program (CAP). Emphasis is on assessment of the integration of knowledge and skill and on the capacity for productive, independent thinking. Anderson describes the development of new forms of assessment in English-language arts, science, mathematics, and history-social science.

417 Annis, David B., and Linda F. Annis. "McPeck on Critical Thinking: A Reply." *Informal Logic* 6 (December 1984): 42-44. [5 Refs.]

Reply to McPeck {443}

The authors argue that McPeck misrepresents researchers in his criticisms of their views on the abilities, definitions, tests, and empirical research of critical thinking and that much of the major research on critical thinking is consistent with McPeck's own conception of critical thinking, rather than the views he criticizes.

418 Arter, Judith A., and Jennifer R. Salmon. *Assessing Higher Order Thinking Skills: A Consumer's Guide*. Portland, OR: Northwest Regional Educational Laboratory, Evaluation and Assessment, 1987. 88 pp.

This source provides background information on the definition and assessment of higher order thinking skills (HOTS), guidelines for choosing appropriate instruments for measuring these skills, and information on specific assessment instruments. Appendix A includes reviews of these instruments categorized by (1) critical thinking, problem solving or decision making tests; (2) developmental tests; (3) creativity tests; (4) achievement tests; (5) ability tests; and (6) observation scales. These reviews include information such as authors' names, descriptions, reliability, validity, useability, availability, and evaluative or critical comments. The same categories used in Appendix A, except for observation scales, are used for a tabular display of information in Appendix B. A list of testing resources organized under (a) local, state, and federal departments of education; (b) colleges, universities, and professional organizations; and (c) books, articles, newsletters, and curriculum reviews is provided in Appendix C. Appendix D is a checklist for selecting higher order thinking skills tests.

419 Baron, Joan Boykoff. "Evaluating Thinking Skills in the Classroom." Chapter 11 in *Teaching Thinking Skills: Theory and Practice*, edited by Joan Boykoff Baron and Robert J. Sternberg, 221-247. New York, NY: W. H. Freeman, 1987. [50 Refs.]

Baron addresses the range of purposes served by evaluations of thinking skills and dispositions. She lists characteristics of effective evaluations and identifies four general dimensions of evaluation types: formative/ summative; product/process; qualitative/quantitative; and experimental/quasi-experimental designs. Evaluations in the classroom should be performed both in the context of the class and of the individual. Baron describes various evaluation approaches and discusses criteria for (a) selecting appropriate evaluation design, (b) judging the reliability and validity of tests, and (c) using standardized norm-referenced achievement tests. She includes a list of general and aspect-specific critical thinking tests compiled by Robert Ennis.

420 Baron, Joan Boykoff, and Bena Kallick. "What Are We Looking For and How Can We Find It?" Chapter 53 in *Developing Minds: A Resource Book For Teaching Thinking*, edited by Arthur L. Costa, 281-287. Alexandria, VA: Association for Supervision and Curriculum Development, 1985. [3 Refs.]

Baron and Kallick provide recommendations for and insights into assessing higher order thinking. They analyze results from the Connecticut Assessment of Educational Progress (CAEP) and discuss other methods for measuring classroom efforts at teaching critical thinking, such as observations, student journals, tape recordings of classroom discussions, and interviews. The authors address briefly the difficulty in establishing criteria for evaluating thinking.

421 Beyer, Barry K. "A Suggested Format for Testing Thinking Skills." *Social Science Record* 24, no. 1 (Spring 1987): 3-5. [6 Refs.]

Beyer contends that tests which reflect thinking skills being taught in the classroom can provide useful information to the teacher for improving instruction and can enhance student motivation in learning skills being tested. He provides step-by-step instructions for constructing a six-item test format useful for testing a single thinking skill and offers suggestions for adapting it for testing various levels of proficiency and multiple thinking skills. He provides sample questions from social studies.

422 Branson, Margaret Stimmann. "Critical Thinking Skills--A Continuum for Grades 3-12 in History/Social Science." *Social Studies Review* 25, no. 2 (Winter 1986): 24-32.

Along with a brief discussion on the Continuum of Critical Thinking Skills in History/Social Science of the California Assessment Program for third through twelfth graders, Branson presents a list of the skills included in the continuum and proposed for statewide assessment. Sample assessment items for grades eight and twelve from the three major clusters of critical thinking skills (Defining and Clarifying the Problem, Judging and Utilizing Information, and Drawing Conclusions) are provided for comparison. Branson addresses the importance of teaching critical thinking and how educators can improve it in students.

423 Brown, Rexford. "Testing and Thoughtfulness." *Educational Leadership* 46, no. 7 (April 1989): 31-33.

The Education Commission of the States investigated the effect of state and local education policies on promoting or inhibiting a higher level of literacy for a broader range of students. The commission conducted case studies of the policies. interviews of administrators, and observations of classrooms for the "Policy and Higher Literacies Project." The investigation revealed (1) that educational success or progress was determined by results on commercial standardized norm-referenced test, (2) a passivity regarding testing of higher order thinking skills, (3) a lackadaisical use of results, and (3) a dependency resulting in curricula and teaching shaped by commercial tests. Brown proposes a new concept of testing that calls for a demonstration of the higher literacies (e.g., critical and creative thinking and problem solving). An article inset provides an outline of testing possibilities.

424 Callahan, Carolyn M., and Mary L. Corvo. "Validating the Ross Test for Identification and Evaluation of Critical Thinking Skills in Programs for the Gifted." *Journal for the Education of the Gifted* 4, no. 1 (Fall 1980): 17-25. [5 Refs.]

The authors describe their study of the structural validity of the Ross Test of Higher Cognitive Processes (1976). Designed to assess the higher level thinking skills of analysis, synthesis, and evaluation as outlined in Bloom's taxonomy, the test is a standardized measure of critical thinking ability of elementary school children. The study involved 154 third through sixth grade gifted students participating in a program in which the development of critical thinking was a primary goal. After various analyses, the authors gathered empirical evidence for the structural validity of the test, found that the test discriminated between gifted and non-gifted students, and determined that it was not an intelligence test. These results support the use of the Ross Test for identifying the academically or intellectually talented and for evaluating elementary gifted and non-gifted programs.

425 Carpenter, C. Blaine, and James C. Doig. "Assessing Critical Thinking across the Curriculum." In *Assessing Students' Learning*, edited by James H. McMillan, 33-46. New Directions for Teaching and Learning, no. 34. San Francisco, CA: Jossey-Bass, 1988. [20 Refs.]

Carpenter and Blaine review techniques and instruments for measuring critical thinking in the classroom and on the institutional level. They emphasize the importance of defining the concept of critical thinking and the processes, skills, and strategies to be assessed before selecting or developing an assessment approach. They also describe five standardized instruments (Cornell Critical Thinking Test--Level 2, New Jersey Test of Reasoning Skills, Watson-Glaser Critical Thinking Appraisal, Ennis-Weir Critical Thinking Essay Test, and Academic Profile) and examples of locally developed performance-based measures at five higher education institutions.

426 Costa, Arthur L. "Thinking: How Do We Know Students Are Getting Better At It?" Chapter 56 in *Developing Minds. Vol. 1: A Resource Book for Teaching Thinking*, rev. ed., edited by Arthur L. Costa, 326-333. Alexandria, VA: Association for Supervision and Curriculum Development, 1991. [4 Refs.]

Costa offers three suggestions for teachers to collect information regarding the intellectual growth of their students. This chapter includes examples of checklists, a sample reporting form for parents, a sample letter for gathering information from parents, and an outline of suggestions to help teachers and parents foster thinking skills.

427 Ennis, Robert H. "Problems in Testing Informal Logic Critical Thinking Reasoning Ability." *Informal Logic* 6 (January 1984): 3-9. [13 Refs.]

Ennis addresses the problems of testing for critical thinking and offers possible resolutions. Using examples from five English language machine-gradeable multiple-choice tests (Watson-Glaser Critical Thinking Appraisal, Ross Test of Higher Cognitive Processes, New Jersey Test of Reasoning Skills, and the Cornell Critical Thinking Tests--Level X and Level Z), Ennis analyzes the tests for critical thinking content (value judgment, induction, and assumption identification) and for testing concerns (internal consistency and validity of data). He finds that philosophical questions related to the meaning of critical thinking and the concepts of value judgment, assumption, and induction underlie the tests.

428 Ennis, Robert H. "Testing Teachers' Competence, Including Their Critical Thinking Ability." In *Philosophy of Education 1987: Proceedings of the Forty-Third Annual Meeting of the Philosophy of Education Society*, edited by

Barbara Arnstine and Donald Arnstine, 413-420. Normal, IL: Philosophy of Education Society, 1988. [17 Refs.]

While expressing reservations about testing the competence of teachers, Ennis believes such testing to be inevitable and addresses the question of what kind of testing should be done. He lists several areas of teacher competency often overlooked in testing, such as reading comprehension, classroom organization and control, the ability to explain things clearly, and the ability to think critically. Ennis provides an outline of the four major categories of critical thinking that could be used as components in teacher-competence testing and uses sample multiple-choice questions from various critical thinking tests to demonstrate the problem of variation in background beliefs and of valid alternative assumptions deemed incorrect by test makers. Ennis suggests ways of creating better test questions.

429 Ennis, Robert H. "Tests That Could Be Called Critical Thinking Tests." *Developing Minds: A Resource Book for Teaching Thinking*, edited by Arthur L. Costa, 303-304. Alexandria, VA: Association for Supervision and Curriculum Development, 1985.

This is an annotated list of eleven tests that could be used to assess critical thinking.

430 Ennis, Robert H., and Stephen P. Norris. "Critical Thinking Assessment: Status, Issues, Needs." Chapter 1 in *Cognitive Assessment of Language and Math Outcomes*, edited by Sue Legg and James Algina, 1-42. Advances in Discourse Processes, vol. 36. Norwood, NJ: Ablex, 1990. [66 Refs.]

Ennis and Norris discuss distinctions between tests and evaluation procedures, aspect-specific and comprehensive assessment, machine-scoreability and scoreability only by a knowledgeable person, subject specific versus general-knowledge-based assessment, abilities and dispositions, critical thinking and reasoning, critical thinking and creative thinking. They provide an annotated list of existing critical thinking tests and discuss other issues related to testing and evaluating critical thinking including: the meaning of critical thinking, the validity of machine-scoreable testing, how to deal with differences in ideological and background beliefs between the test taker and test maker, how to test for critical thinking dispositions, and how to judge what a critical thinking test is actually testing. A chart outlining goals for a critical thinking/reasoning curriculum is included.

431 Facione, Peter A. "Testing College-Level Critical Thinking." *Liberal Education* 72, no. 3 (Fall 1986): 221-231. [8 Refs.]

Addressing the needs of educators in providing effective instruction in critical thinking to undergraduate college students, Facione focuses on the issues of defining and testing critical thinking. Warning against overly broad definitions of critical thinking, Facione offers the following operational definition, "the ability to properly construct and evaluate arguments" (p. 222). Skills associated with constructing, evaluating, and identifying arguments must be differentiated for teaching and must be discriminated among in the testing of critical thinking. Facione outlines the skills that must be taught and discusses the feasibility of testing students for these skills using machine-gradeable examinations.

432 Fontana, D., Gareth Lotwick, Allen Simon, and L. O. Ward. "A Factor Analysis of Critical, Convergent and Divergent Thinking Tests in a Group of Male Polytechnic Students." *Personality and Individual Differences* 4, no. 6 (1983): 687-688. [2 Refs.]

The authors investigated the feasibility of extracting common factors from several different thinking tests. The Watson-Glaser Critical Thinking Appraisal, AH5 Group Test of High Grade Intelligence, and Hudson's Uses of Objects and Meaning of Words Tests (concerned respectively with critical, convergent, and divergent thinking) were given to 71 male polytechnic students. Results showed low to moderately high coefficients of correlation between different test variables and indicated that three factors related to thinking processes could be extracted: (1) verbal-inferential-deductive-interpretative, (2) verbal-spatial reasoning, and (3) a judgment factor.

433 Frederiksen, Norman. "Measuring Skills in Problem Solving." Chapter 2 in *Cognitive Assessment of Language and Math Outcomes*, edited by Sue Legg and James

Algina, 43-91. Advances in Discourse Processes, vol. 36. Norwood, NJ: Ablex, 1990. [127 Refs.]

Frederiksen outlines an information-processing theory of cognition, discussing the roles of memory, automatic processing, pattern recognition, and problem solving processes. He focuses on the nature of ill-structured problems and the instruments and procedures for assessment of problem solving skills. Frederiksen discusses global measures of skill in solving problems, such as multiple-choice tests or essay tests, and suggests a procedure for constructing such tests. He also identifies methods for measuring information-processing skills such as pattern recognition, problem representation, knowledge structure, and skill in information retrieval. In the last sections of the chapter Frederiksen discusses ways both tests for global measures of skill and tests of information-processing skills can be incorporated into the instructional process, a procedure for construct validation of tests, cost considerations for testing, and testing areas that require more research.

434 Haroutunian, Sophie. "A Response to 'Testing for Critical Thinking'." *Philosophy of Education 1985: Proceedings of the Forty-First Annual Meeting of the Philosophy of Education Society*, edited by David Nyberg, 21-25. Normal, IL: Philosophy of Education Society, 1986.

Reply to Petrie {456}

Haroutunian identifies and discusses two difficulties in Petrie's position on how critical thinking should be tested. The first concerns distinguishing critical thinking activities from ordinary thinking and the second is determining whether teachers are better judges of critical thinking ability than objective testers. Haroutunian proposes identifying problems that students should solve and providing situations in which the students can learn and perform the problem solving activities. This approach would overcome the two difficulties Haroutunian identifies in Petrie's position and allow critical thinking to be tested under objective conditions and testers, rather than problematic classroom observations by teachers.

435 Hill, John C. "A Matrix for Curriculum Evaluation: The Author's Approach." *NASSP Bulletin* 73, no. 516 (April 1989): 84.

This is a question analysis matrix for the evaluation of a critical thinking and problem solving curriculum.

436 Kallick, Bena. "Evaluation: A Challenge to Our Critical Thinking." Chapter 57 in *Developing Minds. Vol. 1: A Resource Book for Teaching Thinking*, rev. ed., edited by Arthur L. Costa, 334-337. Alexandria, VA: Association for Supervision and Curriculum Development, 1991. [2 Refs.]

Kallick challenges teachers to apply critical thinking in examining evaluation systems. She suggests beginning with two questions such as: (1) Who are the audiences we are trying to inform from our evaluation? and (2) What are the best methodologies to collect data in order to inform them? Kallick stresses the need for more than one assessment strategy, explores strategies other than tests that might be used in the classroom, and discusses the implications for professional development.

437 Kneedler, Peter E. "Assessment of the Critical Thinking Skills in History-Social Science." *Social Studies Review* 27, no. 3 (Spring 1988): 2-32. [78 Refs.]

Kneedler addresses critical thinking skills (viewed as practical, teachable, and learnable skills essential to a successful democracy) in the context of (a) the California Assessment Program--a statewide assessment of the critical thinking ability of eighth grade students, (b) the knowledge explosion, and (c) re-ordering priorities in social studies. He provides a critical thinking skills process model, outlining fifteen skills essential to critical thinking and desired outcomes of the process. Kneedler outlines, defines, and illustrates the skills with items from the California Assessment Program from the following categories: (1) defining and clarifying problems, (2) judging information related to problems, and (3) solving problems and drawing conclusions. He stresses the importance of instruction in critical thinking at all grade levels and in all content areas and suggests resources and activities for teaching it. The article includes a 78-item bibliography of books, articles, and audiovisual aids related to critical thinking.

438 Kneedler, Peter E. "History-Social Science Assessment in California." *Social Science Record* 24, no. 1 (Spring 1987): 8-9.

Kneedler provides (a) brief descriptions of how the California Assessment Program's history-social science test assesses critical thinking skills, (b) an outline of the results of the test taken by eighth grade students, and (c) recommendations for improving instruction.

439 Kneedler, Peter. "Testing Critical Thinking at Grade Eight." *Social Studies Review* 25, no. 2 (Winter 1986): 78-82.

After stressing the importance of critical thinking, Kneedler provides an overview of the statewide critical thinking skills assessment for eighth graders in California. The assessment consists of objective questions, critical thinking vocabulary, and essay writing. It covers defining problems, judging information related to the problems, drawing conclusions, and solving problems. Kneedler provides an information process model.

440 Landis, Richard E., and William B. Michael. "The Factorial Validity of Three Measures of Critical Thinking within the Context of Guilford's Structure-of-Intellect Model for a Sample of Ninth Grade Students." *Educational and Psychological Measurement* 41, no. 4 (Winter 1981): 1147-1166. [23 Refs.]

Landis and Michael investigated the common factors identifiable among the intercorrelations of three critical thinking measures--the Curry Test of Critical Thinking, Watson-Glaser Critical Thinking Appraisal (Form YM), and the Cornell Critical Thinking Test (Level X)--with Guilford's structure-of-intellect theory of 24 possible critical thinking abilities. Scores from all the measures taken by 235 ninth grade students were calculated for intercorrelations and factor analyses. The abilities identified as associated with critical thinking were the cognition of semantic classes, relations, and systems; the evaluation of semantic units, classes, relations, and transformations; and the convergent production of semantic transformations.

441 Linn, Robert L. "Dimensions of Thinking: Implications for Testing." Chapter 6 in *Educational Values and Cognitive Instruction: Implications for Reform*, edited by Lorna Idol and Beau Fly Jones, 179-208. Hillsdale, NJ: Lawrence Erlbaum, 1991. [74 Refs.]

Linn discusses three concerns with current approaches to the teaching of higher order thinking skills: (1) an overemphasis on factual knowledge, (2) the constraints of standardized testing (i.e., problem structure and efficiency), and (3) tests as devices that direct instruction. He discusses alternative approaches to assessment and addresses improving teacher-directed assessment procedures, ongoing research in reading assessment for state assessment programs in Michigan and Illinois, the California statewide assessment of critical thinking skills in history-social science, constructed response formats, diagnostic testing, assessment of metacognition and specific cognitive strategies, dynamic assessment, and computer simulations.

442 Marzano, Robert J., and Arthur L. Costa. "Questions: Do Standardized Tests Measure General Cognitive Skills? Answer: No." *Educational Leadership* 45, no. 7 (May 1988): 66-71. [22 Refs.]

Marzano and Costa discuss an analysis of the Stanford Achievement Test batteries and the California Test of Basic Skills conducted to determine the general cognitive operations required in the tests and the relationship of these operations with student performance on the tests. Two major findings from the analysis were: (1) that test items included only nine of the 22 general cognitive operations identified by thinking skills theorists and (2) that general cognitive operations required to answer questions had little relevance to student achievement on the tests. Some implications of these findings are that current standardized tests primarily measure factual or declarative information and if students know the concepts, principles, and schemata contained in the items, they will do well on the tests. The authors suggest that standardized tests should be restructured to emphasize more complex process knowledge and teachers should rely on informal techniques of analyzing student thinking skills or cognitive operations important for the information age. The article includes a list of the 22 general cognitive processes used in the analysis.

443 McPeck, John E. "The Evaluation of Critical Thinking Programs: Dangers and Dogmas." *Informal Logic* 6, no. 2 (July 1984): 9-13. [12 Refs.]

A version printed in McPeck {7}, pp. 54-63, 126.
Reply: Annis {417}
See: Miller {446}

In defending his view of critical thinking against critics (e.g., Robert Ennis) looking for empirical substantiation, McPeck argues against the belief that the evaluation of critical thinking is an empirical question. His argument is based on the following factors: (1) that no one has yet established the existence of "critical thinking ability" or "general reasoning skill;" (2) there are different definitions of "critical thinking" which require different criteria of good performance; and (3) there are different views on what constitutes evidence for critical thinking. McPeck notes the fallacy of the Watson-Glaser Critical Thinking Appraisal of taking the description of an achievement as indicative of an ability. He cites a study by David and Linda Annis as an example of how there is an emphasis (1) on equating empiricism with tests and statistical measurement and (2) on the assumption that the sole purpose of education is to develop skills with instrumental value which are considered psychometrically test-measurable. Concerned with the de-emphasis on knowledge and understanding gained from traditional disciplines and the power of the liberal arts to liberate people from ignorance about everyday problems, McPeck advocates improving methods for teaching the traditional disciplines for developing critical thinkers.

444 McPeck, John E. "Reading, Testing and Critical Thinking." Chapter 6 in *Critical Thinking and Education*, 126-151. Issues and Ideas in Education. Oxford: Martin Robertson, 1981. [14 Refs.]

McPeck contends that the Watson-Glaser Critical Thinking Appraisal and Cornell Critical Thinking Tests incorporate a basic skills approach to critical thinking testing similar to reading/literacy tests. He believes that the Watson-Glaser Test confuses the distinction between a proposition (which may be true or false) and an inference (which can only be valid or invalid). While the test claims to be designed to test inferences, which require self-contained questions, the test questions are too often open-ended and ask for true or false answers. For many questions, additional background knowledge is needed and multiple answers may be valid, but are not allowed. In addition, the high correlation between test results for Watson-Glaser and general intelligence tests suggest that the tests are not measuring different things. The Cornell Critical Thinking tests incorporate Robert Ennis's concept of critical thinking as general skills and do not allow for subject context or multiple answers. McPeck outlines four conditions that any critical thinking test should meet: subject specificity, multiple answers, justification, and learned accomplishment. He finds that the tests employed in normal discipline /subject-related courses come closer to matching his requirements than any standardized test.

445 Michael, Joan J., Roberta L. Devaney, and William B. Michael. "The Factorial Validity of the Cornell Critical Thinking Test for a Junior High School Sample." *Educational and Psychological Measurement* 40, no. 2 (Summer 1980): 437-450. [20 Refs.]

The authors describe an investigation designed to obtain empirical evidence regarding the categorical validity of the Cornell Critical Thinking Test, Level X, and the test performance of students at different grade levels. A factorial solution of the intercorrelations among 71 items of the test showed five identifiable dimensions following a verimax rotation: (1) Relevance; (2) Irrelevance; (3) Differentiating Levels of Reliability of Observations or of Authorities; (4) Accuracy of Deduction; and (5) Determination of the Accuracy of an Assumption. Student test results showed a progressive increment of results from one grade level to the next higher one. The factorial results indicated that only the Accuracy of Deduction factor represented one well-defined construct. The other four factors were found to be ill-defined, and could not be readily interpreted. The researchers concluded that the Cornell Critical Thinking Test may be lacking in construct validity.

446 Miller, Richard B. "Toward an Empirical Definition of the Thinking Skills." *Informal Logic* 8, no. 3 (Fall 1986): 113-124. [5 Refs.]

See: McPeck {7} and {443}

Miller addresses McPeck's arguments regarding a general critical reasoning ability and McPeck's criticisms of tests that attempt to measure a small set of abilities. Miller pursues the questions raised by McPeck's criticisms and conducts a study of the internal consistency of the New Jersey Test of Reasoning Skills. He concludes that tests incorporating the differing assumptions on the nature of critical thinking could be used to resolve some of the conceptual disagreements, but must be designed to explicitly test existing reasoning skill taxonomies.

447 Modjeski, Richard B., and William B. Michael. "An Evaluation by a Panel of Psychologists of the Reliability and Validity of Two Tests of Critical Thinking." *Educational and Psychological Measurement* 43, no. 4 (Winter 1983): 1187-1197. [8 Refs.]

The authors describe an investigation into the validity, reliability and measurement error of the Cornell Critical Thinking Test, Level X, and the Watson-Glaser Critical Thinking Appraisal, Form YM. The investigation consisted of a panel of psychologists evaluating the two tests using the ten ESSENTIAL validity standards and the five ESSENTIAL reliability and measurement error standards from the *Standards for Educational and Psychological Tests* (Washington, DC: American Psychological Association, 1974). Both tests were evaluated as meeting the standards between "minimal" or "somewhat." Though the Watson-Glaser Critical Thinking Appraisal was evaluated as a superior instrument in terms of meeting the ESSENTIAL standards for validity and measurement, neither instrument was judged to have met all of the standards completely. The panel recommended that the authors of the tests enhance the reliability and validity of the tests.

448 Morante, Edward A., and Anita Ulesky. "Assessment of Reasoning Abilities." *Educational Leadership* 42, no. 1 (September 1984): 71-74. [5 Refs.]

Morante and Ulesky describe activities toward a statewide assessment of students' thinking skills in New Jersey. The New Jersey Board of Higher Education created a Basic Skills Assessment Program in 1977 to assess basic skills of all first year students entering public colleges in the state and to evaluate the colleges' remedial programs. A Basic Skills Council of higher education faculty created the New Jersey Basic Skills Placement Test to measure critical thinking skills. A Task Force on Thinking developed a taxonomy of thinking skills and analyzed the following measurements of thinking and reasoning: New Jersey Test of Reasoning Skills, Whimbey Analytical Skills Inventory, Cornell Critical Thinking Test (Level X), Cognitive Abilities Test (Form 3, Level 14), Watson-Glaser, and the Ross Test of Higher Cognitive Processes. The measurements were analyzed for clarity (a) in measuring a student's ability to reason and (b) of the aspects of thinking measured by each test. The article includes an outline of the tests in chart form, including author and source of each test and the number and kinds of items on each. More extensive research was done with the Cornell Critical Thinking Test, Whimbey Analytical Skills Inventory, and the New Jersey Test of Reasoning. The authors include the correlations of these tests and the New Jersey Basic Skills Placement Test.

449 Norris, Stephen P. "Controlling for Background Beliefs When Developing Multiple-Choice Critical-Thinking Tests." *Educational Measurement: Issues and Practice* 7, no. 3 (Fall 1988): 5-11. [27 Refs.]

Using sample items from the Watson-Glaser Critical Thinking Appraisal, Norris illustrates how differences in responses on standardized tests might be attributed to differences in background beliefs rather than performance in critical thinking. He states that the Test on Appraising Observations was designed to alleviate the dilemma by having samples of students think aloud about the items on trial versions of the test. Concerned about the validity and fairness in assessing critical thinking through standardized multiple-choice tests, Norris proposes the use of verbal reports of thinking on trial test versions, or other methodology that will account for the diversity of opinions and approaches to problems encouraged by critical thinking.

450 Norris, Stephen R. "Evaluating Critical Thinking Ability." *History and Social Science Teacher* 21, no. 3 (Spring 1986): 135-146. [30 Refs.]

Norris discusses practical and theoretical issues involved in designing and conducting an evaluation of critical thinking ability. He stresses the importance of an evaluation having a purpose and a specified concept of critical thinking. He discusses methods for collecting information, the advantages and disadvantages of five commercially available essay and objective tests, the advantages and disadvantages of naturalistic observation, and three useful categories for evaluation information (instructional, developmental, and decision making). Norris concludes with a listing of six areas to be aware of when conducting an evaluation.

451 Norris, Stephen P. "Informal Reasoning Assessment: Using Verbal Reports of Thinking to Improve Multiple-Choice Test Validity." Chapter 22 in *Informal Reasoning and Education*, edited by James F. Voss, David N. Perkins, and Judith W. Segal, 451-472. Hillsdale, NJ: Lawrence Erlbaum, 1991. [31 Refs.]

Arguing that multiple-choice tests of informal logic or critical thinking are problematic since they typically allow only one correct response, Norris uses examples from the Cornell Critical Thinking Tests and the Watson-Glaser Critical Thinking Appraisal to demonstrate how a sophisticated critical thinker may have valid reasons for choosing a response deemed wrong by the tests' keys. Eliciting verbal responses of reasoning from examinees on select test questions is a way to evaluate the reasoning used by an examinee. The validity and usefulness of verbal reports of thinking and the effect such reports have on examinees' thinking have not been sufficiently studied. Norris presents an investigation of the relevance and reliability of verbal reports of thinking. The results indicate that verbal reports of thinking are relevant and reliable. Norris discusses the implications of the study for critical thinking assessment.

452 Norris, Stephen. "Justifying Nonstandard Multiple Choice Critical Thinking Tests." In *Philosophy of Education 1985: Proceedings of the Forty-First Annual Meeting of the Philosophy of Education Society*, edited by David Nyberg, 27-31. Normal, IL: Philosophy of Education Society, 1986. [5 Refs.]

Reply to Petrie {456}

Norris argues that a multiple choice test based on a different concept than Petrie describes can measure critical thinking ability. Norris admits that essay and oral tests, as well as detailed interviews, are the best means of determining the critical thinking ability of individual students. Tests such as the Cornell Critical Thinking Test, Level X and the Test on Appraising Observations adequately measure overall critical thinking ability of groups of students.

453 Norris, Stephen P., and Robert H. Ennis. *Evaluating Critical Thinking*. The Practitioners' Guide to Teaching Thinking Series, 3. Pacific Grove, CA: Midwest Publications, 1989. 204 pp. [11 Refs.]

This is a practical guidebook on evaluating critical thinking, defined as "reasonable and reflective thinking that is focused upon deciding what to believe or do" (p. 2). In the first chapter, the authors expound upon this definition, list abilities and dispositions of critical thinking, and provide a pictorial representation of critical thinking, as background for information on the types of information-gathering techniques presented in Chapter Two. They discuss advantages and disadvantages of multiple choice tests, constructed-response tests, direct classroom observation, individual interviewing, and student and teacher journals in relation to purpose. Norris and Ennis outline general categories of information gathering techniques based on comprehensiveness of critical thinking coverage. They provide explanations and evidence factors for reliability and validity as indicators of quality of information. Norris and Ennis give a critical review of twelve commercially available tests and seven guidelines for examining tests. They offer recommendations and guidelines for constructing multiple-choice critical thinking tests and open-ended information-gathering techniques, as well as for gathering and using information on critical thinking.

454 Norris, Stephen P., and James Ryan. "Designing a Test of Inductive Reasoning." Chapter 43 in *Argumentation: Analysis and Practices. Proceedings of the Conference on Argumentation 1986*, edited by Frans H. van Eemeren, Rob Grootendorst, J. Anthony Blair, and Charles A. Willard, 394-403. Dordrecht, The Netherlands: Foris Publications, 1987. [19 Refs.]

Norris and Ryan present the procedures followed in researching and designing a test for inferential reasoning. The authors describe the general nature of test design and outline a definition of inferential reasoning that will be the fundamental basis of the test. They discuss three test problem tasks and ways of scoring student responses.

455 Pecorino, Philip A. "Grading Critical Thinking." *Informal Logic* 9, 2-3 (Spring-Fall 1987): 125-129.

Pecorino outlines a procedure he uses to evaluate student performance in his critical thinking and informal logic classes. Students lacking proficiency in critical thinking at the beginning of the course are not penalized as is ordinarily done with grade averaging. The course, divided into nine sections, requires students to master the skills taught in each section to the point when they are able to achieve a grade of 80% or better on each quiz. All quizzes except the course final can be retaken to achieve the passing grade. A brief outline listing the exercises used for quizzes is included.

456 Petrie, Hugh G. "Testing for Critical Thinking." In *Philosophy of Education 1985: Proceedings of the Forty-First Annual Meeting of the Philosophy of Education Society*, edited by David Nyberg, 3-19. Normal, IL: Philosophy of Education Society, 1986. [24 Refs.]

Replies: Norris {452}
Haroutunian {434}

Monitoring and evaluating thought is a key element of critical thinking. According to Petrie, the common elements of this key element include a concept, goal, or standard; a perception of a current situation; and an assessment of the "distance" between the current situation and the concept, goal, or standard. The interrelation between the three elements and experience allows for the adaptation of thoughts, actions, and the perceived situation. Petrie shows how current testing practices fail to (1) assess higher order cognitive skills or critical thinking and (2) allow for adaptation possibilities. Tests are structured for the benefit and from the world view of the tester, rather than the student. Not revising the current approaches to testing will result in such consequences as (1) emphasis on test scores over learning as a goal of education and (2) a two-tier system of those who can and cannot pass multiple-choice tests. Petrie stresses the need for analyzing the concept of critical thinking; understanding monitoring, evaluating, and correcting thought; and understanding how cognitive structures interact with the world to enable us to adapt to it.

457 Quellmalz, Edys S. "Needed: Better Methods of Testing Higher-Order Thinking Skills." Chapter 58 in *Developing Minds. Vol. 1: A Resource Book for Teaching Thinking*, rev. ed., edited by Arthur L. Costa, 338-343. Alexandria, VA: Association for Supervision and Curriculum Development, 1991. [22 Refs.]

Originally printed in *Educational Leadership* 43, no. 2 (October 1985): 29-35.

In exploring the conceptions of higher order thinking skills by philosophers, psychologists, and curriculum theorists, Quellmalz notes the commonality of the cognitive processes of analysis, comparison, inference, and evaluation appearing in the major conceptualizations of problem solving, critical thinking, and intellectual performance. She believes these skills should be the fundamental basis of higher order thinking skills tests.

458 Ramirez, Paul Michael. "Valett Inventory of Critical Thinking Abilities (VICTA)." *Reading Teacher* 41, no. 3 (December 1987): 348-350. [2 Refs.]

Ramirez reviews the Valett Inventory of Critical Thinking Appraisal developed by Robert E. Valett. The test, developed for preschool through early adolescence, consists of 100 items arranged according to Piagetian cognitive development levels. Each level is subdivided according to the ten critical thinking skills derived from Bloom's "Cognitive Taxonomy of Educational Objectives." Ramirez describes three problems with the test: (1) there are only two questions per critical thinking skill per level, (2) the questions have not been qualitatively analyzed, and (3) there is no integrated instructional program based on the test. Ramirez advises caution in using VICTA.

459 Rankin, Stuart C. "Evaluating Efforts to Teach Thinking." Chapter 51 in *Developing Minds: A Resource Book for Teaching Thinking*, edited by Arthur L. Costa, 272-275. Alexandria: VA: Association for Supervision and Curriculum Development, 1985.

Rankin provides guidelines for evaluating efforts to teach thinking. Included is a step-by-step procedure to guide evaluation through design, data collection, and data analysis.

460 Stiggins, Richard J., Evelyn Rubel, and Edys Quellmalz. *Measuring Thinking Skills in the Classroom*. Rev. ed. Washington, DC: National Education Association, 1988. 32 pp. [8 Refs.]

This is a step-by-step guide to learning how to plan for day-to-day assessment of thinking skills in the classroom. The authors present a basic assessment planning chart which combines five types of thinking (recall, analysis, comparison, inference, and evaluation) and three forms of classroom assessment (oral questioning, paper-and-pencil tests, and performance assessment--judgment and evaluation) as a tool for teachers. They use topics from elementary English, junior high social studies, junior high science, and senior high social studies to illustrate how a concept can be assessed for the five thinking skills levels using the three forms of assessment. The authors suggest strategies for effective day-to-day classroom assessment and provide a six-item annotated bibliography of further resources on classroom assessment.

461 Thompson, Bruce, and Janet G. Melancon. "Validity of a Measure of Critical Thinking Skills." *Psychological Reports* 60, no. 3, pt. 2 (June 1987): 1223-1230. [34 Refs.]

Given the inadequacy of the available measures of critical thinking, Thompson developed the Test of Critical Thinking Skills. Three hundred and forty-three undergraduates (343) were subjects for the evaluation of the measurement characteristics of the test items and the construct validity of the test. Results indicated that the test appears to be valid, the items have desirable difficulty and discrimination, and the items measure the constructs of their respective subtests.

462 Tomko, Thomas N., and Robert H. Ennis. "Evaluation of Informal Logic Competence." *Informal Logic: The First International Symposium*, edited by Ralph H. Johnson and J. Anthony Blair, 113-144. Inverness, CA: Edgepress, 1980. [61 Refs.]

This is an overview of evaluating informal logic competence and identifying the standard characteristics and types of tests used for measuring competence. Tomko and

Ennis critically review three tests: the Watson-Glaser Critical Thinking Appraisal, the Cornell Critical Thinking Tests (Levels X and Z), and the Instructional Objectives Exchange Indexes. Each test is evaluated for consistency and accuracy in measuring what it is supposedly testing. The authors discuss general characteristics of criterion-based testing and norm-referenced testing. They examine the concepts of test reliability and test validity, offer suggestions on how to construct a test, and describe the proper use of evaluation instruments.

463 Wasserman, Selma. "Reflections on Measuring Thinking While Listening to Mozart's 'Jupiter' Symphony." *Phi Delta Kappan* 70, no. 5 (January 1989): 365-370. [13 Refs.]

Believing that thinking is a highly complex concept about which much remains to be learned, Wasserman reviews several approaches to measuring thinking skills and follows with a discussion of caveats in choosing such measurements. She advocates systematic, thoughtful daily observation by competent professional teachers as the best assessment tool for gathering data on student thinking. Wasserman suggests that money to be expended on tests should be redirected toward re-training teachers and to higher salaries for attracting better professionals who can foster higher order thinking in students.

464 Wiggins, Grant. "Teaching to the (Authentic) Test." Chapter 59 in *Developing Minds. Vol. 1: A Resource Book for Teaching Thinking*, rev. ed., edited by Arthur L. Costa, 344-350. Alexandria, VA: Association for Supervision and Curriculum Development, 1991. [24 Refs.]

Originally printed in Educational Leadership 46, no. 7 (April 1989): 121-127, without postscript and resource list.

Wiggins advocates "teaching to the test." He believes that standard-setting tests designed to test the capacities considered essential and to test them in context should enhance education. Wiggins advocates awarding diplomas on the basis of performance or exhibition of mastery in which students publicly demonstrate knowledge, initiative, problem solving, and problem posing. He provides an example of a final exhibition and a test of performance, as well as a list of characteristics of authentic tests. In a postscript, Wiggins mentions examples of performance-based measures being used in a number of states.

465 Wilson, Diane Grimard, and Edwin E. Wagner. "The Watson-Glaser Critical Thinking Appraisal as a Predictor of Performance in a Critical Thinking Course." *Educational and Psychological Measurement* 41, no. 4 (Winter 1981): 1319-1322. [9 Refs.]

Determining that little was known about the predictive validity of the Watson-Glaser Critical Thinking Appraisal at the college level, the authors performed a study of its predictive validity relative to the performance of 55 college students in a physics course designed to teach critical thinking. Results indicated that the SAT predicted the criterion physics grades more accurately than the Watson-Glaser test.

466 Wolf, Dennis Palmer. "Portfolio Assessment: Sampling Student Work." Chapter 60 in *Developing Minds. Vol. 1: A Resource Book for Teaching Thinking*, rev. ed., edited by Arthur L. Costa, 351-355. Alexandria, VA: Association for Supervision and Curriculum Development, 1991. [5 Refs.]

> Adapted from the article of the same title printed in *Educational Leadership* 46, no. 7 (April 1989): 116-120.

Wolf advocates the use of portfolios in which students collect a diverse range of works over a period of time as a means of promoting thinking and of assessing development progress. The author illustrates how PROPEL, a consortium of the Pittsburgh Public Schools, Educational Testing Service, and Project Zero at the Harvard Graduate School of Education, uses portfolios.

467 Wood, Carolyn M. "Teaching Thinking and Measuring Competency: How Accountability Assessment Influences Curriculum and Instruction." *Critical Thinking: Language and Inquiry Across the Disciplines*, edited by Mark Weinstein and Wendy Oxman-Michelli, 217-232. Conference 88 Proceedings, Institute for Critical Thinking. Upper Montclair, NJ: Institute for Critical Thinking, 1989. [29 Refs.]

With 48 of the 50 states having established state testing programs or providing for local testing, Wood examines the widespread use of standardized tests, focusing on the California Achievement Test (CAT) used in Maryland's accountability assessment program. Wood argues that such tests fail to measure or address students' critical thinking abilities. She discusses two models of thinking that have been proposed as guides for developing curriculum: Bloom's taxonomy and Dimensions of Thinking. Wood details the components of the Dimensions of Thinking model and argues that standardized tests such as the CAT and the Maryland Functional Reading Test do not address the cognitive processes identified by the model. She believes the educational influence of standardized tests leads teachers to teach for the test. This situation makes it important to examine the limitations of standardized tests and ways such testing can be used to support the teaching of thinking. Wood describes current efforts at providing alternatives to multiple-choice format tests.

468 Young, Robert E. "Testing for Critical Thinking: Issues and Resources." *Fostering Critical Thinking*, edited by Robert E. Young, 77-89. New Directions for Teaching and Learning, no. 3. San Francisco, CA: Jossey-Bass, 1980. [45 Refs.]

Young relates the three fundamental steps of classroom evaluation identified by Groundlund to the testing of critical thinking. These are: (1) identifying and defining the intended learning outcomes, (2) constructing or selecting tests or other evaluation instruments that are relevant to the specified outcomes, and (3) using the results to improve learning and instruction. Young identifies sources of objectives for critical thinking and for defining objectives for testing. He discusses existing tests of critical thinking (teacher-made tests previously used in the classroom and published tests), as well as sources to assist teachers with test construction. Young emphasizes the importance of teachers using test results in conjunction with the process used to obtain the answers and in relation to previous performance in order for tests to become a means of fostering critical thinking.

7

INSTRUCTIONAL METHODS AND APPROACHES

469 Adams, Marilyn Jager. "Balancing Process and Content." Chapter 1 in *Developing Minds. Vol. 2: Programs for Teaching Thinking*, rev. ed., edited by Arthur L. Costa. Alexandria, VA: Association for Supervision and Curriculum Development, 1991. 1-2. [4 Refs.]

Adams addresses the importance of balancing direct instruction of principles and modes of thinking with subject matter and daily living. She contends that this can be done effectively through a course on thinking that focuses on transfer as its primary goal.

470 Adams, Marilyn Jager. "Thinking Skills Curricula: Their Promise and Progress." *Educational Psychologist* 24, no. 1 (Winter 1989): 25-77. [79 Refs.]

Adams provides an overview of thinking skills curricular programs, identifying their process orientation and the major differences in targeted processes, principles, and the materials used for the exercise of these processes and principles. She analyzes the approaches and effectiveness of six programs: CoRT Thinking Materials, Philosophy for Children, the Productive Thinking Program: A Course in Learning to Think, Instrumental Enrichment, Intuitive Math, Odyssey, and Think. Adams discusses how the programs address the issues of transfer, individual differences, useability, and the needs of Chapter I students. She gives special attention to the program Odyssey, which she helped develop.

471 Alcorn, Bonnie, and Annie Wittgen. "The Authority to Think: The Student Centered Classroom." *Contemporary Education* 61, no. 2 (Winter 1990): 91-93. [2 Refs.]

Alcorn and Wittgen argue that traditional forms of teaching are not meeting student needs for diversity. Instead of authority and decisions being solely in the hands of the teacher, classrooms should become student-centered.

Instead of lectures, students should be actively engaged in discussions in which the teacher is a participant, not an authority figure. Such classrooms give students the freedom to create an atmosphere for learning, where student and teacher think, inquire, interpret, and act as peers. The authors include examples from classrooms employing student-centered activities.

472 Arnold, Genevieve H., Alice Hart, and Karen Campbell. "Introducing the Wednesday Revolution." *Educational Leadership* 45, no. 7 (April 1988): 48.

The authors describe the organization and implementation of Socratic or Paideia seminars based on Mortimer Adler's Wednesday Revolution concept. They assert that the seminars enhance critical thinking skills by using teams that combine personnel from an educational organization, elementary and secondary schools, and a university with parents and community members.

473 Baker, John D. "Building Thinking Skills." Chapter 16 in *Developing Minds. Vol. 2: Programs for Teaching Thinking*, rev. ed., edited by Arthur L. Costa, 59-61. Alexandria, VA: Association for Supervision and Curriculum Development, 1991.

Revision of Costa {505}, pp. 236-238.

Baker describes the Midwest Publications Analytic and Critical Thinking Program which developed into the Building Thinking Skills series and the Critical Thinking series. Building Thinking Skills provides a sequential plan of activities for cognitive skill development and analytical reasoning instruction for kindergarten through twelfth grade (K-12). The Critical Thinking series is a course in formal and informal logic for eighth grade through college that is written on a fifth grade reading level. Baker includes information about results of the use of the Building Thinking Skills series and the availability of other thinking skills materials for teachers and administrators.

474 Barbour, Nita H. "Can We Prepackage Thinking?" *Childhood Education* 65, no. 2 (Winter 1988): 67-68. [11 Refs.]

In response to educators' diverse concepts of teaching thinking, Barbour notes that textbook publishers and curriculum developers have constructed prepackaged materials with strategies, tactics, and procedures for teaching thinking. She cautions against using these materials in a manner detrimental to thinking. Barbour encourages open-ended discussion and a classroom environment in which teachers and students are seen as learners.

475 Barell, John. "Reflective Teaching for Thoughtfulness." Chapter 38 in *Developing Minds. Vol. 1: A Resource Book for Teaching Thinking*, rev. ed., edited by Arthur L. Costa, 207-210. Alexandria, VA: Association for Supervision and Curriculum Development, 1991. [26 Refs.]

Barell outlines how reflective teachers can enhance thoughtfulness in students by (1) listening empathically, (2) modeling thinking, (3) collaborating with students, (4) designing learning as problem solving and experimentation, (5) planning, monitoring, and evaluating progress, and (6) empowering students toward self-direction. He suggests and illustrates several teaching strategies.

476 Barell, John, Rosemarie Liebmann, and Irving Sigel. "Fostering Thoughtful Self-Direction in Students." *Educational Leadership* 45, no. 7 (April 1988): 14-17. [8 Refs.]

The authors outline ways teachers can foster an environment in which students are able to develop the requirements for engaging in critical thinking.

477 Bergmann, Sherrell, and Gerald J. Rudman. *Decision-Making Skills for Middle School Students*. Reference & Resource Series. Washington, DC: National Education Association, 1985. 64 pp. [27 Refs.]

This is a guidebook of strategies for developing and implementing a curriculum that will help eleven- to fourteen-year-old-students develop decision making skills. It includes an outline of a sample one-semester program, lists of class objectives, and descriptions and samples of teaching strategies, projects, activities, resources, worksheets, forms, and letters.

478 Berman, Shelley. "Thinking in Context: Teaching for Openmindedness and Critical Understanding." Chapter 3 in *Developing Minds. Vol. 1: A Resource Book for Teaching Thinking*, rev. ed., edited by Arthur L. Costa, 10-16.

Alexandria, VA: Association for Supervision and Curriculum Development, 1991. [13 Refs.]

Berman presents an outline of nine strategies developed by Educators for Social Responsibility for teachers to use to foster clear and independent thinking in students. These strategies represent a "whole language" approach and are intended to encourage students' confidence and empowerment. Underlying the approach is the basic principle that when students' thinking is valued and when their thinking improves their lives, they will become more confident and skilled in their thinking.

479 Beyer, Barry K. *Developing a Thinking Skills Program.* Boston, MA: Allyn and Bacon, 1988. 361 pp. [200 Refs.]

Beyer discusses the issues involved in developing, implementing and maintaining a thinking skills program. He (1) outlines the basic ingredients and rationale for developing a program; (2) examines the nature of thinking, cognitive strategies and cognitive skills; (3) discusses a variety of structures for a thinking skills curriculum (including ways commercially or expert-developed programs can be combined with a locally developed program); (4) presents guidelines for selecting thinking skills and strategies to teach in the program; and (5) outlines a teaching framework that focuses on strategies for explicit instruction in how to execute the thinking operations and develop student metacognition. Beyer identifies elements such as classroom environment, instructional materials, and appropriate staff development that must be addressed in order to successfully implement a program. He also suggests ways to support and maintain a program by developing classroom coaching and teacher support, and ways to assess a program's success in achieving its goal of teaching thinking skills. Two appendices, one outlining the features of selected thinking skills programs and the other describing selected thinking skills and strategies, are included.

480 Beyer, Barry K. "Practice is Not Enough." *Thinking Skills Instruction: Concepts and Techniques*, edited by Marcia Heiman and Joshua Slomianko, 77-86. Building Students' Thinking Skills. Washington, DC: National Education Association, 1987. [29 Refs.]

Beyer believes that the most commonly used methods to teach thinking encourage, stimulate, and provide opportunities for thinking, but do not actually teach thinking. To develop and improve students' thinking skills, practice should be combined with an explicit introduction to thinking skills, guided practice in executing the skills, and instruction in the skills within a variety of contexts. Beyer suggests ways of using these techniques.

481 Beyer, Barry K. *Practical Strategies for the Teaching of Thinking*. Boston, MA: Allyn and Bacon, 1987. 273 pp. [150 Refs.]

Beyer discusses how to directly teach thinking skills and strategies at all grade levels of education. In chapter one, he examines the nature of thinking and outlines two operations performed by a mind when thinking: cognition and metacognition. Beyer presents a functional model of thinking and distinguishes critical thinking from creative thinking, problem solving, decision making and other thinking strategies. In chapter two, he suggests principles and procedures teachers can use to select and define thinking skills and strategies to teach. In chapter three, four different dimensions of the teaching-learning context or environment are identified: (1) the classroom environment, (2) the subject matter, (3) the teaching process, and (4) an instructional framework to introduce a thinking operation and guide the students in transferring the skill to new applications. In chapters four to seven, Beyer focuses on employing the framework to teach various thinking operations. In chapter eight, he addresses how teachers can help students develop metacognitive skills, thinking dispositions, and independent thinking. In chapter nine, Beyer suggests ways to assess student thinking (focusing on classroom evaluations that teachers can do in their own tests) and ways teachers can assess their own thinking. He concludes by discussing the implications the direct teaching of thinking has for teaching in general.

482 Bippus, Stanley L. "Think Before You Ask." *Educational Leadership* 45, no. 7 (April 1988): 50-51.

Bippus describes one school district's approach to improving students' thinking skills by having seventh through twelfth grade students apply their problem solving skills to real problems confronting community organizations.

483 Bonnstetter, Ronald J. "Active Learning Often Starts with a Question." *Journal of College Science Teaching* 18, no. 2 (November 1988): 95-97. [2 Refs.]

In working with undergraduate faculty in three institutions, Bonnstetter noted that teaching styles revealed the absence of a working definition of classroom discussion and of an understanding of the relationship between questioning strategies and the development of critical thinking skills. He provides tips for effective questioning that mentally engages students: do not ask the known, avoid yes/no responses, use appropriate wait time for extended-answer questions while maintaining eye contact, and increase nonevaluative responses by probing into the thinking behind the response.

484 Bransford, John D., Robert D. Sherwood, and Tom Sturdevant. "Teaching Thinking and Problem Solving." Chapter 9 in *Teaching Thinking Skills: Theory and Practice*, edited by Joan Boykoff Baron and Robert J. Sternberg, 162-181. New York, NY: W. H. Freeman, 1987. [19 Refs.]

The authors discuss problem identification as a way to help students learn to use and refine their knowledge, providing them with a framework for understanding the value of concepts and principles. They also discuss five components of thinking found in IDEAL problem solvers: Identification of problems, Definition of problems, Exploration of strategies, Acting on ideas, and Looking at the effects. In exploring topics and research related to the teaching of thinking and problem solving, the authors discuss the problem of inert knowledge, conceptual tools, access to learned information, and teaching across the curriculum. Believing that students should be encouraged to think with important concept and procedures on their own rather than only when explicitly prompted to do so, the authors recommend an approach that recognizes the importance of helping students (1) analyze their own problem solving processes and (2) understand how inventions and discoveries enable important problems to be solved.

485 Bransford, John D., Barry S. Stein, Ruth Arbitman-Smith, and Nancy J. Vye. "Improving Thinking and Learning Skills: An Analysis of Three Approaches." Chapter 4 in *Thinking and Learning Skills. Vol. 1: Relating Instruction to Research*, edited by Judith W. Segal, Susan F. Chipman, and Robert Glaser, 133-206. Hillsdale, NJ: Lawrence Erlbaum, 1985. [74 Refs.]

The authors analyze Whimbey and Lochhead's paired problem solving course, Instrumental Enrichment, and Philosophy for Children. Their analyses include an overview of each program's theoretical foundation, procedures for instruction, and program content, followed by a detailed examination of each program's instructional approaches and procedures. The authors discuss the advantages, disadvantages and effectiveness of each program and review existing evaluation data. They identify basic theoretical issues warranting further research.

486 Bransford, John D., Nancy Vye, Charles Kinzer, and Victoria Risko. "Teaching Thinking and Content Knowledge: Toward an Integrated Approach." Chapter 12 in *Dimensions of Thinking and Cognitive Instruction*, edited by Beau Fly Jones and Lorna Idol, 381-413. Hillsdale, NJ: Lawrence Erlbaum, 1990. [60 Refs.]

Bransford and colleagues explore relationships between general processes of thinking and learning and specific knowledge of particular content. They provide an overview of the literature concerned with the importance of specific knowledge for thinking and learning. The authors argue that the acquisition of new content knowledge is not sufficient for the development of organized knowledge structures for subsequent thinking and using relevant knowledge for related problem solving tasks. They discuss and illustrate the application of an anchored instruction approach that includes the teaching of general processes and specific content in ways that mutually strengthen each.

487 Bratton, Libby. "You Have to Think Real Hard When You Write." *Educational Leadership* 45, no. 7 (April 1988): 62.

Bratton describes activities used in a Maryland school for teaching thinking through writing in subject areas to students from kindergarten through twelfth grade. She provides examples from several classes.

488 Brookfield, Stephen D. *Developing Critical Thinkers: Challenging Adults to Explore Alternative Ways of Thinking and Acting*. San Francisco, CA: Jossey-Bass, 1987. 293 pp. [376 Refs.]

Intended to help professionals, managers, and educators understand and develop critical thinking skills in their colleagues, clients, students, and peers, this text is divided into three parts or groups of chapters covering pertinent information. Part One: Understanding Critical Thinking in Adult Life explores the concept and importance of critical thinking for adults in a democratic society. Part Two: Practical Approaches for Developing Critical Thinkers examines various methods, techniques, approaches, and strategies for facilitating critical thinking in others. Part Three: Helping Adults Learn to Think Critically in Different Arenas of Life focuses on ways in which critical thinking can be fostered in the workplace, personal relationships, political commitments, and television viewing. Case studies and exercises are provided.

489 Brophy, Jere, ed. *Advances in Research on Teaching: A Research Annual*. Greenwich, CT: JAI Press, 1989. 355 pp.

The papers in this volume focus on the thinking or reasoning processes associated with reading, writing, mathematics, and science; metacognition and self-regulated learning; and effective teaching of higher order thinking within content areas. The authors examine research studies, teaching strategies, learning strategies, and instructional programs related to those processes. Following each paper is a brief section in which the authors respond to questions and comments posed by the editor or by the authors of other papers included in the volume.

490 Brown, Sallie. "Three Methods to Teach Thinking Skills." *Social Studies Review* 26, no. 2 (Winter 1987): 59-62.

Brown suggests that teachers begin the teaching of thinking skills by using three methods: modeling, focused recall, and TIPS (topic, ideas, and points).

491 Buehner, Linda J., and Virginia H. Lucas. "MAP: A Model for Teaching Problem-Solving." *B.C. Journal of Special Education* 10, no. 3 (1986): 251-55. [17 Refs.]

After reviewing the literature on brain research and theory, Buehner and Lucas propose a model for teaching problem solving and critical thinking skills to children, especially exceptional children. This model, MAP, consists of three steps: (1) Motivation--teachers must stimulate children to consider a problem by presenting a situation with which students can identify, (2) Association--teachers must encourage students to relate similar problems, and (3) Processing--teachers must encourage students to integrate, judge, and evaluate. The authors suggest teaching methods and strategies for each step and stress the importance of accommodating all learning styles.

492 Carr, Kathryn S. "How Can We Teach Critical Thinking?" *Childhood Education* 65, no. 2 (Winter 1988): 69-73. [15 Refs.]

Stressing the importance of the application and practice of thinking within each content area at every level from elementary through college, Carr reviews various types of thinking skills activities applicable across disciplines. She gives sample reading, writing, and classification activities for developing critical thinking.

493 Castronovo, James. "Effective Thinking in the Social Sciences." *History and Social Science Teacher* 24, no. 2 (Winter 1989): 85-86.

Castronovo suggests ways in which teachers can increase their own awareness of effective thinking, foster critical thinking in students, and evaluate effective thinking.

494 Cederblom, Jerry, and David W. Paulsen. *Critical Reasoning: Understanding and Criticizing Arguments and Theories*. Belmont, CA: Wadsworth, 1982. [61 Refs.]

This textbook was developed for a university critical reasoning course. Chapter One provides background on critical reasoning. Chapters Two through Seven focus on arguments, covering the premises, conclusions, fallacies, emotion versus reason, fallacies, and validity. Chapters Eight through Ten focus on induction, empirical generalizations, empirical theories, and conceptual theories. Chapter Eleven examines creating arguments and theories. Sample problems and exercises are presented throughout the text.

495 Chance, Paul. *Thinking in the Classroom: A Survey of Programs*. New York, NY: Teachers College Press, 1986. 164 pp. [137 Refs.]

Chance presents a survey of eight programs designed to teach thinking: CoRT, Productive Thinking, Philosophy for Children, Problem-Solving and Comprehension, Odyssey, Instrumental Enrichment, Techniques of Learning, and Thoughtful Teaching. He devotes a chapter to each program, outlining the program's assumptions and goals, methods and materials, target audience, teacher training and qualifications, and evaluating the program's strengths and weaknesses. Each chapter includes a chart listing the program's features.

496 Charlton, Ronald E. "The Direct Teaching of Analysis." *Thinking Skills Instruction: Concepts and Techniques*, edited by Marcia Heiman and Joshua Slomianko, 152-159. Building Students' Thinking Skills. Washington, DC: National Education Association, 1987. [2 Refs.]

Advocating that the skill of analysis be taught before students are asked to apply it, Charlton outlines a five-step generic model for teaching three levels of analysis (identifying the elements, relationships, and organizational principles) based on Bloom's taxonomy and Beyer's six-stage teaching framework (readiness, introduction, guided practice, expansion/broadening, guided practice, and application). He illustrates the flexibility of the teaching model with several examples and emphasizes that the skill of analysis can and should be taught in all content areas.

497 Christiansen, Larry A. *Critical Thinking and Effective Expression*. Dubuque, IA: Kendall/Hunt, 1990. 72 pp. [9 Refs.]

Intended as a companion for all students and for possible use by the general population, this handbook consists of two parts of four chapters each. Part One covers the principles of critical thinking, including analyzing information, evaluating information, and reasoning. The concluding chapter provides worksheets and exercises to practice applying these principles. Part Two focuses on the principles of effective written or spoken expression, covering organizing information, gaining the respect and support of audience, and style. The final chapter provides a checklist to help with integrating critical thinking and effective expression. Sample problems and practical exercises are included with most of the chapters.

498 Clark, Wilma. "T-Shirt Tangle." *Exercise Exchange* 32, no. 1 (Fall 1986): 35-37.

Clark outlines an exercise using cutout drawings of differently decorated T-shirts to teach classification.

499 Clarke, John. "Designing Discussions as Group Inquiry." *College Teaching* 36, no. 4 (Fall 1988): 140-143. [7 Refs.]

On the premises that discussion and student involvement promote higher order thinking and learning, Clarke makes recommendations for designing effective, active discussion. Believing that effective discussion follows predictable and logical steps, he expounds upon the following four phases of the inquiry cycle: (1) concept development, (2) concept clarification, (3) verification, and (4) analysis. He suggests techniques such as free-writing, diagrammatic representations of concept relationships, role playing, and postwriting for facilitating active discussion. Clarke also offers suggestions for helping the students become responsible for their own learning and provides sample questions with suggested activities.

500 Clarke, John H. "Graphic Organizers: Frames for Teaching Patterns of Thinking." Chapter 41 in *Developing Minds. Vol. 1: A Resource Book for Teaching Thinking*, rev. ed., edited by Arthur L. Costa, 224-231. Alexandria, VA: Association for Supervision and Curriculum Development, 1991. [12 Refs.]

Clarke discusses the advantages of using graphic organizers in classroom teaching and learning. He provides examples of graphic organizers for inductive and deductive thinking that elementary and secondary school teachers have used with students.

501 Collins, Allan. "Teaching Reasoning Skills." Chapter 26 in *Thinking and Learning Skills. Vol. 2: Research and Open Questions*, edited by Susan F. Chipman, Judith W. Segal, and Robert Glaser, 579-586. Hillsdale, NJ: Lawrence Erlbaum, 1985. [23 Refs.]

Collins presents a summary of the most important strategies used by teachers employing the inquiry method. He groups the strategies under the headings, Systematic

Selection of Cases and Systematic Questioning of Students. Collins also discusses the advantages and disadvantages of the inquiry method.

502 Comber, Geoffrey J., Nicholas Maistrellis, and Howard Zeiderman. "The Touchstones Project: Discussion Classes for Students of All Abilities." Chapter 22 in *Developing Minds. Vol. 2: Programs for Teaching Thinking*, rev. ed., edited by Arthur L. Costa, 85-88. Alexandria, VA: Association for Supervision and Curriculum Development, 1991.

The authors describe the Touchstones Project intended for students of all ability and skill levels from sixth through twelfth grades. The project revolves around texts, small and large student discussion groups, and a teacher as discussion leader rather than a source of information.

503 Cooper, Eric J. "Toward a New Mainstream of Instruction for American Schools." *Journal of Negro Education* 58, no. 1 (Winter 1989): 102-116. [55 Refs.]

Cooper notes that research data indicates that school instruction revolves around poorly developed materials, workbook activities, published instructional material rather than active interaction between students and teachers, and informational responses rather than open responses involving reasoning. He calls for educators to refocus and expand their vision for classrooms in view of the diverse needs of students and problems related to minority performance. This vision should focus upon the thinking patterns by which people from different cultures, backgrounds, skill levels, and languages learn to learn. Cognitive theory, rather than textbooks and tests, should be the theme of a New Mainstream of schooling in which teaching and learning are interwoven. Cooper addresses several teaching and learning strategies for developing higher order cognitive skills, advocating that such strategies be integrated into the curriculum for students at all grade, discipline, and skill levels.

504 Cortés, Carlos E., and Elinor Richardson. "'Why in the World': Using Television to Develop Critical Thinking Skills." *Phi Delta Kappan* 64, no. 10 (June 1983): 715-716.

The authors discuss seven facets of critical analysis and supporting teaching strategies for using the "Why in the World" Public Broadcasting Service television series as the primary instructional resource. This series uses national and international current events to foster critical thinking.

505 Costa, Arthur L., ed. *Developing Minds: A Resource Book for Teaching Thinking*. Alexandria, VA: Association for Supervision and Curriculum Development, 1985. 343 pp.

This is an anthology of 69 papers designed as a resource book to help educational leaders "infuse curriculum, instruction, and school organization with practices that more fully develop children's intellectual potentials." (p. xi). Topics include school conditions for thinking, definitions of thinking, thinking curricula, teaching strategies, programs for teaching thinking, computers and thinking, and accessing thinking abilities.

506 Costa, Arthur L., ed. *Developing Minds. Vol. 1: A Resource Book for Teaching Thinking*. Rev. ed. Alexandria, VA: Association for Supervision and Curriculum Development, 1991. 400 pp.

Revised edition of Costa {505}

This is an anthology of 60 papers designed as a resource book to assist educators in initiating, improving, and evaluating efforts to infuse thinking into educational programs. Topics include creating school conditions for thinking, defining thinking, thinking curricula, teaching strategies, and accessing thinking abilities. A lengthy bibliography of over 400 books, articles, audio and video materials, networks, newsletters, critical thinking tests, and human resources is provided on pages 356 to 371. The appendices include various checklists to assist educators in appraising effectiveness in developing students' thinking skills and in planning for incorporating thinking into teaching and learning.

507 Costa, Arthur L., ed. *Developing Minds. Vol. 2: Programs for Teaching Thinking*. Rev. ed. Alexandria, VA: Association for Supervision and Curriculum Development, 1991. 122 pp.

Revised edition of Costa {505}

A companion to Vol. 1: *A Resource Book for Teaching Thinking*, this volume includes 29 articles on programs designed for teaching thinking and on how to choose an appropriate thinking skills program.

508 Costa, Arthur L. "The Inquiry Strategy." Chapter 53 in *Developing Minds. Vol. 1: A Resource Book for Teaching Thinking*, rev. ed., edited by Arthur L. Costa, 302-303. Alexandria, VA: Association for Supervision and Curriculum Development, 1991. [6 Refs.]

Costa discusses briefly the goals and background of the inquiry strategy, as well as teacher behaviors critical to inquiry.

509 Costa, Arthur L. "Mediating the Metacognitive." Chapter 39 in *Developing Minds. Vol. 1: A Resource Book for Teaching Thinking*, rev. ed., edited by Arthur L. Costa, 211-214. Alexandria, VA: Association for Supervision and Curriculum Development, 1991. [10 Refs.]

Adapted from article of same title in *Educational Leadership* 42, no. 3 (November 1984): 57-62.

Costa outlines twelve strategies teachers can use to develop the metacognitive abilities of students. He contends that such strategies must be infused into teaching methods, staff development, and supervisory processes.

510 Costa, Arthur L. "Teacher Behaviors That Enable Student Thinking." Chapter 37 in *Developing Minds. Vol 1: A Resource Book for Teaching Thinking*, rev. ed., edited by Arthur L. Costa, 194-206. Alexandria, VA: Association for Supervision and Curriculum Development, 1991. [63 Refs.]

Revision of Costa {505}, pp. 125-137.

Asserting that the classroom behavior of teachers greatly affects student learning, Costa analyzes four categories of teacher behaviors: questioning, structuring, responding, and modeling. He suggests ways to design questions, structure class time and classroom environmental resources, use appropriate responsive behaviors to student questions, and model behavior consistent with cognitive goals and objectives in order to motivate student thinking.

511 Costa, Arthur L., Robert Hanson, Harvey F. Silver, and Richard W. Strong. "Other Mediative Strategies." Chapter 25 in *Developing Minds: A Resource Book for Teaching*

Thinking, edited by Arthur L. Costa, 166-170. Alexandria, VA: Association for Supervision and Curriculum Development, 1985. [12 Refs.]

Costa presents a descriptive outline of four strategies for teaching thinking: the Open-Ended Discussion Group, the Inquiry Strategy, the Values Awareness/Clarification Strategy, and the Concept Development Strategies: Concept Formation/Concept Attainment.

512 Costa, Arthur L., and Lawrence F. Lowery. *Techniques for Teaching Thinking*. The Practitioners' Guide to Teaching Thinking Series, 2. Pacific Grove, CA: Midwest Publications, 1989. 105 pp. [118 Refs.]

This volume provides a collection of suggested teacher behaviors, classroom organizational strategies, and instructional strategies determined effective through research and practical experimentation. The seven chapters of this work cover (1) three aspects for structuring the classroom for thinking: clarity of verbal and written instructions, structuring time and energy, and organizational and grouping patterns that affect student thinking; (2) syntactical arrangements of teacher-initiated questions and statements that facilitate student thinking; (3) teacher response behaviors that facilitate student thinking; (4) strategies for enhancing metacognition; (5) teaching thinking skills directly (with a sample lesson on teaching classification and categorization); and (5) assessment of student thinking.

513 Costa, Arthur L., and Robert Marzano. "Teaching the Language of Thinking." *Educational Leadership* 45, no. 2 (October 1987): 29-33. [13 Refs.]

An adapted version is in Costa {506}, pp. 251-254.

Emphasizing the role of language in teaching and learning, Costa and Marzano discuss seven ways in which teachers can enhance cognitive development through language. These include (1) developing a classroom language of cognition by using precise vocabulary and providing specific instruction in thinking skills related to these terms, (2) posing critical questions that encourage appropriate behavior, (3) providing data for autonomous decision making, (4) guiding students through tasks by questioning, (5) probing for specificity of oral language used by students, (6) encouraging thinking about thinking, and (7) having students analyze linguistic cues.

514 Crabbe, Anne B. "Future Problem Solving." Chapter 10 in *Developing Minds. Vol. 2: Programs for Teaching Thinking*, rev. ed., edited by Arthur L. Costa, 40-42. Alexandria, VA: Association for Supervision and Curriculum Development, 1991. [2 Refs.]

Revision of Costa {505}, pp. 217-219.

Crabbe discusses the objectives and components of the Future Problem Solving Program developed by Paul Torrance and based on the work of Alex Osborne and Sidney Parnes. The program involves teams of students, practice problem solving exercises, state competitions, international competitions, and a Scenario Writing Contest for students in grades four through twelve. There is also a non-competitive instructional program for children in kindergarten through third grade.

515 de Bono, Edward. "Beyond Critical Thinking." *Curriculum Review* 25, no. 3 (January-February 1986): 12-16.

De Bono warns against the dangers of believing that dialectic, debate, and critical thinking skills are all that is needed by society. He asserts that society also needs constructive and generative thinking skills. De Bono uses examples from the CoRT Thinking Program to illustrate how such thinking skills can be taught directly. He discusses the advantages of the CoRT program and advocates teaching thinking as a separate subject area rather than an integral part of subject areas.

516 de Bono, Edward. "The Cognitive Research Trust (CoRT) Thinking Program." In *Thinking, the Expanding Frontier. Proceedings of the International, Interdisciplinary Conference on Thinking Held at the University of the South Pacific, January, 1982*, edited by William Maxwell, 115-127. Philadelphia, PA: Franklin Institute Press, 1983. [8 Refs.]

De Bono describes the Cognitive Research Trust (CoRT) Thinking Program, examining the program's theoretical basis, methodologies, structure, and major difficulties encountered with the program's direct, process-oriented method. De Bono outlines the program's six lesson sections and briefly discusses evaluations of the program.

517 de Bono, Edward. "The CoRT Thinking Program." Chapter 10 in *Thinking and Learning Skills. Vol. 1: Relating Instruction to Research*, edited by Judith W. Segal, Susan F. Chipman, and Robert Glaser, 363-388. Hillsdale, NJ: Lawrence Erlbaum, 1985. [22 Refs.]

The author reviews the major features of the CoRT Program of instruction in thinking skills, including the approach used in CoRT lessons, the structure of the lessons, and the skills which are taught. De Bono presents a sample lesson to illustrate the CoRT style. He discusses the effectiveness of the program as evidenced by its use in many school systems and critiques other approaches to teaching thinking skills.

518 de Bono, Edward. "The Direct Teaching of Thinking as a Skill." *Phi Delta Kappan* 64, no. 10 (June 1983): 703-708. [10 Refs.]

Reprinted in Heiman and Slomianko {551}, pp. 217-229 and in Costa {505}, pp. 203-209 Revised in Costa {507}, pp. 27-32.

De Bono defines thinking as "the operating skill with which intelligence acts upon experience" (p. 703) and emphasizes the crucial relationship of perception to thinking. He describes human beings as having self-organizing systems within which perception takes place and experiences are arranged into patterns. He advocates using the CoRT program to improve the clarity, breadth, and creativity of perception. De Bono emphasizes the program's focus on thinking tools that can be transferred to academic and everyday decision making or problem solving.

519 de Bono, Edward. "The Practical Teaching of Thinking Using the CoRT Method." in *Facilitating Cognitive Development: International Perspectives, Programs, and Practices*, edited by Milton Schwebel and Charles A. Maher, 33-47. New York, NY: Haworth Press, 1986. [4 Refs.]

De Bono believes the direct teaching of thinking as a skill should be done through constant practice that focuses on the process of thinking rather than its content. He argues that discussion and simulation type programs emphasize content while the CoRT program emphasizes process. He asserts that content is not transferable to other subjects, the thinking process is. De Bono discusses the CoRT program's usefulness in designing specific thinking tools based on the program's concern with the operative and self-organizing aspects of perceptual thinking. He uses the program's Plus/Minus/Interesting (PMI) "tool" as an example of the "tool" method. He provides lists of the program's six sections and other "tool" methods.

520 de Bono, Edward. "A Technique for Teaching Creative Thinking." *Momentum* 17, no. 3 (September 1986): 17-19.

De Bono asserts that a program designed to teach thinking should be (1) useable by a variety of teachers, (2) simple, and (3) effective. He argues against the teaching of only critical thinking and describes lessons from the CoRT thinking program, covering constructive, creative, generative, and critical thinking. The program uses the "tools" method of teaching in which students practice a thinking skill on several small problems. De Bono outlines three fallacies of thinking that must be dealt with in any program: (1) intelligence is enough and intelligent people make good thinkers, (2) information will do the thinking for you, and (3) debate, argument, and proving someone wrong is a sufficient thinking system.

521 de Sánchez, Margarita. "Developing Thinking Skills." Chapter 26 in *Developing Minds. Vol. 2: Programs for Teaching Thinking*, rev. ed., edited by Arthur L. Costa, 101-106. Alexandria, VA: Association for Supervision and Curriculum Development, 1991. [20 Refs.]

The author provides the background information, purpose, rationale, and description of the Developing Thinking Skills (DTS) program. Initiated in Mexico, the program intends to develop the intellectual abilities of secondary school students so that they can demonstrate excellence in problem solving and decision making and success upon entering college. The program consists of 168 lessons grouped into five levels of courses for the first five semesters of high school. De Sánchez outlines the course content and implementation strategy, including staff development, evaluation, and a curricular development plan.

522 de Sánchez, Margarita. "Teaching Thinking Processes." Chapter 24 in *Thinking: The Second International Conference*, edited by David N. Perkins, Jack Lochhead, and John C. Bishop, 413-430. Hillsdale, NJ: Lawrence Erlbaum, 1987. [17 Refs.]

De Sánchez contends that the ability to think critically is a process that requires the use of knowledge and skill in using that knowledge to generate new products by transforming knowledge content. She outlines a technique for analyzing a thinking process, discusses characteristics that should be found in the teaching of thinking processes, and provides a table outlining the development of thinking skills. De Sánchez discusses a two-step process-oriented model of instruction, entailing the definition of the process from two points of view and the definition of an appropriate method to ensure learning. She describes three programs used in Venezuela's "Programs for the Development of Intelligence Directed at the Formal Educational System": Learning to Learn, Project Intelligence, and Instrumental Enrichment.

523 Dedicott, Wendy. "The Value of Pictures in Encouraging Children's Thinking Strategies." *Reading* 21, no. 1 (April 1987): 53-61. [13 Refs.]

Dedicott describes a project undertaken to demonstrate how pictures can be used to facilitate children's thinking strategies. Consisting of seven lessons, the project includes using exercises with pictures to encourage self-reflection on feelings, justification of actions, and judgmental thinking based on pictorial evidence. Dedicott stresses the importance of teachers developing skills in the art of questioning and in judging when and how students need help.

524 Derrico, Patricia J. "Learning to Think with Philosophy for Children." *Educational Leadership* 45, no. 7 (April 1988): 34.

Derrico briefly relates the successful effects that the use of the Philosophy for Children had on the thinking skills of middle school students and teachers.

525 Derry, Sharon J., Lois W. Hawkes, and Chia-jer Tsai. "A Theory for Remediating Problem-Solving Skills of Older Children and Adults." *Educational Psychologist* 22, no. 1 (Winter 1987): 55-87. [28 Refs.]

These authors describe TAPS (Training Arithmetic Problem-Solving Skills) and the two studies upon which the comprehension theory of problem solving is based. They provide models representing good and bad problem solving behavioral characteristics in diagrammatical illustrations and discuss their characteristics. The authors also describe a TAPS instructional program.

526 Downs, Judy R. "Using Thinkers' Cards." *College Teaching* 37, no. 2 (Spring 1989): 61.

Downs believes that critical thinking is facilitated in college level courses in critical thinking, business communication, and composition through the use of thinkers' cards and minipresentations. Students summarize and analyze textbook material for major points and omissions and develop an open-ended question related to the material. This information is written on index cards and then presented orally to the class. The class participates with responses and reactions. Downs notes that this exercise requires the skills of reading, writing, speaking, listening, and thinking.

527 Eble, Kenneth E. "Getting Students to Think." Chapter 3 in *The Craft of Teaching: A Guide to Mastering the Professor's Art*, 28-41. 2d ed. San Francisco, CA: Jossey-Bass, 1988.

Eble offers five speculations about Galileo's, as well as our own, ways of thinking. Believing that individuals must think a lot in order to think well and that teachers have a fundamental responsibility to provide reasons for thinking, Eble presents practical teaching techniques for stimulating and encouraging thinking in the classroom. He advocates teaching students to think in every course rather than in one course, as the nature of thinking is subject-specific. Eble considers thinking across the curriculum an obvious corollary to writing across the curriculum.

528 Educational Testing Service. "The Thinking to Learn Series." Chapter 25 in *Developing Minds. Vol. 2: Programs for Teaching Thinking*, rev. ed., edited by Arthur L. Costa,

98-100. Alexandria, VA: Association for Supervision and Curriculum Development, 1991.

This chapter provides a description of (1) Strategies for Teaching Critical Thinking across the Curriculum, a two-phase staff development program for secondary school teachers intended to provide methods for integrating the teaching thinking skills into subject area instruction and (2) Inside Story: Dateline Brazil, a three-week instructional unit for sixth and seventh graders that incorporates thinking skills with language arts.

529 Eulie, Joseph. "Teaching Understanding and Developing Critical thinking." *Social Studies* 79, no. 6 (November-December 1988): 260-265. [4 Refs.]

Eulie contends that learning content and developing critical thinking skills are interrelated processes. He suggests strategies of the developmental lesson, decision making, and problem solving for improving the understanding of content and for developing critical thinking in students. He stresses using activities relevant to the lives of students, including four model lessons.

530 Felder, Richard M., and Barbara A. Soloman. "Systems Thinking: An Experimental Course for College Freshmen." *Innovative Higher Education* 12, no. 2 (Spring-Summer 1988): 57-68.

Felder and Soloman describe an experimental interdisciplinary first-level college course, "The Systems Approach to the Universe." Taught at North Carolina State University in Spring 1986, this course had three objectives, including introducing and providing practice in critical questioning and evaluation. The authors provide the course activities and procedures, as well as student and instructors' evaluations. They offer suggestions for teaching such a course.

531 Feuerstein, Reuven. *Instrumental Enrichment: An Intervention Program for Cognitive Modifiability*. Baltimore, MD: University Park Press, 1980. 436 pp. [134 Refs.]

The author presents a detailed description of the Instrumental Enrichment program, describing the concept of cognitive modifiability and mediated learning experience underlying the program, the cognitive deficiencies addressed by the program, the objectives and nature of program materials and instruments, the scope and modality of teacher training provided by the program, and the results of a research study on the program. The program consists of paper-and-pencil exercises divided into fifteen instruments, each focusing on a specific cognitive deficiency while addressing the acquisition of other prerequisites of learning. Teachers must be trained for the understanding and acceptance of the cognitive theory of Instrumental Enrichment; mastery of the program's instruments; and for insight, bridging, and application of the acquired processes. Feuerstein also discusses an experimental evaluation of the program that indicates cognitive modifiability may be achieved and enhanced by appropriate intervention measures.

532 Feuerstein, Reuven, Mildred B. Hoffman, Mogens Reimer Jensen, and Yaacov Rand. "Instrumental Enrichment, An Intervention Program for Structural Cognitive Modifiability: Theory and Practice." Chapter 1 in *Thinking and Learning Skills. Vol. 1: Relating Instruction to Research*, edited by Judith W. Segal, Susan F. Chipman, and Robert Glaser, 43-82. Hillsdale, NJ: Erlbaum, 1985. [5 Refs.]

The authors discuss the Instrumental Enrichment program's underlying theory of structural cognitive modifiability, its approach to the problem of improving retarded performance, and how the program attempts to change the cognitive structure of participating individuals. The discussion delineates the program's conception and use of the mediated learning experience, the nature of its instructional program, and summarizes a study measuring the divergent effects achieved by the program.

533 Feuerstein, Reuven, Mildred B. Hoffman, Yaacov Rand, Mogens R. Jensen, David Tzuriel, and David B. Hoffman. "Learning to Learn: Mediated Learning Experiences and Instrumental Enrichment." *Facilitating Cognitive Development: International Perspectives, Programs, and Practices*, edited by Milton Schwebel and Charles A. Maher, 49-82. New York, NY: Haworth Press, 1986. [77 Refs.]

The authors detail the Instrumental Enrichment program on cognitive modifiability. They discuss the use of the program as a substitute for mediated learning experiences and the characteristics of the program tasks or assignments. The authors give an overview of the program's curriculum with numerous examples of assignments including: orientation in space, family relations, comparisons, and categorization. They discuss the program's implications for educators and provide a list of studies and evaluations of Instrumental Enrichment.

534 Feuerstein, Reuven, Ronald Miller, Mildred B. Hoffman, Ya'acov Rand, Yael Mintzker, and Mogens Reimer Jensen. "Cognitive Modifiability in Adolescence: Cognitive Structure and the Effects of Intervention." In *Thinking Skills Instruction: Concepts and Techniques*, edited by Marcia Heiman and Joshua Slomianko, 189-201. Building Students' Thinking Skills. Washington, DC: National Education Association, 1987. [5 Refs.]

Reprinted from *Journal of Special Education* 15 (Summer 1981): 269-287.

The authors focus on intervention as a means to help children who are victims of cultural deprivation or the inability to learn or modify learning even under conducive learning conditions (e.g., direct exposure to stimuli). Feuerstein and his colleagues believe that this syndrome is the result of insufficient mediated learning experiences in which a mediator interprets the world to a learner. Thus, the learner lacks the cognitive structures that connect, organize, integrate, and relate stimulus information. The authors describe an intervention program, Instrumental Enrichment, designed to help culturally deprived adolescents and cite empirical research supporting the effectiveness of the program.

535 Feuerstein, Reuven, Ya'acov Rand, Mildred B. Hoffman, Moshe Egozi, and Nilly Ben Shachar-Segev. "Intervention Programs for Retarded Performers: Goals, Means, and Expected Outcomes." In *Educational Values and Cognitive Instruction: Implications for Reform*, edited by Lorna Idol and Beau Fly Jones, 139-178. Hillsdale, NJ: Lawrence Erlbaum, 1991. [20 Refs.]

Feuerstein and his colleagues address the "creaming-up" phenomenon in thinking programs designed to enhance the thinking of advantaged students. They argue that these programs are based on the prerequisites of cognitive, emotional, motivational, and functional basic school skills, making them inaccessible to individuals lacking these skills. It is these individuals or retarded performers who most need an intervention program. The authors outline the deficient functions in retarded performance followed by guidelines for the selection and production of tasks programs should include to develop cognitive processes, critical thinking, problem solving behavior, creative thinking, philosophical modes of thinking, and lateral thinking in retarded performers. The authors stress the importance of content-free programs and of training teachers as mediators to meet goals for retarded performers.

536 Fisher, Robert. *Teaching Children to Think*. Oxford, UK: Blackwell, 1990. 272 pp. [240 Refs.]

Fisher discusses the nature of thinking and thinking skills. He examines the concepts of creative thinking, critical thinking and problem solving, and suggests ways these concepts can be taught. Fisher details the teaching methods and approaches used in the Instrumental Enrichment and Philosophy for Children programs. He describes ways thinking can be taught across the curriculum, detailing approaches for language arts and mathematics, and then outlining approaches that can be used in science, design and technology, geography, history, art, music, movement, and computer assisted instruction. Fisher concludes by identifying seven factors in teaching that foster thinking in children: (1) building student self esteem, (2) reaching each child, (3) listening with care, (4) being genuine, (5) being positive, (6) being clear, and (7) being a learner too.

537 Fogarty, Robin. "The Thinking Log: The Inking of Our Thinking." Chapter 42 in *Developing Minds. Vol. 1: A Resource Book for Teaching Thinking*, rev. ed., edited by Arthur L. Costa, 232-242. Alexandria, VA: Association for Supervision and Curriculum Development, 1991. [14 Refs.]

Fogarty describes the value of the thinking log in promoting various higher levels of thinking in students. The article includes illustrations of different types of thinking logs used in the classroom.

538 Fountain, Gwen, and Esther Fusco. "A Strategy to Support Metacognitive Processing." Chapter 45 in *Developing Minds. Vol. 1: A Resource Book for Teaching Thinking*, rev. ed., edited by Arthur L. Costa, 255-258. Alexandria, VA: Association for Supervision and Curriculum Development, 1991. [38 Refs.]

Fountain and Fusco discuss the effectiveness of the series of nine questions they developed to support metacognitive processing in kindergarten to college students.

539 Freie, John F. "Thinking and Believing." *College Teaching* 35, no. 3 (Summer 1987): 89-91. [2 Refs.]

Freie contends that the process of critical thinking leads toward a belief in one position, rather than a consideration of multiple perspectives. He believes that teachers must develop procedures that allow students to experience multiple perspectives. Freire describes Peter Elbow's methodological belief in conjunction with critical thinking. With this procedure, students compare and defend multiple perspectives as if each were true and then apply critical thinking to each perspective. Freie includes one example and lists seven conditions which make the procedure most effective.

540 Gallo, Delores. "Think Metric." *Thinking Skills Instruction: Concepts and Techniques*, edited by Marcia Heiman and Joshua Slomianko, 284-303. Building Students' Thinking Skills. Washington, DC: National Education Association, 1987. [9 Refs.]

Gallo provides an outline of principles and recommendations for creating a classroom climate conducive to cultivating attitudes and traits for critical and creative thinking within a content area. She illustrates incorporating thinking skills into a content area with an interdisciplinary unit on the metric system.

541 Girle, Roderic A. "A Top-Down Approach to the Teaching of Reasoning Skills." In *Thinking, the Expanding Frontier. Proceedings of the International, Interdisciplinary Conference on Thinking Held at the University of the South Pacific, January, 1982*, edited by William Maxwell, 139-147. Philadelphia, PA: Franklin Institute Press, 1983. [16 Refs.]

Girle notes that the most common approach to the teaching of reasoning skills concentrates on detail at the expense of context. This results in a highly negative attitude to reasoning and argument. Girle argues that most reasoning and arguments have an interactive context that should be approached and taught as dialogues rather than isolated abstraction. He sketches the content of a course in reasoning using the dialogue approach.

542 Greenfield, Lois Broder. "Teaching Thinking through Problem Solving." In *Developing Critical Thinking and Problem-Solving Activities*, edited by James E. Stice, 5-22. New Directions for Teaching and Learning, no. 30. San Francisco, CA: Jossey-Bass, 1987. [33 Refs.]

Greenfield reviews the theories, research studies, and methods used to analyze problem solving that have influenced the way problem solving is defined and taught. She outlines seven ways in which educators can help students learn appropriate problem solving processes. The author believes that any attention to problem solving skills and instruction in thinking skills in the classroom leads to an improvement in those skills.

543 Halpern, Diane F. "Thinking across the Disciplines: Methods and Strategies to Promote Higher-Order Thinking in Every Classroom." *Thinking Skills Instruction: Concepts and Techniques*, edited by Marcia Heiman and Joshua Slomianko, 69-76. Building Students' Thinking Skills. Washington, DC: National Education Association, 1987. [6 Refs.]

Halpern provides suggestions and ideas for enhancing higher order thinking in the classroom, for developing a thinking attitude in students, and testing thinking skills through examinations and homework assignments.

544 Hayes, John R. *The Complete Problem Solver*. 2d ed. Hillsdale, NJ: Lawrence Erlbaum Associates, 1989. 357 pp.

This text is designed to help individuals develop problem solving skills and to provide current information on the psychology of problem solving. Suitable as a text for a college-level course on problem solving, this work contains twelve chapters organized by the categories of Problem Solving Theory and Practice, Memory and

Knowledge Acquisition, Decision Making, and Creativity and Invention. Each chapter covers a subtopic of the section theme, exploring findings from research studies, providing examples which illustrate appropriately aspects of the subtopic, and providing practice exercise problems. These chapters cover such topics as understanding problems through the process of representation, protocol analysis, searching for solutions, learning strategies, cost-benefit analysis, and the relationship of social conditions and creativity. Appendices include information on time management and probabilities.

545 Hayes, John R. "Three Problems in Teaching General Skills." Chapter 17 in *Thinking and Learning Skills. Vol. 2: Research and Open Questions*, edited by Susan F. Chipman, Judith W. Segal, and Robert Glaser, 391-405. Hillsdale, NJ: Lawrence Erlbaum, 1985. [11 Refs.]

Hayes discusses three problems confronting the teaching of general skills: (1) proficiency in some general skills may require an accumulation of a body of knowledge that may take years to acquire, (2) the hundreds of learning skills and strategies that may be reasonable to teach, and (3) the problem of transferring those skills or strategies to other applications. Hayes explores the number of years great composers needed to acquire the necessary music knowledge to create great works and argues that this is indicative of most skills and strategies. He lists 50 strategies that he uses in a first level college problem solving course and argues that other strategies should be employed depending on the level of the students, subject of the course, or teacher presenting the material. He also discusses the problem of transfer, suggesting that transfer does not occur unless it is taught.

546 Haynes, John B. "Philosophy for Children and the Critical Thinking Movement: Reply to Mulvaney." *Thinking about Thinking: Proceedings of the Thirty-First Annual Meeting of the South Atlantic Philosophy of Education Society*, edited by Samuel M. Craver, 20-23. Richmond, VA: South Atlantic Philosophy of Education Society, 1987. [8 Refs.]

Reply to Mulvaney {594}

While finding little to criticize in Mulvaney's paper, Haynes questions whether the Philosophy for Children program meets Dewey's investigative criteria which calls for reflection on past experience and future consequences. The criteria require going beyond the learning of formal and informal logic. Haynes also questions whether philosophy should be introduced into the elementary curriculum. He notes that the relative merits and results of the program are still being debated.

547 Haywood, H. Carl, Penelope Brooks, and Susan Burns. "Cognitive Curriculum for Young Children." Chapter 27 in *Developing Minds. Vol. 2: Programs for Teaching Thinking*, rev. ed., edited by Arthur L. Costa, 107-109. Alexandria, VA: Association for Supervision and Curriculum Development, 1991.

The authors describe the goals and six principal components of Cognitive Curriculum for Young Children (CCYC), an educational program designed primarily for use with children from three to six years old who are either handicapped or at-risk. A theory-based curriculum, CCYC was developed for use with a content-focused curriculum to facilitate perceiving, thinking, learning, and problem solving.

548 Heiman, Marcia. "Learning to Learn." Chapter 13 in *Developing Minds. Vol. 2: Programs for Teaching Thinking*, rev. ed., edited by Arthur L. Costa, 51-53. Alexandria, VA: Association for Supervision and Curriculum Development, 1991.

Printed also in Costa {505}, pp. 227-229.

Heiman gives the history and theory behind the Learning to Learn (LTL) system. A system of critical thinking skills originally designed to help educationally disadvantaged college students, it has been adapted for use with junior and senior high school students. It is intended to improve the academic performance of students in content areas and to improve their reasoning, reading, writing, and listening skills.

549 Heiman, Marcia. "Learning to Learn: A Behavioral Approach to Improving Thinking." Chapter 25 in *Thinking: The Second International Conference*, edited by David N. Perkins, Jack Lochhead, and John C. Bishop, 431-452. Hillsdale, NJ: Lawrence Erlbaum, 1987. [40 Refs.]

Heiman discusses the genesis and principle components of the behavioral program Learning to Learn Improvement

System and reviews research conducted on the program. She cites Skinner's writings on thinking to show the framework behaviorism uses in approaching the learning and teaching of thinking. Heiman contrasts the behaviorism approach with the cognitive science approach and argues that behaviorism may have a more internally consistent explanation for the process of thinking than other frameworks. She believes the Learning to Learn System, as an example of how the behavioral analysis of thinking can be applied, shows the success a behavioral program can have in predicting long-term improvement in students' thinking across the academic disciplines.

550 Heiman, Marcia. "Learning to Learn: Improving Thinking Skills across the Curriculum." In *Thinking Skills Instruction: Concepts and Techniques*, edited by Marcia Heiman and Joshua Slomianko, 87-91. Building Students' Thinking Skills. Washington, DC: National Education Association, 1987. [1 Ref.]

Reprinted from *Educational Leadership* 43 (September 1985): 20-24.

Heiman describes the background, components, and effectiveness of the Learning to Learn program. This program, with its three stages: (1) input--gathering information, (2) organization--arranging information for further analysis, and (3) output--student demonstration of mastery of the material, has been effectively implemented in colleges and secondary schools through integration in the classroom content and as separate credit courses.

551 Heiman, Marcia, and Joshua Slomianko. *Critical Thinking Skills*. Analysis and Action Series. Washington, DC: National Education Association, 1985. 48 pp. [44 Refs.]

Heiman and Slomianko view critical thinking as skills inherent in the internal dialogue an individual engages in when listening and reading. After reviewing research studies and programs for improving critical thinking, the authors provide numerous exercises that teachers might use to help improve the critical thinking skills of students, especially middle school through high school. They present each exercise with teaching examples that contrasts the active learning versus passive learning approach, followed by a brief discussion. The authors also include examples for imaginative writing, decision making, and for generating questions and examples. They offer suggestions for providing feedback to students and having students work in pairs.

552 Heiman, Marcia, and Joshua Slomianko, eds. *Thinking Skills Instruction: Concepts and Techniques*. Building Students' Thinking Skills. Washington, DC: National Education Association, 1987. 312 pp.

This compilation of 35 articles and interviews with noted proponents of teaching thinking skills, encompasses a range of ideas, techniques, and programs for fostering thinking skills in the classroom. While most of the articles have general application, some relate specifically to special students or subject areas.

553 Hembrow, Vern. "A Heuristic Approach across the Curriculum." *Language Arts* 63, no. 7 (November 1986): 674-679.

Hembrow describes how an elementary school teacher nurtures his fifth grade students' ability to think for themselves and to take increasing control of their learning process. The teacher uses the heuristic approach across the curriculum, employing the techniques of inquiry, collaborative decision making, investigation, journal writing, peer evaluation, and collaborative projects, to create a community of learners and critical thinkers supportive of each other.

554 Herrenstein, Richard J., Raymond S. Nickerson, Margarita de Sánchez, and John A. Swets. "Teaching Thinking Skills." *American Psychologist* 41, no. 11 (November 1986): 1279-1289. [13 Refs.]

This article describes Project Intelligence, an experimental program administered in Venezuela, designed to teach cognitive skills relative to learning and intellectual performance outside the context of academic subject content. The program focused on enhancing performance in tasks requiring observation and classification, inductive or deductive reasoning, critical use of language, hypothesis generation and testing, problem solving, inventiveness, and decision making. Twenty-four (24) seventh grade classes, representing socio-economically deprived students and six schools, participated in the evaluation of the program. Results showed that students in the program improved their cognitive skills and their ability to deal with multiple choice questions. Although program developers and administrators were uncertain about the long-term benefits of the course, they were convinced that cognitive skills could be taught and enhanced by direct instruction.

555 Hobbs, Deborah E., and Carol L. Schlichter. "Talents Unlimited." Chapter 20 in *Developing Minds. Vol. 2: Programs for Teaching Thinking*, rev. ed., edited by Arthur L. Costa, 73-78. Alexandria, VA: Association for Supervision and Curriculum Development, 1991. [11 Refs.]

Hobbs and Schlichter describe Talents Unlimited, a process model for teaching critical and creative thinking to kindergarten through twelfth grade students (K-12). Based on Calvin Taylor's theory of multiple talent approach, its purpose is to help teachers identify and nurture a range of talent in students in the areas of productive thinking, communication, forecasting, decision making, planning, and traditional academic talent. The authors provide background on the original project and its three components: (1) inservice training for teachers, (2) materials development to support integration of talent processes into regular classroom instruction, and (3) evaluation of student performance.

556 Hoelzel, Norma J. "Basics in Bloom." *Thinking Skills Instruction: Concepts and Techniques*, edited by Marcia Heiman and Joshua Slomianko, 128-133. Building Students' Thinking Skills. Washington, DC: National Education Association, 1987.

Hoelzel uses the six levels of Bloom's taxonomy of thinking skills and a list of appropriate verbs under each to illustrate a means of developing the questioning skills of fifth grade students. After modeling questioning with the verbs listed under Application, Analysis, Synthesis, Evaluation, Knowledge, and Comprehension on a social studies topic being studied, Hoelzel had students follow suit. Students were then given an opportunity to apply the technique to an assignment relating to a topic in science.

557 Hyerle, David. "Expand Your Thinking." Chapter 5 in *Developing Minds. Vol. 2: Programs for Teaching Thinking*, rev. ed., edited by Arthur L. Costa, 16-26.

Alexandria, VA: Association for Supervision and Curriculum Development, 1991. [18 Refs.]

Hyerle describes the Expand Your Thinking program which is designed to introduce fifth through seventh grade students to six thinking processes and graphic tools for applying these processes to content learning while working in cooperative pairs. The article includes illustrations of graphic tools.

558 Idol, Lorna, Beau Fly Jones, and Richard E. Mayer. "Classroom Instruction: The Teaching of Thinking." Chapter 3 in *Educational Values and Cognitive Instruction: Implications for Reform*, edited by Lorna Idol and Beau Fly Jones, 65-119. Hillsdale, NJ: Lawrence Erlbaum, 1991. [171 Refs.]

The authors describe general and subject-specific characteristics of thinking, presenting subject-specific examples in mathematics, science, and language arts. They examine the role of the teacher in cognitive instruction, exploring various functions of the teacher as manager, as a guide to explicit instruction, and as a strategist. They compare selected model programs/approaches in fifteen categories, including efficacy evidence, characteristic thinking skills, targeted population, guidance for program use, expected outcomes, and cost effectiveness. The authors recommend cognitive instruction that includes three goals: (1) immediate relevancy for students, (2) aid in general school achievement, and (3) enhancement of generalized application and learning. The chapter includes a chart detailing the comparison of the selected programs and approaches.

559 Isaksen, Scott G., and Donald J. Treffinger. "Creative Learning and Problem Solving." Chapter 23 in *Developing Minds. Vol. 2: Programs for Teaching Thinking*, rev. ed., edited by Arthur L. Costa, 89-93. Alexandria, VA: Association for Supervision and Curriculum Development, 1991. [4 Refs.]

The authors outline the levels, principles, and components of their Creative Learning and Problem Solving program for young children through adults. Two fundamental principles underlying the program are deferred judgment and affirmative judgment. Isaksen and Treffinger note that their approach is based on extensive research.

560 Johnson, David W., and Roger T. Johnson. "Critical Thinking through Structured Controversy." *Educational Leadership* 45, no. 8 (May 1988): 58-64. [10 Refs.]

The authors describe a structured controversy curriculum program developed to teach critical thinking and higher level reasoning skills. The program requires students to explore, advocate, and discuss assigned positions on selected issues. They outline the six-stepped, four-hour program and discuss the basic format teachers should use when organizing structured controversies. The authors also discuss the prerequisites to constructive controversy and the benefits of a structured controversy program to students. The article includes several charts outlining the program.

561 Johnson, Tony W. "Philosophy for Children and Its Critics--Going beyond the Information Given." *Educational Theory* 37, no. 1 (Winter 1987): 61-68. [17 Refs.]

Johnson defends the Philosophy for Children program against criticism of teaching programs expressed by John McPeck and Jeffrey Kane. Johnson argues that the program meets McPeck's criteria requiring a subject-specific, epistemically-oriented approach and should not be included among the programs McPeck criticizes. Johnson asserts that Kane's critique of Philosophy for Children overemphasizes logic and misrepresents how the Harry Stottlemeier novels are used in the program.

562 Jones, Beau Fly, Annemarie Sullivan Palincsar, Donna Sederburg Ogle, and Eileen Glynn Carr, eds. *Strategic Teaching and Learning: Cognitive Instruction in the Content Areas*. Elmhurst, IL: North Central Regional Educational Laboratory, 1987. 167 pp. [288 Refs.]

The editors present a framework for strategic thinking based on cognitive science and research on teaching. They present strategic thinking as a role and process in which the teacher is constantly thinking and making decisions, has a rich knowledge base of content and strategies for teaching and learning, and acts as a model and mediator in the classroom. The editors discuss six assumptions about how students learn and think: (1) learning is goal oriented, (2) learning is linking new information to prior knowledge, (3) learning is organizing knowledge, (4) learning is strategic, (5) learning occurs in phases and is recursive, and (6) learning is influenced by development. They proceed to explore the parameters of strategic thinking: (1) aligning the variables of instruction, (2) relating content and instruction to learning, (3) developing effective strategy instruction, (4) relating assessment to learning and instruction, and (5) considering contextual factors. The editors discuss the characteristics of the strategic teacher and draw parallels between strategic teaching and learning. They include three planning guides that use strategic teaching and present an example of the process one teacher used to plan for strategic teaching. The last half of the book includes descriptions of strategic teaching and learning used in four content areas: science, social studies, mathematics, and literature.

563 Karmos, Joseph S., and Ann H. Karmos. "Strategies for Active Involvement in Problem Solving." *Thinking Skills Instruction: Concepts and Techniques*, edited by Marcia Heiman and Joshua Slomianko, 99-110. Building Students' Thinking Skills. Washington, DC: National Education Association, 1987. [6 Refs.]

The authors describe specific problem-solving strategies, such as thinking aloud, trial and error, and working backwards, as well as classroom procedures to encourage students to become active problem solvers. They emphasize the importance of students having practice and guidance in problem solving and of problem solving skills being an integral part of the curriculum in all subject areas.

564 Kealey, Robert J. "The Present Task: Thinking and Valuing Skills." *Momentum* 17, no. 3 (September 1986): 14-16. [3 Refs.]

Kealey notes that the role of the Roman Catholic school is not only to provide students with the skills to become independent learners, but also to enable them to deepen their commitment to Christian values. He believes that helping students form values is inherent in helping them acquire critical thinking skills. Students learn critical thinking skills through content material by which teachers have opportunities to focus on specific values raised in the material. Kealey proposes a program of critical thinking skills; presents a listing of critical thinking skills under four broad headings (Identification, Evaluation, Manipulation, and Expression); and suggests teaching methods to be used by schools.

565 Lane, N. R., and S. A. Lane. "Rationality, Self-Esteem and Autonomy through Collaborative Enquiry." *Oxford Review of Education* 12, no. 3 (1986): 263-275. [51 Refs.]

The authors contend that the best way for developing reasoning skills in children is through a teaching strategy that combines the teaching of reasoning skills with a non-authoritarian, inquiry-based approach that encourages discussion and collaboration between teacher and students. They believe using this approach increases student autonomy and self-esteem. The approach is employed in the Philosophy for Children program of Matthew Lipman which has successfully taught reasoning skills to primary school students. The authors attribute the failure of other programs that have tried to introduce more democratic teaching strategies to teacher training that emphasizes an authoritarian/knowledge-based approach.

566 Lehrer, Richard. "Logo as a Strategy for Developing Thinking?" *Educational Psychologist* 21, no. 1-2 (Winter/Spring 1986): 121-137. [72 Refs.]

Lehrer explores the debate over the utility and effectiveness of Logo as an instructional strategy for developing thinking or increasing intelligence by examining conceptions of intelligence through the root metaphors of mechanism and contextualism. Computational models of intelligence and developmentally oriented theories of intelligence are associated with mechanism and with variations of contextualism, respectfully. Lehrer discusses ideal learning and instructional practices for Logo within the context of both the mechanist and contextualist perspectives. The discussion covers problem solving skills, discovery learning, and the transfer of skills, knowledge, and ideas to other contexts. Lehrer proposes reconciling the two perspectives and developing an understanding of Logo as a strategy for developing thinking by distinguishing among three levels of cognitive processing: cognition, metacognition, and epistemic cognition.

567 Link, Frances R. "Instrumental Enrichment." Chapter 3 in *Developing Minds. Vol. 2: Programs for Teaching Thinking*, rev. ed., edited by Arthur L. Costa, 9-11. Alexandria, VA: Association for Supervision and Curriculum Development, 1991.

Printed also in Costa {505}, pp. 193-195.

Link describes the Instrumental Enrichment program developed by Reuven Feuerstein for altering the cognitive style of retarded performers in upper elementary, middle, and secondary school levels from passivity and dependence to active, self-motivated, independent thinkers. The program emphasizes the process of learning rather than specific skills and subject matter. The article includes an outline of a three-year sequence of the program.

568 Link, Frances R. "Instrumental Enrichment: A Strategy for Cognitive and Academic Improvement." Chapter 5 in *Essays on the Intellect*, edited by Frances R. Link, 89-106. Alexandria, VA: Association for Supervision and Curriculum Development, 1985. [12 Refs.]

This is a review of the Instrumental Enrichment program for improving cognitive performance through identifying and addressing cognitive deficiencies. Link outlines the program's major goals and strategies, and contrasts them to other programs and positions. She describes the components of the three year Instrumental Enrichment curriculum and discusses its use of mediated learning. The paper includes specific examples of the successful implementation of the program into schools.

569 Link, Frances R. "Thinking to Write: Assessing Higher-Order Cognitive Skills and Abilities." Chapter 4 in *Developing Minds. Vol. 2: Programs for Teaching Thinking*, rev. ed., edited by Arthur L. Costa, 12-15. Alexandria, VA: Association for Supervision and Curriculum Development, 1991.

Link describes the Thinking to Write program in which the Student Work Journal serves as an evaluation instrument for students and teachers. Through this weekly mediated, structured writing experience, students' anxiety over writing is reduced; students gain insight into their cognitive processes; teachers can assess students' understanding of concepts, principles, and strategies used in problem solving;

and teachers can evaluate organizational skills, summative behavior, and awareness of the mental processes used in structured writing experiences.

570 Lipman, Matthew. "Philosophy for Children." Chapter 8 in *Developing Minds. Vol. 2: Programs for Teaching Thinking*, rev. ed., edited by Arthur L. Costa, 35-38. Alexandria, VA: Association for Supervision and Curriculum Development, 1991. [3 Refs.]

Revision of Costa {505}, pp. 212-214.

Lipman describes the goals, materials, training, and effectiveness of the Philosophy for Children program. The program provides opportunities for students from kindergarten through high school to read, discuss, and apply thinking skills.

571 Lipman, Matthew. "Some Thoughts on the Foundations of Reflective Education." Chapter 8 in *Teaching Thinking Skills: Theory and Practice*, edited by Joan Boykoff Baron and Robert J. Sternberg, 151-161. New York, NY: W. H. Freeman, 1987. [11 Refs.]

Lipman outlines the components of the Philosophy for Children program, reviewing its disciplinary and methodological sources and the cognitive skills it is designed to sharpen.

572 Lipman, Matthew. "Thinking Skills Fostered by Philosophy for Children." Chapter 2 in *Thinking and Learning Skills. Vol. 1: Relating Instruction to Research*, edited by Judith W. Segal, Susan F. Chipman, and Robert Glazer, 83-108. Hillsdale, NJ: Lawrence Erlbaum, 1985. [24 Refs.]

Lipman summarizes the major features of the Philosophy for Children program, including an overview of its basic ideas and assumptions, its use of modeling as a teacher training technique, how it encourages group dialogue, and the methods employed for teaching thinking skills apart from knowledge acquisition and problem solving. He outlines several evaluation studies of the Philosophy of Children Program and identifies 30 thinking skills the program aims to teach.

573 Lipman, Matthew, Ann Margaret Sharp, and Frederick S. Oscanyan. *Philosophy in the Classroom*. Philadelphia, PA: Temple University Press, 1980. 231 pp. [139 Refs.]

The authors argue that philosophy should be taught as an integral, but separate, discipline in the elementary through primary school curriculum. The authors describe the Philosophy for Children program which aims to help children learn to think for themselves by engaging in classroom philosophical discussions on topics presented in novels written for the program. The classroom discussions enable students to improve their reasoning skills and creativity and develop their ability to find meaning in experience through active participation in a community of inquiry. The authors relate teacher training, attitudes and behavior conducive to guiding classroom discussions, and helping students engage in philosophical reasoning. In the final unit of the book, the authors discuss how formal logic is used in the program and the relationship of moral education and ethical inquiry to philosophical inquiry. Two appendices are included. Appendix A outlines a teacher education program that prepares teachers for integrating philosophy into the school curriculum and encouraging philosophical thinking. Appendix B outlines four research studies on the educational significance of the Philosophy for Children program.

574 Lochhead, Jack. "Teaching Analytic Reasoning Skills through Pair Problem Solving." Chapter 3 in *Thinking and Learning Skills. Vol. 1: Relating Instruction to Research*, edited by Judith W. Segal, Susan F. Chipman, and Robert Glaser, 109-131. Hillsdale, NJ: Lawrence Erlbaum, 1985. [25 Refs.]

Lochhead describes the pair problem solving approach which he and Whimbey developed. The approach requires students to work together in pairs on assigned problems. One partner reads and thinks aloud, while the other listens. Lochhead provides examples of problems. He outlines the cognitive theory behind the use of pair problem solving and, in particular, the role played by verbalization. Lochhead summarizes an evaluation study of the program and suggests means for conducting future evaluations.

575 Lochhead, Jack, and Arthur Whimbey. "Teaching Analytical Reasoning through Thinking Aloud Pair Problem Solving." In *Developing Critical Thinking and Problem-Solving Abilities*, edited by James E. Stice, 73-92.

New Directions for Teaching and Learning, no. 30. San Francisco, CA: Jossey-Bass, 1987. [19 Refs.]

Lochhead and Whimbey describe and illustrate a problem solving method effective for developing thinking skills. This method, Thinking Aloud Pair Problem Solving (TAPPS) requires students to work in pairs, one student serves as problem solver and the other as listener. The listener analyzes the process, initialing the steps, diversions, and errors, used by the problem solver who recounts everything that goes through his/her head while solving the problem. The authors provide a checklist of the sources and types of errors in problem solving. They devote most of the article to the application of TAPPS to teaching analytical reasoning in reading and mathematics, providing sample problems.

576 Lown, Jean M. "Teaching Issue Analysis and Critical Thinking through Role Playing." *Journal of Education for Business* 62, no. 1 (October 1986): 20-23. [8 Refs.]

Lown advocates using role playing as a means for fostering communication, reasoning, and analytical skills and demonstrating influences on public decision making. Recommending a legislative hearing as the format for this activity, the author offers suggestions and guidelines for preparing for the exercise, selecting topics, providing handouts, and debriefing. A sample issue example illustrates role playing possibilities.

577 Makau, Josina M. "Perspectives on Argumentation Instruction." Chapter 41 in *Argumentation: Analysis and Practice. Proceedings of the Conference on Argumentation 1986*, edited by Frans H. van Eemeren, Rob Grootendorst, J. Anthony Blair, and Charles A. Willard, 376-385. Dordrecht, The Netherlands: Foris Publications, 1987. [24 Refs.]

Makau believes that good argumentation instruction teaches critical thinking, reading, listening, speaking, and writing skills necessary for full participation in democratic institutions. The author identifies five key characteristics found in good argumentation instruction: (1) ethical considerations, (2) focus on critical thinking, (3) recognition of audience and context as central to good argumentation, (4) attention to the central role values and emotions play in good reasoning, and (5) the teaching of oral and written advocacy skills. Makau compares three competing North American pedagogical approaches: the informal logic approach, the traditional debate perspective, and the "new rhetoric" view. The informal logic approach focuses on the development of critical thinking skills, but neglects to teach students to consider fully the role audience plays in argument formulation and analysis. The traditional debate school focuses on oral advocacy skills and neglects written advocacy skills and the evaluation of written texts. The "new rhetoric" school teaches both critical thinking and advocacy skills, and stresses the importance of oral and written argumentation and analytical skills. The latter approach also stresses ethical considerations, as well as the audience. Makau argues that it is the only approach that contains all five of the characteristics of good argumentation instruction.

578 Makau, Josina M. *Reasoning and Communication: Thinking Critically about Arguments*. Belmont, CA: Wadsworth, 1990. 251 pp. [125 Refs.]

Intending to assist individuals in acquiring and developing organized knowledge, understanding, and skills, Makau organized this text into three parts: Critical Thinking Process, Argumentation Skills, and Applications. In Part 1: The Critical Thinking Process, Makau focuses on the definition and elements of critical thinking (e.g., questioning skills, viewing skills, and listening skills) as background for Part 2: Argumentation Skills. In Part 2, Makau explores the meaning of argumentation, its elements, and contexts in which it effectively contributes to decision making, and follows with discussion, exercises, and examples helpful in preparing arguments and in evaluating argumentation. In Part 3: Applications, Makau provides exercises for applying the principles in Parts 1 and 2 to family life issues.

579 Marzano, Robert J. "Tactics for Thinking: A Program for Initiating the Teaching of Thinking." Chapter 18 in *Developing Minds. Vol. 2: Programs for Teaching Thinking*, rev. ed., edited by Arthur L. Costa, 65-68. Alexandria, VA: Association for Supervision and Curriculum Development, 1991. [5 Refs.]

Marzano describes Tactics for Thinking as a way for individual teachers, school, and districts to explore the teaching of thinking by selecting tactics most useful for the particular content area or classroom. The program is not intended to be implemented as a complete program. The program includes strategies for the development of 22 cognitive skills which are arranged into three categories: learning-to-learn strategies, content thinking strategies, and reasoning strategies.

580 Marzano, Robert J., Ronald S. Brandt, Carolyn Sue Hughes, Beau Fly Jones, Barbara Z. Presseisen, Stuart C. Rankin, and Charles Suhor. "Critical and Creative Thinking." Chapter 3 in *Dimensions of Thinking: A Framework for Curriculum and Instruction*, 17-31. Alexandria, VA: Association for Supervision and Curriculum Development, 1988.

As a part of the framework for teaching thinking, the authors emphasize the complementary nature of critical and creative thinking. Both types of thinking should be integrated within regular academic instruction. Included within this chapter are goals for a critical thinking curriculum, strategies and techniques for integrating both types of thinking in the classroom and an exploration of the implications of critical and creative thinking.

581 McCarty, T. L., Stephen Wallace, and Regina Hadley Lynch. "Inquiry-Based Curriculum Development in a Navajo School." *Educational Leadership* 46, no. 5 (February 1989): 66-71. [9 Refs.]

This is a report of a curriculum project to develop a bilingual, bicultural, inquiry-based curriculum at Rough Rock Demonstration School on the Navajo Reservation in Arizona. The curriculum emphasizes open-ended questioning and inductive inquiry and incorporates culturally meaningful concepts and experiences. The curriculum is based on the three-phase process of inductive inquiry outlined by Hilda Taba: questions for developing concepts, questions for developing main ideas, and questions for applying ideas and generalizations. The project was not completed due to funding problems.

582 McGuinness, Carol. "Talking about Thinking: The Role of Metacognition in Teaching Thinking." Chapter 20 in *Lines of Thinking: Reflections on the Psychology of Thought. Vol. 2: Skills, Emotion, Creative Processes, Individual*

Differences and Teaching Thinking, edited by K. J. Gilhooly, M. T. G. Keane, R. H. Logie, and G. Erdos, 301-312. New York, NY: John Wiley, 1990. [57 Refs.]

McGuinness explores three instructional traditions used in teaching the thinking curriculum, focusing on the role played by metacognition and metacognitive tools in the thinking skills courses of each tradition. The three approaches examined are cognitive strategies, critical thinking, and knowledge restructuring. McGuinness outlines the theoretical traditions, methods of instruction, variations in programs within each tradition, and the use of metacognition in each program. The metacognitive emphasis of each approach is with the individual learner. The author outlines an approach of cognitive apprenticeship and modeling which emphasizes social interaction, dialogues, and mediating models.

583 McPeck, John E. "A Second Look at de Bono's Heuristics for Thinking." In *Thinking, the Expanding Frontier. Proceedings of the International, Interdisciplinary Conference on Thinking Held at the University of the South Pacific, January, 1982*, edited by William Maxwell, 163-175. Philadelphia, PA: Franklin Institute Press, 1983. [10 Refs.]

McPeck criticizes the CoRT and PO programs designed by Edward de Bono. He argues that the CoRT program assumes thinking to be a generalized skill separate from any subject content. Its exercises emphasize the quantity rather than quality of responses and overlooks the need for background knowledge in order to judge what responses are relevant to the exercise. Neither the CoRT or PO programs contain an account for response criteria nor recognize the important role knowledge and subject-content have in thinking.

584 McTighe, James J. "Teaching for Thinking, Of Thinking, and About Thinking." *Thinking Skills Instruction: Concepts and Techniques*, edited by Marcia Heiman and Joshua Slomianko, 24-30. Building Students' Thinking Skills. Washington, DC: National Education Association, 1987.

McTighe describes three distinct and complementary approaches effective for developing and improving students' thinking abilities: teaching for thinking, teaching of thinking, and teaching about thinking. McTighe includes examples of applications of these approaches in the classroom.

585 McTighe, Jay, and Frank T. Lyman, Jr. "Cueing Thinking in the Classroom: The Promise of Theory-Embedded Tools." *Educational Leadership* 45, no. 7 (April 1988): 18-24. [26 Refs.]

An adapted version in Costa {506}, pp. 243-250.

McTighe and Lyman describe six teaching/learning devices that promote thinking in the classroom. Based on theoretically valid teaching/learning ideas, these devices or tools are a means of combining theory and practice in the classroom. The authors provide examples and uses of Think-Pair-Share, Questioning/Discussion Strategies Bookmark, Thinking Matrix, Ready Reading Reference, Problem-Solving Strategies Wheel, and Cognitive Mapping. Such instructional tools are effective in that they serve as memory aids, provide a common frame of reference, readily combine theory and practicality, and offer an inherent permanence.

586 Mechanic, Janevive Jean. *The Logic of Decision Making: An Introduction to Critical Thinking*. American University Studies. Series V., Philosophy, vol. 9. New York, NY: Peter Lang, 1988. 205 pp. [12 Refs.]

The author intends this book for students and practitioners in such fields as business, law, medicine, and education, and for anyone wishing to improve the quality of his/her decisions. The text emphasizes the nature of decision making and the application of critical thinking in professional and personal life. According to Mechanic, the ideal procedure for decision making consists of a cycle of nine phases: (1) collecting background information, (2) recognizing and defining a problem, (3) collecting and organizing relevant information, (4) formulating tentative solutions, (5) presenting factors to support and oppose alternatives, (6) evaluating alternative solutions and choosing the most promising one, (7) estimating possible adverse consequences of tentative decisions and reconsidering decisions, (8) implementing decisions, and (9) following up. Mechanic uses situations from newspapers, magazines, and personal experience as examples and exercises for applying critical thinking.

587 Meeker, Mary N. "Structure of Intelligence (SOI)." Chapter 2 in *Developing Minds. Vol. 2: Programs for Teaching Thinking*, rev. ed., edited by Arthur L. Costa, 3-8. Alexandria, VA: Association for Supervision and Curriculum Development, 1991. [6 Refs.]

Revision of Costa {505}, pp.187-192.

Meeker describes the Structure of Intellect (SOI), based on Guildford's theory of intelligence. She emphasizes its use in differentiating between basic thinking skills and higher-level critical thinking abilities, identifying learning abilities necessary for success in specific subject areas, and providing developmental plans for critical thinking competency through curricula.

588 Meichenbaum, Donald. "Teaching Thinking: A Cognitive-Behavioral Perspective." Chapter 18 in *Thinking and Learning, v.2: Research and Open Questions*, edited by Susan F. Chipman, Judith W. Segal, and Robert Glaser, 407-426. Hillsdale, NJ: Lawrence Erlbaum, 1985. [93 Refs.]

Meichenbaum reviews literature illustrating the importance of instructing and training children in self-management skills such as goal setting, strategy planning, self-monitoring, and metacognition. He presents general guidelines for teaching thinking based on cognitive behavior modification and metacognition. Meichenbaum discusses the influence and implications that feelings have for the teaching of thinking and the pedagogical implications of the cognitive behavior modification approach.

589 Melchior, Timothy M., Robert E. Kaufold, and Ellen Edwards. "Using CoRT Thinking in Schools." *Educational Leadership* 45, no. 7 (April 1988): 32-33.

The authors report success in using de Bono's CoRT program over a five-year period in a junior high school. They discuss seven of the CoRT tools and provide examples of how the tools can be used with various assignments in different disciplines. The authors include an example of educators using CoRT tools outside of the classroom.

590 Meyers, Chet. *Teaching Students to Think Critically: A Guide for Faculty in All Disciplines*. San Francisco, CA: Jossey-Bass, 1986. 131 pp. [59 Refs.]

Intended primarily to assist undergraduate college faculty with approaches for developing critical thinking in students, this work is based on the concept that critical thinking incorporates logical reasoning and problem solving, processes which take different forms in the context of different academic disciplines. Meyers calls for the direct teaching of critical thinking in all disciplines and for different approaches to teaching it within various disciplines. He stresses the need for a basic framework for analysis of materials in a discipline or a perspective that organizes and makes the discipline meaningful for students. Meyers provides practical suggestions for structuring classes and designing effective assignments for the promotion of critical thinking and includes sample program and exercise models. He describes model critical thinking seminars for faculty development used at various universities.

591 Miller, Robert. "Teaching Students to Evaluate Materials That Contain Judgments." *Teaching English in the Two-Year College* 12, no. 3 (October 1985): 207-209. [2 Refs.]

Miller proposes a method for helping high school and community college students learn to make rational judgments about opinion articles. The method requires students to summarize the main idea and supporting points. Students must determine whether the article is based on fact or opinion, reflects authorial bias, if their experiences conflict with the author's, and whether they accept, reject, or defer judgment on the article. Miller presents this concept in a model of critical power, a modification of a pyramid of reading power.

592 Mirman, Jill, and Shari Tishman. "Infusing Thinking through 'Connections'." *Educational Leadership* 45, 7 (April 1988): 64-65. [7 Refs.]

Mirman and Tishman discuss Connections, a program to assist teachers in integrating the teaching of thinking into all subjects. Connections consists of a set of thinking strategies for decision making, problem solving, communication, and understanding. Students apply the strategies through subject matter lessons.

593 Moore, Brooke Noel, and Richard Parker. *Critical Thinking: Evaluating Claims and Arguments in Everyday Life*. Palo Alto, CA: Mayfield, 1986. 413 pp.

A practical textbook of formal and informal logic intended for students within the first two years of college. Part One: Claims consists of seven chapters on understanding and evaluating claims, explanations, pseudoreasoning, and nonargumentative persuasion with numerous sample exercises based primarily on examples from media (including letters to editors, opinion magazine articles, television news programs, and advertising). Part Two: Arguments consists of five chapters on understanding and evaluating arguments, covering deductive arguments, inductive reasoning, causal arguments, and moral reasoning and including appropriate exercises. Answers and suggestions for some of the exercises are included in the back of the book.

594 Mulvaney, Robert J. "Philosophy for Children and the Critical Thinking Movement." *Thinking about Thinking: Proceedings of the Thirty-First Annual Meeting of the South Atlantic Philosophy of Education Society*, edited by Samuel M. Craver, 12-19. Richmond, VA: South Atlantic Philosophy of Education Society, 1987. [10 Refs.]

Mulvaney argues that criticisms of the Critical Thinking Movement by McPeck, Sternberg, and Adler, while valid for many of the Movement's programs, are not applicable to Matthew Lipman's Philosophy for Children program. Mulvaney holds that the program avoids many of the criticisms by having as its subject the teaching of thinking about thinking, the characteristic of most philosophical thought. He asserts that since philosophical problems are found in every area of human discourse, the program, through its emphasis on real-life problems and group discussion, is cross-disciplinary. Mulvaney views Philosophy for Children as a complement to Adler's Paideia program, and urges its introduction into elementary school curriculum as early as possible. He contends that studies show student improvement in reading comprehension, logic, mathematics, and linguistic skills after participation in the program.

595 Mulvaney, Robert J. "Philosophy for Children and the Modernization of Chinese Education." *Thinking* 7, no. 2 (1987): 7-11.

Mulvaney discusses the nature of the Philosophy for Children Program, outlining the major features and educational goals of the program, and tracing its link to educational reform in the United States. He argues that the program's approach and goals epitomize many of the educational goals of China and should be introduced into Chinese education.

596 Munro, George, and Allen Slater. "The Know-How of Teaching Critical Thinking." *Social Education* 49, no. 4 (April 1985): 284-292.

Munro and Slater present a framework for learning critical thinking skills that can be used for curriculum development. The framework defines teachers' learning expectations for students, organizes the learning outcomes for teachers, and illustrates the relationships among the various types of learning. The authors use the skill of distinguishing between fact and opinion to illustrate the steps used in planning for teaching critical thinking. These general steps include: (1) classifying the skill as a learning outcome, (2) identifying what knowledge and skills students need to perform the thinking skill, and (3) identifying the characteristics of the concepts students must know and use in executing the critical thinking skill. Munro and Slater provide graphic illustrations of (1) the framework for learning, (2) using the framework to analyze critical thinking skills, and (3) a model for teaching critical thinking skills.

597 Nardi, Anne H., and Charles E. Wales. "Thinking Skills: Making a Choice." Chapter 11 in *Developing Minds. Vol. 2: Programs for Teaching Thinking*, rev. ed., edited by Arthur L. Costa, 43-47. Alexandria, VA: Association for Supervision and Curriculum Development, 1991. [2 Refs.]

Revision in Costa {505}, pp. 220-223.

The authors contend that the decision making process should be the focus of teaching and learning. They believe that the process should be directly and explicitly taught at all levels and integrated throughout the curriculum. Nardi and Wales recommend Guided Design, a teaching strategy that provides step-by-step guidance for teaching the decision making process at any level.

598 Nickerson, Raymond S. "Project Intelligence: An Account and Some Reflections." *Facilitating Cognitive Development: International Perspectives, Programs, and Practices*, edited by Milton Schwebel and Charles A. Maher, 83-102. New York, NY: Haworth Press, 1986. [5 Refs.]

Nickerson describes Project Intelligence's background, curriculum materials, program objectives, problems encountered, and evaluation of student progress. He reflects on several aspects of teaching thinking, including teacher competence and enthusiasm, the institutional context in which a teaching program is to be introduced, transferability of thinking skills, thinking skills versus knowledge, the need to use real-life problems, freedom versus structure in the classroom, and the need to integrate what is taught in thinking skills courses into the rest of the curriculum.

599 Nilsen, Alleen, Ken Donelson, Don Nilsen, and Marie Donelson. "Humor for Developing Thinking Skills." *Et Cetera* 44, no. 1 (Spring 1987): 63-75. [5 Refs.]

The authors contend that humor can entice people into thinking in terms that are investigative, seeking, grasping, and filled with trial and error. They believe that humor should be incorporated into the curriculum of English, journalism, and communication classes to aid in the development of student thinking abilities. They provide examples of how humor may be used to improve thinking skills and offer suggestions for incorporating humor into the classroom.

600 O'Flahavan, J. F., and Robert J. Tierney. "Reading, Writing, and Critical Thinking." Chapter 2 in *Educational Values and Cognitive Instruction: Implications for Reform*, edited by Lorna Idol and Beau Fly Jones, 41-64. Hillsdale, NJ: Lawrence Erlbaum, 1991. [48 Refs.]

O'Flahavan and Tierney argue that reading and writing are powerful ways to promote critical thinking because of the synergistic and symbiotic nature of integrated reading and writing engagements. The authors summarize two characteristics of the reading/writing connection: (1) how the cognitive operations involved in the composing acts of reading and writing vary and (2) how reading and writing contribute to critical thought. They explore how and why a self-initiating learner engaged in complex learning situations depends on the acts of reading and writing, using an example of a hospital administrator. The authors discuss the implications the reading/writing connection has for instruction and research.

601 Olson, Carol Booth. "The California Writing Project." Chapter 9 in *Developing Minds. Vol. 2: Programs for Teaching Thinking*, rev. ed., edited by Arthur L. Costa, 39. Alexandria, VA: Association for Supervision and Curriculum Development, 1991.

Printed also in Costa {505}, pp. 215-216.

Booth provides a brief description of the University of California at Irvine Thinking/Writing Project intended as a development approach to foster critical thinking skills through writing. The project involves curriculum development, teacher training, and evaluation.

602 Page, Helen Ward. "Literature across the College Curriculum." *Journal of Reading* 31, no. 6 (March 1988): 520-523. [2 Refs.]

Page provides descriptions of community college courses in applied psychology, environmental science, and accounting. These courses were redesigned to incorporate literature as a means for promoting understanding of content and developing critical thinking skills.

603 Parker, Walter C. "Teaching Thinking: The Pervasive Approach." *Journal of Teacher Education* 38, no. 3 (May-June 1987): 50-56. [38 Refs.]

Parker asserts that thinking should be incorporated throughout the curriculum as a means for learning subject matter, acknowledging that the amount of content taught will have to be reduced to accommodate the time required for thinking. Since content can be thought about in various ways, teachers must employ diverse strategies for engaging students in thinking. Most of this article is devoted to the advantages and limitations of two strategies (concept formulation and critical reasoning) for infusing thinking into the kindergarten through twelfth grade curriculum, and for developing critical thought. Parker stresses that there is no one best strategy, but advocates using a combination of the two strategies in conjunction with metacognition.

604 Parnes, Sidney J. "Creative Problem Solving." Chapter 14 in *Developing Minds. Vol. 2: Programs for Teaching Thinking*, rev. ed., edited by Arthur L. Costa, 54-56. Alexandria, VA: Association for Supervision and Curriculum Development, 1991. [4 Refs.]

Revision of Costa {505}, pp. 230-232.

Parnes outlines the objectives of the Creative Problem Solving (CPS) program which is based on the work of Alex F. Osborn. The program focuses on developing abilities and attitudes for creative learning, problem sensing, and problem solving. Parnes notes the effectiveness of the program as shown through research studies. The program is intended for middle school students (especially gifted students) and secondary school students.

605 Pauker, Robert A. "School Interest in Thinking is More Than a Fad." *School Administrator* 44, no. 1 (January 1987): 16-19.

Pauker provides vignettes of thinking skills programs in eight districts across the nation as an aid to others designing and implementing programs. Each vignette concludes with a suggestion from the district. This activity represents part of the force behind the 1980's thinking movement which, Pauker asserts, was not present in previous thinking movements over the past four decades.

606 Paul, Richard W. "Dialogical and Dialectical Thinking." Chapter 49 in *Developing Minds. Vol. 1: A Resource Book for Teaching Thinking*, rev. ed., edited by Arthur L. Costa, 280-289. Alexandria, VA: Association for Supervision and Curriculum Development, 1991. [10 Refs.]

Paul stresses the importance of fostering dialogical and dialectical thinking in schools. He identifies four things teachers need to learn: (1) how to identify and distinguish multilogical from monological problems and issues, (2) how to teach Socratically, (3) how to use dialogical and dialectical thought to master content, and (4) how to assess dialogical and dialectical thought. Paul notes that these can be mastered only over an extended period of time. He discusses each of the areas, providing examples of learning and teaching strategies. Paul also stresses the importance of moving instruction in the direction of dialogical and dialectical thinking slowly and carefully with a long-term staff development plan.

607 Paul, Richard W. "Ethics without Indoctrination." *Educational Leadership* 45, no. 8 (May 1988): 10-19. [9 Refs.]

Paul asserts that moral education in public schools usually attempts to indoctrinate students into a particular ethical perspective or dogma. He argues that such indoctrination can be avoided by incorporating critical thinking into the moral education curriculum. He discusses integrating consideration of moral issues into other subjects such as literature, science, and history. Paul outlines the implementation of an inservice design for the integration of critical thinking and ethical reasoning. He calls for administrators to lead the way in fostering critical thinking and moral education. The article includes several charts listing moral reasoning skills and moral virtues that may be taught.

608 Paul, Richard. "Teaching Critical Thinking in the Strong Sense." Chapter 16 in *Developing Minds. Vol. 1: A Resource Book for Teaching Thinking*, rev. ed., edited by Arthur L. Costa, 77-84. Alexandria, VA: Association for Supervision and Curriculum Development, 1991. [6 Refs.]

Paul outlines the elements of critical thought as micro-skills, macro-abilities, and traits of mind. He advocates teaching with a strong-sense approach to critical thinking. Teachers should develop students' micro-skills and macro-abilities in the context of intellectual standards and values. Paul outlines nine traits essential to critical thinking: (1) independence of mind, (2) intellectual curiosity, (3) intellectual courage, (4) intellectual humility, (5) intellectual empathy, (6) intellectual integrity, (7) intellectual perseverance, (8) faith in reason, and (9) fair-mindedness. He explores the interdependence of these traits and suggests ways of teachers can foster these traits in their students.

609 Paul, Richard. "Teaching Critical Thinking in the 'Strong' Sense: A Focus on Self-Deception, World Views, and a Dialectical Mode of Analysis." *Informal Logic* 4, no. 2 (May 1982): 2-7. [9 Refs.]

Paul distinguishes between teaching critical thinking in the "weak" sense and the "strong" sense, and discusses the dangers of the former and the advantages of the latter. Rather than teaching "a battery of atomistic technical skills independent of egocentric beliefs and commitments" (p. 3), i.e., teaching critical thinking in the "weak" sense, Paul advocates teaching critical thinking in the strong sense, focusing on world views and a dialectical/dialogical approach to arguments through multicategorical ethical issues. The author provides a theoretical basis for the "strong" sense approach and describes sample assignments.

610 Paul, Richard W., A. J. A. Binker, Karen Jensen, and Heidi Kreklau. *Critical Thinking Handbook: 4-6th Grades. A Guide for Remodelling Lesson Plans in Language Arts, Social Studies, and Science*. Rohnert Park, CA: Center for Critical Thinking and Moral Critique, Sonoma State University, 1990. 442 pp. ED 325 804.

This guidebook is intended to help fourth through sixth grade teachers incorporate critical thinking into their classroom instruction through remodeling lesson plans in various subject areas and through understanding the theoretical background of critical thinking. The first part contains eight chapters with examples and applications of remodeling strategies and illustrations of 52 traditional or standard lesson plans remodeled to facilitate critical thinking. Part II, with seven chapters, covers the definitions and theories of critical thinking, learning, knowledge, and literacy and includes staff development possibilities. The appendices include recommended readings and other resources for teaching critical thinking.

611 Paul, Richard W., A. J. A. Binker, Douglas Martin, and Ken Adamson. *Critical Thinking Handbook: High School. A Guidebook for Redesigning Instruction*. Rohnert Park, CA: Center for Critical Thinking and Moral Critique, Sonoma State University, 1989. 424 pp. ED 325 805.

This guidebook is intended to help secondary school teachers incorporate critical thinking into their classroom instruction through remodeling lesson plans in various subject areas and through understanding of the theoretical concepts and background related to critical thinking. Part I, containing seven chapters, covers remodeling strategies with suggestions, examples, and applications and illustrates 64 remodeled lessons in social studies, language arts, science, mathematics, Spanish, typing, physical education, work experience, and interdisciplinary areas. Part II, containing seven chapters, covers the definitions and theories of critical thinking, learning, knowledge, and literacy and offers staff development possibilities. The appendices include recommended readings and other resources for teaching critical thinking.

612 Paul, Richard W., A. J. A. Binker, Douglas Martin, Chris Vetrano, and Heidi Kreklau. *Critical Thinking Handbook: 6-9th Grades. A Guidebook for Remodelling Lesson Plans in Language Arts, Social Studies, & Science*. Rohnert Park, CA: Center for Critical Thinking and Moral Critique, Sonomo State University, 1989. 328 pp. ED 308 481.

This guidebook is intended to help sixth through ninth grade teachers incorporate critical thinking into their classroom instruction through remodeling lesson plans in various subject areas and through an understanding of the theoretical concepts and background of critical thinking. The guidebook is divided into two parts, with Part I covering remodeling strategies and their applications, as well as illustrations of standard lesson plans remodeled to facilitate critical thinking. Part II covers the definitions and theories of critical thinking, knowledge, learning, and literacy and provides staff development possibilities.

613 Paul, Richard W., A. J. A. Binker, and Daniel Weil. *Critical Thinking Handbook: K-3rd Grades. A Guide for Remodelling Lesson Plans in Language Arts, Social Studies, & Science*. Rohnert Park, CA: Center for Critical Thinking and Moral Critique, Sonoma State University, 1990. 420 pp. ED 325 803.

This guidebook is intended to help kindergarten through third grade teachers incorporate critical thinking into their classroom instruction through remodeling lesson plans in various subject areas and through understanding the theoretical background information of critical thinking. Part I, containing nine chapters, provides examples and applications of numerous remodeling strategies and illustrates ways of changing traditional or standard approaches found in 69 lesson plans to approaches that facilitate critical thinking. These lesson plans cover social sciences, language arts, science, mathematics, and a thematic unit. Part II, containing seven chapters, covers the definitions and theories of critical thinking, learning, knowledge, and literacy and staff development possibilities. The appendices include recommended readings and other resources for teaching critical thinking.

614 Perkins, D. N. *Knowledge as Design*. Hillsdale, NJ: Lawrence Erlbaum, 1986. 247 pp. [110 Refs.]

According to Perkins, conceiving of knowledge as design means viewing pieces of knowledge as "structures adapted to a purpose" (p. 4) rather than as mere information. Knowledge is embedded rather than disconnected from its contexts of application. Perkins outlines a systematic approach to using the theme of design as a tool for understanding knowledge. The approach entails the posing of four questions intended to open the nature of any design: (1) what is its purpose or purposes, (2) what is its structure, (3) what are model cases of it, and (4) what are arguments that explain and evaluate it. Perkins presents several examples to demonstrate how to apply each question. He discusses other topics such as how to recognize and evaluate designs, reading and writing by design, art and design, models, and argument by design. Perkins offers suggestions for instruction using knowledge as design and discusses the use of the design approach to teach for transfer of learning from subject to subject and context to context. Each chapter concludes with suggestions of activities for learners or teachers.

615 Pfeiffer, Kenneth, Gregory Feinberg, and Steven Gelber. "Teaching Productive Problem-Solving Attitudes." Chapter 8 in *Applications of Cognitive Psychology: Problem Solving, Education, and Computing*, edited by Dale E. Berger, Kathy Pezdek, and William P. Banks, 99-107. Hillsdale, NJ: Lawrence Erlbaum, 1987. [14 Refs.]

The authors suggest general techniques for teaching skills such as problem solving and describe general characteristics or attitudes of good problem solvers. The teacher must provide an environment that gives students relevant practice and motivates them to practice. Teachers should also be good models of problem solving. Common characteristics or attitudes found in good problem solvers include: inquiry, open-mindedness, belief in one's own problem solving abilities, seeing problems as challenges, and seeing problems in a larger perspective. The teacher should provide facts, appropriate models, motivation, practice exercises, and feedback to cultivate the acquisition of problem solving skills and attitudes.

616 Pickering, Debra, and Karen Harvey. "Toward an Integrating Framework for Teaching Thinking." *Educational Leadership* 45, no. 7 (April 1988): 46. [1 Ref.]

This one-page article covers the efforts in the Cherry Creek Schools (CO) for maintaining thinking skills as a lasting integral part of the instructional program, including practical staff development activities, a coaching program, and a proposal for the adoption of a thinking skills framework modeled after *Dimensions of Thinking* {278}.

617 Pogrow, Stanley. "Helping Students to Become Thinkers." *Electronic Learning* 4, no. 7 (April 1985): 26-29, 79.

Progrow describes a Higher Order Thinking Skills (HOTS) project using computers to help increase critical thinking skills. He outlines the four primary techniques of the program: (1) working a basic concept through a number of different computer environments, (2) using tasks that require the use and synthesis of information from a variety of subject areas, (3) linking ideas discovered in the computer lab to concepts presented in the regular classroom, and (4) having students teach recent classroom content to the computer. Results of field tests using the HOTS curriculum indicate that improved thinking ability is attained when students are not substantially deficient in both reading and math. Progrow includes charts listing computer hardware and software used for the HOTS lab and briefly discusses other computer-assisted HOTS programs.

618 Pogrow, Stanley. "HOTS." Chapter 17 in *Developing Minds. Vol. 2: Programs for Teaching Thinking*, rev. ed., edited by Arthur L. Costa, 62-64. Alexandria, VA:

Association for Supervision and Curriculum Development, 1991. [4 Refs.]

Revision of Costa {505}, pp. 239-240.

Pogrow provides a description of the Higher-Order Thinking Skills (HOTS) program designed specifically for at-risk students in fourth through seventh grades in Chapter 1 and Learning Disabilities (LD) programs. The program involves computers, Socratic teaching strategies, and specially designed curricular materials. The program is also being used for gifted students in kindergarten and first grade and for the early detection of gifted minority students in first and second grades.

619 Pogrow, Stanley. "Learning Dramas: An Alternative Curricular Approach to Using Computers with At-Risk Students." Chapter 46 in *Developing Minds. Vol. 1: A Resource Book for Teaching Thinking*, rev. ed., edited by Arthur L. Costa, 259-265. Alexandria, VA: Association for Supervision and Curriculum Development, 1991. [12 Refs.]

Adapted from the chapter by the same title in *Technology in Today's Schools*, edited by Cynthia Warger, (Alexandria, VA: Association for Supervision and Curriculum Development), 1990, pp. 103-118.

Pogrow describes the Higher-Order Thinking Skills (HOTS) curricular program he developed for using computers with at-risk students, especially for those in fourth through seven grades. The approach combines the use of Socratic dialogue, drama, computer software, and information processing theories of learning. Pogrow describes a technique called learning dramas which he uses with HOTS.

620 Pogrow, Stanley. "A Socratic Approach to Using Computers with At-Risk Students." *Educational Leadership* 47, no. 5 (February 1990): 61-66. [10 Refs.]

Recognizing the ineffectiveness of computer-assisted instruction in meeting the needs of at-risk students beyond the third grade, Pogrow developed a HOTS (higher order thinking skills) program. The four components of the program: (1) computers as problem-solving settings, (2) dramatic techniques, (3) Socratic conversations, and (4) thinking skill development are discussed. Computer software was used for its motivational quality and for presenting interesting activities rather than content or technical expertise. Pogrow argues that computers should not be viewed as deliverers of instruction, but as means for developing creative and sophisticated curricula and pedagogical practices. He suggests techniques for developing students' thinking skills of metacognition, decontextualization, inference from context, and information synthesis using software.

621 Pogrow, Stanley. "Teaching Thinking to At-Risk Elementary Students." *Educational Leadership* 45, no. 7 (April 1988): 79-85. [1 Ref.]

Pogrow describes success in using a Higher Order Thinking Skills (HOTS) program with a wide range of students, especially in developing the thinking skills of at-risk students. From experience with and evidence from the program, Pogrow discusses conclusions about the conditions required for using thinking skills programs with at-risk students. Emphasis is on helping at-risk students develop a sense of understanding before integrating thinking skills into the curriculum.

622 Polette, Nancy. "Minireaps! Mini Research Papers That Make Kids Think." *School Library Media Activities Monthly* 4, no. 4 (December 1987): 24-26. [2 Refs.]

Polette discusses the benefits of using one-page research reports to develop thinking, reading, and writing skills. She provides detailed examples of assignments and evaluative criteria.

623 Polson, Peter G., and Robin Jeffries. "Instruction in General Problem-Solving Skills: An Analysis of Four Approaches." Chapter 12 in *Thinking and Learning Skills. Vol. 1: Relating Instruction to Research*, edited by Judith W. Segal, Susan F. Chipman, and Robert Glaser, 417-455. Hillsdale, NJ: Lawrence Erlbaum, 1985. [67 Refs.]

The authors analyze two programs, the Productive Thinking Program and CoRT Thinking Lessons, and two textbooks, *Patterns of Problem Solving* by Moshe Rubinstein (Englewood Cliffs, NJ: Prentice-Hall, 1975), and *How to Solve Problems: Elements of a Theory of Problems and Problem Solving* by Wayne A. Wickelgren (New York, NY: W.H. Freeman, 1973).

624 Porter, Thomas E., Charles Kneupper, and Harry Reeder. *The Literate Mind: Reading, Writing, Critical Thinking.* Dubuque, IA: Kendall/Hunt, 1987. 216 pp.

The authors focus on teaching reading and writing from three perspectives: exposition, argumentation, and self-expression. Emphasis is on integrating reading and writing using critical thinking and the general heuristic methodologies of topoi and tagamenics. The application of these methodologies are demonstrated for writing and for understanding and interpreting narrative, drama, and poetry. This book is based on CACTIP (Composition, Analysis of Texts, Critical Thinking Integrated Program), a program initiated by the University of Texas at Arlington in 1985. The authors characterize the literate mind as reflective, methodical, inventive, curious, flexible, confident, recursive, and dialogic.

625 Presseisen, Barbara Z. *Thinking Skills throughout the Curriculum: A Conceptual Design.* Bloomington, IN: Pi Lambda Theta, 1987. 109 pp. [155 Refs.]

Presseisen provides a guidebook for establishing, designing, and implementing a thinking skills program in the kindergarten through twelfth grade curriculum. She includes sample activities, lessons, lesson plans, and evaluation forms for instructional materials and programs, and an outline of a thinking skills program.

626 Pritchard, Michael S. *Philosophical Adventures with Children.* New York, NY: University Press of America, 1985. 155 pp. [7 Refs.]

This book is primarily a collection of excerpts from student discussions during an after-school enrichment program Pritchard developed and taught to select fifth graders. The program used Matthew Lipman's novel, *Harry Stottlemeier's Discovery*, as a basis for the classroom discussions. Topics covered in the discussions include elementary informal logic, personal identity, evidence, brain and mind, and self-knowledge. Pritchard augments the discussions with his own interpretations of what occurred in the student dialogues. He includes examples of discussions with fifth and sixth graders in a different school district.

627 Queenan, Margaret. "Finding the Grain in the Marble." *Language Arts* 63, no. 7 (November 1986): 666-673. [7 Refs.]

Using the research process of professional researchers as a model, Queenan's students in "The Research Paper" course used primary sources (e.g., eyewitnesses and experts) for their research topics. The author emphasizes the importance of allowing time for students to reflect and come to conclusions. She describes some of the ways that she helps students reflect through peer conferences and learning logs. Queenan asserts that the research process is not enough to satisfy researchers or students; the product is also important.

628 Quellmalz, Edys S., and Janita Hoskyn. "Making a Difference in Arkansas: The Multicultural Reading and Thinking Project." *Educational Leadership* 45, no. 7 (April 1988): 52-55. [2 Refs.]

With the collaboration of teachers and state department reading specialists, a three-year project to develop critical thinking abilities and increase cultural awareness was implemented in fourth, fifth, and sixth grades in seven school districts. This project, Multicultural Reading and Thinking, focused on the following four categories of reasoning skills: analysis, comparison, inference/ interpretation, and evaluation for designing instructional lessons and on the direct instruction approach. The instructional approach guided students through an inquiry process involving nine components. Quellmalz provides information on the means and results of assessing this project.

629 Roberts, Ernestine W. "Using Vocabulary Study to Generate Thinking." In *Thinking Skills Instruction: Concepts and Techniques*, edited by Marcia Heiman and Joshua Slomianko, 202-207. Building Students' Thinking Skills. Washington, DC: National Education Association, 1987. [2 Refs.]

Roberts suggests vocabulary study as a means of teaching thinking skills in all secondary education disciplines. She provides a number of exercises that can be used in various disciplines for vocabulary enrichment and for practice in thinking.

630 Rosen, Joan G. "Problem-Solving and Reflective Thinking: John Dewey, Linda Flower, Richard Young." *Journal of Teaching Writing* 6, no. 1 (Spring 1987): 69-78. [6 Refs.]

Rosen links Richard E. Young's *Rhetoric: Discovery and Change* (New York, NY: Harcourt, Brace, Jovanovich, 1970) and Linda Flower *Problem-Solving Strategies for Writing* (New York, NY: Harcourt, Brace, Jovanovich, 1981) to Dewey's theory of inquiry. She compares the methods proposed in both works to Dewey's five phases of reflective thought. Rosen finds significant similarities in all three approaches.

631 Rubin, Ronald Lee. "Developing Students' Thinking Skills through Multiple Perspectives." In *Thinking Skills Instruction: Concepts and Techniques*, edited by Marcia Heiman and Joshua Slomianko, 230-235. Building Students' Thinking Skills. Washington, DC: National Education Association, 1987.

This chapter includes numerous activities which use divergent questioning for developing students' thinking skills by helping them appreciate and understand multiple perspectives. These activities are intended for grades six through twelve, but Rubin believes that they could be adapted for younger or older students. In addition to developing thinking skills, these activities foster creativity, research skills, and various abilities associated with social studies and language arts curricula.

632 Rubinstein, Moshe F., and Iris R. Firstenburg. "Tools for Thinking." In *Developing Critical Thinking and Problem-Solving Abilities*, edited by James E. Stice, 23-36. New Directions for Teaching and Learning, no. 30. San Francisco, CA: Jossey-Bass, 1987. [11 Refs.]

The authors believe that problem solving ability depends on the enrichment of a knowledge base, a repertoire of thinking tools, and cultivation of attitudes that allow for a productive integration of knowledge and thinking. They focus on guides or heuristics for acquiring knowledge, for presenting and restructuring a problem, and for solving a problem. Emphasis is on allowing time for reflection on a problem in order to consider alternative solutions and new perspectives before moving toward a solution.

633 Rudinow, Joel, and Richard Paul. "A Strategy for Developing Dialectical Thinking Skills." In *Thinking Skills Instruction: Concepts and Techniques*, edited by Marcia Heiman and Joshua Slomianko, 92-98. Building Students' Thinking Skills. Washington, DC: National Education Association, 1987. [20 Refs.]

Rudinow and Paul define dialectical thinking skills as reflective self-criticism and reasoning sympathetically within alternative frames of reference. Emphasizing the importance of teaching dialectical thinking skills in critical thinking courses, the authors discuss the nature of these skills and present an instructional strategy for exercising and developing them. The instructional strategy involves dividing a class into groups corresponding to their initial positions on an issue, each group preparing a defense of their position, and each group preparing a defense for a position it initially opposed. Defenses are presented and discussed with the class.

634 Ruggiero, Vincent Ryan. *The Art of Thinking: A Guide to Critical and Creative Thought*. 2d. ed. New York, NY: Harper & Row, 1988. 233 pp.

Ruggiero designed this text to be used in thinking courses. He believed that a text on thinking should: (1) emphasize what to do more than what to avoid doing, (2) introduce students to the principles and techniques of creative thinking, (3) teach students how to critique ideas, and (4) teach students how to persuade others. The work includes fifteen chapters, covering analytical skills, the creative process, expressing problems or issues, investigating problems or issues, producing ideas, the role of criticism, evaluating arguments, and communicating ideas. Each chapter includes warm-up exercises and applications exercises. The appendices include guides to composition, conversation and group discussion, and logic.

635 Ruggiero, Vincent Ryan. *Teaching Thinking across the Curriculum*. New York, NY: Harper & Row, 1988. 225 pp. [173 Refs.]

Designed to aid in preparing teachers to teach thinking skills, this book presents a holistic approach to the teaching of thinking, integrating creative and critical thinking into a single heuristic for problem solving and issue analysis. Ruggiero addresses questions frequently asked about the teaching of thinking and identifies (a) obstacles to cognitive development, (b) instructional objectives and methods for developing dispositions associated with effective thinking, (c) developing the habits and skills that enhance the production and evaluation of ideas, (d) guidelines for evaluating student progress in thinking, and (e) suggestions for developing thinking skills programs. Ruggiero discusses his holistic heuristic of exploration, expression, investigation, idea production, and evaluation/refinement as a model for encouraging engagement in classroom discussions and promoting independent thinking. He presents suggestions for developing general thinking exercises for courses on thinking, courses that include thinking as a secondary objective, and exercises of general significance to particular academic disciplines.

636 Sadler, William A., Jr. "Holistic Thinking Skills Instruction: An Interdisciplinary Approach to Improving Intellectual Performance." In *Thinking Skills Instruction: Concepts and Techniques*, edited by Marcia Heiman and Joshua Slomianko, 183-188. Washington, DC: National Education Association, 1987.

Sadler discusses the effectiveness of holistic instruction in thinking skills. Such instruction combines analytical thinking practice with communication throughout the curriculum as a means of improving students' intellectual skills. He shares practical information on implementing such a program gained from experiences at Bloomfield College (NJ) and Paul Robeson High and Middle School (Chicago).

637 Sadler, William A., Jr., and Arthur Whimbey. "A Holistic Approach to Improving Thinking Skills." *Phi Delta Kappan* 67, no. 3 (November 1985): 199-203. [25 Refs.]

Whereas Beyer proposes teaching thinking skills as a variety of skills based on a taxonomy ({205} and {206}), Sadler and Whimbey advocate using a holistic approach to teach thinking skills. The authors share six principles which they formulated for a holistic approach in use at Robeson High School (Chicago) and Bloomfield College (NJ). Based on psychological research and ten years of classroom teaching, these six principles are: (1) teaching active learning, (2) articulating thinking, (3) promoting intuitive understanding, (4) structuring courses developmentally, (5) motivating learning, and (6) establishing a positive social climate for learning. Suggested teaching techniques accompany discussions of the principles.

638 Salinger, Terry. "Critical Thinking and Young Literacy Learners." Chapter 16 in *Teaching Thinking: An Agenda for the Twenty-First Century*, Edited by Cathy Collins, and John N. Mangieri, 319-332. Hillsdale, NJ: Lawrence Erlbaum, 1992. [23 Refs.]

In order to develop classroom environments that encourage critical thinking, teachers should assume that children are active thinkers who attempt to construct knowledge about school-related subjects. Teachers should develop appropriate instructional experiences that encourage students to use their emerging critical thinking skills. Using literacy as an example, Salinger identifies and discusses three classroom components that must be carefully planned and initiated to encourage student critical thinking: (1) the teacher's theoretical stance regarding how they teach, how students learn, classroom structure, and teacher expectations; (2) the teacher's role as a model of thinking strategies, and poser/answerer of questions; and (3) classroom activities and opportunities that allow students to exercise their critical thinking. Salinger suggests that such activities include drawing, shared literacy experiences, supportive group discussions of learning, and extensive experience with the writing process.

639 Scales, Peter. "All Children Need to Think Critically." *PTA Today* 12, no. 7 (May 1987): 8-10.

Scales lists ten critical thinking skills that children need to develop and suggests ways critical thinking can be taught at home. He mentions the efforts of Hawaii and California to promote critical thinking programs.

640 Schiever, Shirley W. *A Comprehensive Approach to Teaching Thinking*. Needham Heights, MA: Allyn and Bacon, 1991. 315 pp. [13 Refs.]

Schiever presents the Spiral Model of Thinking which illustrates the continual developmental and interrelational aspects of cognitive processes. She discusses the developmental thinking processes of classification, concept development, deriving principles, drawing conclusions, and making generalizations. Schiever examines the transference and application of these processes to other tasks requiring complex cognitive strategies, such as problem solving, critical thinking, creative thinking, decision making, and evaluation. She illustrates curricular applications of the Spiral Model, including techniques, curriculum planning, the use of questioning and classroom discussion, methods of self-evaluation for teachers and students, and models for improving teaching skills. Shiever concludes the book with a lengthy discussion of the Hilda Taba Teaching Strategies of concept development, interpretation of data, application of generalizations, and resolution of conflict. Samples for planning, implementing, and applying each strategy are included.

641 Schlichter, Carol L., Deborah Hobbs, and W. Donald Crump. "Extending Talents Unlimited to Secondary Schools." *Educational Leadership* 45, no. 7 (April 1988): 36-40. [4 Refs.]

The authors describe the implementation of Talents Unlimited, a teaching thinking model within secondary schools in New Mexico, Arkansas, and Alabama. The program involves instruction in basic academic skills and in nineteen thinking skills concerning productive thinking, communication, planning, forecasting, and decision making. Its staff development component emphasizes strategies for integrating thinking skills practice and subject content.

642 Schmeck, Ronald R. "Improving Learning by Improving Thinking." *Educational Leadership* 38, no. 5 (February 1981): 384-385.

Schmeck notes that research indicates that people remember and understand information better when they process it deeply and elaboratively by devoting more attention to the possible meanings and classifications of a word or symbol, rather than to the word or symbol itself. He suggests several techniques for encouraging a deep and elaborative style of learning and thinking.

643 Schon, Donald A. "The Design Process." In *Varieties of Thinking: Essays from Harvard's Philosophy of Education Research Center*, edited by V. A. Howard, 110-141. New York, NY: Routledge, 1990. [15 Refs.]

Schon argues that the conception of design as a problem-solving process or rational decision is incomplete due to its reliance on a well-formed design structure; its division into components of selection and generation, which cannot account for important kinds of learning through designing; and its view of rational decision making as individual rather than social or dialectical. Schon analyzes the model of design as rational decision, exploring the theory's division of the design process into components of generation or creation of admissible alternatives for problem solving, and selection or recognizing one alternative as the best. He criticizes the alternative views of random generation and systematic search. Schon then posits his own theory of generative metaphor which focuses on problem setting and problem solving and eliminates the distinction between generation and selection. He conceives designing as a conversation with the materials of a situation, using a metaphor plus the dialogue of its translation into a new situation to yield design structure. The process can be taught as storytelling, i.e., having students tell a diagnostic/prescriptive story about the new situation or system indicating what is wrong and how it may be corrected. Students engage in a social dialogue in which different students or designers frame the situation in different ways and learn to talk across the divergent frames. As generative metaphor, Schon believes that the design process can contribute to an epistemology of problem solving.

644 Schreiber, Anne. "Fire Up Those Brain Cells." *Instructor* 98, no. 3 (October 1988): 62-64.

To help elementary school teachers incorporate a critical thinking program into their lesson plans, Schreiber proposes beginning with three categories of learning goals: communication, creativity, and problem solving. She proceeds by providing three lessons for each of the categories. Five resources are provided at the end of the article.

645 Segal, Judith W., Susan F. Chipman, and Robert Glaser, eds. *Thinking and Learning Skills. Vol. 1: Relating Instruction to Research*. Hillsdale, NJ: Lawrence Erlbaum, 1985. 554 pp.

This is the first of a two volume anthology of presentations given at a conference sponsored by the National Institute of Education on educational practices and scientific research on the cognitive abilities of students. Volume one contains descriptions of programs or approaches to the teaching of thinking that have been implemented in schools. Each chapter was written by the developers of the particular program, and addresses the program's goals, methods, implementation, and relation to research on cognitive functions. The presentations are organized into three sections: Intelligence and Reasoning, Knowledge Acquisition, and Problem Solving. At the end of each section a concluding chapter gives a detailed analysis and comparison of the programs described in that section. A final unit presents educators' experiences in implementing several of the programs.

646 Seiger-Ehrenberg, Sydelle. "Concept Development." Chapter 50 in *Developing Minds. Vol 1: A Resource Book for Teaching Thinking*, rev. ed., edited by Arthur L. Costa, 290-294. Alexandria, VA: Association for Supervision and Curriculum Development, 1991. [3 Refs.]

Revision of Costa, pp. 161-165.

Seiger-Ehrenberg discusses the concept development approach for teaching thinking. The author examines the meaning of concept, suggests strategies for teaching concepts, identifies common elements to concept-learning strategies, and outlines criteria for selecting and evaluating curriculum materials to promote concept development.

647 Sharp, Ann Margaret. "What is a 'Community of Inquiry'?" *Journal of Moral Education* 16, no. 1 (January 1987): 37-45. [12 Refs.]

Sharp explores the characteristics of a classroom community of inquiry. She discusses how a community of inquiry may be created and the role of such a community in fostering rational thinking.

648 Sheingold, Karen. "Keeping Children's Knowledge Alive through Inquiry." *School Library Media Quarterly* 15, no. 2 (Winter 1987): 80-85. [25 Refs.]

The process of inquiry encompasses the comprehensive thinking and learning skills critical to living in an information-based society. Inquiry as an educational model views the learner as an active constructor of his/her own understandings, developed from interactions with the human, physical, and symbolic world. In this model, libraries and media centers are central to the inquiry process and librarians and media specialists are experts in guiding learners through the inquiry process. Sheingold contrasts the traditional model of research assignments in schools with the inquiry model. She addresses the importance of motivation, questioning, and metacognition in the inquiry process, suggesting ways of promoting these elements.

649 Shibles, Warren. *Lying: A Critical Analysis*. Whitewater, WI: Language Press, 1985. 242 pp. [137 Refs.]

Shibles explores the meaning and usage of the term "lying." He examines the characteristics, explanations, and consequences of lying, as well as the relationship between language and thinking. Shibles designed his exploration of "lying" not only to clarify the word, but also to develop the critical thinking skills of the reader. He includes quotations from scholars and examples from actual life situations in support of his examination. Exercises are provided periodically within many chapters. The book is designed to be used either in a classroom or for individual study.

650 Shlesinger, B. Edward, Jr. "I Teach Children to be Inventors." *Educational Leadership* 37, no. 7 (April, 1980): 572-573. [1 Ref.]

Schlesinger outlines a process for teaching children to become better problem solvers through inventing solutions. The process entails identifying a problem, collecting relevant information, asking questions, identifying limitations that may influence a solution, and using imagination as a problem solving tool.

651 Shor, Ira. *Critical Teaching and Everyday Life*. Boston, MA: South End Press, 1980. [80 Refs.]

Shor discusses how critical teaching empowers students by teaching them to think critically. He emphasizes the effect such teaching has upon working class students, enabling them to overcome their educational alienation. He reviews the history of working class entry into higher education and the role played by community colleges and the Open Admissions program at the City University of

New York. Shor outlines a system of liberatory education based on Freirian teaching theories and on his own experiences in the Open Admissions' program. Shor's system promotes discussion founded on experienced-based dialogue and the development of critical thought. The teacher, no longer a coercive lecturer, assumes the roles of fellow discusser, peer, explorer, and advisor. Critical reflection emerges from exploring the concrete practices of everyday life. In the last four chapters, Shor provides examples of his teaching experiences, involving explorations of social life that include critical literacy, conceptual thought and learning, and social inquiry through the use of poetry, drama, and language. Examples of student manuscripts are included in an appendix.

652 Shulik, Jacqueline P. "Project IMPACT in Elementary Schools." *Educational Leadership* 45, no. 7 (April 1988): 41.

Shulik describes briefly the adaptation and implementation of Project IMPACT for second through fifth grade students in Howard County, Maryland.

653 Skorpen, Erling. "The Art of Socratic Reasoning." In *Thinking Skills Instruction: Concepts and Techniques*, edited by Marcia Heiman and Joshua Slomianko, 304-312. Building Students' Thinking Skills. Washington, DC: National Education Association, 1987.

Skorpen illustrates the art of Socratic reasoning with an outline of a dialogue on defining religion. This dialogue incorporates student questions, rationale, and refutation within the classic pattern of definition by example, general definition, and definition by genus and difference. A sample exercise on defining love follows the outline.

654 Slesnick, Twila. "Creative Play: An Alternative Use of the Computer in Education." *Simulation & Games* 14, no. 1 (March 1983): 11-19. [8 Refs.]

Slesnick describes Creative Play, a computer curriculum designed to integrate computer activities with current elementary school curricula. Creative Play provides activities that stimulate the development and sharpening of critical thinking skills. These activities are divided into eight conceptual units containing a number of educational computer games and some related noncomputer activities:

(1) Word Games, (2) Number Games, (3) Coordinate Games, (4) Simulations, (5) Mapping Games, (6) Mazes, (7) Symmetry, and (8) Looking Back.

655 Smith, Carl B. "Two Approaches to Critical Thinking." *Reading Teacher* 44, no. 4 (December 1990): 350-351. [2 Refs.]

Smith highlights two different approaches to teaching critical thinking offered by theorists: (1) open and nonstructured and (2) directed and structured. He suggests using both approaches. Descriptions of four related ERIC documents are given.

656 Sternberg, Robert J. "Five Ways to Think about Thinking Skills." *Instructor* 97, Special Issue (Winter 1987): 32-33.

Sternberg offers the following five tips as ways for improving effectiveness in teaching thinking skills: (1) make the most of textbooks and teacher's manuals containing material designed to foster thinking skills, (2) when presenting problems to students, remember that not all problems are neatly structured, (3) help students learn how to identify and define problems by letting them recognize and define their own problems, (4) make greater use of dialogical instruction, and (5) become sensitive to children's thinking and learning styles.

657 Sternberg, Robert J. "Instrumental and Componential Approaches to the Nature and Training of Intelligence." Chapter 10 in *Thinking and Learning Skills. Vol. 2: Research and Open Questions*, edited by Susan F. Chipman, Judith W. Segal, and Robert Glaser, 215-243. Hillsdale, NJ: Lawrence Erlbaum, 1985. [43 Refs.]

This chapter is a comparison of Reuven Feuerstein's Instrumental Enrichment program and Robert Sternberg's Componential Training Program. The author examines the conceptions of intelligence underlying each program, and compares the different approaches and methods each program uses for training information processing and improving intellectual functioning. He sees value in both programs and believes they represent promising starts toward intellectual training that is routine and successful.

658 Sternberg, Robert J. "Intelligence Applied: A Triarchic Program for Training Intellectual Skills." Chapter 21 in *Developing Minds. Vol. 2: Programs for Teaching Thinking*, rev. ed., edited by Arthur L. Costa, 79-84. Alexandria, VA: Association for Supervision and Curriculum Development, 1991.

Sternberg described his Intelligence Applied program for developing intellectual skills of secondary and college students. It consists of a student's text of narrative material and exercises and a teacher's guide of materials to be used to maximize the effectiveness of the program. Sternberg outlines the five parts of the student text, *Intelligence Applied: Understanding and Increasing Your Intellectual Skills* (New York, NY: Harcourt, Brace, Jovanovich, 1986) and the eight sections within the corresponding chapters of the teacher's guide.

659 Sternberg, Robert J. "Teaching Critical Thinking, Part 1: Are We Making Critical Mistakes?" *Phi Delta Kappan* 67, no. 3 (November 1985): 194-198. [14 Refs.]

See: Sternberg {660}

In this first article of a two-part series, Sternberg addresses the discrepancies between what is taught in critical thinking programs and the problems that require critical thinking in the real world. He outlines ten areas in which the problems used in critical thinking programs differ from those in adulthood. Recognizing a problem exists is the first and often difficult step in everyday problem solving. In the classroom, students are trained to solve problems already posed for them. Sternberg expresses concern that students are not being prepared to meet the demands of everyday life.

660 Sternberg, Robert J. "Teaching Critical Thinking, Part 2: Possible Solutions." *Phi Delta Kappan* 67, no. 4 (December 1985): 277-280. [3 Refs.]

See: Sternberg {659}

In this second article of a two-part series, Sternberg proposes ways to prepare students for solving problems in everyday life, including his self-designed Intelligence Applied program. He responds to the ten areas of discrepancy discussed in Part 1 with sample problems from the program, designed to alleviate and avoid differences between what the student learns to do in the classroom and what is demanded of him/her in life outside the classroom.

661 Sternberg, Robert J., and Marie Martin. "When Teaching Thinking Does Not Work, What Goes Wrong?" *Teachers College Record* 89, no. 4 (Summer 1988): 555-578. [11 Refs.]

Sternberg and Martin present four models of possible problems contributing to the lack of the transmission of thinking skills to students. These involve teaching style, presentation of thinking skills material in textbooks, instructional model, and kinds of problems presented to students. Among the authors' suggestions for improving the transmission process of higher order thinking skills are a dialogical teaching style; an integration of thinking skills within problems in a textbook and of thinking skills materials within text content; and direct instruction using practical, everyday type problems and group and individual problem solving methods.

662 Stice, James E., ed. *Developing Critical Thinking and Problem-Solving Abilities*. New Directions for Teaching and Learning, no. 30. San Francisco, CA: Jossey-Bass, 1987. 115 pp.

This work contains seven chapters written by experts in problem solving skills who believe that such analytical skills can and should be taught. The authors explore options and offer suggestions for teaching problem solving. They also review the research, theories, and experience upon which the options and suggestions are based.

663 Stice, James E. "Further Reflections: Useful Resources." In *Developing Critical Thinking and Problem-Solving Abilities*, edited by James E. Stice, 101-109. New Directions for Teaching and learning, no. 30. San Francisco, CA: Jossey-Bass, 1987. [13 Refs.]

Stice emphasizes the importance of teaching the process of analytical reasoning and giving students practice problems. He describes using the Think Aloud Problem Solving method and shares resources useful for teaching and using analytical reasoning skills.

664 Stonewater, Jerry K. "Strategies for Problem Solving." In *Fostering Critical Thinking*, edited by Robert E. Young, 33-57. New Directions for Teaching and Learning, no. 3. San Francisco, CA: Jossey-Bass, 1980. [36 Refs.]

Stonewater discusses four approaches to teaching problem solving: Guided Design, ADAPT program, Moshe Rubinstein's *Patterns of Problem Solving* (Englewood Cliffs, NJ: Prentice-Hall, 1975) and remedial and developmental education. For each approach, the author describes the strategy, role of the professor, role of the student, results, and applications. Stonewater identifies five components of effective problem solving instruction as (a) the development of formal operational thinking, (b) self-paced, mastery instruction, (c) systematic design of instruction, (d) feedback to students, and (e) use of group learning.

665 Swartz, Robert J. "Infusing the Teaching of Critical; Thinking into Content Instruction." Chapter 34 in *Developing Minds. Vol. 1: A Resource Book for Teaching Thinking*, edited by Arthur L. Costa, 177-184. Alexandria, VA: Association for Supervision and Curriculum Development, 1991. [28 Refs.]

Swartz advocates integrating instruction in thinking into the content areas. He discusses two approaches to the direct teaching of thinking: (1) using lessons to explicitly teach thinking skills and have students apply the thinking skills within content lessons and (2) infusing the teaching of thinking skills explicitly within content instruction. The latter involves restructuring content lessons. Swartz provides examples of lessons that infuse core critical thinking skills into instruction in American history, library research, primary school stories, English, and science. He also outlines four basic instructional strategies to consider when designing infused lessons.

666 Swartz, Robert J. "Making Good Thinking Stick: The Role of Metacognition, Extended Practice, and Teacher Modeling in the Teaching of Thinking." Chapter 34 in *Thinking across Cultures: The Third International Conference*, edited by Donald M. Topping, Doris C. Crowell, and Victor N. Kobayashi, 417-436. Hillsdale, NJ: Lawrence Erlbaum, 1989. [33 Refs.]

Swartz outlines a framework for infusing teaching for critical thinking into regular classroom instruction rather than special programs. This framework entails a restructuring of the way traditional curriculum materials are used. Students should be helped to become aware of their thinking and assimilate ways of thinking that are used when called for in and outside of the classroom. Swartz examines the nature of metacognition and ways metacognition can be taught and used to classify and analyze thinking. He discusses ways in which thinking skills lessons can be enhanced by including additional examples and exercises to help students transfer their thinking skills to other areas. Teachers should model important thinking attitudes to help students develop those techniques. Classroom activities should engage students in the active use of thinking skills, metacognitive reflection, and extended practice with the acquired skills.

667 Swartz, Robert J. "Restructuring What We Teach to Teach for Critical Thinking." In *Thinking Skills Instruction: Concepts and Techniques*, edited by Marcia Heiman and Joshua Slomianko, 111-118. Building Students' Thinking Skills. Washington, DC: National Education Association, 1987. [7 Refs.]

Swartz gives examples of teachers integrating critical thinking into their teaching by restructuring the content they have traditionally taught. Referred to as the conceptual-infusion approach, it is considered to be the most powerful approach for bringing teaching for critical thinking into classroom activities. Teaching for critical thinking involves not only teaching skills, but also helping students develop attitudes of thought, such as open-mindedness, consideration for other points of view, and investigating all available evidence.

668 Thomas, Dene Kay. "*Why* Questions and *Why* Answers: Patterns and Purposes." *Language Arts* 65, no. 6 (October 1988): 552-556.

Thomas stresses the importance of the why question in stimulating thinking. In responding to the why questions of students, Thomas feels that it is important that teachers develop patterns of responding that rely on logic or reasoning abilities. She lists and illustrates eight common patterns of responding. Thomas suggests that two of them are particularly valuable for encouraging curiosity, while the remaining six can discourage questioning as a mode of learning if used too often.

669 Tishman, Shari. "Connections." Chapter 19 in *Developing Minds. Vol. 2: Programs for Teaching Thinking*, rev. ed., edited by Arthur L. Costa, 69-72. Alexandria, VA: Association for Supervision and Curriculum Development, 1991.

Tishman describes Connections, a program to help teachers infuse the teaching of thinking into the subject areas that they teach. The program is based on teaching higher order thinking in the context of real problems in standard school subjects. Three thinking strategies are taught: Decision making, Deep Understanding, and Inventive Thinking. The program materials are intended for third through sixth grades, but the strategies are appropriate for any grade level.

670 Tyler, Sydney Billig. "Thinking, Reading, and Writing." Chapter 24 in *Developing Minds. Vol. 2: Programs for Teaching Thinking*, rev. ed., edited by Arthur L. Costa, 94-97. Alexandria, VA: Association for Supervision and Curriculum Development, 1991. [3 Refs.]

Tyler emphasizes experiential learning for developing thinking, reading, and writing skills. Illustrations from Tyler's Young Think, Just Think, and Stretch Think programs for teaching thinking from pre-school through eighth grade are provided.

671 Warc, Herbert W. "Thinking Skills: The Effort of One Public School System." Chapter 16 in *Thinking and Learning Skills. Vol. 1: Relating Instruction to Research*, edited by Judith W. Segal, Susan F. Chipman, and Robert Glaser, 515-527. Hillsdale, NJ: Lawrence Erlbaum, 1985. [2 Refs.]

Ware summarizes the efforts of the Arlington, Virginia, public schools in implementing an instructional thinking skills program in the mid-1970s. He outlines the history of these efforts, describes the leading impediments and teacher resistance to the program, and presents examples of successful accomplishments made by program specialists and teachers. Ware contrasts the mixed results of the thinking skills program with those of a more successful writing project implemented in the same school district.

672 Watson, Edward D. "How to Ask Better Questions." *Learning* 17, no. 2 (September 1988): 94.

Watson suggests four techniques for asking open-ended questions that foster a higher level of thinking in students. He includes sample questions.

673 Watson, Jim, and Neal Strudler. "Teaching Higher Order Thinking Skills with Databases." *Computing Teacher* 16, no. 4 (December-January 1988-89): 47-50, 55. [8 Refs.]

Watson and Strudler believe that instructional database activities offer opportunities for the teaching and learning of higher order thinking skills. They provide excerpts from a concluding lesson in a database unit on the fifty U.S. states. This lesson, based on Hilda Taba's Inductive Thinking model of teaching, was designed to help students (a) synthesize, evaluate, and apply what they have learned through brainstorming about problems related to a topic; (b) sort and interpret data by prioritizing, exploring relationships, and making predictions and judgments; (c) reviewing their problem solving process; and (d) apply the process to other problems. Watson and Strudler outline the five steps of the lesson and activities, as well as the three steps of Taba's model. They include question sets, question templates, and sample questions with possible responses. Watson and Strudler emphasize that the database is only a medium to use for enhancing thinking skills and that the use of effective teaching strategies to engage students in higher order thinking is the critical aspect when using databases.

674 Weaver, Frederick Stirton, ed. *Promoting Inquiry in Undergraduate Learning*. New Directions for Teaching and Learning, no. 38. San Francisco, CA: Jossey-Bass, 1989. [95 Refs.]

This is a collection of essays on the inquiry-based curriculum at Hampshire College (MA). After a general, introductory essay on the inquiry approach to undergraduate education, planning and organizing an inquiry curriculum, inquiry and liberal education, and brief descriptions of the components of the Hampshire College curriculum, the following ten essays focus on specific course offerings and approaches. Coverage includes teaching experiences with the inquiry approach in introductory science; cognitive psychology; nature literature; experimental science; calculus, finite mathematics, and computer science; literature and anthropology; introductory statistics; and bibliographic instruction.

675 Weinter, Elizabeth Hirzler, ed. *Unfinished Stories for Facilitating Decision Making in the Elementary Classroom*. Washington, DC: National Education Association, 1980. 78 pp.

This collection of brief stories without endings reflect situations, problems, questions, and inner conflicts which confront young children. Intended for use with elementary school children, each story poses the question of what the protagonist should do and is followed by possible discussion questions. The stories are organized into the following three categories: Responsibility and Commitment to Oneself and Others, Personal Shortcomings, and Shortcomings of Others. Weiner offers suggestions in the foreword for using the stories to assist young children with decision making.

676 Welds, Kathryn. "Cultivating Critical Questioning and Intellectual Self-Direction: A Sub-Agenda for Educational Formats." *Continuum* 50, no. 2 (Spring 1986): 111-116. [17 Refs.]

Welds emphasizes the importance of cultivating intellectual skills of inquiry and evaluation through instructional designs. She describes an instructional model, intended to foster intellectual responsibility, self-reliance, and critical thinking, which was used in a multicultural situation with college undergraduates and continuing education adults. The model includes collaborative learning, team efforts, and oral and writing activities.

677 Whimbey, Arthur. "The Key to Higher Order Thinking Is Precise Processing." *Educational Leadership* 42, no. 1 (September 1984): 66-70. [21 Refs.]

Whimbey sees the division of single versus multiple factor approaches to teaching thinking skills as a recapitulation of the earlier division of single versus multiple factor theories in the science of measuring. He reviews some of the research and theories behind single and multiple factor skills, emphasizing the failure to isolate different reasoning skills. Focusing on precise processing as the key to higher order thinking skills, Whimbey suggests methods for teaching analytical reasoning skills, using either course content materials or materials designed to teach specific thinking skills.

678 Whimbey, Arthur. "Students Can Learn to Be Better Problem Solvers." *Educational Leadership* 37, no. 7 (April, 1980): 560-565. [8 Refs.]

Whimbey contends that the difficulty in observing the thinking processes of learners can be overcome by having them think aloud while participating in small, problem solving groups. This approach allows students to communicate their thoughts to others and become more aware of flaws in the way they approach problems. Whimbey believes that analytical reasoning should not be confined to one course, but should be reinforced throughout the curriculum. He includes examples of schools that have successfully initiated problem solving or thinking programs using the think aloud and small group approach.

679 Whimbey, Arthur, and Jack Lochhead. *Problem Solving & Comprehension*. 4th ed. Hillsdale, NJ: Lawrence Erlbaum, 1986. 342 pp.

Designed to be used individually or as a classroom textbook, this book is intended to improve analytical thinking skills. The first chapter includes the Whimbey Analytical Skills Inventory (WASI Test) and is followed in the second chapter by a discussion of common errors made on the test due to faulty analysis and reasoning. Other chapters cover problem solving methods, verbal reasoning problems, myths about reading, analogies, writing relationship sentences, analysis of trends and patterns, and mathematical word problems. Practice exercises are included within most of the chapters. The final chapter includes a posttest.

680 Wilkerson, LuAnn, and Grahame Feletti. "Problem-Based Learning: One Approach to Increasing Student Participation." In *The Department Chairperson's Role in Enhancing College Teaching*, edited by Ann F. Lucas, 51-60. New Directions for Teaching and Learning, no. 37. San Francisco, CA: Jossey-Bass, 1989. [19 Refs.]

Wilkerson and Feletti believe that the problem-based approach to teaching and learning increases participation of students, as they take responsibility for their own learning, and changes the traditional role of the teacher as controller to challenger and supporter. Students learn facts, concepts, and thinking processes in disciplines as they confront problems, engage in independent study, and return to problems with new information and insight. Wilkerson and Feletti discuss the different formats in which the problem-based approach works. This approach is advantageous to teachers in providing feedback and in assessing students. The role of the department chair in promoting problem-based teaching is as (a) catalyst for change; (b) linker of the personal, financial, and informational resources to support faculty replanning and experimentation; and (c) facilitator for change by providing appropriate spaces, schedules, and materials for program-based activities.

681 Will, Howard. "The Junior Great Books Program of Interpretive Reading and Discussion." Chapter 15 in *Developing Minds. Vol. 2: Programs for Teaching Thinking*, rev. ed., edited by Arthur L. Costa, 57-58. Alexandria, VA: Association for Supervision and Curriculum Development, 1991.

Revision of Costa {505}, pp. 233-235.

Will provides the background and a description of the Junior Great Books program which focuses on higher level reading and thinking skills for elementary and secondary school students. The program involves interpretive reading and shared inquiry discussion. Will also notes future developments in the program for students of varying reading ability and for younger readers.

682 Winocur, S. Lee. "Developing Lesson Plans with Cognitive Objectives." Chapter 16 in *Developing Minds: A Resource Book for Teaching Thinking*, edited by Arthur L. Costa, 87-93. Alexandria, VA: Association for Supervision and Curriculum Development, 1985. [12 Refs.]

Winocur discusses the framework used in the IMPACT program's curriculum models for teaching critical thinking, focusing on three factors that affect teacher decisions regarding lesson planning: content, constructs, and conditions.

683 Winocur, S. Lee. "IMPACT." Chapter 7 in *Developing Minds. Vol. 2: Programs for Teaching Thinking*, rev. ed., edited by Arthur L. Costa, 33-34. Alexandria, VA: Association for Supervision and Curriculum Development, 1991.

Revision of Costa {505}, pp. 210-211.

Winocur describes the components, training, and materials of the IMPACT (Improving Minimal Proficiencies by Activating Critical Thinking) program. The program identifies critical thinking skills and teacher behaviors essential to effective instruction and involves the infusion of thinking skills into the content areas.

684 Wolfe, Rosemary Fanti. "The Supplemental Instruction Program: Developing Learning and Thinking Skills." *Journal of Reading* 31, no. 3 (December 1987): 228-232. [4 Refs.]

Wolfe discusses her participation in studies on the effectiveness of the University of Missouri-Kansas City Supplementary Instruction Reading Program (SI) at a community college. The program's purpose is to develop better study and critical questioning skills through participation in after-class workshops conducted by an SI leader. Wolfe examines the methods used in the program's review sessions and compares the achievements of SI participants and non-participants in her class section.

685 Wood, Larry E. "An 'Intelligent' Program to Teach Logical Thinking Skills." *Behavior Research Methods & Instrumentation* 12, no. 2 (April 1980): 256-258. [5 Refs.]

To help students improve their logical thinking skills, a computer program based on the game, *Mastermind*, was developed. The program consists of two games. The first follows the rules of *Mastermind*, using numbers instead of colored pegs. The second game provides more feedback regarding possible guesses of the player. A game providing increasingly difficult sequences was tested using the Watson-Glaser Critical Thinking Appraisal and found to increase reasoning skills moderately.

686 Woods, Donald R. "How Might I Teach Problem Solving?" In *Developing Critical Thinking and Problem-Solving Activities*, edited by James E. Stice, 55-71. New Directions for Teaching and Learning, no. 30. San Francisco, CA: Jossey-Bass, 1987. [44 Refs.]

Woods contends that knowledge or information is basic to problem solving, but how information is learned affects how an individual solves problems. Woods believes that good problem solvers possess carefully developed, organized, hierarchical knowledge, not memorized unstructured facts or ideas. He also believes that problem solving is a domain of knowledge or experience that can be taught. Woods reviews research that enumerates negative and positive issues in the actual teaching of problem solving, reviews the pros and cons of eight options for teaching problem solving, and offers five general suggestions for teaching problem solving.

687 Woods, Donald R. "Teaching Thinking and Ideas about Assessment." *Journal of College Science Teaching* 18, no. 5 (March-April 1989): 338-340.

Woods emphasizes information from Lauren Resnick's *Education and Learning to Think* (Washington, DC: National Academy Press, 1987), including definitions of and instructional programs for higher order thinking skills. He stresses the importance of infusing higher order thinking skills into all subjects and disciplines at all grade levels. Woods emphasizes the importance of relating the development of motivation with higher order thinking skills. He concludes with suggestions for ways teachers can start addressing these issues immediately in their classrooms.

688 Worsham, Antoinette. "A 'Grow As You Go' Thinking Skills Model." *Educational Leadership* 45, no. 7 (April 1988): 56-57. [1 Ref.]

Reprinted in Costa {506}, pp. 141-142.

Worsham describes the use of the Inclusion Process as an instructional model for incorporating thinking skills at a middle school. This model can be used for all grade levels, kindergarten through twelfth grade.

689 Wright, Elena Dworkin. "Odyssey: A Curriculum for Thinking." Chapter 12 in *Developing Minds. Vol. 2: Programs for Teaching Thinking*, rev. ed., edited by Arthur L. Costa, 48-50. Alexandria, VA: Association for Supervision and Curriculum Development, 1991. [4 Refs.]

A revision of Costa {505}, pp. 224-226.

Wright describes the Odyssey approach to teaching thinking, the scope of materials, and the design of the lessons. The program is intended to teach a range of generalizable thinking skills to upper elementary and middle school students. The lessons incorporate various teaching strategies for teaching the processes of divergent, synthetic, inductive, deductive, convergent, and analytic thinking.

690 Young, Michael, James Van Haneghan, Linda Barron, Susan Williams, Nancy Vye, and John Bransford. "A Problem-Solving Approach to Mathematics Instruction Using an Embedded Videodisc." Chapter 28 in *Developing Minds. Vol. 2: Programs for Teaching Thinking*, rev. ed., edited by Arthur L. Costa, 110-113. Alexandria, VA: Association for Supervision and Curriculum Development, 1991. [24 Refs.]

Adapted version of article under same title in *Technology and Learning* 3, no. 4 (1989): 1-4.

The authors describe the use of videodisc format, embedded data, and everyday context problems to help students develop confidence, skills, and knowledge necessary for problem solving. They describe the principles underlying the design of the videodisc, *The Adventures of Jasper Woodbury: Episode One*, intended to provide a problem solving environment in which middle school students must generate and solve several subproblems in order to solve an overall problem. This is the first in a series of videos planned by the Learning Technology Center at Vanderbilt University.

691 Young, Robert E., ed. *Fostering Critical Thinking*. New Direction for Teaching and Learning, no. 3. San Francisco, CA: Jossey-Bass, 1980. 103 pp.

The themes and issues that surround fostering critical thinking in higher education are addressed in this collection of essays. Contributors present different perspectives on the concept, teaching, and evaluation of critical thinking in colleges and universities. They also present teaching approaches, strategies, and resources.

692 Zenke, Larry, and Larry Alexander. "Teaching Thinking in Tulsa." *Educational Leadership* 42, no. 1 (September 1984): 81-84.

The authors describe the design and implementation of the Think (or Strategic Reasoning) program in two Tulsa middle schools. They cite a study conducted after the first year of the program which indicated significant improvement in student test scores and notable progress of Chapter 1 students in reading and writing skills.

8

TEACHING IN SUBJECT AREAS

Reading and Writing

693 Allen, Elizabeth Godwin, Jone Perryman Wright, and Lester L. Laminack. "Using Language Experience to ALERT Pupils' Critical Thinking Skills." *Reading Teacher* 41, no. 9 (May 1988): 904-910. [27 Refs.]

The authors propose ALERT, a strategy which combines the language experience approach with the use of commercial messages from radio, television, newspaper, and magazines for helping students develop critical listening, reading, and thinking skills. They give a step-by-step description of the strategy (Advance Organizer, Listen/Learn, Examine/Explain, Restate/Read, and Think/Test/Talk) and suggest follow-up activities.

694 Bean, John C. "Summary Writing, Rogerian Listening, and Dialectic Thinking." *College Composition & Communication* 37, no. 3 (October 1986): 344-346.

Bean describes a program of summary writing assignments designed to foster dialectic thinking. In addition to helping students overcome egocentrism, summary writing insures careful reading, allows students to view the effects of egocentric vision, teaches research and writing skills, and develops thinking skills.

695 Beck, Isabel L. "Reading and Reasoning." *Reading Teacher* 42, no. 9 (May 1989): 676-682. [6 Refs.]

Beck contends that reasoning accompanies reading and that a reading program is an appropriate means for developing and enhancing reasoning. Reading is a constructive act within which background knowledge and language comprehension are essential for making inferences that are important to reasoning and problem solving. Given the lack of transfer of some knowledge, higher order thinking should be incorporated into every school subject from the kindergarten level. Using folktales appropriate for first and third graders, Beck illustrates how higher order thinking can be incorporated into reading instruction by applying a reasoning and problem solving approach.

696 Bird, Michael D. "Helping Students Think and Read More Critically." *Journal of Reading* 32, no. 8 (May 1989): 743-745. [9 Refs.]

Bird briefly reviews several suggested teaching techniques and programs for improving the reading and critical thinking abilities of college students. Some suggestions focus specifically on developmental students. Bird addresses a skills approach versus a general contextual approach.

697 Birdsong, Theda P., and Wanda Sharplin. "Peer Evaluation Enhances Students' Critical Judgment." *Highway One* 9, no. 1 (Winter 1986): 23-28. [8 Refs.]

Birdsong and Shraplin describe how they have incorporated peer evaluation of student papers into writing courses. They discuss how the approach affected student writing and critical thinking skills. The authors also review student evaluations of the program.

698 Brock, Sue. "Talking Helps Young Writers." *Australian Journal of Reading* 10, no. 2 (June 1987): 106-119.

Brock argues that talk plays an important role in the development of young writers. She demonstrates how writing and discussion are enhanced in her classroom by having students participate in small groups. The bulk of the article consists of excerpts from student writings and group discussions.

699 Chimombo, Moira. "Towards Reality in the Writing Class." *ELT Journal* 41, no. 3 (July 1987): 204-210. [4 Refs.]

Chimombo presents a series of lessons that employ letters to the editor in local newspapers to teach argumentation and writing. The lessons provide the opportunity for students to engage in writing for a genuine purpose and audience, as well as presenting examples that use everyday language. The lessons consist of a series of assignments that require analysis of the arguments used in the letters, classroom discussion and debate, and writing response letters.

700 Didsbury, Kendall. "Teaching Precise Processing through Writing Instruction." *Thinking Skills Instruction: Concepts and Techniques*, edited by Marcia Heiman and Joshua Slomianko, 167-173. Building Students' Thinking Skills. Washington, DC: National Education Association, 1987.

Didsbury describes developing the writing expository skills and analytical skills of high school junior English students by incorporating Whimbey's thinking strategy or "precise processing" idea to the conference-based writing program. Building on Whimbey's framework, students are given assignments through which they are taught five types of writing problems: classifying information, comparison and contrast, analysis of structure, analysis of character, and problem solving.

701 Doyle, Michelle L. "This 'Buzz' Has Wings." *Momentum* 19, no. 4 (November 1988): 48-50.

Doyle emphasizes the importance of teaching process writing and critical thinking throughout the curriculum in elementary school. She describes briefly the Critical Writing program in a Virginia elementary school which combines the teaching of critical thinking and the writing process. Doyle offers teaching ideas for combining these two concepts.

702 Farrar, Mary Thomas. "Four Conceptions of Literacy." *Reading Psychology* 7, no. 1 (1986): 43-55. [53 Refs.]

To provide a framework that teachers might use to reflect on various aspects of their reading programs, Farrar identifies four conceptions of literacy that have evolved since the 19th century: (1) decoding, (2) story structure comprehension, (3) elaborative comprehension to construct textual meaning, and (4) literacy as reasoning or critical thinking. She relates each conception to a teaching method.

703 Flemming, Paula K. "Questioning in a Writing Program to Develop Thinking." *Thinking Skills Instruction: Concepts and Techniques*, edited by Marcia Heiman and Joshua

Slomianko, 255-261. Building Students' Thinking Skills. Washington, DC: National Education Association, 1987. [7 Refs.]

Flemming focuses on using the strategy of questioning within the context of writing to develop the critical thinking skills of students. She presents examples of the strategy used with elementary school children and provides a list of questions for different purposes that teachers might use with students at various writing stages.

704 Flynn, Linda L. "Developing Critical Reading Skills through Cooperative Problem Solving." *Reading Teacher* 42, no. 9 (May 1989): 664-68. [11 Refs.]

Flynn proposes a model for incorporating problem solving strategies with reading through the use of cooperative learning techniques and the IDEAL approach. The IDEAL approach, developed by John D. Bransford and Barry S. Stein in *The Ideal Problem Solver* (NY: W.H. Freeman, 1984), is a five-step problem solving process which focuses on the skills of Identifying, Defining, Exploring, Acting, and Looking. Flynn suggests presenting problems through mystery stories and role-playing that are based on problems and issues from newspapers, journals, short stories, or novels. She describes activities illustrating the application of the model, provides a graphic illustration of the model, and suggests teaching materials.

705 Glatthorn, Allan A. "Thinking and Writing." Chapter 4 in *Essays on the Intellect*, edited by Frances R. Link, 67-88. Alexandria, VA: Association for Supervision and Curriculum Development, 1985. [52 Refs.]

Glatthorn examines the relationship between thinking and writing and the educational implications of that relationship through a review of research findings. He briefly explores the role played by writing in the development of thinking and the role played by thinking in writing. Glatthorn also reviews programs using writing to facilitate thinking and discusses how knowledge of thinking can be used to facilitate writing.

706 Goleman, Judith. "Getting There: A Freshman Course in Social Dialectics." *Journal of Education* 169, no. 3 (1987): 48-57. [6 Refs.]

Goleman describes a freshman writing course in language awareness that she developed. Through an analysis and interpretation of speech acts found in writing, reading, and speaking which culminates in written essays that are reviewed and discussed in class, students learn to see the social construction of their lives and language. An analytical instrument, SPEAKING (setting, participants, ends, act sequence, key, instrumentalities, norms, genre) is used to examine speech acts. Goleman argues and demonstrates how pedagogy for critical literacy helps students establish or reclaim authority in their own writing and their own lives. She presents an example of an essay within the context of the class discussion.

707 Haggard, Martha Rapp. "Developing Critical Thinking with the Directed Reading-Thinking Activity." *Reading Teacher* 41, no. 6 (February 1988): 526-533. [18 Refs.]

Haggard describes the following five steps in the Directed Reading-Thinking Activity: (1) Identifying purposes for reading, (2) Adjustment of rate to purposes and material, (3) Observing the reading, (4) Developing comprehension, and (5) Fundamental skill development. She provides classroom examples and the appropriate activities for the steps. Advantages of the Directed Reading-Thinking Activity include (1) increased comprehension through predictions, speculations, and conclusions generated by students using prior knowledge and experience; and (2) the promotion of critical thinking through identifying a problem, generating hypotheses, gathering evidence, testing hypotheses, and drawing conclusions.

708 Hahn, Stephen. "Counter-Statement: Using Written Dialogue to Develop Critical Thinking and Writing." *College Composition and Communication* 38, no. 1 (February 1987): 97-100. [2 Refs.]

Hahn argues that college students do not associate academic written discourse with ongoing debates and, therefore, do not perceive themselves as participants in debates when reading and writing. To raise their awareness, he proposes using a counter-statement to prompt written dialogue that is eventually used for extended writing assignments requiring analysis and argumentation. Hahn gives examples of counter-statements and resulting written dialogues and suggests extended writing assignments.

709 Harris, Theodore L., and Eric J. Cooper, eds. *Reading, Thinking, and Concept Development: Strategies for the Classroom*. New York, NY: College Entrance Examination Board, 1985. 280 pp.

This collection of fifteen articles provides an array of techniques for developing reading comprehension skills in elementary through secondary school levels. The collection consists of five parts, forming general theme categories for the articles. Part I, Explicit Comprehension Skills Teaching emphasizes the direct teaching of comprehension skills such as identifying the main idea. A proposed model of teaching the skills of categorizing and classifying as a means of teaching the concept of main idea is explained and illustrated through examples. Instructional activities for developing an understanding of anaphoric relationships for facilitating comprehension are suggested. Part II, Precomprehension an Postcomprehension Strategies includes an article on a three-phase, problem-oriented prereading plan (PReP) that focuses on using classroom discussion to help students become aware of their knowledge and experience and help them recall and reflect on both for comprehending texts. It also includes an article on Ausubel's concept of the advance organizer with illustrations on to how to construct and apply the advance organizer. Other articles include descriptions and applications of instructional activities on building students' background knowledge prior to reading and helping students articulate responses to questions on reading selections through oral and written discussion (response instruction). Part III, Interactive Comprehension Strategies focuses on metacognition and instructional approaches designed to help students develop responsibility for structuring effective comprehension processes. Articles emphasizing a holistic approach to teaching comprehension, integrating process and content are found in Part IV, Integrative Comprehension Strategies. Descriptions and illustrations of strategies especially appropriate for improving thinking and study processes in the middle and upper grades are provided. Text selection for comprehensibility, quality, instructional soundness, and effectiveness for teaching is the theme of Part V, Readability and the Future of the Textbook.

710 Heller, Mary F. "Modeling Critical Thinking in the English Classroom." *Highway One* 9, no. 2 (Spring 1986): 87-90. [3 Refs.]

Heller describes a classroom modeling activity that teaches students to monitor their reading comprehension and to describe their own thinking process. The techniques of thinking aloud, discussion, and writing help students think about the concepts of a reading assignment before and after reading it. Teachers model the activity by sharing the metacognitive strategies they used while reading and thinking about the reading assignment.

711 Herber, Harold L. "Levels of Comprehension: An Instructional Strategy for Guiding Students' Reading." In *Reading, Thinking, and Concept Development: Strategies for the Classroom*, edited by Theodore L. Harris and Eric J. Cooper, 195-211. New York, NY: College Entrance Examination Board, 1985. [14 Refs.]

Herber advocates integrating the teaching of reading comprehension, reading skills, and reasoning. This holistic model of teaching provides for the literal, interpretive, and applied levels of comprehension of content material. He suggests instructional guides which model or simulate the comprehension process as a means for promoting these comprehension levels by helping students become aware of their thought processes during reading. Herber provides sample guides for social studies, literature, and mathematics designed for sixth grade and eighth grade students. He also offers suggestions for constructing such guides.

712 Herendeen, Warren. "Of Tricksters and Dilemmas in ESL Writing Classes: An Epistolary Account." *Journal of Basic Writing* 5, no. 2 (1986): 49-58.

In this article which is written in the form of a letter, Herendeen describes using trickster and dilemma tales drawn from cultural myths and stories to develop critical listening, critical and creative thinking, and writing skills of ESL students. A few suggestions of teaching approaches and sources of tales are given.

713 Hill, Carolyn. "Beyond the Enthymeme: Sorites, Critical Thinking, and the Composing Process." *Fortieth Annual*

Meeting of the Conference on College Composition and Communication, Seattle, WA, March 16-18, 1989. ED 307 612.

Hill describes a writing exercise designed to develop critical thinking, self-discovery, constructive knowledge, and a connection between writer and audience. After an analysis of enthymemes (specific argumentative figures), sorites (two or more enthymemes), claims, reasons, and conclusions from reading and freewriting, students choose an enthymeme as the basis for a paper.

714 Hollis, Karyn. "Building a Context for Critical Literacy: Student Writers as Critical Theorists." *Writing Instructor* 7, no. 3-4 (Spring-Summer 1988): 122-130. [11 Refs.]

Hollis advocates using *The Idea of a Critical Theory: Habermas and the Frankfurt School* by Raymond Geuss (New York, NY: Cambridge University Press, 1968) as the basis for teaching critical theory and critical literacy in composition courses. Hollis reviews some of the research on literacy acquisition responded to by Geuss. This research shows an interaction between literacy and the context within which it is acquired. Geuss' work explains the differences between critical theory and empirical knowledge and critical theory and scientific method and outlines the components of critical theory. Hollis shares this information in the article and presents suggestions on applying Geuss' methodology in the classroom. She suggests using examples in the class to demonstrate the methodology orally first before giving group assignments for research papers. Hollis provides a scenario of an oral demonstration of the methodology, using the issue of care for the elderly. Through careful analysis, argumentation, and exposition in writing, students enter into the context of literacy, learning to recognize social constructions and ideologies underlying them.

715 Hull, Glynda Ann. "Research on Writing: Building a Cognitive and Social Understanding of Composing." Chapter 6 in *Toward the Thinking Curriculum: Current Cognitive Research*, edited by Lauren B. Resnick and Leopold E. Klopfer, 104-128. 1989 Yearbook of the Association for Supervision and Curriculum Development.

[Alexandria, VA]: Association for Supervision and Curriculum Development, 1989. [28 Refs.]

Hull notes that due to research over the past twenty years the concept of writing and of instruction in writing has evolved from a product requiring response and correction to a complex cognitive process requiring authentic tasks and social interaction. She provides examples of the application of the current concept of writing in classrooms. Emphasis is on understanding the writing process and how social context affects the acquisition of knowledge, thinking, and writing.

716 Jones, Beau Fly, Margaret B. Tinzmann, Lawrence B. Friedman, and Beverly Butler Walker, eds. *Teaching Thinking Skills: English/Language Arts*. Washington, DC: National Education Association, 1987. 104 pp. [114 Refs.]

The authors present a framework for cognitive instruction focusing on teaching the thinking processes in the language arts. They discuss the parallel research findings concerning the thinking processes of writing, listening, and speaking, in particular the nonlinear process of constructing meaning from text, strategic learning, and the characteristics of textual organizational patterns common in each field. The authors address strategic learning, defining the role of the teacher in cognitive instruction as manager, executive, and instructor. They describe specific instructional strategies for teaching thinking and outline several instructional approaches. Planning guides follow each of the first three chapters. The second part of the book includes a description of five extended examples for teaching specific content and skills objectives which can be used as models for sequencing instruction.

717 Langer, Judith A., and Arthur N. Applebee. "Learning to Write: Learning to Think." *Educational Horizons* 64, no. 1 (Fall 1985): 36-38. [19 Refs.]

Langer and Applebee advocate writing and thinking activities across the curriculum to help students learn to use basic writing skills to communicate ideas, learn new information, and solve problems. The authors outline suggestions for initiating change at the district level and how to proceed with the planning and implementation of a program. They provide sample writing and thinking activities for science and social studies.

718 Lehr, Fran. "Developing Critical Reading and Thinking Skills." *Journal of Reading* 25, no. 8 (May 1982): 804-807. [6 Refs.]

Lehr reviews the research and study found in ERIC documents on instructional techniques to help students become better readers through lessons that develop critical thinking skills. She explores (1) questioning strategies, (2) an instructional strategy for teaching both comprehension and critical reading, and (3) a teaching technique, based on L. Rosenblatt's transactional analysis, that allows students to discover how writers generate, develop, clarify, and organize critical ideas.

719 Marzano, Robert J. *Cultivating Thinking in English and the Language Arts*. Urbana, IL: National Council of Teachers of English, 1991. 88 pp,. [117 pp.]

Marzano discusses a framework for cultivating thinking, focusing on English and language arts instruction in grades seven through twelve. The framework assumes that there are generic thinking skills as well as skills that are subject specific. Marzano identifies four categories of thinking that should be taught: (1) contextual thinking, (2) thinking that aids in the construction of meaning, (3) thinking that facilitates knowledge change, and (4) thinking that is both higher order and dispositional in nature. He discusses each type of thinking in separate chapters and identifies key features of thinking such as contextual framing, transactional responses, cognitive operations, and dispositions. Marzano provides several teaching approaches that focuses the form and function of instruction in English and language arts on the four categories of thinking.

720 Meeks, Lynn Langer. "Developing Metacognition in Composition with Peer Response Groups." *Thinking Skills Instruction: Concepts and Techniques*, edited by Marcia Heiman and Joshua Slomianko, 119-127. Building Students' Thinking Skills. Washington, DC: National Education Association, 1987. [34 Refs.]

Meeks explains the purpose and concept of peer response groups, students meeting with other students as partners or as groups to help each other with writing. The author contends that this method of teaching writing develops students' metacognition and internal locus of control. As students are empowered to create, revise and evaluate text, they become aware of their own writing process and how it relates to the larger writing process. By working in peer response groups, students begin internalizing the questions their peers asked when compositions were read aloud during their own writing and revising processes.

721 Meyers, G. Douglas. "Teaching Critical Thinking in the Technical Writing Class." *Journal of Advanced Composition* 6, (1985-86): 97-103. [14 Refs.]

Meyers argues for the importance of incorporating critical thinking into the technical writing course in relation to the tasks performed by professionals in a technological era. Using David N. Dobrin's definition of technical writing, "'writing that accommodates technology to the user,'" Meyers discusses ten critical thinking skills natural to technical writing.

722 Miccinati, Jeannette L. "Mapping the Terrain: Connecting Reading with Academic Writing." *Journal of Reading* 31, no. 6 (March 1988): 542-552. [27 Refs.]

Miccinati believes that representing ideas presented in reading matter through the visual notetaking procedure of mapping requires critical thinking skills and serves as a catalyst for focused thinking and writing. She reviews research findings that support the advantages of mapping as an instructional method. Miccinati describes the procedures used with first level college students in preparing them for mapping, evolving from creating planning maps and preliminary maps to choosing or adapting one of various mapping formats for a final product. These procedures involve analyzing, evaluating, critical reasoning, and metacognitive skills. Miccinati provides sample assignments with corresponding mapping formats.

723 Neilsen, Allan R. *Critical Thinking and Reading: Empowering Learners to Think and Act*. Bloomington, IN: ERIC Clearinghouse on Reading and Communication Skills; Urbana, IL: National Teachers of English, 1989. 54 pp. [68 Refs.]

Arguing for learner-centered schools, Neilsen contrasts the attitudes incorporated in pedagogy emanating from a mechanistic world view versus an organic world view and outlines implications for reading instruction. Transmission pedagogy, based on a mechanistic world view, perpetuates dependence and compliance. In the mechanistic world view, knowledge is seen as fact, teachers as the central figures in the classroom, and reality as discrete elements that must be understood in order to understand reality as a whole. Transaction pedagogy, based on an organic world view, perpetuates independence, questioning, and transfer of knowledge. In the organic world view, knowledge is seen as relative and temporary, learners as the central figures in the classroom, and reality as a continual stream of experience in which people, things, and situations have meaning only in the context of other people, things, and situations. Neilsen advocates transaction pedagogy in which teachers provide opportunities for students to transact in real life circumstances or contexts. Reading and thinking are processes, isolated skills, for making meaning. In transaction pedagogy, reading becomes a fundamental part of critical thinking. To help students become independent thinkers, readers, and learners, teachers should provide them with opportunities to become actively involved in the learning process; provide consequential contexts for learning; and provide opportunities for learners to collaborate.

724 Niles, Olive S. "Integration of Content and Skills Instruction." In *Reading, Thinking and Concept Development*, edited by Theodore Harris and Eric J. Cooper, 177-193. New York, NY: College Entrance Examination Board, 1985. [32 Refs.]

Niles advocates the integration of process and content in the teaching of reading comprehension and proposes comprehension monitoring through intervention of the reading process. The intervention procedure entails teacher pre-selection of stopping points where students reflect on what they are doing through process and content questions. She describes several ways in which the intervention procedure can be accomplished in the classroom and provides sample during-reading lessons.

Niles recommends this procedure for use at any grade level with textbooks that are used daily and consistently until there is evidence of transfer of learning.

725 Palincsar, Annemarie Sullivan, and Ann L. Brown. "Instruction for Self-Regulated Reading." Chapter 2 in *Toward the Thinking Curriculum: Current Cognitive Research*, edited by Lauren B. Resnick and Leopold E. Klopfer, 19-39. 1989 Yearbook of the Association for Supervision and Curriculum Development. [Alexandria, VA]: Association for Supervision and Curriculum Development, 1989. [39 Refs.]

Focusing on the premise that how students respond to classroom activities reflects, in part, their awareness of the variables important to learning and their ability to control their learning environment, Palincsar and Brown suggest ways to provide students with the knowledge of the variables important to reading comprehension and knowledge of strategies that facilitate comprehension. This knowledge leads to self-regulation of the activity of reading. Thus, the student becomes a self-regulated learner--one who is able to use "real-world" knowledge, metacognition knowledge, and knowledge of strategies for accomplishing learning tasks efficiently. The authors discuss six strategies which foster and monitor comprehension. These strategies involve (1) using background knowledge, (2) evaluating content, (3) allocating attention to focus on major content, (4) clarifying purposes of reading to determine appropriate approaches, (5) using monitoring activities to determine if comprehension is occurring, and (6) making and using inferences. Emphasis is on linking the contexts of literacy in the home and community with the classroom and the school and integrating strategy instruction into the classroom and curriculum. The authors discuss three approaches to strategy instruction: Informed Strategies for Instruction, Responsive Elaboration, and Reciprocal Teaching.

726 Palincsar, Annemarie Sullivan, and Ann L. Brown. "Reciprocal Teaching: Activities to Promote 'Reading with Your Mind'." In *Reading, Thinking, and Concept Development: Strategies for the Classroom*, edited by

Theodore L. Harris and Eric J. Cooper, 147-159. New York, NY: College Entrance Examination Board, 1985. [9 Refs.]

Palincsar and Brown advocate four strategies (question-generating, summarizing, predicting, and demanding clarity) and the instructional technique of reciprocal teaching as means of helping students think about their reading comprehension strategies. In reciprocal teaching, the teacher models the four strategies and students are given opportunities to assume the role of the teacher in leading dicussion on text. The authors describe and illustrate applications of these strategies, reciprocal teaching, and the extension of reciprocal teaching to peer-tutoring.

727 Paris, Scott G. "Using Classroom Dialogues and Guided Practice to Teach Comprehension Strategies." In *Reading, Thinking, and Concept Development: Strategies for the Classroom*, edited by Theodore L. Harris and Eric J. Cooper, 133-146. New York, NY: College Entrance Examination Board, 1985. [15 Refs.]

Paris believes that reading comprehension activities, such as understanding the purposes of reading, activating relevant background knowledge, giving attention to main ideas, critical evaluation, monitoring comprehension, and drawing inferences, are important to developing self-directed learning. He describes guided instruction as an effective means of informing students about the existence of reading strategies and internalizing the regulation of comprehension skills through modeling, feedback, and persuasion. Interactive learning techniques such as reciprocal teaching, group discussion, and classroom dialogues are ways in which students can learn about their thinking, reading, and study skills and gain in three categories of metacognitive knowledge (declarative, procedural, and conditional). Paris describes and provides sample lessons from Informed Strategies for Learning, a program for teaching comprehension strategies to third and fifth graders.

728 Puglisi, Guy J. "FUTURES in Reading." *Catholic Library World* 59, no. 3 (November-December 1987): 122-124.

Puglisi describes a supplemental reading program, FUTURES, which emphasizes the development of critical thinking skills. Developed for Roman Catholic elementary schools in New York, this program involves the participation of teachers, students, and parents; the use of value-based materials which promote moral development; and practical exercises intended to link thinking, decision making, and responsible moral action.

729 Sardy, Susan. "Thinking about Reading." In *Reading, Thinking, and Concept Development: Strategies for the Classroom*, edited by Theodore Harris and Eric J. Cooper, 213-229. New York, NY: College Entrance Examination Board, 1985. [48 Refs.]

Sardy contends that the opportunity that texts offer for contemplation and reconsideration distinguishes reading comprehension from many other problem solving activities. To help students take advantage of this opportunity, Sardy suggests teaching students to examine texts critically and to distinguish information from the presentation of it. She advocates the Directed Thinking about Reading approach as a means for teaching this to students in primary through secondary school levels. This approach encourages critical reading and raises an awareness of the relationship between writing and reading comprehension processes. Sardy outlines the assumptions underlying this approach and the steps for planning and implementing it in the classroom. She stresses the importance of teacher preparation and text selection. Sardy provides a checklist for text evaluation and a visual illustration of the parallelism between the writing and reading comprehension processes.

730 Simpson, Mary K. "What Am I Supposed to Do While They're Writing?" *Language Arts* 63, no. 7 (November 1986): 680-684. [2 Refs.]

Simpson enumerates the nine tasks that define her role as a participant in a writing-workshop classroom environment. She describes these tasks and how she performed them by maintaining sensitivity, questioning, modeling, and helping students learn about the writing process from each other through peer evaluation and comments.

731 Slattery, Patrick. "Encouraging Critical Thinking: A Strategy for Commenting on College Papers." *College Composition and Communication* 41, no. 3 (October 1990): 332-335. [4 Refs.]

Slattery suggests using William Perry's cognitive development model as a strategy for commenting on students' papers. He demonstrates the value of this strategy in fostering critical thinking in students through supportive and challenging comments by providing representative examples of the three types of papers--dogmatic, nonjudgmental, and analytical--that college students tend to write when confronted with multiple viewpoints.

732 Spiegel, Dixie Lee. "Critical Reading Materials: A Review of Three Criteria." *Reading Teacher* 43, no. 6 (February 1990): 410-412. [4 Refs.]

Spiegel applies three criteria for reviewing instructional materials (content validity, transfer potential, and amount of reinforcement) to four commercially produced instructional critical thinking resources designed for teaching critical reading.

733 Tremblay, Paula Y. "Writing Assignments for Cognitive Development." *College Composition & Communication* 37, no. 3 (October 1986): 342-343.

Tremblay outlines the three-step structure of a series of writing assignments designed to help students make the transition from concrete to formal operations, as defined by Piaget. With these assignments, students develop the details of an experience, analyze their perceptions, and synthesize details, acquiring various levels and types of thinking. The article includes sample assignments.

734 Zeiger, William. "A Dialectical Model for College Composition." *Freshman English News* 16, no. 2 (Fall 1987): 14-16. [14 Refs.]

Zeiger proposes a dialectical form of writing as an alternative to the conventional thesis-support approach. The dialectical approach calls for a discussion of fiction and non-fiction essays during which a thesis and antithesis are developed and then synthesized. Zeiger believes this approach develops student willingness to examine opposing viewpoints and appreciate the ambiguity in conflicting views.

735 Zeller, Robert. "Developing the Inferential Reasoning of Basic Writers." *College Composition and Communication* 38, no. 3 (October 1987): 343-346.

Zeller describes a sequence of assignments in a basic writing course that incorporate a group of photographs, a photograph of E.B. White, White's essay "Education", and sources of brief biographical information about White, as well as the instructional techniques of group work, class discussion, and writing. The assignments require students to analyze information, make inferences, support inferences, synthesize information, and examine thinking processes.

Library Instruction

736 Bechtel, Joan. "Developing and Using the Online Catalog to Teach Critical Thinking." *Information Technology and Libraries* 7, no. 1 (March 1988): 30-40.

Bechtel stresses basing the design of and instruction in online catalogs on the needs of students and faculty engaged in learning and research. Online catalogs should encourage discrimination in choosing a topic and instruction should focus on the critical thinking process involved in the research process rather than on the mechanics of the system. Bechtel presents illustrations of student searches in which features of an online catalog were used to formulate a topic, to discriminate between primary and secondary sources, to discover multiple viewpoints, and to make an initial decision on the appropriateness of materials based upon knowledge of authors, subject, date, and format.

737 Berkowitz, Bob, and Joyce Berkowitz. "Thinking is Critical: Moving Students beyond Location." *School Library Media Activities Monthly* 3, no. 9 (May 1987): 25-27, 50. [1 Ref.]

The authors argue that integrating a library curriculum focusing on critical thinking skills into the content curriculum would (1) help students develop information-use skills, (2) provide students with opportunities to demonstrate abilities associated with the application and interpretation of information, (3) involve library media specialists in the development and implementation of the total school curriculum, and (4) strengthen the partnership between teachers and library media specialists. The authors suggest using Benjamin Bloom's six levels of cognition as the framework for their suggested curriculum. They present examples of questions associated with each level and terms useful in writing appropriate questions. The authors provide sample information analysis sheets and suggest ways to construct such sheets.

738 Bodi, Sonia. "Critical Thinking and Bibliographic Instruction: The Relationship." *Journal of Academic Librarianship* 14, no. 3 (July 1988): 150-153. [17 Refs.]

Bodi provides a brief review of critical thinking definitions, outlines Walter Perry's four stages of intellectual and ethical development of college students, and discusses the implications of critical thinking for bibliographic instruction and teacher training. She describes a bibliographic instruction session in a teacher education program at a liberal arts college that incorporates critical thinking. In the session, the professor and librarian debate a controversial issue, lead the class in a discussion of the debate, and demonstrate how search strategies helps students look more critically at issues and research.

739 DeHart, Florence E., and Gerrit W. Bleeker. "Helping Young Adults Use Information in Problem Solving." *Journal of Youth Services in Libraries* 1, no. 3 (Spring 1988): 305-309. [6 Refs.]

DeHart and Bleeker explore ways librarians can help young adults develop skills for seeking and using information for problem solving. The authors provide suggestions for professional development, professional research, and library services and programs.

740 Engeldinger, Eugene A. "Bibliographic Instruction and Critical Thinking: The Contribution of the Annotated Bibliography." *RQ* 28, no. 2 (Winter 1988): [15 Refs.]

Engeldinger believes an annotated bibliography assignment not only helps acquaint students with the literature of a discipline, but also allows for the teaching of library research skills, a systematic way of evaluating information, and the writing of critical annotations. Engeldinger sees the assignment as a natural way for librarians and teachers to work together in helping students find and evaluate information, facilitating critical thinking skills. He presents and discusses a guideline of nine questions (developed at the McIntyre Library, University of Wisconsin-Eau Claire) to help students evaluate what they read and write critical annotations. Engeldinger recommends employing the guideline within a class discussion approach and presents a list of pointers for using the approach.

741 Feinberg, Richard, and Christine King. "Short-Term Library Skill Competencies: Arguing for the Achievable." *College & Research Libraries* 49, no. 1 (January 1988): 24-28. [14 Refs.]

Feinberg and King question the possibility of teaching long-term library skill competencies. They propose teaching for short-term competency based on the specific needs of students. The approach uses short classroom presentations followed immediately by students applying this information to their research assignments. The authors believe their method provides an opportunity for the student to work individually with the librarian and course instructor.

742 Gibson, Craig. "Alternatives to the Term Paper: An Aid to Critical Thinking." *Reference Librarian* 24 (1989): 297-309. [8 Refs.]

Gibson sees an opportunity for reference and instruction librarians to become agents for change in higher education by actively developing alternative library-based assignments to the term paper. Using Robert Ennis's critical thinking goals and Chet Meyers's features of effective critical thinking assignments, librarians can design alternative assignments that foster the development of critical thinking. Gibson offers several examples of alternative assignments.

743 Huston, Mary M., and Susan L. Perry. "Information Instruction: Considerations for Empowerment." *Research Strategies* 5, no. 2 (Spring 1987): 70-77. [16 Refs.]

Based on the premise that pedagogy can affect students' achievement of self-reliance, Evergreen State College (WA) developed a course to foster self-reliance in libraries for an outreach program of predominantly urban Black students. The course employs techniques for developing problem solving skills needed for research planning, actual research, and evaluation. Instructors focus on empowering students through collaborative work, experience in applying problem solving skills, and instructor sensitivity to their needs, interests, and values.

744 Krapp, JoAnn Vergona. "Teaching Research Skills: A Critical-Thinking Approach." *School Library Journal* 34, no. 5 (January 1988): 32-35. [5 Refs.]

Krapp believes scheduled library sessions for classes, individuals, and groups offer an opportune time to introduce students to critical thinking skills. She recommends beginning with the fifth or sixth grade. Krapp adapts the results of several studies on problem-solving into guidelines for introducing critical thinking into those grades. She gives two examples utilizing worksheets to direct the student in asking questions and conducting independent research.

745 MacAdam, Barbara. "Information Literacy: Models for the Curriculum." *College & Research Libraries News* 51, no. 10 (November 1990): 948-951. [4 Refs.]

MacAdam presents curriculum models for developing information literacy in undergraduates and for teaching librarians how to incorporate information literacy in bibliographic instruction. These models emphasize conceptual frameworks for gathering information in a technological era based on problem solving, question analysis, and critical thinking. MacAdam includes a sample search strategy and model for biographical information.

746 McCormick, Mona. "Critical Thinking and Library Instruction." *RQ* 22, no. 4 (Summer 1983): 339-341. [10 Refs.]

McCormick advocates incorporating critical thinking in library instruction by emphasizing how to evaluate and use information rather than how to find it. She outlines characteristics of a critical thinker and suggests that librarians can assist students in becoming critical thinkers by promoting the evaluation of authorities, people, publications, and criticism. Attention should be given to the possibilities of promoting critical thinking in all aspects of library user education, including reference desk encounters, tours, classes, and lectures.

747 Minnich, Nancy P., and Carrol B. McCarthy. "The 'Clipping Thesis': An Exercise in Developing Critical Thinking and Online Database Searching Skills." *School Library Media Activities Monthly* 2, no. 8 (April 1986): 45-50. [1 Refs.]

"Clipping Thesis" is an assignment for high school students that requires thoughtful reading and writing about current events. Students are required to read articles from current newspapers and magazines on a specific topic, write proper bibliographic citations for the articles, write a summary of the chosen topic, and develop a bibliography. Minnich and McCarthy describe a cycle of four assignments, each requiring the use of a different form of information, and provide instructions for the assignments.

748 Nash, Stan, and Myoung Chung Wilson. "Value-Added Bibliographic Instruction: Teaching Students to Find the Right Citations." *RSR: Reference Services Review* 19, no. 1 (Spring 1991): 87-92. [4 Refs.]

Nash and Wilson conducted a study to determine the range of problems that undergraduates face in critically evaluating the results of CD-ROM searches. Their preliminary investigation consisted of (1) a survey, completed to find out the amount of time a student spent at a CD-ROM workstation and their satisfaction with the results and (2) in-depth interviews with a limited number of undergraduate CD-ROM users. Based on their findings, the authors conclude that students need to be taught to apply critical thinking skills to information sources and propose a two-tier instructional model for doing so.

749 Oberman, Cerise. "Avoiding the Cereal Syndrome, or Critical Thinking in the Electronic Environment." *Library Trends* 39, no. 3 (Winter 1991): 189-202. [32 Refs.]

With advances in technology and movement toward "supercatalogs" in libraries, library users are presented with numerous options from which to choose to satisfy their information needs. Oberman contends that a multiplicity of choices or an excess of information "can lead to intellectual distress" (p. 194). To prevent information overload in this online information environment, bibliographic education must focus on teaching students the critical thinking skills of analysis, synthesis, and evaluation. Oberman addresses the need for a new combination of methodology and pedagogy by instruction librarians in order to prepare students for the current world of information.

750 Plum, Stephen. "Library Use and the Development of Critical Thought." In *Increasing the Teaching Role of Academic Libraries*, edited by Thomas G. Kirk, 25-33. New Directions for Teaching and Learning, no. 18. San Francisco, CA: Jossey-Bass, 1984. [16 Refs.]

Plum asserts that using the context of the discipline as a framework for bibliographic instruction will help students develop patterns of critical thought. Using examples from American and English literature and science, Plum illustrates how the process of original research in a discipline and the use of a discipline's literature and library information systems is an important structure for bibliographic instruction. Students who understand the structure of a discipline and its literature and are encouraged to use research strategies reflective of the discipline know how to approach topic selection, determine appropriate evidence, and to evaluate information sources quickly.

751 Rankin, Virginia. "One Route to Critical Thinking." *School Library Journal* 34 (January 1988): 28-31.

Rankin describes an approach to teaching seventh grade language arts classes library research and critical thinking skills based on the premises that students must be allowed time to plan a research strategy and reflect on their own thought processes. The teaching methods employed in the approach include group and individual idea generation and journal writing.

752 Sheridan, Jean. "The Reflective Librarian: Some Observations on Bibliographic Instruction in the Academic Library." *Journal of Academic Librarianship* 16, no. 1 (March 1990): 22-26. [31 Refs.]

Sheridan reviews criticism directed toward the ineffectiveness of the traditional modes of professional-client interactions, higher education teaching, academic-librarian-student interactions at the reference desk, and bibliographic instruction. Considering this criticism in relation to Donald Schon's reflection-in-action behavior style (*The Reflective Practitioner*, New York, NY: Basic, 1983) and the call for holistic education by presenters at

American Association of Higher education meetings, Sheridan concludes that collaborative learning is the appropriate teaching method. She outlines the characteristics and essential ingredients for successful collaborative learning and provides examples of its practical application in the classroom. Sheridan offers numerous suggested applications to bibliographic instruction and addresses the appropriateness of the method to nontraditional or special needs college students.

Humanities

753 Alvermann, Donna E., and James R. Olson. "Discussing Read-Aloud Fiction: One Approach for Motivating Critical Thinking." *Reading Horizons* 28, no. 4 (Summer 1988): 235-241. [8 Refs.]

Alvermann and Olson describe how Paula Danziger's novel, *This Place Has No Atmosphere* (1986), was used to enhance critical thinking and responding by middle school students. The techniques of reading aloud, discussion, role-playing, and an analytical web were used in conjunction with the text of the novel.

754 Ashby-Davis, Claire. "Improving Students' Comprehension of Character Development in Plays." *Reading Horizons* 26, no. 4 (Summer 1986): 256-261. [3 Refs.]

Ashby-Davis discusses how the direct teaching of thinking, or inductive reasoning, can be incorporated into the teaching of reading comprehension in relation to plays. She suggests strategies for teaching students how to infer the personalities of characters and for teaching inductive reasoning.

755 Berquist, Goodwin, Virginia Tiefel, and Beth Waggenspack. "Coping with the Critical Essay in a Large Lecture Course." *Communication Education* 35, no. 4 (October 1986): 396-399.

The authors describe a college course, "The Rhetoric of Western Thought," that used critical bibliography and essay assignments as a means for students to demonstrate reading, writing, information retrieval, and decision making skills. The course required students to apply their knowledge of rhetorical theory to a specific communication event. The authors address student performance on and reactions to the assignments.

756 Brod, Harry. "Logic and Politics: An Approach to Teaching Informal Reasoning." *Teaching Philosophy* 5, no. 3 (July 1982): 211-219. [10 Refs.]

Clarity of thought and an informal citizenry are presented as the primary goals of educational institutions and as rationale for teaching logic. Insight is assumed to lead to action or to be the motivation for action. Brod believes that most students do not act upon their insight into thinking or into political matters. He argues that student political apathy stems from life experiences which teach the futility of attempting to act. Brod advocates a teaching approach to informal reasoning and politics that stresses the relation of informal logical to the politics of daily living before addressing the larger controversial political issues. The approach develops an understanding of the politicization of logic and the logic of politicization. Brod provides examples that can be used in teaching with the approach.

757 Cianciolo, Patricia J. "No Small Challenge: Literature for the Transitional Readers." *Language Arts* 66, no. 1 (January 1989): 72-81. [2 Refs.]

Cianciolo reviews selected literature which will extend the reading comprehension and critical thinking skills of eight-year-old to eleven-year-old readers. She also discusses the developmental characteristics of this transitional age group and the characteristics of the literature they tend to enjoy. The article includes a bibliography of other appropriate literary selections.

758 Cohen, Elliot D. *Making Value Judgements*. Malabar, FL: Krieger, 1985. [10 Refs.]

This is a textbook designed to be used as a supplement in applied logic and ethics courses. Cohen discusses the relation between value judgments and logic or sound reasoning. He explains the traditional standards of logic, and shows how these standards have evaluative dimensions. Cohen applies these standards to the making of value judgments and outlines justificatory, attitudinal, and emotional safeguards and pitfalls for sound reasoning about value judgments. Each chapter concludes with exercises.

759 Colicelli, Olga M., and Carol Summer. "Critical Thinking Via Literature." *School Library Journal* 34, no. 2 (October 1987): 46.

This one-page article describes the collaboration of a school media specialist and reading specialist in a program that used book discussion and question writing activities to improve reading skills, broaden reading interests, and develop higher level thinking skills in students.

760 Commeyras, Michelle. "Using Literature to Teach Critical Thinking." *Journal of Reading* 32, no. 8 (May 1989): 703-707. [3 Refs.]

Commeyras illustrates a strategy for using fiction or drama to promote critical thinking. She contends that a question grid designed to engage students in inductive reasoning about characters in literary works can promote the following critical thinking dispositions and abilities: (1) the disposition to focus on the original or basic concern, (2) the disposition to withhold judgment when there is insufficient evidence and reasons, (3) the ability to see similarities and differences, (4) the ability to investigate for seeking evidence and counterevidence, (5) the disposition and ability to seek reasons, (6) the ability to judge credibility or reliability of a source, and (7) the ability to determine whether a generalization is warranted. The article includes a sample grid.

761 Faulconer, James E., Richard N. Williams, and Dennis J. Packard. "Using Critical Reasoning to Teach Writing." *Teaching Philosophy* 11, no. 3 (September 1988): 229-244. [4 Refs.]

The authors discuss a syllabus that is based on using reasoning to teach writing in introductory philosophy courses. The syllabus integrates instruction in grammar, logic, and rhetoric by emphasizing four rhetorical strategies for each development: (1) arguments on how a belief is false, (2) formulating and defending one's own beliefs, (3) strategies for applying beliefs, and (4) strategies for formulating and applying belief. The authors recommend recognition and imitation of patterns as the basic instructional technique for meeting their goals. They provide a statistical comparison of results obtained in courses using their syllabus with those in their university's traditional English composition courses which indicates the use of the syllabus produces statistically higher results. An appendix of the article contains the non-essay portion of the final exam used with the syllabus.

762 Foss, Sonja K. "Rhetorical Criticism as the Asking of Questions." *Communication Education* 38, no. 3 (July 1989): 191-196. [2 Refs.]

Since the primary goal of an undergraduate rhetorical criticism course is to teach students to think rhetorically, Foss proposes and illustrates a question-asking approach to teaching such a course. She contends that this approach develops critical thinking skills and introduces students to the process by which knowledge is constructed within a discipline. Foss describes the structure of a course designed around three major questions, a four-step approach, and the incorporation of both rhetorical methods and artifacts. An outline of teaching methods used in the course is given.

763 Frankenbach, Charlie. *Teaching Poetry: Generating Genuine, Meaningful Responses*. ERIC Digest. Bloomington, IN: ERIC Clearinghouse on Reading and Communication Skills, 1989. [8 Refs.] ED 307 609.

This is an analysis of some sources in the ERIC database regarding the teaching of poetry. The sources emphasize student involvement, an inquiry approach, and the value of studying poetry in enhancing the use of critical thinking skills in responding to advertising and in enhancing the reasoning skills of law students.

764 Fritz, Paul A., and Richard L. Weaver, II. "Teaching Critical Thinking Skills in the Basic Speaking Course: A Liberal Arts Perspective." *Communication Education* 35, no. 2 (April 1986): 174-182. [91 Refs.]

The divisions of classical rhetoric provide a framework for teaching critical thinking skills in a basic speech communication course. Fritz and Weaver describe a series of tested exercises and teaching methods for developing the skills inherent in framing, scenario, organization, self-analysis, audience analysis, composition, memory, delivery, and imaging that are important for analyzing and presenting written and oral messages.

765 Gambell, Trevor J. "Literature: Why We Teach it." *English Quarterly* 19, no. 2 (Summer 1986): 85-91. [2 Refs.]

Gambell provides a review of literature defending the teaching of literature as a way of teaching language, values, culture, writing, and critical thinking.

766 Garoian, Charles R. "Teaching Critical Thinking through Art History in High School." *Design for Arts in Education* 90, no. 1 (September-October 1988): 34-39. [9 Refs.]

Garoian asserts that art history can be a means of developing critical thinking skills in secondary school students. He believes that historical and experiential perspectives--the ability to identify with visual qualities, describe, analyze, interpret, and evaluate--are required in the understanding of art. Using Gauguin's *Where do I come from? Who am I? Where am I going?*, Garoian illustrates how art history is relevant to the uncertain conflict-ridden period of adolescence and how Gauguin's questions can be used as guidelines for examining the past, present, and future of students" own lives in relation to the history of humankind. Garoian compares Bloom's taxonomy of educational objectives with Edmund B. Feldman's stages of art criticism found in *Varieties of Visual Experience* (Englewood Cliffs, NJ: Prentice-Hall, 1972) to further justify how critical thinking is facilitated through the study of art history. He offers suggestions for teaching art history and gives recommendations for a secondary school art history curriculum.

767 Groarke, Leo, and Christopher Tindale. "Critical Thinking: How to Teach *Good* Reasoning." *Teaching Philosophy* 9, no. 4 (December 1986): 301-317. [25 Refs.]

The authors decribe a systematic approach to teaching critical thinking. The approach focuses on the criteria for constructing good arguments rather than how to avoid fallacies and mistakes. Fallacies are reconstructed into positive criteria for how good arguments may be created, rather than as means for identifying bad arguments. Segments of the approach are discussed: introducing argument, propositional logic, ordinary language, semantics, ordinary argument forms, and extended arguments. The discussion includes examples and suggested exercises.

768 Gronbeck, Bruce E. "Rhetorical Criticism in the Liberal Arts Curriculum." *Communication Education* 38, no. 3 (July 1989): 184-190. [19 Refs.]

Gronbeck advocates teaching rhetorical criticism from a liberal arts perspective. Dating back to Isocrates, this perspective envisions an educated citizen as one conversant with theory, history, criticism, and the skills necessary to generate and consume communicative messages. It demands that skill and social knowledge be taught simultaneously, so that all training and education take place within cultural contexts. Instructional goals for rhetorical criticism should be the same as general education: developing students' abilities to discourse accurately about the world by learning a technical vocabulary, to view the world in perspective by putting public communication habits and processes into contexts, and to make and defend knowledgeable and reasoned judgments. Gronbeck proposes that introductory public speaking courses include rhetorical criticism to develop vocabularies and critical dispositions and that a formal rhetorical criticism course on examining critical perspectives be offered.

769 Hayward, Albert W. "Reconstructing Arguments from Editorials." *Teaching Philosophy* 9, no. 1 (March 1986): 61-70.

Hayward describes simplification exercises he uses in teaching informal logic arguments.

770 Healy, Paul. "Critical Reasoning and Dialectical Argument: An Extension of Toulmin's Approach." *Informal Logic* 9, no. 1 (Winter 1987): 1-12. [43 Refs.]

Healy asserts that Toulmin's model for assessing practical arguments is limited by its single perspective approach. By merging features of the dialectical assessment of argumentation (which considers criticisms from multiple perspectives) with Toulmin's model, Healy develops a model that overcomes those limitations.

771 Hepler, Susan. "A Guide for the Teacher Guides: Doing it Yourself." *New Advocate* 1, no. 3 (Summer 1988): 186-195. [17 Refs.]

As teachers and administrators increasingly agree on the worthiness of incorporating literature throughout the curriculum, Hepler notes the increasing need for suggestions on selecting and teaching literature. This article provides information on commercially available teaching guides, evaluating guides, and the advantages of teachers constructing their own. Hepler describes the process she and her colleagues followed in developing their own guides. Emphasis is on evaluating and developing guides that enhance reader satisfaction and enjoyment and that stimulate critical thinking.

772 Hitchcock, David. *Critical Thinking: A Guide to Evaluating Information*. Toronto, Ontario: Methuen, 1983. 283 pp. [32 Refs.]

This is an informal logic text intended to help students critically assess what they read and hear. Chapters cover topics such as argument structure, inferences, reasoning, clarifying meaning, and evaluating claims. Each chapter concludes with self-testing exercises.

773 Hoaglund, John. *Critical Thinking: An Introduction to Informal Logic*. Newport News, VA: Vale Press, 1984. [229 pp.]

This text is designed to improve student reasoning skills in an introductory informal logic course. The material presented is adapted from propositional logic and covers logical relations of statements, consistency, assumptions, definitions, arguments, categories, and syllogisms. Included are examples using ordinary language and everyday contexts, exercises, and suggested further readings.

774 Kielkopf, Charles. "Forms for 'Informal Logic'." *Informal Logic* 6 (January 1984): 21-25. [4 Refs.]

Kielkopf believes that providing a list of fallacy forms is a helpful method for teaching students to organize arguments by critical analysis. He contends that two additional forms covering irrelevant conclusion fallacies should be added to the traditional list. Kielkopf labels these two additional forms as affirmative irrelevant argumentation and negative irrelevant argumentation. He presents examples of how these new fallacies may be used in evaluating arguments.

775 Kielkopf, Charles. "Relevant Appeals to Force, Pity & Popular Pieties." *Informal Logic* 2 (April 1980): 2-5.

Kielkopf discusses the need to teach students the distinction between reasons for thinking and reasons for acting. He argues that the relation of conclusions to premises may be considered fallacious and irrelevant as reasons for thinking, but non-fallacious and relevant as reasons for acting. He analyzes examples of arguments to demonstrate the need for the distinction.

776 Kistner, W. "A Note on Formal Logic in Teaching Critical Thinking." *South Africa Journal of Philosophy* 7, no. 2 (1988): 123-125. [19 Refs.]

Traditionally, formal logic has been used to teach critical thinking courses, but the current trend is toward informal logic. Kistner explores the weaknesses of formal and informal logic as teaching mechanisms for critical thinking. The author concludes by advocating the strengthening of the weak points in teaching with formal logic, rather than replacing it with informal logic which tests for acceptability rather than validity of arguments.

777 Knickerbocker, Joan L. "A Literature Infusion Model for College Reading Improvement Classes." *Journal of Reading* 31, no. 6 (March 1988): 524-532. [19 Refs.]

To add variety, promote motivation, and foster analytical skills, Knickerbocker proposes the incorporation of literature into a college reading improvement course traditionally based on college reading textbooks. She outlines the Literature Infusion Model, a five-phase sequenced developmental program designed to promote (1) understanding and appreciation of fiction through oral reading, (2) the story structure approach to analyzing fiction, (3) individualized reading by the student, and (4) written and oral responses based on the literary criticism approach.

778 Kruise, Carol Sue. "Using Children's Literature in Critical Thinking Skills." *School Library Media Activities Monthly* 4, no. 2 (October 1987): 27-29. [3 Refs.]

Using Benjamin Bloom's taxonomy of cognitive learning (knowledge, comprehension, application, analysis, synthesis, evaluation) as a guide for defining questions and activities, Kruise discusses ways library media specialists can teach critical thinking through children's literature, using examples of specific works of children's literature.

779 Levitsky, Ronald. "Simulation and Thinking." *Thinking Skills Instruction: Concepts and Techniques*, edited by Marcia Heiman and Joshua Slomianko, 262-271. Building Students' Thinking Skills. Washington, DC: National Education Association, 1987. [6 Refs.]

Levitsky advocates using simulation in the history classroom to promote thinking among adolescents. He discusses its suitability with adolescents who are at Piaget's formal operation stage and addresses the arguments of educators and parents opposing the use of simulation. Levitsky provides an example of a simulation used successfully in an eighth grade United States history class.

780 Maker, William. "Teaching Informal Logic as an Emancipatory Activity." *Informal Logic* 5 (December 1982): 17-20.

Maker argues that informal logic fulfills the objectives of philosophical and traditional education by teaching the basic techniques of critical thinking, which aims for intellectual emancipation from aperspectivism, distorted communication, and authoritarianism. Informal logic produces justification for a criteria of rationality that supplies many of the rules and guidelines for proper human action. Maker discusses the teaching techniques he uses and provides examples of how teaching informal logic has emancipated his own thinking.

781 Manlove, Colin N. *Critical Thinking: A Guide to Interpreting Literary Texts*. London, UK: Macmillan, 1989. 188 pp. [4 Refs.]

Manlove attempts to show the reader how to go about forming ideas and critical interpretations of literature. He encourages the reader to work more closely with the text and textual evidence, entering the work and feeling "its movements, harmonies, jars and jolts" (p. 12). Manlove works toward these objectives by actively analyzing selected sections of poems, literature, and plays. By engaging in actual analyses of texts, rather than discoursing on the nature of textual interpretation, Manlove hopes to engage the reader in actively analyzing and interpreting the sample selections as they read his own attempts.

782 Markle, Aldeen. "Developing Critical Thinking Skills through Literature." *School Library Media Quarterly* 16, no. 1 (Fall 1987): 43-44. [10 Refs.]

Markle believes that students who learn to think critically about literature, learn the consequences of behavior and how to clarify values. To enhance the development of these skills, the author advocates reading aloud and providing challenging questions and activities to children and adolescents. Markle suggests resources for teachers, librarians, and parents.

783 Matthews, Gareth B. "What Did the Universe Appear *On*?" *Journal of Thought* 20 (Summer 1985): 14-20. [3 Refs.]

See: Schrag {802}

Matthews presents examples of reasoning excerpted from discussions in a philosophy discussion class for third and fourth graders. He asserts that philosophical discussions similar to the examples help children develop critical thinking skills. He believes a philosophy course should be offered in elementary schools to teach critical thinking. Such a course would nurture a pursuit that is natural to children, be exciting and rewarding for both students and teachers, and be valuable for developing a mutually respectful and interactive relationship between teachers and students that would foster growth for everyone involved.

784 McBride, Lawrence W., and Gary E. McKiddy. "The Oral Tradition and Arab Narrative History: An Exercise in Critical Thinking." *Teaching History: A Journal of Methods* 14, no. 1 (Spring 1989): 3-17. [2 Refs.]

The authors discuss their use of variant oral histories of the 1902 capture of Riyadh by the Saudis to teach how critical thinking skills are used in analysis and evaluation of historical sources. The authors relate relevant background information, three versions of the event, and critical thinking questions a teacher should pose concerning the different historical accounts.

785 McCarty, Richard. "Media Projects for Introductory Logic." *Teaching Philosophy* 8, no. 4 (October 1985): 325-329. [1 Ref.]

McCarty describes how newspapers and video recordings of television material can be used in logic instruction. Included are suggestions on how to find the time that selected commercials and political speeches and debates will be aired and the copyright restrictions on such materials. McCarty outlines his method for teaching students about the world views presented in newspapers that result from the selection and editing of stories. Students are to perform the same task of selecting and editing their own front page and headlines.

786 McGonigal, Elizabeth. "Correlative Thinking: Writing Analogies about Literature." *English Journal* 77, no. 1 (January 1988): 66-67.

McGonigal advocates the use of word analogies to promote an appreciation for and critical thinking about literature. After practicing how to complete and interpret analogies generated in class, students begin constructing their own analogies, gaining confidence in relying on their instincts and experience in providing critical interpretations of literature. Feeling ownership of their critical ideas, students then write with authority and power, supporting their analogies with elements from the literature.

787 McMillan, Merna M., and Lance M. Gentile. "Children's Literature: Teaching Critical Thinking and Ethics." *Reading Teacher* 41, no. 9 (May 1988): 876-878.

McMillan and Gentile assert that children's literature, with its abundance of themes, is an excellent vehicle for teaching critical thinking. Posing dilemmas and characters in the classroom setting allows for open discussion of alternatives and predictions and the development of the ability to think critically and ethically. While basal reading instruction helps children learn the mechanics of reading, children's literature provides them with a wide range of information and stirs their imagination and creativity.

788 Mebane, John S. "Teaching Interpretive Skills through Testing in Literature Courses." *Exercise Exchange* 32, no. 1 (Fall 1986): 7-10. [3 Refs.]

Mebane describes a testing method based on open-ended study questions distributed at the beginning of a course for enhancing critical thinking skills in literature. He advocates challenging students to examine their ideas systematically, emphasizing independent thinking, interpretive skills, argumentation, and justification. Mebane provides sample questions.

789 Miller, Douglas E. "Cooperative Critical Thinking and History." *Social Studies Review* 28, no. 3 (Spring 1989): 55-68. [4 Refs.]

Miller argues that high school history textbooks lack consistent, logical, and coherent formats; contain abstract, technical terms and dense paragraphs; and present an array of facts without analysis. These features complicate the learning of history. Miller advocates combining findings from reading research and cooperative learning as a way of teaching history. He demonstrates the approach in a sample history lesson. Miller includes a teacher's guide, teacher's handouts, student handouts, and exercises for this lesson.

790 Moberg, Dale. "Appraising Argumentative Texts: Justificatory and Defensive Components." *Informal Logic* 5 (December 1982): 20-23. [3 Refs.]

A common approach to argument appraisal uses diagramming an argument to separate premises, conditionals, and conclusions for analysis of validity and soundness. Moberg argues that this approach is seriously limited due to the existence of argument components that can not be diagrammed. He advocates an epistemic conception of argumentation which combines the diagramming approach with the anticipation of objections and conflicting positions. Moberg provides examples of this combined approach.

791 Nodelman, Perry. "Teaching Children's Literature: An Intellectual Snob Confronts Some Generalizers." *Children's Literature in Education* 17, no. 4 (Winter 1986): 203-214. [2 Refs.]

Nodelman describes his attempts at countering his students' persistence in approaching children's literature through generalizations about children based on conclusions drawn from research studies which they believed to be unquestionable facts. By revealing his assumptions and expectations openly to students and confronting his students' assumptions through their responses to critical reading, Nodelman provided a successful critical thinking experience through which students earned a new way of thinking.

792 O'Reilly, Kevin. "Infusing Critical Thinking into United States History Courses." Chapter 31 in *Developing Minds. Vol. 1: A Resource Book for Teaching Thinking*, rev. ed., edited by Arthur L. Costa, 164-168. Alexandria, VA: Association for Supervision and Curriculum Development, 1991. [5 Refs.]

O'Reilly describes infusing critical thinking into an eleventh grade United States history course. He illustrates approaches and methodologies for incorporating the skills of identifying and evaluating sources of information, assessing cause-and-effect reasoning, and analyzing comparisons or analogies. O'Reilly also addresses the issues of evaluation, content coverage, and the time necessary to write lessons.

793 O'Reilly, Kevin. "Spotlight on Critical Thinking." *New England Journal of History* 45, no. 2 (Summer 1988): 26-29.

O'Reilly presents a lesson plan for teaching analytical thinking skills that uses the issue of whether the public played a significant role in the formulation and ratification of the U.S. Constitution. A sample lesson is included.

794 Paccione, Paul. "Critical Thinking for Composers." *Journal of Music Theory Pedagogy* 4, no.1 (Spring 1990): 73-84. [7 Refs.]

Paccione explores the relationship between critical thinking and music composition. He applies Bloom's taxonomy and Paul's concepts of technical reason and emancipatory or dialectical reason to composition and the teaching of composition. Paccione sees analysis, synthesis, and evaluation as forming the dialectic of composition or as the critical-creative-reflective process in which analysis is concept-generating, synthesis is concept-using, and evaluation is personal and global reflection. Since composers have no set of generally established principles within which to work, each compositional question requires reasoning, decision making, self-criticism, and reflection.

reasoning, decision making, self-criticism, and reflection. Paccione presents six exercises he has used to foster critical thinking in beginning composition students.

795 Parks, Michael E. "How Does the Work Mean?" *Art Education* 41, no. 3 (May 1988): 55-61. [5 Refs.]

Parks advocates using a framework for discussion modeled after the art critic's discussion of a work of art which includes referring to other works of art in order to establish a perspective on its value. He believes comparing and contrasting works through class discussion can be used as an instructional method with students possessing limited background knowledge in the arts. Through this method, students learn to relate the propensities of a work with its themes and concepts. Parks suggests sample art works and the corresponding elements that could be addressed through the discussion framework for comparing and contrasting works.

796 Pecorino, Philip A. "How Does an Informal Logician Analyze an Argument?" In *Conference 85 on Critical Thinking, Christopher Newport College*, edited by John Hoaglund, 83-97. Newport News, VA: Christopher Newport College Press, 1985. [4 Refs.]

The analysis and evaluation of extended ordinary language arguments is a valuable, though controversial, activity of critical thinking. Pecorino presents a six step method for teaching extended argument analysis: (1) identify the argument, (2) analyze the argument, (3) criticize the premises, (4) criticize the inferences, (5) introduce and consider other relevant arguments, and (6) oral evaluation, grading, and final judgment.

797 Peeno, Larry N. "Art Education: A Curriculum." *Design for Arts in Education* 90, no. 2 (November-December 1988): 41-43. [7 Refs.]

Peeno argues for incorporating discipline-based art education at appropriate levels throughout the curriculum. Discipline-based art education is an attempt to present art education as an academic discipline with content that can be taught, learned, and evaluated. Art educators must be aware of learning styles, teaching strategies, higher thinking skills, and the relation of objectives and skills to the kindergarten through twelfth grade curriculum. Teaching curriculum objectives as ends in themselves results in fragmented thinking and ignores the relation of learning with prior knowledge.

798 Perkins, D. N. "Art as An Occasion of Intelligence." *Educational Leadership* 45, no. 4 (December 1987-January 1988): 36-43. [23 Refs.]

Perkins believes that students need to look at works of art actively and systematically, incorporating their knowledge and experience, in order to develop an appreciation of art. He sees three counterforces in education blocking the development of "intelligent looking" (p. 37) at art and other subjects: (1) students' naive concepts or mistaken beliefs of particular subject matter concepts, (2) schooling's neglect of intelligent behavior (or failure to develop students' thinking abilities), and (3) counterproductive disciplinary traditions such as emphasis on studio art or important elements of art history and art criticism, rather than on topics and ideas that foster the development of art appreciation in novices. To counteract these dilemmas in education, Perkins and colleagues developed an experimental art appreciation course, "Invisible Art," for upper elementary and middle school students. The course incorporates a set of four thinking frames to guide students' thinking about art. These frames emphasized aesthetic effects (e.g., surprise and motion); contrast between real and suggested effects; contrast between specific and overall features; and the mechanisms or tactics used by artists to convey messages, impressions, and effects. Perkins advocates using similar approaches in other subject matter courses.

799 Pogonowski, Lee. "Developing Skills in Critical Thinking and Problem Solving." *Music Educators Journal* 73, no. 5 (February 1987): 37-41. [4 Refs.]

Pogonowski stresses the importance of experience in teaching and learning. He emphasizes the importance of the experience of problem solving with musical materials to the development and application of critical thinking skills in music. He illustrates using musical problem solving in teaching pitch through experience. Pogonowski addresses the importance of prospective teachers understanding the significance of classroom environment, recognizing and analyzing their own attitudes toward music, and having their own critical thinking experiences in music education programs.

800 Ramsland, Katherine. "Teaching Critical Reasoning through Group Competition." *Teaching Philosophy* 9, no. 4 (December 1986): 319-326.

Ramsland describes strategies for teaching a critical reasoning course requiring active participation, group competition, and practical applications through speaking, writing, and listening activities. The first part of the course sets the foundation for argumentation through lecture and exams, while the second part involves group and individual work. Ramsland argues that the approach is effective in teaching students practical argumentation and critical reasoning skills, developing social skills, and responsibility, and exposing students to numerous critical perspectives.

801 Reahm, Douglas E. "Developing Critical Thinking through Rehearsal Techniques." *Music Educators Journal* 72, no. 7 (March 1986): 29-31.

Reahm advocates teaching students in secondary school music performance classes that musicianship involves critical decision making. He suggests involving students in an analysis of performance options, experimentation, conducting, and the teacher's interpretation of choral, band, and orchestral pieces to teach critical thinking skills and demonstrate the critical decision making involved in music performance.

802 Schrag, Francis. "Response to Gareth Matthews." *Journal of Thought* 20 (Summer 1985): 21-24. [1 Ref.]

Reply to Matthews {783}

Schrag identifies two features aiding in the success of Matthews' philosophy sessions with children: (1) the setting was voluntary and (2) the number of students was small. The author discusses the possible inhibitions to success that large classrooms would have on a required course in philosophy. Schrag expresses concern that introducing philosophy to children may impede a balanced development of intellect and feeling in favor of a superficial adeptness at logic and pedantry, leading to sophistry.

803 Sheridan, James J. "Teaching Thinking: The Mission of the Humanities." *Community, Technical, and Junior College Journal* 58, no. 1 (August-September 1987): 18-21. [5 Refs.]

With over 55% of American workers in jobs requiring information-related activities and the short time span within which half the knowledge base of some fields will become obsolete, Sheridan believes that it is imperative that community, technical, and junior colleges teach students how to think and that the humanities reclaim its historical mission to teach individuals to become independent thinkers. Sheridan describes his approach to teaching the thinking process through techniques such as prewriting, PMI (Plus, Minus, Interesting), AWOL (Alternate Ways of Thinking), focused free-writing, brainstorming, prioritizing, discussion, and critical analysis.

804 Small, Ann R. "Music Teaching and Critical Thinking: What Do We Need to Know?" *Music Educators Journal* 74, no. (September 1987): 46-9. [3 Refs.]

Small asserts that incorporating critical thinking into music training will foster the development of critical performers and consumers of music. She outlines how critical thinking can be applied to music teaching through defining the musical problem, identifying what is and what is not related to a subject, recognizing underlying assumptions, and detecting inconsistencies. To help students develop thinking skills, Small suggests that teachers establish an atmosphere of cognitive challenge, plan an incident of intellectual dissonance, and help students develop a repertoire of questions to activate reasoning. She discusses a few examples of teaching activities.

805 Stroble, Elizabeth J., and Paul E. Stroble. "Simulated Garbage: Leaps of Inference from Artifacts." *Exercise Exchange* 34, no. 1 (Fall 1988): 3-5. [3 Refs.]

The authors describe using a strategy that engages students in creative problem solving and critical thinking. This strategy, called Simulated Garbage, presents a list of items found in a household garbage can on a particular date and requires student groups to make inferences regarding the number of individuals in that household and the occupations, hobbies, and lifestyles of these individuals.

The strategy was first used with gifted and talented middle school students and then adapted for college students in a world religions course in which inferences were to be made about a civilization's religious beliefs from a list of objects supposedly discovered by an archaeological expedition.

806 Svinicki, Marilla D., and Richard H. Kraemer. "Critical Thinking: Some Views from the Front Line." In *Fostering Critical Thinking*, edited by Robert E. Young, 59-75. New Directions for Teaching and Learning, no. 3. San Francisco, CA: Jossey-Bass, 1980. [9 Refs.]

This article presents reactions from administrators, students, instructors, and teaching assistants on their involvement in an interdisciplinary course that emphasized critical thinking. The course, "The American Experience," was team-taught by faculty from the departments of history and government at the University of Texas. The reactions reflect the positive and negative aspects inherent in making the goal of critical thinking a practical reality.

807 Tymoczko, Maria. "Using Literature to Develop Critical Thinking Skills." In *Thinking Skills Instruction: Concepts and Techniques*, edited by Marcia Heiman and Joshua Slomianko, 246-254. Building Students' Thinking Skills. Washington, DC: National Education Association, 1987.

Tymoczko illustrates how literature can be used as a vehicle for teaching the following four types of critical thinking: induction, deduction, constructing sound arguments, and model building and theory formulation. She presents strategies and techniques for teaching critical thinking through literature.

808 Weinstein, Mark. "Musclebuilding for Strength in Critical Thinking." *Informal Logic* 5 (December 1982): 13-17. [3 Refs.]

Weinstein describes pedagogical techniques for integrating the teaching of strong sense critical thinking (Paul {609}) into a logical thinking course designed for the development of the basic skills of reading, writing, and speaking in undergraduate students. The author believes that the "theory of critical teaching theory is, necessarily, bound to the analysis of students as readers, speakers, and writers" (p.17).

809 Wicks, Robert J. "Clarity and Obscurity: Critical Thinking and Cognitive Therapeutic Principles in the Service of Spiritual Discernment." *Thought* 63, no. 248 (March 1988): 77-85. [20 Refs.]

Wicks views critical thinking as "squarely grounded in the process of reflection and reflexion" (p. 79) which makes it applicable to spiritual decision making for Christians striving for Truth. Knowing cognitive psychotherapeutic principles will help spiritual directors facilitate people seeking clarity in their spiritual decision making and suffering from distorted perceptions, thinking, and beliefs.

810 Yaffe, Stephen H. "Drama as a Teaching Tool." *Educational Leadership* 46, no. 6 (March 1989): 29-32.

Yaffe provides examples of using dramatic improvisation with kindergartners, gifted and talented fifth graders, and at-risk twelfth graders to demonstrate that drama can effectively develop thinking skills, enhance comprehension of subject matter, connect the written word and the reader, and make learning fun.

811 Yeager, Natalie C. "Teaching Thinking to Teach Literature While Teaching Literature to Teach Thinking." In *Thinking Skills Instruction: Concepts and Techniques*, edited by Marcia Heiman and Joshua Slomianko, 134-144. Building Students' Thinking Skills. Washington, DC: National Education Association, 1987. [29 Refs.]

Yeager illustrates how students can develop critical thinking skills through literature and how using the skills will lead to a greater understanding of literature. She presents numerous examples from literature and suggests techniques for teaching translation, interpretation, application, analysis, synthesis, and evaluation.

Social Sciences

812 Adams, Dennis, and Mary Hamm. "Changing the Texture of Learning." *Journal of Epsilon Pi Tau* 14, no. 1 (Winter-Spring 1988): 28-30. [9 Refs.]

The authors assert that electronic media, like print, are based on a symbol system and rely upon the reader's or viewer's ability to interpret abstract symbols. Interpreting and processing visual images requires critical thinking and visual literacy skills. Adams and Hamm suggest several practical teaching techniques for helping students develop these skills. They advocate a cross-media curriculum.

813 Allen, Rodney F. "Image and Reality: The Critical Use of Tourist Brochures in World Geography Classes." *Journal of Geography* 88, no. 1 (January-February 1989): 6-9, 10.

Allen presents ways to use travel brochures to teach critical thinking. Students are to evaluate the gap between the brochure images and the reality of the area, then contact relevant government agencies or embassies for comments. Addresses for U.N. consuls and select foreign embassies are included.

814 Allen, Rodney F., and David E. LaHart. "Critical Thinking Skills and Energy: Using Energy Error Cards in Geography Classes." *Journal of Geography* 80, no. 2 (February 1981): 64-70. [1 Refs.]

The authors describe twelve situations involving arguments or decisions pertaining to energy matters that contain fallacious understanding, beliefs, or reasoning. They recommend presenting these situations on cards to secondary school students and, when appropriate, including relevant matter such as charts, maps, tables or graphs. Each situation contains an error in the arguments or actions of individuals. The students must discover this error. Allen and LaHart contend that by using these energy error cards, geography teachers can teach current, relevant, and useful information to students and help develop critical thinking skills.

815 Bennett, James R. "Corporate Sponsored Image Films." *Journal of Business Ethics* 2 (Fall 1983): 35-41. [84 Refs.]

Bennett discusses the proliferation of corporate sponsored educational films, most of which implicitly advocate certain social policies favoring the corporate sponsor. He believes the scaling back of government regulations addressing the information imbalance of such films in the 1980s increases the need for individuals to learn how to analyze the ideas presented in the films. Bennett discusses the approach he uses for such analysis, using the Chesebrough-Pond Corporation's film, "Family," as his example. His approach entails asking questions that make the individual think critically about the film and focus on the credibility of the film's sponsor and message. The approach combines awareness of the speaker in any communication, knowledge of informal fallacies, and the intensify/downplay method endorsed by the National Council of Teachers of English Committee on Public Doublespeak.

816 Beyer, Barry K. "Teaching Critical Thinking: A Direct Approach." *Social Education* 49, 4 (April 1985): 297-303. [24 Refs.]

A version of this printed in Costa {505}, pp. 145-150.

Advocating the direct instruction of critical thinking skills, Beyer provides a five-stage framework for teaching these skills in social studies. Based on research findings, this framework entails providing opportunities for students to recognize the application of a skill, to learn the components of the skill in detail through demonstration, to practice a skill under instructional guidance, to broaden the contexts of the skill, and to apply the skill beyond the context used when introduced. Beyer illustrates inductive and directive strategies for introducing the critical thinking skill of detecting bias in written documents in world history, outlines guidelines for using these strategies, and provides two strategies for guided practice. He emphasizes the importance of a critical thinking skill being taught over a period of years and a sequence of courses.

817 Brandhorst, Allan, and Fred Splittgerber. "Social Studies and the Development of Thinking: The State of the Art." *Southern Social Studies Quarterly* 13, no. 2 (Fall 1987): 20-41. [21 Refs.]

In order to more clearly define the nature of thinking in social studies, the authors examine four alternative methods for teaching thinking: reflective thinking, inquiry, critical thinking, and critical theory. They identify general principles for instruction in thinking found in current cognitive science research and discuss the teacher's role in teaching thinking.

818 Brookfield, Stephen. "Media Power and the Development of Media Literacy: An Adult Educational Interpretation." *Harvard Education Review* 56, no. 2 (May 1986): 151-70. [37 Refs.]

Brookfield describes the presentations of bias in television, emphasizing the important function of media literacy in adult education, especially for educators attempting to foster critical thinking. To develop media literacy in adult learners, Brookfield proposes exercises for deconstructing and decoding the text of programs, analyzing the content, and analyzing life portrayal of television programs.

819 Clausing, Carolyn. "Simulations for Critical Thinking." *Louisiana Social Studies Journal* 14, no. 1 (Fall 1987): 18-20.

Clausing discusses the use of critical thinking simulations in the social studies classroom. She believes that unlike factual simulations, critical thinking simulations involve students as leaders in planning, organizing, and presenting. Students learn the importance of asking good questions and of research skills. They demonstrate an understanding of facts through role-playing which requires them to think critically about the information gathered. Clausing provides a description of a critical thinking simulation involving the U.S. Constitution presented through a simulated television news program.

820 Copa, Patricia, Francine Hultgren, and Joan Wilkosz. "Critical Thinking as a Lived Activity." Chapter 36 in *Developing Minds. Vol. 1: A Resource Book for Teaching Thinking*, edited by Arthur L. Costa, 188-192. Alexandria, VA: Association for Supervision and Curriculum Development, 1991. [9 Refs.]

The authors stress the importance of critical thinking being the core of teaching and learning in home economics classes designed to improve the well-being of individuals and families. Critical thinking as an academic exercise is not sufficient. It must be translated into taking action to solve practical problems or human problems. Such problems involve moral decisions and require ethical thinking. The authors describe staff development programs and curricula projects for home economics developed in Minnesota and Wisconsin.

821 Cradler, John. "Three Messages Regarding Technology." *Social Studies Review* 25, no. 3 (Spring 1986): 8-29.

Cradler describes two projects: the California History-Social Science Technology in Curriculum Project and Project CompuTHINK. The California History-Social Science project assists teachers in selecting computer software and instructional television programs that can expand the history/social science curriculum and help to develop specific skills in students. Cradler outlines the project's program analysis procedure and its resource guide for history and social science. CompuTHINK assists teachers in integrating technology into their instruction and in selecting instructional computer and television programs for the teaching of critical thinking and problem solving skills. Cradler details the CompuTHINK resource guide and includes diagrams of the program's cognitive framework, analysis process and cognitive skills matrix. Sample pages from the resource guide are included. Cradler includes an analysis of technology program reviews and recommendations for future technology development provided by the California History-Social Science Technology in Curriculum Project.

822 Curtis, Charles K. "Using Radio 'Hot-Line' Programs to Teach Critical Thinking." *History and Social Science Teacher* 15, no. 4 (Summer 1980): 268-272. [6 Refs.]

Curtis illustrates a critical thinking exercise that uses a tape recorded radio broadcast of a discussion on housing issues, such as rent controls, interest rates, and government intervention. Curtis describes using this exercise with students in secondary social studies classes who were investigating the housing problems of their communities. The exercise lessons incorporate critical thinking skills identified by Robert Ennis, contemporary societal problems, the inquiry method. and evaluative criteria for making judgments.

823 Davis, Arda B., and Sandra J. Gill. "Teaching Critical Thinking through Questioning and Concept Attainment." *Illinois Teacher of Home Economics* 32, no. 3 (May-June 1989): 169, 186-187. [8 Refs.]

Despite recommendations by several studies that students need to be taught thinking skills, Davis and Gill find educators continue to lecture and teach for factual learning. The authors affirm their support for instruction in thinking and review several classroom factors that influence thinking. They provide two examples from home economics that illustrate the teaching of thinking, emphasizing the type of conceptual questions to be asked by the teacher.

824 Duckett, Jasmin. "Back to Basics in Business Writing." *Business Education Forum* 42, no. 8 (May 1988): 16-18.

Duckett describes two ways the teaching of business writing can be used to develop critical thinking skills by focusing on the development and expression of control ideas. One method employs B.O.W.E.R. (Brainstorming, Outline, Write, Edit, Refine), the other a "recipe" writing list in which students list the steps to follow in completing a specific practice application problem.

825 Estaville, Lawrence E., Jr. "Debate: A Teaching Strategy for Geography." *Journal of Geography* 87, no. 1 (January-February 1988): 2-4. [5 Refs.]

Estaville describes using classroom debate as a teaching method in geography courses as a means of stimulating students to think critically about important issues, to enhance student ability to express ideas logically, and to improve students' verbal articulation and writing skills. Estaville provides guidelines for using debate effectively in the classroom, including outlines of topics, procedures, and evaluation criteria used in his classes.

826 Evans, Eileen B., and Roberta Supnick. "Evaluating Evidence of Critical Thinking Skills." *Business Education Forum* 43, no. 6 (March 1989): 16-18. [5 Refs.]

The authors contend that business writing requires that students seek solutions to problems, attend to audience needs, and apply critical thinking in problem solving. By beginning with an analysis of paragraph components that reflect critical thought, students will be able to relate problem solving skills with a written presentation of the problem solving process. Evans and Supnick provide a checklist to be used by students for determining the extent of the evidence of critical thinking found through an analysis of topic sentence, audience analysis, paragraph coherence and logic, sentence logic, parallelism, and subordination. They explain how these components can provide evidence of progress in students' critical thinking skills development.

827 Fair, Jean, and Grace Kachaturoff. "Teaching Thinking: Another Try!" *Social Studies* 79, no. 2 (March-April 1988): 64-69. [16 Refs.]

This is an overview of the various aspects and concepts of thinking and their manifestations in thinking skills programs. Addressing thinking skills programs, generally, and in social studies, specifically, the authors emphasize the need for curriculum revision rather than the addition of separate thinking skills programs. They stress the importance of integrating knowledge and thinking, and recommend less coverage of context to allow time for activities to develop higher order intellectual processes. Fair and Kachaturoff suggest activities for teaching thinking in social studies in accordance with student capabilities based on Piaget's four stages of cognitive development. They provide general suggestions for teaching materials and questioning techniques and include an eight-item bibliography of readings for teachers.

828 Feeser, John M. "The Pre-Contact Time American Indian: A Study in the Meaning and Development of Culture--A Teaching Unit." *Thinking Skills Instruction: Concepts and Techniques*, edited by Marcia Heiman and Joshua Slomianko, 272-283. Building Students' Thinking Skills. Washington, DC: National Education Association, 1987.

The author discusses a teaching unit "designed to introduce students to the various and unique cultures developed by the aboriginal inhabitants of the Americas prior to European contact" (p. 272). The activities outlined are intended to help high school students develop such skills as analysis, deductive reasoning, critical reading, and synthesis. Each unit mentions a number of resources. The book also includes a 23-item bibliography of books useful for completing some of the activities.

829 Feinberg, Walter. "Civic Education: Lessons from the Iran-Contra Affair." *Theory into Practice* 27, no. 4 (Fall 1988): 270-274. [4 Refs.]

In preparation for inevitable inadequate coverage of the Iran-Contra affair in future textbooks, Feinberg advocates the use of textbooks as vehicles for critical thinking about social affairs. He suggests using the Iran-Contra hearings to help students develop skills in collecting and judging facts, understanding the use of symbols and media in shaping public opinion, and understanding alternative views. Suggested exercises and class projects are included.

830 Ferguson, Norman B. L. "Encouraging Responsibility, Active Participation, and Critical Thinking in General Psychology Students." *Teaching of Psychology* 13, no. 4 (December 1986): 217-218. [2 Refs.]

Ferguson describes how he revised his teaching methods in General Psychology to encourage students to become more actively involved in class and have more responsibility for their own learning. Socratic dialogue became the format for each class session and student-generated questions, evaluated by peers, formed the basis for class discussion and exam questions. To develop different levels of questioning, Ferguson requires students to use Benjamin Bloom's six levels of objectives within the cognitive domain.

831 Freese, Sara. "Exploring Propaganda in Advertising: A Critical Thinking Unit for Grades Four to Six." *School Library Media Activities Monthly* 4, no. 8 (April 1988): 26-27.

The authors present a curriculum unit on propaganda in advertising which teaches elementary school students to critically evaluate mass media advertising. Freese includes a list of propaganda techniques that students are to identify in advertising. The unit incorporates group and individual instructional activities.

832 Friman, H. Richard. "The Crisis of Teaching Crisis Decision Making." *Political Science Teacher* 2, no. 2 (1989): 14-16.

Friman describes the decision making under crisis simulation exercise used in an introductory international relations course. In the exercise student groups use background material and additional information supplied during discussion time to discuss a crisis situation. Friman provides sample materials and information on procedures used with the exercise.

833 Giroux, Henry A. "Teaching Content and Thinking through Writing." *Social Education* 43, no. 3 (March 1979): 190-193. [12 Refs.]

Giroux outlines an approach to teaching specific social studies subjects. The approach uses writing as a tool for learning thinking skills and subject content. The writing and reading assignments require students to analyze, discuss, and synthesize content while writing the subject, rather than "merely write" about the subject.

834 Goldstone, Bette P. "Visual Interpretation of Children's Books." *Reading Teacher* 42, no. 8 (April 1989): 592-595. [16 Refs.]

Goldstone argues that interpreting visual images from pictorial or media sources requires abstract thinking skills and prepares children for interpreting the printed page. She suggests several strategies and resources for teaching visual literacy through children's book illustrations. Goldstone asserts that visual literacy promotes creative and analytical thinking.

835 Gross, Richard E. "Reasons for the Limited Acceptance of the Problems Approach." *Social Studies* 80, no. 4 (September-October 1989): 185-186. [4 Refs.]

Gross outlines and discusses eleven reasons why the problem-oriented approach has limited acceptance in social studies teaching. The reasons outlined include the belief among some educators that the approach should be built upon background information, teachers believing teaching materials are not commonly problem-oriented, and a devotion to broad content coverage.

836 Haas, Mary E. "Encouraging Student Thinking through Participation Activities." *Social Studies Journal* 17 (Spring 1988): 32-36. [4 Refs.]

Haas suggests four activities requiring classroom participation and decision making by high school students: a ranking exercise, consequences exercise, concept relations exercise and a small group activity involving an examination of causal factors or consequences. The activities are described and illustrated using U.S. history topics. Haas provides suggestions for writing assignments and addresses the role of the teacher in student participation activities.

837 Haas, Mary E. "What is the Name of the Mystery Nation?" *Social Studies and the Young Learner* 1, no. 2 (November-December 1988): 19-20.

Haas finds that exercises requiring students to identify a country by using clues provided by the instructor can stimulate thinking in a geography classroom. She outlines several sample exercises.

838 Halden-Sullivan, Judith. "Business Basics: Using a Cognitive Approach in the Business Communication Class." *Bulletin of the Association for Business Communication* 50, 4 (December 1987): 11-15. [6 Refs.]

The author asserts that the goal of business communication classes should be to strengthen thinking abilities, thereby, enabling students to meet the demands of work and the world. She presents a representative list of cognitive competencies, with suggested teaching activities, that should be pursued in business communication classes. These competencies include generating possibilities, inferential reasoning, analyzing, classifying, prioritizing, abstracting, problem solving, understanding complex relationships, metaphoric and analogical reasoning, hypothetical reasoning, decision making, coherent argumentation, and reflecting upon internal processes.

839 Hastedt, Glenn. "Estimating the U.S. and Soviet Strategic Threat." *Political Science Teacher* 2, no. 1 (Winter 1989): 11-12. [38 Refs.]

Hastedt presents the intelligence estimating process as a way of engaging students in the learning process and helping them understand the nature of the U.S. and Soviet strategic threat. Through this approach, students develop their own intelligence estimate which requires problem definition and information collection, processing, analysis, and evaluation.

840 Hickey, Gail. "Creative Activities for Fostering Critical Reading in Elementary Social Studies." *Georgia Social*

Science Journal 19, no. 2 (Fall 1988): 20-21. [3 Refs.]

Hickey presents a listing of ideas to foster critical reading skills in elementary school social studies. The suggested activities include "You Are There" exercises, "Believe It or Not" exercises, and "In the News" reading assignments.

841 Hobbs, Heidi H., and Dario V. Moreno. "'Bureaucratic Bargaining': An American Foreign Policy Simulation." *Political Science Teacher* 1, no. 1 (Winter 1988): 6-9. [4 Refs.]

Hobbs and Moreno describe "Bureaucratic Bargaining," a simulation of decision making in American foreign policy, the first of a series of simulations entitled American Foreign Policy Simulations (AFPS). They provide instructions for pre-game and post-game activities, including testing for students' belief systems and general debriefing. The article includes a belief system questionnaire, a simulation summary, game rules, and a simulation text.

842 Hultgren, Francine. "Leaping into the Neighborhood Where Thinking Resides." *Illinois Teacher of Home Economics* 30, no. 4 (March-April 1987): 147-149. [11 Refs.]

Hultgren addresses the importance of viewing critical thinking from different frameworks of knowledge which uses different kinds of reasons, evidence, and modes of justification for inquiry and investigation. She proposes an emancipatory framework through which the familiar is viewed in different ways and in which thinking is approached from more intuitive modes. Hultgren introduces articles from students in her course on critical thinking and home economics that show students reflecting about the concept of thinking and practicing what they learned about thinking.

843 Kolar, Jane E. "Teaching Problem Solving in Interior Design." *Illinois Teacher* 32, no. 4 (March-April 1989): 147-150. [7 Refs.]

Kolar views critical thinking as essential to effective problem solving in all facets of home economics. She outlines the problem solving process within the context of interior design. As a part of the problem solving process, Kolar includes J. Parry's six stages of the Design Process.

Kolar suggests that teaching problem solving should stress the importance of developing questions for the client interview. She gives four possible assignments for teaching critical thinking.

844 Kownslar, Allan O. "What's Worth Having Students Think Critically About?" *Social Education* 49, no. 4 (April 1985): 304-307.

Incorporating critical thinking into social studies instruction should teach students to generalize and transfer critical thinking skills to a variety of areas other than history and government. Students should be critical thinkers even when they are no longer in school. Kownslar gives ten key questions that can be asked in social studies. The questions are designed to be used by students in other courses, non-academic concerns, or for later tasks. Kownslar includes samples of various social studies materials to which the ten questions can be applied for class discussion.

845 Laster, Janet F. "A Practical Action Teaching Model." *Journal of Home Economics* 74, no. 3 (Fall 1982): 41-44. [13 Refs.]

Laster presents a teaching model for home economics. She views home economics as a practical science which critically examines the cognitive content of values, the influence of values on actions, and the consequences of actions. The teaching model incorporates cooperative group interaction, contemporary problems, and critical and creative thinking. Laster uses a family housing problem to illustrate the four-phase teaching model (problem identification, practical reasoning, action, and reflection).

846 Lett, James. "A Field Guide to Critical Thinking." *Skeptical Inquirer* 14, no. 2 (Winter 1990): 153-160. [8 Refs.]

Concerned about the ineffectiveness of public education in teaching students critical thinking skills, Lett developed an elective course called "Anthropology and Paranormal" to help students learn these essential skills. To teach students the anthropological perspective for evaluating evidence, Lett presents them with six rules that simplify the scientific method: (1) falsifiability, (2) logic, (3) comprehensiveness, (4) honesty, (5) replicability, and (6) sufficiency. He then shows how to apply these rules to paranormal claims.

847 Lilley, Stephen. "Social Inquiry and the Civil Rights Movement." in *Critical Thinking: Focus on Social and Cultural Inquiry. Conference 1989 Proceedings*, edited by Wendy Oxman-Michelli and Mark Weinstein, 331-336. Montclair, NJ: Institute for Critical Thinking, Montclair State College, 1991. [8 Refs.]

Lilley contends that college students should be encouraged to explore and participate in the production of knowledge in order to develop investigative and cognitive skills, become personally involved in an issue, and develop a deep understanding of a social phenomenon. Lilley suggests a course structure for engaging students in the discovery of the Civil Rights Movement and civil rights and for helping them develop the capacity to consider civil rights in different cultures and under divergent conditions.

848 Lounsbury, John H. "Middle Level Social Studies: Points to Ponder." *Social Education* 52, no. 2 (February 1988): 116-118. [19 Refs.]

Lounsbury calls for a reassessment of the curriculum and instructional practices in social studies at the middle school level. He believes the curriculum should emphasize issues of immediate concern in the present day world and teach skills valuable to functioning day to day as an adult. Lounsbury questions the concepts and practices of ability-grouping and scope and sequence. He notes the unmet social studies objectives and the inadequate attention to critical thinking skills. Lounsbury provides brief bibliographies for sources of information on middle school education, generally, and on social studies in middle school education, specifically.

849 Mathews, Fred, and Tom Nowak. "Getting Students into the 'Reaction Paper'." *History and Social Science Teacher* 18, no. 3 (March 1985): 163-165. [1 Ref.]

The reaction paper provides a means of evaluating the development of a student's thinking skills and creates a dialogue between student and teacher. The authors identify the forms included in the concept of reaction paper. They provide general examples of reaction papers and a detailed example of the use of reaction papers in social studies to foster the development of critical thinking.

850 Mayer, Jan. "Teaching Critical Awareness in an Introductory Course." *Teaching Sociology* 14, no. 4 (October 1986): 249-256. [25 Refs.]

Mayer describes his design for an introductory sociology course that teaches critical awareness of the nature of social structures and of the relationship between structures and individuals. Each three-hour class session uses a diversity of instructional approaches to address various learning methods. Mayer emphasizes the importance of fostering student involvement, making the class relevant to the real world, and giving students a feeling of success.

851 Mayer, Richard E., and Fiona M. Goodchild. *The Critical Thinker: Thinking and Learning Strategies for Psychology Students*. Dubuque, IA: Wm. C. Brown, 1990. 80 pp. [11 Refs.]

This self-contained tutorial is intended to help students taking an introductory psychology course become more effective and critical processors of information found in introductory psychology textbooks. The six-hour tutorial guides the student in exploring strategies for critical thinking in psychology and applying these strategies to exercises containing passages from introductory psychology textbooks. The tutorial focuses on understanding and evaluating arguments.

852 McFarland, Mary A. "Critical Thinking in Elementary School Social Studies." *Social Education* 49, no. 4 (April 1985): 277-280.

McFarland presents two strategies for teaching critical thinking skills: word associates and defending a point of view. She describes each strategy's purpose, procedures, and guidelines for applying. McFarland includes comments about the strategy and its relationship to the critical thinking skill of distinguishing relevant from irrelevant information.

853 McGarvey, Jack. "Cross-Examining the Commercial: The Language of TV Advertising." *Media & Methods* 16, no. 5 (January 1980): 47-49.

McGarvey describes five activities he has used successfully in a junior high school classroom to teach students to listen to and analyze television commercials.

854 McKee, Saundra J. "Preparing the College-Bound Student in Social Studies." *Social Studies* 79, no. 2 (March-April 1988): 51-52. [4 Refs.]

Based on an informal survey of faculty in various social science departments at Marshall University, McKee asserts that conceptual knowledge, note-taking and test-taking skills, and critical thinking skills are desirable in incoming freshmen. Since the survey indicated that the faculty's greatest concern was for critical thinking skills, McKee suggests ways in which teachers might foster critical thinking in their students and provide opportunities for students to engage in critical thinking.

855 McKinney-Browning, Mabel C. "Law-Related Education: Programs, Process, and Promise." *International Journal of Social Education* 2, no. 2 (Fall 1987): 7-14. [4 Refs.]

This article provides an overview of law-related education, its importance to the development of critical thinking, citizenship and basic skills, and its incorporation into social education curricula. The author discusses student learning outcomes in law-related education, and emphasizes having active student participation in the classroom.

856 Melamed, Lanie. "Sleuthing Media 'Truths': Becoming Media Literate." *History and Social Studies Teacher* 24, no. 4 (Summer 1989): 189-193. [6 Refs.]

Television, film and video inundate us with words and images that require the application of critical thinking to discriminate between the illusions and realities of the messages presented. Melamed outlines several key concepts of media literacy and suggests ways to help students develop a critical approach to media.

857 Moreland-Young, Curtina. "Teaching Analytical and Thinking Skills in a Content Course." *Revitalizing Teaching through Faculty Development*, editor Paul A. Lacey, 41-47. New Directions for Teaching and Learning, No. 15. San Francisco, CA: Jossey-Bass, 1983. [1 Ref.]

As a participant in the postdoctoral teaching fellows program at Jackson State University (MS), Moreland-Young explored and experimented with the teaching of analytical and creative thinking skills in college level political science. She describes the incorporation of thinking skills in an "Introduction to Comparative Politics" course through classroom exercises, exams, and research papers. Such an undertaking necessitates re-orienting the student, who is accustomed to memorization and regurgitation, and the faculty member, who is accustomed to teacher-centered and content-coverage focused classrooms.

858 Murad, Turhon A. "Teaching Anthropology and Critical Thinking with the Question 'Is There Something Big Afoot?'." *Current Anthropology* 29, no. 5 (December 1988): 787-789. [18 Refs.]

Murad illustrates how critical thinking can be incorporated into an anthropology class by describing her course, "Bigfoot and Other Monsters: Myth or Reality?." The course requires students to explore evidence and claims for the existence of bipedal manlike monsters such as Bigfoot.

859 Nelson, Jack L. "Critical Thinking in Social Education: The Genocide Example." *Social Science Record* 24, no. 2 (Fall 1987): 60-62. [12 Refs.]

Though critical thinking is cited as a goal in many social studies curriculum guides, Nelson found few guides contained examples showing how to introduce critical thinking into the social studies classroom. He addresses this oversight by illustrating how critical thinking may be incorporated into a class discussion of genocide. Nelson examines the definition of genocide adopted by the United Nations and discusses alternative views to that definition.

860 Paul, Richard W. "Critical Thinking and Social Studies." *Teaching K-8* 19 (October 1988): 53-55.

Paul argues that modern social studies textbooks contain deficiencies that inhibit student critical thinking. Teachers can and should overcome such deficiencies by remodeling the approach they use with the textbooks. Paul includes an example of how a lesson plan from *The United States and*

Its Neighbors by Timothy M. Helmus and others (Morristown, NJ: Silver Burdett, 1984) was remodeled to encourage critical thinking.

861 Postman, Neil. "Critical Thinking in the Electronic Era." *National Forum* 65, no. 17 (Winter 1985): 4-8, 17.

Believing that "there can be no liberty for a community which lacks the critical skills to tell the difference between lies and truth" (p. 4), Postman emphasizes the importance of having critical thinking skills to apply to information expounded from electronic media. He presents examples of the techniques and methods used by the media to influence thinking, political beliefs, and social relations, as well as how it disseminates misleading information. Postman proposes that a college course on the study of information environments be introduced.

862 Rinaldo, Angie. "The Constitution is a Living Document: A Current Events-Based Strategy." *Social Studies Review* 27, no. 2 (Winter 1988): 67-70.

Rinaldo lists 23 activities appropriate for helping middle school and junior high school students develop an understanding and awareness of the role the U.S. Constitution plays in the lives of Americans. These activities involve reading, analyzing, and evaluating daily newspapers and weekly news magazines to foster critical and creative thinking.

863 Rooze, Gene E. "Developing Thinking Using Databases: What's Really Involved?" *Social Studies Texan* 5, no. 1 (Spring-Summer 1989): 26-28. [6 Refs.]

Rooze describes two strategies for teaching thinking skills in social studies through the development and use of computer databases. The author also outlines requirements for teaching thinking strategies.

864 Rosenbaum, Roberta. "Teaching Critical Thinking in the Business Mathematics Course." *Journal of Education for Business* 62, no. 2 (November 1986): 66-69.

Rosenbaum stresses the importance of being able to understand, evaluate, and interpret information obtained from quantitative data in the business world and in everyday. She suggests strategies, illustrated with sample problems, for teaching critical thinking in a business mathematics course that enhance students' performance in accounting, management, data processing, and marketing.

865 Ross, E. Wayne, and Lynne M. Hannay. "Reconsidering Reflective Inquiry: The Role of Critical Theory in the Teaching of Social Studies." *Southern Social Studies Quarterly* 13, no. 2 (Fall 1987): 2-19. [25 Refs.]

The authors explore the problems related to the interpretation and implementation of the reflective inquiry model in social studies curricula. They contend that it is counterproductive to view reflective inquiry as a highly structured problem solving procedure that can be taught as a series of steps. As an alternative approach, Ross and Hannay propose a concept of reflective inquiry based on critical theory that encourages dialogical thinking based on Dewey's concepts of open-mindedness, responsibility and wholeheartedness. This alternative would emphasize social knowledge, practical skills and critical discourse, and create a classroom environment open to divergent and alternative solutions.

866 Schoettinger, Nancy L. "Upgrading the Marketing Curriculum: The Integration of Higher-Order Skills." *Marketing Educators' Journal* 11, no. 1 (Fall 1985): 52-58. [17 Refs.]

Schoettinger calls for an integration of higher order skills, such as reasoning, critical thinking, problem solving, and decision making, into vocational education curricula in general and in marketing education of the secondary level in particular. The author cites changes brought about by technology in the workplace, where teamwork and group problem solving techniques are now encouraged among and between labor and management, as the basis for integrating higher order skills training into the curriculum. She asserts that these higher order skills are especially important in the secondary marketing education curriculum, given the growth of areas in the field and the competition with college graduates. Schoettinger argues that although secondary marketing education programs are not equivalent to college marketing programs they can still provide relevant training for various marketing occupations if the curriculum incorporates the higher order skills.

867 Schukar, Ron. "Teaching Foreign Policy and Intervention: An Integrated Problems Approach." *Social Science Record* 25, no. 1 (Spring 1988): 63-66. [6 Refs.]

Schukar believes that foreign policy and intervention studies provide an appropriate means for helping students become informed, competent citizens in a global society. Schukar recommends teachers use an integrated problems approach which requires examining and determining solutions to problems using concepts, generalizations, and data from a variety of social science disciplines to identify problems and determine possible solutions. Such an approach teaches students the importance of acting on understanding and helps them develop the skills to act.

868 Scover, Linda, and Barbara Shapley. "Newspapers and Economics." *Social Studies Teacher* 8, no. 1 (September-October 1986): 11.

Scover and Shapley present exercises that use newspapers to help students develop thinking skills in economics. They provide addresses for information on additional ways to use newspapers in the classroom.

869 Shelly, Ann C., and William W. Wilen. "Sex Equity and Critical Thinking." *Social Education* 52, no. 3 (March 1988): 168-172. [38 Refs.]

To encourage critical and creative thinking about men and women from Western and non-Western cultures, Shelly and Wilen advocate the use of five strategies from the Models of Teaching Program--social inquiry, concept attainment, role-playing, advance organizer, and social simulation--which offer the instructional variety important to enhancing student learning. Sample lesson plans incorporating each strategy for the teaching of sex equity and a bibliography of sources are included.

870 Smith, David E. "Observer and Observed: Collaboration between Literature and Anthropology." In *Promoting Inquiry in Undergraduate Learning*, edited by Frederick Stirton Weaver, 73-77. New Directions for Teaching and Learning, no. 38. San Francisco, CA: Jossey-Bass, 1989. [5 Refs.]

Smith discusses a team effort to integrate the writings and theories of literature and cultural anthropology in an undergraduate course. Using an inquiry-based approach,

Smith and a colleague have students explore problems of mutual concern in both disciplines, such as the relationship between observer and observed, reader and text, and the nature of anthropological understanding and literary analysis. They include a discussion of narrative point of view to illustrate the inquiry approach.

871 Smith, Jane Bandy. "Higher Order Thinking Skills and Nonprint Media." *School Library Media Quarterly* 16, no. 1 (Fall 1987): 38-44. [10 Refs.]

Smith stresses that it is important that the media specialist promote the development of higher order thinking skills, especially since they are information-related skills. In discussing instructional methods for thinking skills, she notes similarities between the integration of thinking skills into the classroom and the methods used for teaching library skills. Smith focuses on the use of nonprint media in teaching thinking skills, suggesting ways in which various media formats, such as slides, realia, computer programs, and films, can be incorporated into thinking skills instruction.

872 Splaine, John. "Televised Politics and the 1988 Presidential Election: A Critical View." *Georgia Social Science Journal* 19, no. 2 (1988): 1-7. [25 Refs.]

Splaine identifies eight biases inherent in television communication and includes examples of how political campaigns use these biases to communicate a manipulated message. He discusses the critical viewing and thinking skills that viewers should learn and use when viewing television in order to better participate in a democratic society.

873 Stark, Sheila. "Developing Critical and Creative Thinking through the Use of the Synectics Teaching Model." *Illinois Teacher of Home Economics* 30, no. 4 (March-April 1987): 154-156. [2 Refs.]

Stark describes using the Synectics Model developed by William J.J. Gordon (*Synectics*. New York: Harper & Row, 1961) in a Family and Communication course to develop undergraduate students' creativity, empathy, and problem-solving abilities. Through reflection on feelings, analogies, writing, and class discussion exercises, students deal with the topic of understanding family relationships and increase their awareness of alternative ways of thinking and valuing. Stark believes that by using this model, students become more creative and critical in problem solving and in viewing themselves, others, and society in general.

874 Sullivan, David. "Using a Textbook for Critical Thinking: An Introductory Lesson for Identifying Point of View." *New England Social Studies Bulletin* 43, no. 2 (Winter 1986): 31-36. [2 Refs.]

Sullivan presents an outline of a lesson designed to teach students to recognize points of view (particularly those of textbooks) and to identify alternative perspectives.

875 Swartz, Robert J. "Teaching for Thinking: A Developmental Model for the Infusion of Thinking Skills into Mainstream Instruction." Chapter 6 in *Teaching Thinking Skills: Theory and Practice*, edited by Joan Boykoff Baron and Robert J. Sternberg, 106-126. New York, NY: W.H. Freeman, 1987. [19 Refs.]

Swartz discusses three examples of ways teachers have restructured classroom material, using the conceptual-infusion approach for teaching thinking, in a secondary school American history course, a social studies course, and in an upper elementary/middle school classroom unit on a historical novel. In an attempt to infuse thinking skills into the curriculum, each teacher developed a conceptual understanding of specific attitudes and skills and the relation between these and other ingredients they wanted to include. Swartz discusses ways of teaching for specific critical thinking skills that recognize the complementary nature of critical and creative thinking, structure classroom activities to promote good thinking attitudes, and help students to uncover and evaluate different points of view.

876 Taylor, William M. "Teaching Critical Reading As A Way of Teaching Critical Thinking." *Informal Logic* 9, no. 2-3 (Spring-Fall 1987): 111-115.

To help students develop critical thinking skills in a community college political science class, the author devised a series of five writing assignments emphasizing informal logic. The writing assignments require, in progressive order, a student to: clarify the nature of facts and opinions found in an article, determine the author's point of view, detect fallacies, compare and contrast two articles that take different positions on the same issue, and, in the final paper, to use all the skills learned in the previous papers to analyze and evaluate an assigned article. Taylor believes this approach will teach students to think for themselves when confronted with experts and politicians trying to win their support.

877 Warner, Stanley L., and Myrna M. Breitbart. "Plant Closings and Capital Flight: A Computer-Assisted Simulation." In *Promoting Inquiry in Undergraduate Learning*, edited by Frederick Stirton Weaver, 25-32, no. 38. San Francisco, CA: Jossey-Bass, 1989. [14 Refs.]

Warner, an economics professor, and Breitbart, a geography and urban studies professor, describe student assignments given in their course "Capital Versus Community." The authors focus on an assignment in which each student is given the role of an individual in a corporation and provided with pertinent background information in order to proceed through the three stages of a simulation (two of which are computer-assisted): (1) predicting corporate closure, (2) assessing community impact of job loss, and (3) designing alternative responses to capital flight. This simulation emphasizes discovery, exploration, and choice and facilitates problem solving.

878 Watts, Nancy A. "Developing Higher-Order Thinking Skills in Home Economics: A Lesson Plan." In *Thinking Skills Instruction: Concepts and Techniques*, edited by Marcia Heiman and Joshua Slomianko, 241-245. Building Students' Thinking Skills. Washington, DC: National Education Association, 1987. [2 Refs.]

Watts presents a lesson plan for an eighth grade home economics class which develops students' higher order thinking skills while they learn about fabric construction. She includes sample assignment sheets.

879 Wilen, William W., and Patrick McKenrick. "Individualized Inquiry: Encouraging Able Students to Investigate." *Social Studies* 80, no. 2 (March-April 1989): 51-54. [3 Refs.]

The authors suggest using individualized inquiry as a technique for involving motivated, intellectually capable, and responsible students in both independent study and inquiry. This technique, which has been successfully used with junior high and senior high school students, allows an individual student to explore and research a topic of interest, analyze a problem using inductive and deductive reasoning, and apply a variety of critical thinking skills. The authors recommend that the teacher and student develop a contract specifying the conditions of the individualized inquiry. An example of the implementation of an individualized inquiry is given.

880 Wright, Ian. "Citizenship Education and Decision Making." *International Journal of Social Education* 3, no. 2 (Fall 1988): 55-62. [16 Refs.]

Wright believes young children are capable of dealing with citizenship concerns. Since citizenship concerns involve decision making and value judgments, children should be taught how to make decisions based on the principles of good practical reasoning. Wright outlines these principles in the context of a hypothetical example relevant to elementary school students. He describes four ways of evaluating the use of these principles.

881 Zeller, Richard A. "On Teaching about Discrimination." *Teaching Sociology* 16, no. 1 (January 1988): 61-66. [4 Refs.]

Zeller describes an assignment designed to enhance critical thinking skills in college introductory sociology and social problems courses by enhancing student understanding of the relationship between inference and evidence. The assignment involves a created situation and contrived data on the major concepts of equality, inequality, and sexual discrimination at a hypothetical university at which men and women faculty members are claiming sex discrimination. The author discusses the opportunities and risks in using contrived data in assignments. A copy of the assignment is provided.

Science and Mathematics

882 Aide, Michael T. "Teaching Critical Thinking in a Soil Classification and Genesis Course." *Journal of Agronomic Education* 18, no. 1 (1989): 37-39. [10 Refs.]

Critical thinking methods were introduced into a soil science class in order to improve comprehension of content, problem solving skills, and transference of concepts and principles from other sciences. Aide describes the course format and its effectiveness. Tables outlining the content and goals of the course lectures, tests, and laboratory assignments are included.

883 Anderson, Carol P. "The Mystery of Consumer Chemistry." *Journal of Chemical Education* 65, no. 3 (March 1988): 217.

Anderson describes an exercise in consumer chemistry presented to students in the form of a murder mystery story. Students determine which household product caused a death by gathering facts through library research and chemical calculations, organizing the gathered facts into an analysis of the problem, and presenting their final analysis in a technical report.

884 Bandman, Elsie, and Bertram Bandman. *Critical Thinking in Nursing*. Norwalk, CT: Appleton & Lange, 1988. 313 pp.

The three parts of this text stress the importance of critical thinking skills in enhancing the effectiveness of the nursing process and everyday decision making in nursing. Part I focuses on the structure, dynamics, and fallacy aspects of argumentation. Part II addresses scientific reasoning, decision making, some controversial issues and assumptions found in nursing and health care, and ways of resolving controversial issues. Part III focuses on deductive, syllogistic, symbolic, inductive reasoning, as well as cause-effect relationships, evidence, and probability. The authors designed the book for use on the undergraduate or graduate level as a text for a critical thinking course or a supplementary text in clinical courses. Each of the thirteen chapters is preceded by a list of objectives or intended outcomes and followed by a list of references. Diagrams and practical exercises are interspersed throughout the text.

885 Bean, Thomas W., and Vicki Soderberg. "Reasoning Guides for Critical Comprehension." *Reading Horizons* 23, no. 2 (Winter 1983): 108-112. [6 Refs.]

Advocating an interactive teaching and learning approach to media used in the classroom, the authors discuss the effectiveness of using reasoning guides to transform a passive situation into an interactive one. The reasoning guides consist of statements developed by teachers for student responses and are to be arranged sequentially for developing student critical comprehension skills: identification, interpretation, and application of information. The authors provide reasoning guides used with sixth graders viewing a filmstrip used in a science unit on ecosystems.

886 Beyer, Barry K., and Ronald E. Charlton. "Teaching Thinking Skills in Biology." *American Biology Teacher* 48, 4 (April 1986): 207-212. [20 Refs.]

The authors focus on ways of integrating the teaching of thinking skills in biology. They illustrate direct and inductive strategies for introducing a skill, as well as for providing instructional guidance and student practice of the skill. Although lessons on the skill of classifying to illustrate these strategies are used, the authors note that these strategies are neither content nor skill specific and so may be used to teach any course at any grade level.

887 Bodner, George M. "Consumer Chemistry: Critical Thinking at the Concrete Level." *Journal of Chemical Education* 65, no. 3 (March 1988): 212-213. [11 Refs.]

Bodner emphasizes the importance of teaching concepts of consumer chemistry and their everyday applications rather than teaching consumer chemistry from a mathematical perspective. The goals of such a course include helping students relate chemistry to their everyday lives, preparing them to make educated decisions on science and technology issues, and fostering the development of critical thinking skills.

888 Boring, John R., III, and Donald O. Nutter. "Analytic Thinking: Educating Students for the Practice of Modern Medicine." *Journal of Medical Education* 59 (November 1984): 875-880. [14 Refs.]

The authors argue that medical education emphasizes factual knowledge and rote skills and does not prepare individuals to use the scientific method, to be independent learners, to evaluate medical information, or to make logical decisions concerning the use of diagnostic techniques and therapeutic agents. Boring and Nutter describe a course employed at Emory University's School of Medicine intended to rectify many of the deficiencies in medical education. The course has four objectives: (1) to help students become aware of the inaccuracy inherent in medical date and the probabilistic nature of the medical decision process, (2) to help students master the techniques for assessing the validity of patient information and of research studies, (3) to help students learn to use medical data in decision analysis, and (4) to introduce the computer as a clinical tool for data banking, display, and analysis.

889 Brandt, Dietrich, and Robert Sell. "The Development of Problem Solving Skills in Engineering Students in Context." *European Journal of Engineering Education* 11, no. 1 (1986): 59-65. [16 Refs.]

The authors outline a problem solving engineering course offered at a technical university. The two-semester course is designed to improve student problem solving skills and study skills by teaching sequential phases of problem solving, group interaction, and ill-structured or real-life problems. Preliminary results of the authors' research on the structure of studying are included.

890 Byrne, Michael S., and Alex H. Johnstone. "Critical Thinking and Science Education." *Studies in Higher Education* 12, no. 3 (1987): 325-39. [29 Refs.]

Byrne and Johnstone explore the concepts of scientific attitudes, specifically critical-mindedness and critical thinking as related to science education through research and theoretical literature. They view critical thinking as a contextual or subject-related skill, and critical mindedness as the propensity to exercise critical thinking. The authors find that a narrow view of the nature of scientific inquiry and scientist behavior underlies many definitions of the scientific attitude. To develop a more broadly applicable scientific critical-mindedness, Byrne and Johnstone propose that science students study science in the context of social, economic, and applied problems.

891 Chancellor, Dinah. "Higher-Order Thinking: A 'Basic' Skill for Everyone." *Arithmetic Teacher* 38, no. 6 (February 1991): 48-50. [7 Refs.]

Using Benjamin Bloom's taxonomy of cognitive domain and Frank Williams's student behaviors of cognitive-intellective factors and affective-feeling factors, Chancellor provides a framework for designing exciting and challenging mathematics activities to engage the intellect of all elementary school students. She includes sample activities for primary and intermediate school mathematics classes.

892 Clark, Mary E., and Linda D. Holler. "Teaching Science within the Limits of Science." *Journal of College Science Teaching* 16, no. 1 (September-October 1986): 8-9, 56-57.

The authors briefly discuss several limits to science that form the boundaries in which scientific investigation of the world is valid. They suggest ways for teaching science that acknowledge those boundaries.

893 Cordeiro, Patricia. "Playing with Infinity in the Sixth Grade." *Language Arts* 65, no. 6 (October 1988): 557-566. [20 Refs.]

Cordeiro describes how a class of eleven sixth graders learned the mathematical concept of infinity through playful exploration, shared learning, and freewriting. She uses this experience to argue for personal involvement and play as teaching and learning strategies for mathematical concepts associated with higher order thinking. She supports her argument by citing the research of individuals such as Piaget and Bloom.

894 Cowan, John. "Are We Neglecting Real Analytical Skills in Engineering Education?" *European Journal of Engineering Education* 11, no. 1 (1986): 67-73. [5 Refs.]

Cowan asserts that engineering courses and tests over-emphasize numerical or quantitative responses that can be answered through the use of algorithms rather than demonstrating a mastery of engineering concepts. The author discusses exercises that require demonstration of analytical or qualitative reasoning as well as quantitative skills. He concludes that there is a cognitive distinction between qualitative and quantitative understanding, and recommends that both be taught and tested in engineering courses. Examples of exercise questions are included.

895 Crow, Linda W., and Sue G. Haws. "Logic-Integrated Geology for Nonscience Majors." *Journal of College Science Teaching* 16, no. 1 (September-October 1986): 25-27. [12 Refs.]

The authors describe the incorporation of several principles of logic into a geology course for non-majors. Learning the principles enhanced student reasoning and critical thinking.

896 Demetrulias, Diana Mayer. "(Creatively) Teaching the Meanings of Statistics." *Clearing House* 62, no. 4 (December 1988): 168-170. [7 Refs.]

The author describes several teaching approaches that foster critical thinking in statistics. She advocates using original and playful questions to foster creative thinking. Such an approach requires that students be given enough time to explore and play intellectually with statistical ideas and concepts and be given opportunities to speculate, hypothesize, generate alternatives, and seek multiple perspectives. This approach promotes the integration of learning and appreciation for statistics.

897 Ewert, Alan. "Decision Making in the Outdoor Pursuits Setting." *Journal of Environmental Education* 20, no. 1 (Fall 1988): 3-7. [10 Refs.]

Ewert analyzes the types of decisions and factors influencing decisions of outdoor leaders. He examines aspects of outdoor leadership decision making and outlines paradigms of decision making. Ewert provides guidelines for facilitating better decision making by outdoor leaders and stresses the importance of devoting more time to studying and developing the decision making skills of leaders.

898 Hill, John W. "Using Chemical Principles to Encourage Critical Thinking in Consumer Chemistry." *Journal of Chemical Education* 65, no. 3 (March 1988): 209-210.

Hill suggests having students apply the scientific principles, such as the structure-property relationship in organic chemistry and the reproducibility of evidence, to advertising claims concerning topics such as weight-loss diets or over-the-counter drugs.

899 Hoover, Steven M. "The Purdue Three Stage Model as Applied to Elementary Science for the Gifted." *School Science and Mathematics* 89, no. 3 (March 1989): 244-250. [7 Refs.]

Hoover describes the Purdue Three Stage Model that was designed to help gifted, talented, or high ability students develop basic thinking skills, more adequate self concepts, intellectual and creative abilities, and independence and effectiveness as learners. Stage I instructional activities teach convergent and divergent thinking, especially skills in fluency, flexibility, originality, and elaboration. Stage II trains students in creative problem solving techniques, such as brainstorming, SCAMPER (Substitute, Combine, Adapt, Modify, Put to different uses, Eliminate, or Reverse), Synectics, morphological analysis, and forced relationships. Stage III focuses on independent research on a self-selected topic or problem. Hoover incorporated the concepts of this model, science content, and science process skills to create a model for elementary science education for the gifted. This model is outlined and illustrated.

900 Kameenui, Edward J., and Cynthia C. Griffin. "The National Crisis in Verbal Problem Solving in Mathematics: A Proposal for Examining the Role of Basal Mathematics Programs." *Elementary School Journal* 89, no. 5 (May 1989): 575-593. [112 Refs.]

Through a review of the research literature on mathematical problem solving, the authors provide a basis for evaluating mathematical word problem solving instruction. They propose an evaluation consisting of three separate, concurrent levels of analyses: (a) the kinds of word problems contained in basal programs, (b) the textual characteristics of word problems, and (c) the instructional features for teaching word-problem solution.

901 Kaplan, Rochelle G., Takashi Yamamoto, and Herbert P. Ginsburg. "Teaching Mathematics Concepts." Chapter 4 in *Toward the Thinking Curriculum: Current Cognitive Research*, edited by Lauren B. Resnick and Leopold E.

Klopfer, 59-82. 1989 Yearbook of the Association for Supervision and Curriculum Development. [Alexandria, VA]: Association for Supervision and Curriculum Development, 1989. [37 Refs.]

Based on the premise that education must consider the child's contribution to the learning process in order to be effective, the authors present research findings regarding the nature of children's mathematical thinking and discuss how these findings can lead to more effective teaching practices. They explore the acquisition of informal and formal mathematical knowledge, how children's mathematical thinking is influenced by beliefs about the nature of mathematics and about teachers' expectations, and how research on the nature and development of children's mathematical thinking should have an impact on educational practices. The authors offer examples of teaching methods and techniques that take the psychology of children's mathematical thinking into account.

902 Kooser, Robert G. "Value Issues in Consumer Chemistry." *Journal of Chemical Education* 65, no. 3 (March 1988): 204-206. [4 Refs.]

Kooser proposes a realistic and relevant approach to consumer chemistry courses for nonmajors that calls for the inclusion of information on business ethics and a re-evaluation of teaching goals. The approach entails communicating a general appreciation of the relevance of chemistry to peoples' lives and the study of nature, teaching a mastery of consumer skills related to consumer chemistry (e.g., reading and understanding labels), and how to discriminate between the scientific and pseudo-scientific.

903 Lawson, Michael J. "The Case for Instruction in the Use of General Problem-Solving Strategies in Mathematics Teaching: A Comment on Owen and Sweller." *Journal for Research in Mathematics Education* 21, no. 5 (November 1990): 403-410. [26 Refs.]

Reply to Owen and Sweller {913}

Reply: Sweller {177}

Lawson asserts that Owen's and Sweller's position regarding the inclusion of problem solving strategies instruction in mathematics teaching implies that attention should be toward domain-specific knowledge rather than problem solving strategies. He believes Owen and Sweller understate the importance of the integration of the different types of general problem solving strategies with content-specific teaching in mathematics classes. Lawson argues that Owen and Sweller need to modify their position in light of studies done on alternative views of general problem solving transfer that support inclusion of problem solving strategies instruction. He discusses the implications such studies have for mathematics education and distinguishes three types of problem solving strategies: task orientation strategies, executive strategies, and domain-specific strategies.

904 Lieu, Van T., and Gene E. Kalbus. "Incorporation of Consumer Products in the Teaching of Analytical Chemistry." *Journal of Chemical Education* 65, no. 3 (March 1988): 207-108. [7 Refs.]

The authors describe several laboratory experiments involving the use of common consumer products used in an analytical chemistry course. The experiments can be used to illustrate the basic principles and techniques of several methods of analysis, to increase students' awareness of the importance of chemistry in consumer products, and to exercise independent thought processes for fostering critical thinking. The authors outline methods for facilitating critical thinking. They believe the experiments can also be used in organic or nutritional chemistry courses.

905 Lochhead, Jack. "Thinking About Learning: An Anarchistic Approach to Teaching Problem Solving." In *Thinking Skills Instruction: Concepts and Techniques*, edited by Marcia Heiman and Joshua Slomianko, 174-182. Building Students' Thinking Skills. Washington, DC: National Education Association, 1987. [18 Refs.]

Reprinted from *Journal of Learning Skills* Winter 1982.

Lochhead suggests that students be allowed to choose or construct their own problem solving techniques, rather than follow a specific method. He cites the effectiveness of the Whimbey approach to teaching problem solving, which stresses attitudes, rather than a method. Such an approach provides structure while forcing students to choose and evaluate their problem solving method. Lochhead shows how this approach is effective in teaching problem solving in physics.

906 Mason, David H. "Dr. Quincy Move Over: The Crash Site." *Science Activities* 25, no. 1 (February-March 1988): 18-21. [4 Refs.]

Mason reviews a series of exercises requiring students to reason about a crash site. The exercises are designed to teach life science students about the human skeletal system, environmental poisoning, and bone growth patterns.

907 McKone, Harold T., and Barbara A. Banville. "Developing the Critical Thinking Skills of Adult Learners through Consumer and Environmental Applications." *Journal of Chemical Education* 65, no. 3 (March 1988): 218. [2 Refs.]

McKone and Banville describe how assigning position papers on consumer and environmental topics in their adult learner science education course helps students understand scientific concepts, the scientific method, and critical thinking process.

908 Mestre, Jose P., William J. Gerace, Pamela T. Hardiman, and Jack Lochhead. "Promoting Thinking in Physics and Algebra: Incorporating Cognitive Research Findings into Software Design." In *Thinking Across Cultures: The Third International Conference*, edited By Donald M. Topping, Doris C. Crowell, and Victor N. Kobayashi, 455-466. Hillsdale, NJ: Lawrence Erlbaum, 1989. [29 Refs.]

Two areas of cognitive research in mathematics and science learning have implications for instruction and educational software design: research on misconceptions and research on differences between expert and novice problem solvers. The authors provide a broad overview of the research literature on misconception and describe a computer-based instructional approach designed to teach students how to translate algebraic word problems into equations. The authors review research findings on the differences between expert and novice problem solving, and outline the Hierarchical Analysis Tool, a computer-based instructional approach, which emphasizes the application of concepts and general strategies used by experts to solve problems and promotes student analysis of physics problems in expert-like ways.

909 Miller, John A. "Consumer Chemistry in an Organic Chemistry Course." *Journal of Consumer Education* 65, no. 3 (March 1988): 210-211. [10 Refs.]

Miller gives several suggestions for incorporating consumer chemistry into the teaching of basic organic chemistry concepts.

910 Minstrell, James A. "Teaching Science for Understanding." Chapter 7 in *Toward the Thinking Curriculum: Current Cognitive Research*, edited by Lauren B. Resnick and Leopold E. Klopfer, 129-149. 1989 Yearbook of the Association for Supervision and Curriculum Development. [Alexandria, VA]: Association for Supervision and Curriculum Development, 1989. [28 Refs.]

Students come to the classroom with ideas and concepts, but have difficulty applying a concept in various contexts and differentiating between related ideas. Minstrell argues that restructuring students' existing knowledge should be a goal for science teachers. He demonstrates, using sample lessons on the concept of force, how experience in the classroom and knowledge of research on cognitive processes guide his teaching practices in physics. Minstrell stresses the importance of relating information to the daily life experiences of students and ensuring that what students learn in the classroom is transferred to everyday life and work situations. He advocates an instructional design that has activities requiring students to use new ideas in multiple contexts and a classroom environment which encourages questioning.

911 Narode, Ronald, Marcia Heiman, Jack Lochhead, and Joshua Slomianko. *Teaching Thinking Skills: Science* Washington, D.C.: National Education Association, 1987. 48 pp. [47 Refs.]

The authors believe developing critical thinking skills in science requires active learning in problem solving activities. Classrooms must be reorganized away from teacher-centered organizations to student-centered ones in which conceptual understanding rather than memorization of formulae is taught. The authors review ways active, critical thinking activities can be brought into science classrooms. Approaches reviewed include paired problem solving to create a Socratic learning environment, integrating science process skills into the curriculum, activity-based elementary science instruction, using student misconceptions to teach thinking, and multiple representations.

912 Nicely, Robert F., Jr. "Higher-Order Thinking Skills in Mathematics Textbooks." *Educational Leadership* 12, no. 7 (April 1985): 26-30. [15 Refs.]

An analysis of secondary and elementary school mathematics textbooks published between 1961 and the mid-1980's reveals an increased emphasis on lower order cognitive behaviors from the 1960's through the 1970's followed by a slight decrease in the 1980's. Nicely concludes that educators must focus on supplemental instructional materials and teaching methods in planning for effective mathematics instruction.

913 Pizzini, Edward L., Sandra K. Abell, and Daniel S. Shepardson. "Rethinking Thinking in the Science Classroom." *Science Teacher* 55, no. 9 (December 1988): 22-25. [12 Refs.]

To develop student thinking skills in the science classroom, the authors believe that instruction should (a) provide opportunities and time for comparing and analyzing data, observations, and information sources, (b) emphasize processing and output levels of thinking and require students to hypothesize, speculate, generalize, create, and evaluate, (c) provide opportunities for identifying and solving problems, including problems that are real and of interest and concern to students, and (d) emphasize student involvement, with the teacher serving primarily as a facilitator of the learning process by guiding students through problem solving. The authors describe and illustrate a problem solving model for science instruction.

914 Postiglione, Ralph. "An Exercise in Critical Thinking: Pattern Recognition." *Science Activities* 25, no. 2 (April-May 1988): 25-27.

Postiglione presents a pattern recognition activity designed for middle school and high school students which uses bar codes or proof-of-purchase scanning lines. Sample questions for pattern recognition, considered inherent in critical thinking, are given.

915 Radack, Kenneth L., and Barbara Valanis. "Teaching Critical Appraisal and Application of Medical Literature to Clinical Problem-Solving." *Journal of Medical Education* 61 (April 1986): 329-331. [9 Refs.]

Radack and Valanis describe a program for teaching fourth-year clinical clerks to critically appraise medical literature. The 1984-85 program involved small-group sessions and problem-oriented materials, including case scenarios, relevant articles, and reviews or pertinent methodological criteria. Based on the results of an evaluative study of the program, the authors recommend that tutorials in critical evaluation of medical literature be introduced in the second year of medical school.

916 Regan-Smith, Martha G. "Teaching Clinical Reasoning in a Clinical Clerkship by Use of Case Assessments." *Journal of Medical Education* 62, no. 1 (January 1987): 60-63. [6 Refs.]

The author describes a problem-based program for third-year students in an internal medicine clerkship. The program uses small group teaching sessions in which students present cases of recently admitted patients and submit a case write-up. Other students in the group provide an evaluation and critique of the case presentation and of the write-up, as well as their own assessment of the case presented. In participating in these activities, students demonstrate their problem solving, critical thinking, clinical judgment, and reasoning skills. Regan-Smith asserts that this approach has produced increased scores on an internal medicine subtest of the National Board of Medical Examiners examination and better performance in clerkships.

917 Reimer, Wilbert. "The Domino Effect: Problem Solving with Common Table Games." *Mathematics Teacher* 82, no. 4 (April 1989): 240-245.

Reimer demonstrates how a problem solving approach in a principles of mathematics class evolved from a single problem into more complex problems and board games due to active participation by the teacher and students. The article includes tables illustrating approaches to solving problems and a list of investigations the class pursued.

918 Robertson, Graham, and Andrew Tannahill. "Important Pursuit: A Board Game for Health Education Teaching." *Medical Teacher* 8, no. 2 (1986): 171-173.

Robertson and Tannahill describe a board game devised as a participatory learning method in health education for the medical education of postgraduate medical students. Intended to encourage clarification and development of students' beliefs, attitudes, and values, this game presents questions on important health education issues. The authors provide a list of questions used in the game.

919 Roth, Kathleen J. "Science Education: It's Not Enough to 'Do' or 'Relate'." *American Educator* 13, no. 4 (Winter 1989): 16-22, 46-48. [15 Refs.]

Traditional textbook-based science teaching presents science as a body of knowledge to be taught through rote memorization. Efforts at reforming this approach in favor of teaching to think scientifically have taken three distinct directions: (1) teaching science as inquiry, which emphasizes scientific thinking skills relatively isolated from a conceptual context, (2) the Science-Technology-Society Perspective (STS) which teaches science in relation to its effects on society, and (3) the conceptual change perspective which teaches the development of meaningful, conceptual understandings of science, scientific processes and scientific conceptions. Roth describes each perspective, and discusses the problems contained in each approach. She finds the conceptual change perspective the most successful at interweaving conceptual knowledge and scientific processes and believes it holds the most promise for teaching students to understand science and scientific thinking.

920 Schoenfeld, Alan H. "Teaching Mathematical Thinking and Problem Solving." Chapter 5 in *Toward the Thinking Curriculum: Current Cognitive Research*, edited by Lauren Resnick and Leopold E. Klopfer, 83-103. 1989 Yearbook of the Association for Supervision and Curriculum Development. [Alexandria, VA]: Association for Supervision and Curriculum Development, 1989. [21 Refs.]

Citing the work of Max Wertheimer and the 1988 report of the Mathematical Sciences Education Board's (MSEB) Curriculum Task Force, Schoenfeld argues that education must focus on the development of mathematical power or the development of the abilities to understand mathematical concepts and methods, discern mathematical relations, reason logically, and to apply mathematical concepts, methods and relations to solve a variety of non-routine problems. He emphasizes the role of the teacher in problem-solving instruction, particularly stressing the importance of establishing a classroom atmosphere that facilitates the development of mathematical power. Schoenfeld identifies research findings supporting his position that mathematics can be taught in a problem-based way so that students experience the subject as a discipline of reason developed because of the need to solve problems and for intellectual curiosity. He includes several examples of mathematic problems and discusses approaches for solving them.

921 Self, Charles C., Mary Anne Nally Self, and David C. Self. "Science as a Process: Modus Operandi." *American Biology Teacher* 51, no. 3 (March 1989): 159-161. [17 Refs.]

The authors describe a classroom technique designed to develop students' critical thinking and reasoning skills and their understanding of biology as a process. The technique combines the analysis of scientific studies, the use of small learning groups, and the development of an experimental study. The technique has been effectively used in a community college introductory biology course.

922 Swartz, Robert J. "Structured Teaching for Critical Thinking and Reasoning in Standard Subject Area Instruction." Chapter 21 in *Informal Reasoning and Education*, edited by James F. Voss, David N. Perkins, and Judith W. Segal, 415-450. Hillsdale, NJ: Lawrence Erlbaum, 1991. [21 Refs.]

Swartz discusses a conceptual-infusion approach to teaching critical thinking. The approach restructures standard curricular content into activities that (1) engage students in thinking, (2) require causal reasoning, (4) interweave content knowledge and reasoning skills, and (5) foster metacognition. Swartz uses examples of forming hypotheses on how a mouse died to illustrate the principles and methods of the approach. He provides a lesson plan for a biological science class, identifies basic principles about good thinking, and presents a list of thinking skills and subskills, abstracted from the taxonomies of Robert Ennis and Benjamin Bloom, that can be taught across the curriculum.

923 Taylor, Beverly A. P. "Teaching Scientific Reasoning to Underprepared Students." In *Revitalizing Teaching through Faculty Development*, edited by Paul A. Lacey, 7-17. New Directions for Teaching and Learning, no. 15. San Francisco, CA: Jossey-Bass, 1983. [14 Refs.]

This essay is a description of Taylor's development of a pre-physics course. The purpose of the course was to help underprepared undergraduate science majors develop the reasoning skills and the ability to understand abstract representations, such as diagrams and equations, required for the introductory physics course. Taylor illustrates the teaching methods she used to meet these objectives and discusses coming to terms with her conflicts regarding the teaching of such a course for college level credit.

924 Tyser, Robin W., and William J. Cerbin. "Critical Thinking Exercises for Introductory Biology Courses." *BioScience* 41, no. 1 (January 1991): 41-46. [5 Refs.]

Tyser and Cerbin describe exercises designed to teach college students a model for evaluating information in science articles found in popular media, including newspapers, general news magazines, and science news magazines. The three-step model involves identifying evidence, evaluating validity of claims, and writing a logically persuasive line of reasoning. Tyser and Cerbin describe how they incorporate these exercises in a large one-semester freshman-level introductory biology course. They address the issues of procedures, grading, quizzes, time requirement, limitations, and effectiveness.

925 Uno, Gordon E. "Teaching College and College-Bound Biology Students." *American Biology Teacher* 50, no. 4 (April 1988): 213-216. [11 Refs.]

Uno enumerates reasons why freshman non-science majors experience difficulty in college introductory biology courses and presents several ways biology instructors can address the difficulties: (1) promote student self-discipline and learning, (2) broaden student perceptions and improve student attitudes toward science and biology, (3) train students to use critical thinking skills, and (4) provide a background in biological concepts. Uno provides suggestions for enacting these proposals and stresses the importance of interrelating the subject matter with the real world.

926 Wales, Charles E., Anne H. Nardi, and Robert A. Stager. "Do Your Students Think or Do They Memorize?" *Engineering Education* 78, no. 7 (April 1988): 682-688. [6 Refs.]

The authors note that research shows that students need to be explicitly taught thinking skills and processes over a period of time in various subjects. They believe that faculty who want students to think rather than just memorize must be able to (1) teach higher level thinking skills and processes, (2) relate these skills and processes to each other, and (3) work independently and in cooperation with colleagues to teach these skills and processes. The authors provide several exercises illustrating how five operations of decision making (defining the situation, stating the goal, generating ideas, preparing a plan, and taking action) can be used to teach engineering students creative and critical thinking.

927 Ward, Alan. "Organized Curiosity: Problem-Solving Ideas for Older Juniors." *Science Activities* 25, no. 2 (April-May 1988): 32-33.

Ward presents 25 ideas for problem solving tasks appropriate for fifth through eighth grade students.

928 Waterman, Margaret A., and Jane F. Rissler. "Use of Scientific Research Reports to Develop Higher-Level Cognitive Skills." *Journal of College Science Teaching* 11, no. 6 (May 1982): 336-340. [12 Refs.]

The authors provide generic, systematic procedures for studying scientific research reports. The approach entails analyzing the parts of the report by using a modification of Gowin's categories or research paper components: question, explanatory theories, procedural theories, and objects. After analysis of the paper, the underlying concepts of the work are obtained by synthesizing specific statements from the paper. Once both analysis and synthesis have been completed, the quality of the work is evaluated by comparing the results of analysis and synthesis with standards of scientific excellence. The authors describe how the approach was used in a graduate course in plant pathology.

929 Wellman, Bruce. "Making Science Learning More Science-Like." Chapter 30 in *Developing Minds. Vol. 1: A Resource Book for Teaching Thinking*, rev. ed., edited by Arthur L. Costa, 159-163. Alexandria, VA: Association for Supervision and Curriculum Development, 1991. [15 Refs.]

Wellman outlines six aspects of a complete science program: (1) Concept Framework, (2) Content Information, (3) Cognitive Skills Development, (4) Affective Skills Development, (5) Mechanical Skills Development, and (6) Process Skills Development. He also outlines the science learning cycle: (1) Activating and Engaging, (2) Exploration and Discovery, (3) Processing for Meaning, and (3) Assessment for Understanding. Wellman stresses the importance of involving students in meaning-making activities.

930 Woodhull-McNeal, Ann. "Teaching Introductory Science as Inquiry." *College Teaching* 37, no. 1 (Winter 1989): 3-7. [12 Refs.]

This paper describes a college level introductory science course designed to engage science majors and nonmajors in inquiry during their first semester. Through guided reading and discussion of primary scientific literature, students learn scientific concepts, terms, and inquiry in preparation for independent reading, thinking, and exploration of their chosen project topic.

AUTHOR INDEX

Numbers refer to annotated entries.

SUBJECT INDEX

Numbers refer to annotated entries.

NOTTINGHAM
UNIVERSITY LIBRARY

ABOUT THE AUTHORS

JERIS CASSEL is Reference Librarian and Online Services Coordinator at the Kilmer Area Library, Rutgers University. She has an M.S. in Library Science from The Catholic University of America, an M.A. in English from Mankato State University, and a B.A. in English and Education from Longwood College.

ROBERT CONGLETON is Serials Acquisitions Librarian and Philosophy Bibliographer at Paley Library, Temple University in Philadelphia, Pennsylvania. He earned his M.L.S. from Rutgers University, his M.A. in history from the University of Connecticut, and his B.A. in history and philosophy from Rider College.